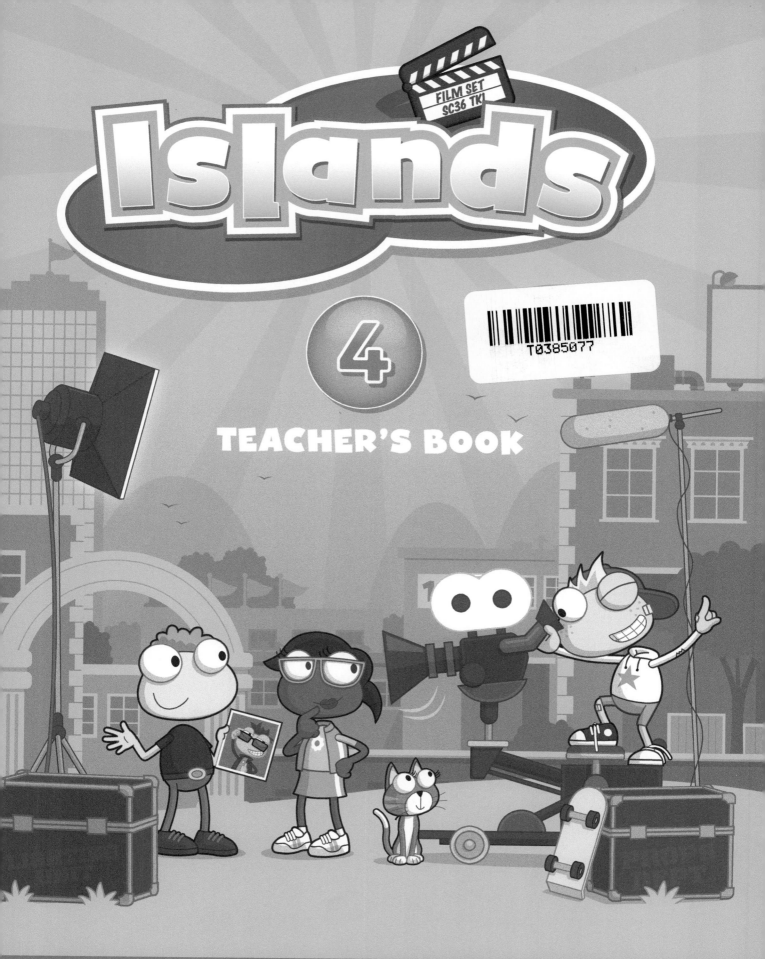

Islands

FILM SET
SC36 TK1

4

Teacher's Book

T0385077

Contents

Scope and sequence

Welcome

Vocabulary	**Time:** morning, afternoon, evening, night **Numbers:** fifty, sixty, seventy, eighty, ninety, one hundred **Simple comparatives:** tall – taller, short – shorter, big – bigger, small – smaller, young – younger, old – older, fast – faster, clever – cleverer
Structures	Hi! My name's (Ann). I'm (10) and I like (football). This is my sister, (Jenny). Do you like (films/Daniel Radcliffe)? Yes, I do. / No, I don't. / Sorry, I don't know him/her. What's your favourite number? My favourite number is (77). What about you?	I'm (taller) than Sam/you/him/her. He's/She's (taller) than Sam/you/me. You're (taller) than Sam/me/him/her. My hands are (bigger).

① Free time

Vocabulary	**Leisure activities:** skiing, cooking, watching TV, playing the guitar, playing computer games, skateboarding, reading the newspaper, chatting online, skipping, painting, playing hockey, reading magazines, watching films, surfing the internet, walking the dog, riding a scooter **Special houses:** lighthouse, stairs, sea	**CLIL:** Social sciences (Special houses) **Wider World:** At the weekend **Values:** Set goals **Phonics:** ou, ow (out, loud, shout, cloud, low, snow, blow, yellow)
Structures	What do you/they like doing? I/We/They like (skiing). What does he/she like doing? He/She likes (skiing). I/We/They don't like (skiing). He/She doesn't like (skiing).	Do you/they like (skipping)? Yes, I/we/they do. No, I/we/they don't. Does he/she like (skipping)? Yes, he/she does. / No, he/she doesn't.	

② Wild animals

Vocabulary	**Wild animals/food:** giraffe, elephant, lion, monkey, hippo, crocodile, leaves, grass, fruit, meat, crab, camel, zebra, panda, gorilla **Habitats:** river, desert, grassland, forest, rainforest **The food chain:** herbivores, carnivores, omnivores, grass, grasshopper, mouse, snake, eagle, lion cubs, orangutans	**CLIL:** Science (The food chain) **Wider World:** Wildlife parks **Values:** Protect wildlife **Phonics:** all, aw (call, wall, tall, small, saw, draw, claw, yawn)
Structures	(Giraffes) eat (leaves). Do (giraffes) eat (leaves)? Yes, they do. / No, they don't. What do (crabs) eat? They eat (worms). Where do (crabs) live? They live in (rivers).	How many (teeth) have (gorillas) got? They've got (32 teeth). How much (fish) do (crocodiles) eat? They eat (a lot of fish).	

③ The seasons

Vocabulary	**Weather:** warm, humid, wet, stormy, lightning, thunder, temperature, degrees **Seasonal activities:** go camping, go water skiing, go hiking, go snowboarding **Seasons:** spring, summer, autumn, winter **Natural disasters:** hurricane/typhoon/cyclone, wave, earthquake, tornado	**CLIL:** Science (Hurricanes) **Wider World:** Natural disasters **Values:** Be a good friend **Phonics:** ew, y (new, dew, chew, stew, my, try, fly, sky)
Structures	What's the weather like today? It's (warm). / There's (thunder and lightning). What's the temperature today? It's (25) degrees.	I/We/They go (camping) in (spring). He/She goes (camping) in (spring). What was the weather like (last summer)? It was (sunny). What was the weather like (yesterday)? It was (windy).	

4 My week

Vocabulary	**Activities:** have music lessons, have ballet lessons, do karate, do gymnastics, practise the piano, practise the violin, learn to draw, learn to cook, study English, study Maths **Time:** morning, midday, afternoon, evening, a quarter past 2, half past 2, a quarter to 3 **Going to school:** road, radio, plane, snowmobile		**CLIL:** Social sciences (Going to school) **Wider World:** Daily routines and timetables **Values:** Develop new interests **Phonics:** ie, ue (pie, tie, lie, fried, blue, glue, true, tissue)
Structures	What do you do on (Saturdays)? I (have music lessons) on (Saturdays). What does he/she do on (Saturdays)? He/She (has music lessons) at (2 o'clock). When do you (have music lessons)? I (have music lessons) in the (morning). When does he/she (have music lessons)? He/She (has music lessons) at (a quarter past 2).	She (always) has ballet lessons in the morning. She (often) goes to parties. She (never) walks.	

5 Jobs

Vocabulary	**Jobs:** builder, firefighter, police officer, basketball player, film star, ballet dancer, astronaut, singer, model, journalist, photographer, carpenter, mechanic, lawyer, athlete **Future jobs:** famous, champion, Olympic Games, train, coach, brave		**CLIL:** Social sciences (Future jobs) **Wider World:** My hero **Values:** Study hard, work hard and play hard **Phonics:** le, y (jungle, tickle, little, paddle, happy, funny, sunny, rainy)
Structures	What do you want to be? I want to be (a builder). What does he/she want to be? He/She wants to be (an astronaut). I don't want to be (an astronaut). He/She doesn't want to be (a builder). Do you want to be (a lawyer)? Yes, I do. / No, I don't. Does he/she want to be (a carpenter)? Yes, he/she does. / No, he/she doesn't.	Why does he/she want to be (an athlete)? He/She wants to be (an athlete) because he (can run fast).	

6 In the rainforest

Vocabulary	**Nature:** hut, bridge, nest, waterfall, valley, mountain, vines, lake, sea, coast, hills **Prepositions:** over, across, near, between – and –, around, through, towards, past **The Amazon Rainforest:** nectar, hummingbirds, giant tarantulas, tapirs, parrots		**CLIL:** Geography (The Amazon Rainforest) **Wider World:** World forests **Values:** Be prepared **Phonics:** ce, ci, cir (centre, princess, ice, rice, prince, city, circus, circle)
Structures	Where's the (hut)? It's (over) the (mountain). It's (across) the (bridge). Where are the (huts)? They're (near) the (waterfall). They're (between) the (mountain) (and) the (lake). (Could) you (walk) around the lake? Yes, I could. / No, I couldn't. I (could walk) around the lake but I (couldn't swim) across it.	Yesterday I (walked) through the hills. Last week he/she (talked) to the teacher. climb – climbed, hike – hiked, jump – jumped, listen – listened, look – looked, play – played, stay – stayed, walk – walked	

7 Feelings

Vocabulary	**Actions/emotions:** crying, shouting, yawning, frowning, laughing, blushing, smiling, shaking, nervous, proud, relieved, surprised, relaxed, embarrassed, worried		**CLIL:** Social sciences (Music, films and feelings)
	Cultural traditions: lantern, dragon dance, traditional dress		**Wider World:** Cultural traditions
Structures	Why are you (crying)? I'm (crying) because I'm (sad). Why is he/she (smiling)? He's/She's (smiling) because he's/she's (happy). What's the matter? I'm (nervous). How do you feel? I feel (ill/sick). What makes you (feel nervous)? (Tests) make me (feel nervous).	Help (me)! I can help (you). Put (it) in the box. Give (them) a hug. I – me, you – you, he – him, she – her, it – it, we – us, they – them	**Values:** Help others in need
			Phonics: ge, dge (gem, gentleman, page, large, edge, badge, hedge, bridge)

8 Action!

Vocabulary	**Outdoor activities and equipment:** snorkelling, snorkel, surfing, surfboard, sailing, life jacket, kayaking, paddle, fishing, fishing rod, horse-riding, riding boots		**CLIL:** Science (Save the reefs!)
	Emotions: fond of, crazy about, bored with, scared of, terrified of		**Wider World:** Summer camps
	Extreme sports: rafting, bungee jumping, rock climbing, scuba diving, hang gliding, beach volleyball		**Values:** Enjoy all your activities
	Coral reefs: save, coral reef, skeleton, seahorse, starfish, global warming, dead, sea snake, butterfly fish, parrot fish		
Structures	Let's go (snorkelling)! Great idea! I love (snorkelling). Let's go (horse-riding)! Sorry, I don't like (horse-riding). Have you got (riding boots)? Yes, I have. / No, I haven't. What are you (fond of)? I'm (fond of) (rafting).	What are you going to do (next month)? I'm going to go (surfing). What's he/she going to do (this summer)? He's/She's going to (visit his/her grandparents).	**Phonics:** ph, wh (phone, dolphin, elephant, alphabet, wheel, white, whale, whisper)

Goodbye

Structures	He/She wants to be a (film star). Sam likes (playing football).	Who's your favourite (film star)? Why do you like him/her? What country is he/she from?

Festivals

Vocabulary	**Halloween:** moon, owl, skeleton, monster, bone
	Christmas Day: Christmas crackers, Christmas pudding, Christmas lunch, open presents, play with presents, snowman, snowball
	Easter: chocolate bunny, jelly beans, Easter eggs, trail
	Mother's Day: breakfast in bed, toast, tea, rose, box of chocolates
	Pancake Day: toss, frying pan
	Earth Day: recycle plastic, reuse paper, don't use plastic bags, recycle cans, reuse glass bottles, give old clothes to other people

Islands is a multiple-level course for children learning English as a foreign language in Primary schools. The level, content and pace make it suitable for use in primary schools with typically five or more lessons of English per week. *Islands* offers best practice methodology in the classroom whilst also offering teachers and pupils an innovative digital environment.

The key course features are:

High level content — *Islands* vocabulary and grammar syllabus has been developed in line with external exam topics, vocabulary and grammar to help pupils who are preparing for external English exams for young learners (*CYL, Trinity* and *KET for schools*).

Phonics/Literacy syllabus — *Islands* offers an integrated programme of phonics across the whole series.

CLIL and cultural references — Integrated within each unit, this provides links to other school subjects and offers the opportunity to study children's lives and culture in other parts of the world.

Enriched digital offer — An Online World, the Active Teach Interactive Whiteboard Software and Digital Activity Book provide opportunities to enrich pupils' learning both in school and at home.

Islands can be used as a blended learning course and takes into account the current movement towards using an increased amount of technology in the classroom and also at home as more and more families have home computers and want safe, effective, educational material for their children.

Islands motivates children by introducing them to a group of characters in an Online Island that mirrors the Island in their English book. Pupils follow the characters on a quest through their book whilst listening to stories, singing songs, communicating and playing games along the way. Most importantly, pupils will enjoy themselves and make their own discoveries in English. In *Islands* learning is an adventure!

On *Film Studio Island*, the main characters Jenny, her brother John, Ruby and Sam are visiting a film studio on a school trip. Pupils follow the stories of two film stars: Favolina Jolly and Madley Kool. They must help Favolina to find all the missing charms from her bracelet. As they move around *Film Studio Island* they quickly realise that Madley Kool, Jenny's favourite film star is missing from a film set so they go on a quest looking for him with the help of Cleo, the cat. They visit a lot of different film sets, having fun along the way and eventually find Madley Kool trapped in a tank of water with a shark! Cleo saves the day and rescues Madley and the Director takes him back to the film set and they finish the film with the children and Cleo watching and waiting for autographs.

Methodology and skills

Islands methodology builds on the traditional '3Ps' (Presentation, Practice, Production) approach. This is a tried and tested approach which is favoured by many teachers in the Primary classroom. The lesson sequence is clear and easy to follow and works in a structured way. The *Islands* '5Ps' approach adds also Personalisation and Pronunciation.

Presentation is the first stage. In each unit there are two grammar points and three vocabulary presentations – two sets of key topic words and an additional set of CLIL and culture related content. The teacher demonstrates the key language (often in illustrated form or using gesture) while providing a model (on audio CD or Active Teach) for pupils to hear the correct pronunciation. Teachers can use the flashcards and wordcards at this stage of the lesson.

Practice is provided in the form of controlled and more open activities using the presented language. Within each level skills are worked on from unit to unit and across the various components (with a focus on oral in the Pupil's Book and written in the Activity Book) and then built up gradually from level to level. Reading skills are further developed with a range of texts increasing in length and variety to offer pupils 'real' reading opportunities.

Production activities encourage pupils to use the language either to speak or write something. These activities encourage pupils to become more autonomous and to manipulate the language in order to communicate.

Personalisation activities are also included in the lesson structure to engage the pupils further with the unit language and to help them with language recall. At the end of each unit there is an opportunity for pupils' self assessment.

Pronunciation of English sounds is a key literacy area which is addressed in the phonics lessons (Lesson 6). *Islands* Level 4 introduces some consonant sounds and diphthongs.

LITERACY

On *Film Studio Island,* reading is introduced in the Pupil's Book and the Activity Book in the form of short paragraphs and texts. Vocabulary labels, speech bubbles, songs and chants are also included. In the Activity Book pupils write short sentences to practise the new language. Specific reading tasks such as drawing, colouring, matching, unscrambling, etc. are also included. There is also a section for Extensive reading that helps pupils develop reading strategies progressively.

The phonics lessons in *Islands* provide a comprehensive and complete phonics syllabus, designed to aid literacy. In Level 4, pupils are introduced to some diphthongs and consonant sounds. Each sound is presented individually, then blended together into simple words, using current methods for teaching literacy.

Components for the pupil

PUPIL'S BOOK

The Pupil's Book provides materials to effectively present and practise the target language. It introduces new language in lively and engaging contexts. A wide variety of practice tasks lead from controlled language activities through to production and personalisation activities. Extensive further practice is provided in the Activity Book. Each unit includes listening, speaking, reading and writing activities, ensuring that pupils develop their skills and are able to practise new language in a broad range of contexts. There is also a high level of cross-curricular and cultural content, so that language learning can be integrated into the Primary curriculum (CLIL). Additionally the Pupil's Book contains songs, chants, stories, games, listening and reading texts and communicative activities to ensure lessons are varied, motivating and effective. The Pupil's Book is organised as follows:

- A **Welcome unit** of six lessons. This introduces pupils to the group of characters and the island, as well as some key introductory language. It also introduces the quest for the Level.
- **Six units** divided into **ten distinct lessons**.
- A **Goodbye unit** of four lessons. This rounds up the quest as well as offering plenty of recycling opportunities.
- **Six festival lessons** at the back of the book for use on Halloween, Christmas Day, Easter, Mother's Day, Pancake Day and Earth Day.
- A **Grammar summary** for pupils' reference.

The **Access code** printed at the back of the book gives pupils and parents unique and safe access to *Film Studio Island Online* via the internet.

ACTIVITY BOOK

The Activity Book provides reinforcement and consolidation of the language presented in the Pupil's Book. It contains controlled and freer practice plus personalisation and further listening and reading texts. It is organised as follows:

- A **Welcome unit** of four lessons, for use after the corresponding Pupil's Book pages.
- **Eight units** divided into **ten lessons** (as in the Pupil's Book).
- A **Goodbye unit** of four lessons (as in the Pupil's Book).
- **Four festival lessons** at the back of the book for use at Halloween, Christmas Day, Easter and Mother's Day.
- **Review activities**. These are linked to the Grammar summaries in the Pupil's Book and can be used for evaluation or additional practice.
- A **Picture Dictionary** at the back of the book to aid pupils in remembering the target language.

Full details of when to use the Activity Book are given in the teaching notes.

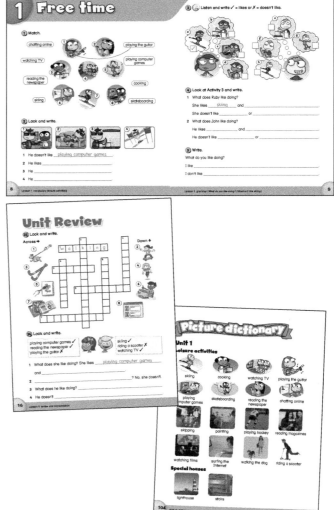

DIGITAL ACTIVITY BOOK

The Digital Activity Book is a version of the Activity Book that contains all the activities from the printed book. It also has picture cards, story cards, a picture dictionary and the songs and chants for the relevant level of the course (with karaoke versions).

ONLINE ISLAND

Islands includes a unique Online Island component. This provides a safe, engaging, highly-motivating environment where the pupils meet the characters from the Pupil's Book plus a host of other exciting characters and follow them on an adventure. Pupils encounter and practise target language from the course in a stimulating environment. They will engage in safe 'closed-chat' dialogues with the characters they meet and follow instructions and guidance to help them solve clues and puzzles and engage in supplementary language games along the way. It's a great way to make learning happen in an interactive environment and further consolidates and extends the language-learning process. Most of all, pupils will enjoy the experience of learning through play and will absorb English without realising it!

READING AND WRITING BOOKLET

The Reading and Writing Booklet includes four pages per unit to target these specific skills. The first page focuses on reading and the second on comprehension with a range of texts further to those offered in the CLIL and Wider World pages of the Pupil's Book. The third page offers reading and writing activities based on revising the key vocabulary and, using the fourth page, pupils have the opportunity to write texts which practice punctuation, syntax and structure. An answer key is provided at the back of the Teacher's Book where required.

GRAMMAR BOOKLET

The Grammar Booklet offers four pages per unit to further practise the grammatical points covered in the corresponding Pupil's Book unit. Tip! boxes are provided for exercises and key vocabulary is reinforced. The last page of each unit provides opportunities for consolidation and review of all key grammatical points. An answer key is provided at the back of the Teacher's Book where required.

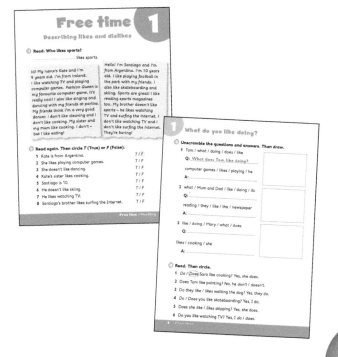

Components for the teacher

The Teacher's Book provides the following:

- An introduction highlighting the main features of the course. It includes a 'tour' of a unit, giving advice for how the different features and components are woven into each unit. Advice is also provided for how to use the digital components, the Active Book and the Online Island effectively in class.
- A summary map for each unit. As well as highlighting the linguistic content of the unit, this lists the cross-curricular, cultural and phonological elements, as well as summarising how the eight basic competences have been integrated.
- Step-by-step lesson plans covering all the course material. Each lesson is clearly structured into stages, with activities included for starting and ending the lesson. There are further optional activities suggested for fast finishers or extension work. The Audioscript and Answer Key is provided at the end of each unit.
- Answer Keys for the Reading and Writing Booklet, the Grammar Booklet, the Photocopiables notes and the Test Booklet. There is also a page for recording your pupils' test scores.
- A Games bank providing procedure for all the games suggested in the lesson notes. There is also a useful summary of classroom language at the back of the book.

The Access code printed at the back of the book gives the teacher special access to *Film Studio Island Online*.

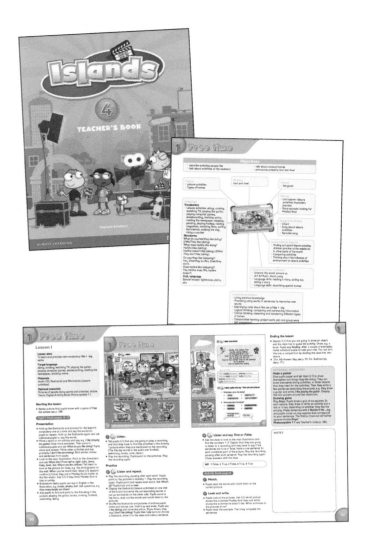

TEST BOOKLET

The Test Booklet contains initial placement tests, progress tests for each unit and practice tests, testing all four skills – reading, writing, listening, speaking – using question types from external exams (*CYL*, *Trinity* and *KET for schools*). Audio recordings are provided on the Class audio CDs and teaching notes, an Answer Key and page to record test results are provided at the back of the Teacher's Book. The audioscript for all the listening activities can be found in the Active Teach.

ONLINE WORLD

Teachers have special access to the *Online Island* using the Access code provided in the Teacher's Book. This takes them into *Film Studio Island Online* with the pupils, plus gives access to an easy to use Progress Review System (PRS) where the teacher can monitor the progress of their pupils. There are step-by-step help guides detailing all aspects of game play, plus log in and classroom management through the PRS. These are available both on screen and as a download to print. Teachers will also find report cards showing each pupil's progress that they can print out for the class and parents. Teachers will find further information on page 34.

AUDIO CDs

The CDs contain all the chants, songs, stories and listening comprehension activities. Karaoke versions of the songs and chants are available via the Active Teach.

ACTIVE TEACH

Islands Active Teach provides software for use on any Interactive Whiteboard (IWB). It eases classroom management as it contains direct links to all of the Pupil's and Activity Book pages, digitally transformed to create more opportunities for interaction between the pupil, teacher and the material. It includes 'hide' and 'reveal' answers, links to further practice activities and games that recycle the language of the unit and previous units and links to audio and video content without the need of a separate CD or DVD player. It has stimulating and engaging digital board games with spinners, flashcards and posters. Digital story cards are also included with 'hide' and 'reveal' speech bubbles and a 'make a story' feature where pupils' own stories can be made with their own speech bubbles for use in the classroom.

On each level of *Islands Active Teach* there are four animated story episodes. Each episode can be used to reinforce and extend the language of the course, focusing on the topics and language of two units. There are songs introduced by three young presenters, Sally, Jack and Albert. And there are animated stories, showing further adventures of the *Film Studio Island* characters.

PHOTOCOPIABLES

Sixty-four pages of photocopiable material are offered via the Active Teach to give maximum flexibility and variety throughout the teaching year. The material includes:

- A Welcome unit photocopiable for introducing the Quest
- Seven photocopiables for use in each unit. These include games, puzzles and activities, vocabulary cards, mini story cards, phonics letter and wordcards, as well as material for exploring the CLIL and cultural themes in the unit
- A Goodbye unit photocopiable
- Three photocopiables for use with the festival lessons
- Notes for these on page 286
- A course certificate
- A cover pupils can use for their portfolio.

FLASHCARDS

There are 185 flashcards at Level 4 illustrating the two main target vocabulary sets and phonics sounds for each unit. The lesson plan and Games bank in the Teacher's Book clearly explain how the flashcards can be used to present, practise and consolidate language through games and activities.

WORDCARDS

A set of wordcards matching the flashcards are provided at each level. The lesson plan and Games bank in the Teacher's Book clearly explain how these can be used for helping with reading and literacy, through games and activities.

PHONICS CARDS

Within the flashcards and wordcards there are also sets to be used specifically with the Phonics lessons (Lesson 6 in each unit). The plan for each of these lessons in the Teacher's Book clearly explains how these should be used for presenting, practising and blending sounds for literacy.

STORY CARDS

The story cards contain a frame from the *Film Studio Island* story and teaching notes comprising 'Before listening' and 'After listening' activities plus the audioscript for the story frame. The story cards are on A4 cards, making them easy to use even in large classes.

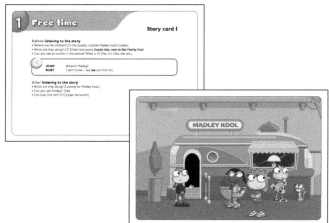

There are four posters to accompany each level of *Islands*. The posters provide an additional resource for the vocabulary, phonics, CLIL and cultural elements of each unit. There is also a generic poster at each level which helps pupils with vocabulary they will need for external exams.

Join us at the Great Teachers' Primary Place

Find inspiring ideas for your Primary classroom, discover new techniques and solutions that work, connect with other Primary teachers, and share your own stories and creativity.

The Great Teacher's Primary Place is the place to go for free classroom resources and countless activities for Primary teachers everywhere.

Go to **www.pearsonelt.com/primaryplace** and register for membership.

Members of The Great Teachers' Primary Place will receive exclusive access to:
- Free articles on current trends in the Primary classroom

- Free reproducible activity sheets to download and use in your classroom

- Free Teacher Primary Packs filled with posters, story cards and games

- Exclusive access to professional development via print materials and web conferences.

Islands provides three different ways of assessing pupils' progress.

1 Formative (or informal) evaluation

The teacher monitors pupils' progress throughout the unit as they carry out the activities in class. This guide includes an Pupil's evaluation chart (also available in the *Islands* Active Teach) which the teacher can use to evaluate pupils' performance in the different classroom activities.

2 Summative (or formal) evaluation

Eight Progress Check lessons are provided, one at the end of each unit in the Pupil's Book.
In addition, the Test Booklet contains: a diagnostic test for the beginning of the school year; three end-of-term tests which enable the teacher to carry out a cumulative assessment if the teacher considers it necessary; and an end-of-year test. The tests are classified as A and B to cater for mixed-ability classrooms.

3 Self evaluation

At the end of each unit in the Activity Book pupils evaluate their own participation in the different classroom activities. This helps them to become aware of how they are progressing and to start to develop a realistic appreciation of their own skills, knowledge and learning objectives.

Portfolio

The Council of Europe promotes the use of a *European Language Portfolio* as a means of encouraging language learning and of providing an internationally recognised record of language achievement.

Islands adapts the European Language Portfolio so that pupils can keep a record of what they are learning in class in a way that is appropriate to their age and their stage of cognitive development.

The Portfolio for *Islands* consists of a selection of the work which pupils have carried out throughout the year. It is the pupils themselves who decide which pieces of work they want to include (for example, the ones they think represent their best work). Pupils' portfolios should preferably be kept in the classroom; pupils can take them home to show to their parents when they wish.

Pupils will need a box or a large folder to store the work which they have done throughout the year. They should put their name on the portfolio cover included in the Photocopiables on the Active Teach and decorate it as they wish, then stick it onto the outside of their box or folder. Pupils can include some of the following in their portfolio:

- The Portfolio project for each unit.
- The posters they have made, their All About Me projects and photocopiable worksheets, cards and other material that they have completed during the year.

- Their end-of-unit and end-of-term tests.

Pupil's evaluation chart

Unit _____   Topic _____

Term _____   Number of sessions/teaching hours _____

Objectives		
	Degree of achievement	**Notes/comments**
Lesson 1	Low/Medium/High	
Lesson 2	Low/Medium/High	
Lesson 3	Low/Medium/High	
Lesson 4	Low/Medium/High	
Lesson 5	Low/Medium/High	
Lesson 6	Low/Medium/High	
Lesson 7	Low/Medium/High	
Lesson 8	Low/Medium/High	
Lesson 9	Low/Medium/High	
Lesson 10	Low/Medium/High	

Primary school work areas	
Reading	
Writing	
Listening	
Speaking	

Material used	in the classroom	delivered to the family
Pupil's Book		
Activity Book		
Photocopiables		
Flashcards		
Posters		
Digital Activity Book		
Active Teach		
Other		

Connections with tutor
Comments:

Unit evaluation	liked most	liked least
Teacher		
Pupils		

At Level 4, there is an introductory unit of four lessons *(Welcome)* followed by eight main teaching units, divided into ten lessons. Consolidation and round up is then provided in a four-lesson *Goodbye* unit. The six *Festival* lessons can be used at Halloween, Christmas Day, Easter, Mother's Day, Pancake Day and Earth Day. There are grammar and speaking summaries at the back of the Pupil's Book.

As well as linguistic and skills practice, the Activity Book provides opportunities for self-evaluation and personalisation. There are also Review activities at the back of the Activity Book and a Picture Dictionary.

The eight main teaching units consist of 10 lessons as follows:

Lesson I
Presentation and practice of vocabulary with audio support

Pupils listen to the key topic vocabulary in context, e,g, a dialogue between the characters. They also listen and repeat the new vocabulary and listen for it receptively in the unit chant. The target vocabulary is highlighted and labelled on the main illustration.

Pupils practise new vocabulary in the Activity Book.

Flashcards and wordcards can be used to present new words and practise them in a variety of games.

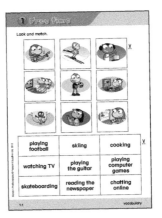

Extra practice of target vocabulary is offered through the photocopiables available on the Active Teach.

Lesson 2
Presentation and practice of Grammar with audio support

Additional grammar practice is offered through the Grammar Booklet.

The new structure is presented and practised in a chant and task listening activity and there is further practice of vocabulary. A karaoke version of the chant is also provided on the Active Teach. Pupils also find and circle the quest item for the unit on the main illustration and sing the quest song. The new grammar content for this lesson is summarised in a Look! box on the Pupil's Book page.

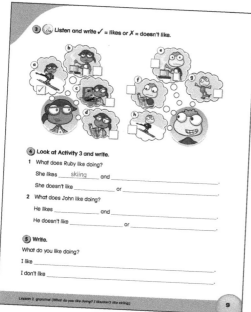

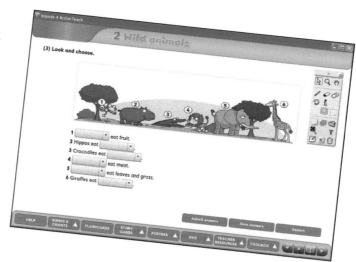

The Active Teach uses digital editions of the flashcards and wordcards to reinforce the language.

Lesson 3
Presentation and practice of vocabulary with audio support

A second group of flashcards and wordcards is provided for the new vocabulary set.

Pupils learn a second set of target vocabulary, which is linked to the unit topic. This may be additional words or it may be a separate vocabulary set. The language of the unit is then presented and practised in a song. Karaoke versions of the songs are included in the audio files on the Active Teach.

Written practice of both vocabulary sets is provided via the Activity Book activities and also on a worksheet available on the Active Teach.

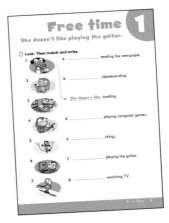

Pupils can further practise the key vocabulary and grammar through the reading and comprehension tasks offered in the Reading and Writing Booklet.

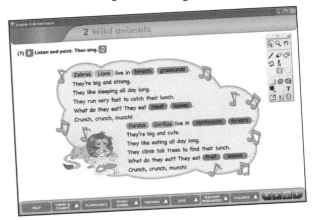

Pupils can sing the karaoke version of the song and use the song photocopiable available on the Active Teach.

A photocopiable to practise the grammar and the song are available on the Active Teach.

Lesson 4
Presentation and practice of grammar with audio support

Additional grammar practice is offered through the Grammar Booklet.

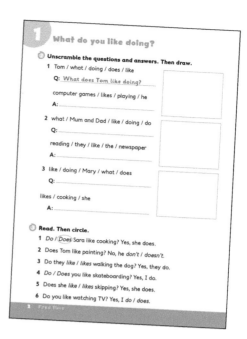

The new structure is presented with a task listening activity and practised with a skills activity. Further practice is included of all the vocabulary and grammar. A karaoke version of the chant is also provided on the Active Teach. The new grammar content for this lesson is summarised in a Look! box at the top of the Pupil's Book page.

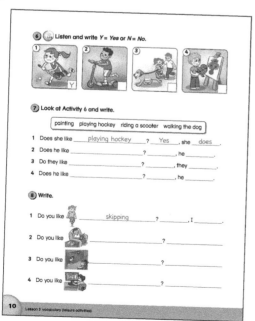

The Activity Book provides pupils with further practice of the new grammar structures with a literacy focus on reading and writing.

Lesson 5
Story and values

Story cards provide visual and verbal prompts to reinforce the target language and structures.

The story is provided as a cartoon strip with speech bubbles and audio support. It recycles vocabulary and structures from previous lessons and introduces some new language.

The values topic for the unit is usually linked to the story and is summarised in the Values box on the Pupil's Book page. There is also a Home-School Link connected with the values topic to encourage parental involvement.

A photocopiable available on the Active Teach supports further work on the story.

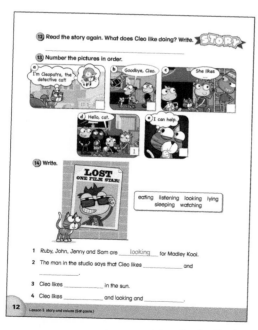

The Activity Book provides activities for both story comprehension and for the values content of the lesson.

Extra reading and writing practice activities focused on the vocabulary are offered in the Reading and Writing Booklet.

Lesson 6
Phonics with audio support

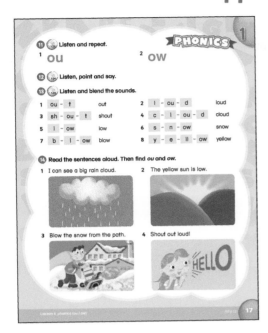

Additional phonics flashcards and wordcards provide further support for phonics lessons.

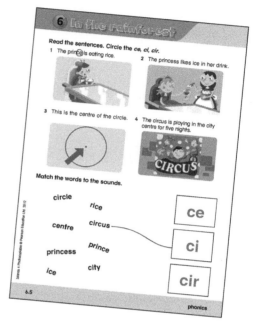

Three or four key letter sounds are introduced in each lesson. In Level 4 these cover some diphthongs and consonant sounds. Each phonics lesson is very clearly staged, with repeated activities and procedures that pupils will quickly become familiar and comfortable with. Each letter sound is presented individually, then blended into words, using only the new letters or letters that have been presented in previous phonics lessons.

A phonics photocopiable is provided on the Active Teach.

The Phonics poster presents the key phonics sounds for each unit.

Written practice is available in the Activity Book.

Lesson 7
CLIL (cross-curricular content)

The CLIL poster presents cross-curricular vocabulary and consolidates the key vocabulary seen in the unit.

New language is presented through a cross-curricular topic in English. This lesson also presents new structures and vocabulary when necessary. It also practises new and recycled language from previous lessons. The material may be related to Science, the Social Sciences, Maths, Arts and Crafts, or Music. In this way, a range of topics which the pupils are learning about in other curricular subjects are revised and developed. A Mini-project encourages further exploration of the CLIL topic and production of the unit language.

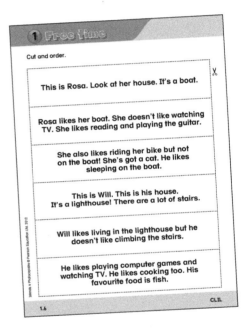

A photocopiable is provided on the Active Teach which offers additional practice of CLIL vocabulary.

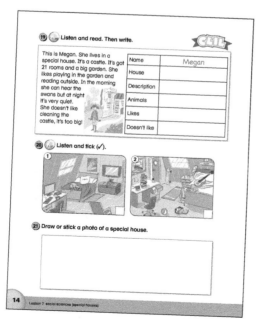

The Activity Book offers reading and writing practice of new vocabulary.

Lesson 8
Wider World (Cultural focus)

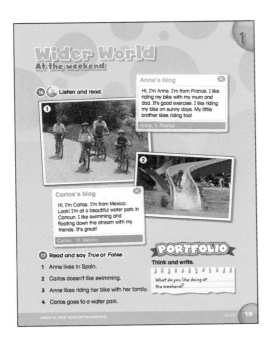

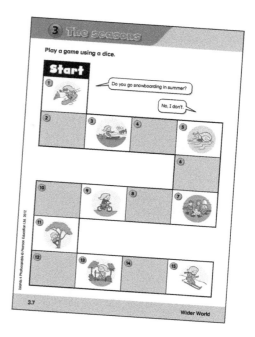

A photocopiable is provided on the Active Teach which offers additional practice of cultural-focus vocabulary.

Pupils read a text that explores an element of international culture linked to the unit topic. In the early levels, this is often through the eyes of a child of their own age. Vocabulary and language is recycled and there is sometimes additional new language which is taught in the context of the text. The Portfolio project encourages pupils to explore the cultural topic further and apply it to themselves.

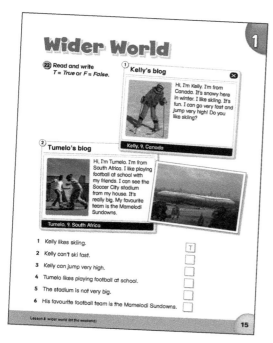

The Activity Book offers reading and writing practice of new vocabulary.

Lesson 9
Review and consolidation

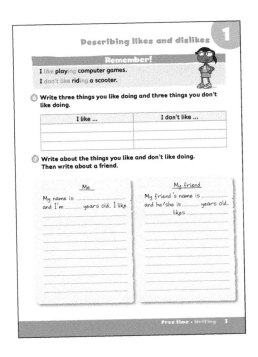

Extra writing practice activities are offered in the Reading and Writing Booklet.

Pupils practise the unit language through a fun language game. There is also a TPR activity providing further practice of the unit language. Pupils are invited to look at the Picture Dictionary in this lesson.

The Activity Book provides reading and writing activities to review the whole unit.

Lesson 10
Self assessment and evaluation

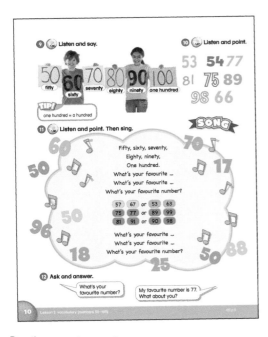

Pupils complete a Progress check activity in the Pupil's Book. They are also invited to self evaluate what they now can do in English after the unit. The unit ends with a link to show teachers when to take pupils to *Film Studio Island Online*.

The Activity Book provides an opportunity for pupils to personalise the language of the unit with a guided drawing and writing activity.

In addition there is a Review which revises the key unit contents.

The key grammar points covered in the unit are provided as a clear reference for pupils.

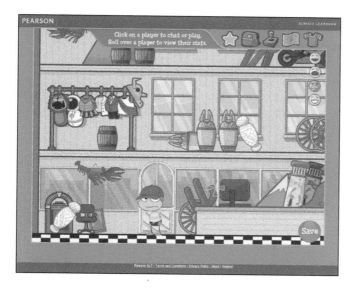

The cat, Cleo, appears on one of the Pupil's Book pages in each unit (Lesson 4), holding a picture of an item from *Film Studio Island Online*. Pupils have to find the item that Cleo is holding online, click on it and complete the supplementary language activity based on the vocabulary of the unit. The lesson notes in the Teacher's Book give the precise location of each online clue.

Additional grammar practice is offered through the Grammar Booklet.

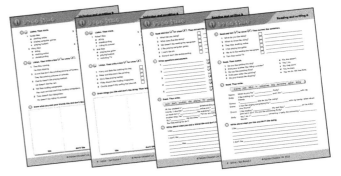

End-of-unit reading, writing, listening and speaking tests are provided in the Test Booklet.

How to use posters

Posters can play a key role in the English language lesson as they are such a powerful visual tool. They can be a valuable way to focus pupils' attention, allowing pupils to consolidate and extend the language already learnt. In addition, the *Islands* posters help develop a pupil's speaking ability as they interact with visually appealing characters, authentic 'real-world' photos and captivating scenes. The interactive posters provide even greater scope as the interactive elements can be moved around and a wider variety of language can therefore be practised.

General poster activities

- Before displaying the poster for the first time, pupils can anticipate and predict who and what they will see within a topic area and then see how many items they guessed correctly once the poster is visible.
- Pupils can create their own posters, based on a similar topic.
- Using a large piece of paper placed over the top of the poster (with a 5 cm hole cut out), pupils can be asked to identify what they can see through the hole.
- Through description, pupils can identify objects that are being described orally, e.g. *It's orange. It's a food. Yum, it's tasty.*
- With a time limit, pupils can look at the posters and try to remember as much language and content as possible and then, in pairs or led by the teacher, they can try to recall the content through questions and answers, e.g. *Is there a flower? What colour is it?*
- By pointing to an object and making a statement, pupils can reply *Yes* or *No* if the information is correct or incorrect, e.g. *This is my bedroom.*
- In teams or pairs, pupils can write down as many words as possible for the items in each poster.

Poster 1 Film Studio Island Map

This is a visual representation of the Online Island for Level 4. It can be used to check pupils' progress through *Film Studio Island Online*, to check where they have located the items presented in each unit of the Pupil's Book in order to play the supplementary vocabulary game and to stimulate language production. Pupils are taken further into *Film Studio Island* as they meet new characters in new settings not represented in the stories in the Pupil's Book.

The map shows the nine main areas which the pupils will pass through:
- Outside the studios
- The trailers
- The Wildlife Studio
- The Special Effects Studio
- The recreational area
- The Costume Studio
- The Dinosaur Park Studio
- The Wild West Studio
- The beach

Poster 2 Phonics

The phonics poster shows a summary of all sounds covered for the level broken down unit by unit.

Poster 3 CLIL

This poster offers a summary of all the CLIL content areas offered within a level and represents key CLIL vocabulary.

Poster 4 General/Exam preparation

This poster offers supporting information that can be useful throughout the year. For Level 4 it shows numbers up to 100.

Specific poster activity

- At the beginning of each lesson, unit or term ask pupils where they are in *Film Studio Island Online* asking them to point on the map. This allows instant feedback as to which pupils are engaging with the Online Island and which pupils are perhaps progressing at a different speed to others.

New technologies in the classroom

The use of new technologies can considerably improve the learning and teaching experience in the English classroom.

Islands Active Teach is a software package for interactive whiteboards. Active Teach is very easy to use, and allows the teacher to get the most out of the possibilities afforded by new technologies in the English classroom.

Active Teach includes:

- Interactive versions of both the Pupil's Book and the Activity Book which makes it possible to teach the material using an interactive whiteboard. In this way, the teacher can monitor the attention and progress of the class at all times.
- All the listening material in the course plus karaoke versions (not on the class audio CD) of the songs and chants which can be easily accessed – either directly from the bottom toolbar, or by clicking on the symbols on the pages of the interactive Pupil's Book.
- Digital versions of the flashcards, wordcards and story cards, which can be used with the interactive whiteboard in a more flexible way than the physical cards; an added advantage is that the recording can be played at the same time as the cards are displayed on the interactive whiteboard.
- Animated stories to reinforce the target language.
- PDFs of all the posters for each level.
- A section of downloadable PDFs which include editable versions of all the course tests and photocopy masters for the supplementary activities suggested in the Teaching notes.

How to use the animated stories

Episode	Target Language
1	snowing, rainy, sunny, windy; spring, summer, autumn, winter; swimming, playing the guitar, playing soccer
2	dancing, skateboarding, playing piano, karate, soccer, gymnastics; horror movie, ghost, monster; days of the week
3	firefighter, astronaut, ice skater, deep-sea diver, ballet dancer; I want/don't want to be a ...
4	weather; What are you doing? Where are we going? Why are you happy? Because ... I feel sad/happy/angry; I'm going (surfing).

The animated stories give the language of *Islands* a new context. Sally, Jack and Albert provide a song and there is an animated story from *Film Studio Island*. Each episode also contains a Language Moment – a short focus on one language point.

- **Song** Pupils watch, listen and follow the actions. As they grow more confident, they can join in with the song.
- **Story** Watch the story. Ask pupils (in L1) what happened in the story. Watch again, stopping at key points, and ask them about the language, the images or the story. Ask pupils to act out the story. Assign the different roles to confident speakers and let other pupils play the other parts. Encourage them to say as much of the dialogue as they can and prompt them where necessary.
- **Language Moment** This reinforces a common language point with short, humorous animation. Some Last Words are interactive, and pupils can use the DVD player controls to answer questions.

How to use the Digital Activity Book at home

New technologies at home

The Digital Activity Book is a version of the Activity Book that contains all the activities from the printed book. An **Access code** for this is supplied in the Activity Book. It has been designed to be used by pupils at home, so that parents can take part in their learning experience.

The Digital Activity Book allows pupils to:
- Work interactively with their Activity Book
- Play at recognising words with the flashcards and wordcards
- Listen to the stories contained in the units, which are presented with interactive versions of the story cards
- Practise songs and chants
- Revise language with the Picture Dictionary for each unit.

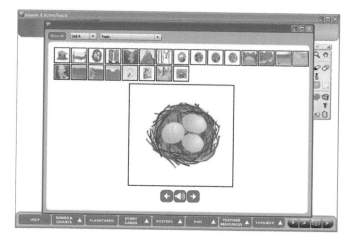

Young Learners and technology

Research shows that appropriate use of computer technology in education is beneficial for pupils (Clements and Sarama, 2003; Waxman, Connell, and Gray, 2002; Byrom and Bingham, 2001). Broadly speaking, pupils can learn *from* computers and *with* computers. Pupils learn *from* computers when the computer assumes the role of a tutor, with the goal of imparting and increasing basic knowledge and skills. Pupils learn *with* computers when the computer serves as a facilitating tool, with the goal of developing critical thinking skills, research skills and the creative imagination (Ringstaff and Kelley, 2002).

Computer activities should be age-appropriate and foster instruction in ways that increase learning, motivation, personal productivity and creativity. For example, Perry (2009) noted that "Children three to five years old are natural 'manipulators' of the world – they learn through controlling the movement and interactions between objects in their world – dolls, blocks, toy cars, and their own bodies." Children are naturally curious and willing to interact with computers, and they enjoy their ability to control the type, pace and repetition of an activity. In some cases, children have even managed to learn how to use a computer with no instruction at all, through their own curiosity, fearlessness and persistence. (Mitra, 1999).

Computers in the English language classroom

The decision to use computers in the language classroom, including the English language classroom, requires the establishment of both technological goals and language-learning goals. For young children, goals such as the following facilitate a path to focused learning.

Technology objectives	Language objectives
To become familiar with the parts of a computer (GPU, screen, keyboard, mouse, cursor, printer and so on).	To use English to interact in the classroom and to communicate in social situations.
To become familiar with approved software programs for the classroom.	To use English to describe self, family, community and country.
To become familiar with operations (select, drag, save, delete and so on).	To use learning strategies to increase communicative competence.
To become familiar with finding, filing, tracking and organising information.	To develop these skills: listening, speaking, reading and writing.
To share information and collaborate with others.	To pronounce English words, phrases and sentences intelligibly.
To develop learner autonomy.	To use appropriate register.

International Society for Technology in Education (2000). *National Educational Technology Standards for Students: Connecting Curriculum and Technology.*

Teachers of English to Speakers of Other Languages, Inc. (1997). *ESL Standards for Pre-K–12 Students.*

Diane Pinkley (former Director of the Teachers College TESOL Certificate Program in the TESOL Program, Department of Arts and Humanities, at Teachers College, Columbia University in New York. A well-known teacher trainer and author in ELL/EFL, she has trained teachers and presented academic papers at conferences around the world).

In addition, she has made major contributions to the best-selling *On Target* and *In Charge* for adults, *Letters to Parents ESL,* and *Backpack and Spin* for children. Formerly the Director of the Institute of North American studies in Barcelona, Spain, and Curriculum Coordinator at the Michigan Language Center in Ann Arbor, Michigan, she has taught all levels of ESL and EFL.

References

Byrom, E., and Bingham, M. (2001). "Factors Influencing the Effective Use of Technology for Teaching and Learning: Lessons Learned from SEIR-TEC Intensive Site Schools, 2nd Edition." Greensboro, NC: SERVE.

Clements, D. H., and Sarama, J. (2003). "Strip Mining for Gold: Research and Policy in Educational Technology – A Response to 'Fool's Gold.'" *Educational Technology Review, 11*(1), 7–69.

Kneas, K. M., and Perry, B. D. (2009). "Using Technology in the Early Childhood Classroom." *Early Childhood Today.* (Retrieved November 5, 2009, from the World Wide Web.) Scholastic.

Mitra, S. (1999). "Hole in the wall – can kids learn computer literacy by themselves?" Generation YES Blog. (Retrieved November 5, 2009, from the World Wide Web.)

Ringstaff, C., and Kelley, L. (2002). "The Learning Return on Our Educational Technology Investment." San Francisco, CA: WestEd.

Waxman, H. C., Connell, M. L., and Gray, J. (2002). "A Quantitative Synthesis of Recent Research on the Effects of Teaching and Learning with Technology on Student Outcomes." Naperville, IL: North Central Regional Educational Laboratory.

Islands Online is an immersive world which accompanies the *Islands* series. It is a ground-breaking digital product, combining the methodologies of classroom-based ELT and games-based learning and is a safe learning environment, suitable for young learners which can be:

- used on individual computers at school or at home
- used in groups at school
- used through the Active Teach IWB software

It provides immediate feedback on performance and contains features that appeal to young learners, such as colourful attractive visuals, clear audio providing excellent pronunciation models, animation and game-like activities, all of which play a part in pupil motivation. It is carefully calibrated to appeal to children between the ages of 4 and 11. The target vocabulary and grammar directly reinforces the syllabus of the course. Because tasks are intuitive and clear, and because pupils receive immediate audio and visual feedback on their progress, the programme builds learner confidence and independence.

Islands Online was authored by a team of ELT specialists and multimedia games developers and offers rich and engaging digital worlds which build on the language and aims contained within the books. The main emphasis is on expanding vocabulary while the pupils learn through playing language games and achieving tasks. New language is introduced gradually and contextualised so that pupils feel confident and motivated to complete each level. The key concepts which have guided the design are:

- **Immersion**. The online world takes pupils out of their classroom or home environment and immerses them in a coherent and believable context. Engaging content and beautiful design hold the pupil's interest and motivate them to continue with the game. Research conducted with the online world indicates that even very young children are able to maintain concentration and enthusiasm for lengthy periods of time.
- **'Just in time' learning.** The starting point in the creation of the online world is the syllabus on which the Pupil's Books and course are based. Each scene of the online world maps to the corresponding Pupil's Book unit in terms of learning aims, lexis and structures. At each stage, pupils are given just enough information and new language to complete each task. In other words, tasks are scaffolded, just as they are in the Pupil's Book. At the same time, support materials such as the Online Picture Dictionary are constantly available, giving pupils the support and confidence that they can complete each task.

- **Stealth learning**. One of the key concerns of the publishing team was that the online world should be enjoyable, and that the learning should take place almost without the pupils being aware of it. Rather than mirroring the type of tasks in the Pupil's Book, pupils learn via interactions with characters in the game. They are presented with real-world tasks, giving them a sense of responsibility and active involvement which is extremely motivating. Learning takes place through listening and reading comprehension of speech bubbles, and through exposure to the target lexical sets via speech bubbles, chatroom dialogues, the Picture Dictionary and supplementary language games.
- **Mastery.** Striking the right balance of challenge and achievability is a key component in any game. The online world has been carefully designed to introduce the key skills needed to complete the task at the start of each level, and then by slowly building the complexity of the language pupils encounter. It is important that pupils find the tasks within the game sufficiently challenging. Pupils with prior exposure to digital games expect to fail at complex tasks several times before achieving them. This makes the tasks more, not less, satisfying, once achieved. The model of 'try, fail, repeat, succeed' is also important because it gives repeated exposure to the target language, ensuring that pupils comprehend the language before they move on.
- **Control.** Pupils love immersive worlds because they feel free within them. They can move their avatar around at their own speed and in their own chosen direction. They are also free to experiment and to fail without censure or observation. This gives them confidence and motivation. The online world has been designed to allow children sufficient freedom to enjoy the game, but at the same time to carefully channel them towards the learning outcomes and to expose them gradually to the target language. A carefully controlled gating system means they must achieve certain tasks before progressing into new parts of the game. A starred report card system motivates them to complete all the tasks within a scene, but gives them some freedom to determine when and how they do this.
- **Reward.** The online world includes many of the most popular features of existing games, such as collectible items, costumisation, avatar design and 'hidden' rewards such as new characters who appear once certain tasks are complete as well as audio and visual feedback to a task.

Skills

The online world is designed first and foremost to be a vocabulary booster. Although it could be completed in isolation, it is designed to complement and extend the language presented in the Pupil's Book. Extra vocabulary pertinent to the context of each level is presented and such items are included in the Picture Dictionary to give extra support.

Pupils interact with characters in the game by reading speech bubble text and hearing a corresponding audio file. Listening and reading comprehension are key skills required in order to progress through the game. Children do not type or write anything, but for some tasks they use the mouse to manipulate text or tick boxes to create simple documents such as emails.

Children do not need to speak in order to complete any tasks within the game, but in some tests we have observed children speaking spontaneously to the characters on screen, either repeating what they said or attempting to anticipate what they will say next. This type of outcome demonstrates the motivational and confidence-building aspects of immersive online environments.

Task types

There are a large variety of different task types within the online world. These can be broken down into the following types:

- Following instructions. A character within the world may tell the player to perform a task, such as finding people with certain skills or items. In order to complete such a task, the player will need to comprehend the target language in each instruction, which may be a gerund (*Find someone who likes skateboarding.*) or a noun (*Please get me an apple.*).
- Choosing the correct response. A character within the world may ask the pupil a question. They will then be presented with a variety of answers to choose from. In order to complete the task, they need to understand the target language in both the question and answer, and they most often have to explore the scene in order to find the answer. For example, a character might ask the player what another character is doing. The pupil must then look through some binoculars to find out what activity the character in question is performing. To discourage pupils from clicking random answers, answer selections can be randomised, or the pupil may be forced to restart the whole task if they get three answers in a row wrong.
- Manipulating items within the game. These tasks add a physical aspect to the game. For example, the pupil may have to collect certain items to fix a broken machine. Once they have done this, a character may

direct them on how to use the machine. They must comprehend the language and then manipulate their avatar in the right way (for example, by jumping on a red lever instead of a blue lever).
- Traditional games. These can be accessed as multi-player games in the chatroom, or at various points in each scene as 'hidden' games which the child can find by looking at a picture clue in their Pupil's Book. These include spelling games such as Hungry Shark (a version of Hangman) and Spell Drop (a version of Tetris). There are a number of picture matching games such as Photoshoot and Match Card. There is also a Quiz game with a multiple-choice or True/False version. These language games sometimes form a major task within a scene, but more often they are supplementary or reward activities which are designed to be completed after the main tasks.

Progression through the game

The game is designed to encourage pupils to work through each scene in a linear fashion, building their vocabulary and language comprehension as they do so. Support includes visual, as well as verbal, clues and the Picture Dictionary, which is available at all times in the top right corner of the screen, and allows pupils to check the meaning of any unfamiliar vocabulary. Once they have completed all of the tasks in a scene, they are given a silver star in their progress chart. Once they have completed all of the supplementary activities and the tasks in a scene, they are given a gold star.

Teacher support

We recognise that many teachers are likely to be unfamiliar with this type of component and have developed a series of help guides both online and as a download to be printed to help teachers gain confidence in using the Online Island in the classroom, assisting pupils with queries about the tasks, or setting parts of the game for home study.

In conjunction with this we plan to develop video walkthroughs of each level, which teachers can fast forward through to answer queries about specific sections of the game. These videos can also act as an introduction to the game, or provide quick support for teachers who can't spare the time to work through the Online Island themselves.

All teachers will receive an individual PIN code to the Online Island and, unlike the pupil version it will contain a map, allowing them to skip back and forward between scenes. For ease of classroom management we have included a Progress Review System (PRS) where teachers can register their classes and monitor their progress. Parents can also view pupil's progress via the Report Card online.

Is set on a fun island where the pupils visit a Wildlife Studio, a Special Effects Studio and a Dinosaur Studio among others. Pupils follow the stories of two film stars: Favolina Jolly and Madley Kool, whom they will recognise from the Pupil's Book. They must help Favolina to find all the missing charms from her bracelet as well as having fun and helping other characters in all the different film sets along the way. As they move around *Film Studio Island* they will bump into and be able to interact with characters they recognise from their books, such as Jenny, John, Ruby and Sam.

The adventure begins with an introductory tutorial *Scene Zero* with a simple activity. The aim is to familiarise the pupils with the layout and computer controls, and to provide some context for the following scenes. This also contains the chatroom, where the pupils can interact and play games with other pupils such as Spell Drop, etc. the chatroom contains sample dialogue matching the language aims of each unit at this level. The pupils can return to the chatroom at any stage during the adventure to test their mastery of the language.

The pupils then progress to the first scene. Each scene contains one, two or three tasks (such as moving an object out of the way or finding the parts of a broken machine). Within each scene there are some supplementary activities such as Match Card or Hungry Shark to further test vocabulary. One of the supplementary activities in each scene is flagged by an image in the Pupil's Book, held by Cleo, the cat. This is not linked in with the task and the pupils can complete this at any time. Players can move freely through Scenes 1–3, but they cannot progress to Scenes 4–6 until they have completed all the tasks from Scenes 1–3. Progression to Scenes 7–8 is similarly dependent on the pupil having completed all the tasks in Scenes 4–6. The Level ends with an Outro scene, which occurs automatically and doesn't require interaction from the pupils. The purpose of this scene is to 'round off' the Level, and to reward the pupils for completing all the tasks.

Film Studio Island Unit 2 Lesson Plan

Film Studio Island Online can be used safely by children at home, if they have a computer and internet access. If you wish to incorporate *Film Studio Island Online* into your lessons, below is an easy-to-follow lesson plan which shows how simple it is to manage it in class.

Learning aim

- To distinguish between different wild animals (*lion, snake, monkey, giraffe, crocodile, bird*) and types of food (*insects, leaves, meat, grass*). *What do lions eat? Lions eat meat. Where do lions live? Lions live in Africa.*
- Receptive language: *I'm the animal keeper. What's the problem? The animals have gone. That's the last one, thank you so much! What's this? It looks like a bracelet charm ... so beware!*

Lesson plan

- Carry this out as part of Lesson 5, after the pupils have completed the PB/AB activities. Pupils may have already found the book/online link item that Cleo is holding up on the PB page at the end of Lesson 4 (film studio light) and may have therefore completed the supplementary language activity based on the vocabulary in this unit. If not, the teacher can 'walk' the pupils through this now. The film studio light is the one in the roof at the top near Jungle Man's treehouse.
- Online: Using the IWB or a computer screen visible to the class, go to *Film Studio Island Online* and access Scene 2, the Wildlife Studio.
- 'Walk' pupils through the first part of the quest. Find and talk to the animal keeper (she is at ground level right hand side of the studio). Then find Jungle Man by walking back to the left and climbing a tall tree until you see him next to the tree house. Answer Jungle Man's first question *What do lions eat?* Have pupils choose the correct answer (*Lions eat meat*), then bring the meat to the lion and return the lion to the animal keeper.
- Divide the class into three groups. Choose a pupil from each group to take over the mouse, answering one of Jungle Man's questions and bringing the food to the correct animal keeper. (*Monkeys eat fruit. Giraffes eat leaves. Elephants eat grass*).
- Talk to the animal expert, Raymond Meerkat and complete the true or false quiz (accessed via the arcade machine to the right of the animal cages, based on the language and facts learnt in this scene).
- Alternatively, once you have completed an example online with the whole class, direct pupils to individual or shared computers, or have them access the task at home for homework.
- End the lesson as detailed in the main lesson notes.

Online Island access code record

Class: _____

Pupil's name	Access code

Pronunciation table

Consonants			Vowels	
Symbol	Keyword		Symbol	Keyword
p	pen	short	ɪ	bit
b	back		e	bed
t	ten		æ	cat
d	day		ɒ	dog
k	key		ʌ	cut
g	get		ʊ	put
f	fat		ə	about
v	view		i	happy
θ	thing		u	actuality
ð	then	long	iː	sheep
s	soon		ɑː	father
z	zero		ɔː	four
ʃ	ship		uː	boot
ʒ	pleasure		ɜː	bird
h	hot	diphthongs	eɪ	make
x	loch		aɪ	lie
tʃ	cheer		ɔɪ	boy
ʤ	jump		əʊ	note
m	sum		aʊ	now
n	sun		ɪə	real
ŋ	sung		eə	hair
w	wet		ʊə	sure
l	let		uə	actual
r	red		iə	peculiar
j	yet			

Welcome

Islands presentation

Lesson aims
To find out about the characters and the context of the story

Materials
Audio CD; Story cards; *Film Studio Island* poster

Optional activity materials
Soft ball or small bean bag; pictures of famous people with a variety of looks/hair colour/clothes

Starting the lesson

- Play a game. With a small class, sit in a circle on the floor and have pupils throw a ball or bean bag to each other. With a larger class, keep the usual seating arrangement and ask pupils to stand up and give the ball to each other. Explain (L1) that pupils should ask *What's your name?* when they throw or give the ball to another pupil. When a pupil catches or receives the ball they should call out *I'm (name)* or *My name's (name)* before passing the ball to the next person. The game continues around the class until everyone has introduced themselves.

Pupil's Book pages 6–7

Presentation

1   **Listen and read.**

- Hold up the *Film Studio Island* poster. Tell pupils (L1) that they are going to follow the adventures of Madley Kool and Favolina Jolly on the island, visit different places and collect the missing charms from Favolina's bracelet.
- Point to the characters in the story and say their names (guard, Sam, Jenny, John, Ruby, Cleo, Madley Kool). Tell pupils to pay attention to the faces of the children in the pictures. You can use the *Island* poster for this.
- Point to the characters and ask *Who's this?* Point to the skateboard and ask *What has Sam got?* Pupils answer (L1). Echo their answer in English: *Yes, a skateboard.* Pupils repeat the English word.
- Point to the children's clothes and ask *Is (Ruby) wearing (trousers)? What colour are her (shoes)?* etc.
- Play the recording. Pupils listen and read the story.

Practice

- Say a line and do a mime to represent each character in random order, e.g. wave and say *Hello!* for Ruby, and mime skateboarding and say *Do you like my skateboard?* for Sam. Pupils say the name, then copy the mime and repeat the line after you.
- Divide the class into pairs. Pupil A mimes and speaks; Pupil B says the character's name.

Island presentation – Film Studio Island

OPTIONAL ACTIVITIES

Who is it?

Stick on the board some pictures of famous people with different coloured hair, clothes, etc. Ask *Who is it?* for each picture. Make a sentence describing one of the people and the pupils say the name. Individual pupils then take over your role, or they can continue the activity in pairs.

Lesson 1

Lesson aims
To revise vocabulary and structures

Revision
Introductions and greetings
Hello. My name's Sally.
I'm 10 and I like football.
This is my brother, Jack.

Materials
Audio CD; Story cards, *Film Studio Island* poster;
Photocopiable W.1

Starting the lesson

● Say *Hello. My name's (name). What's your name?*
Check the meaning and elicit some answers. Then say
I like films. Do you like films? They say names of films
they know.

Pupil's Book page 8

Presentation

2 **Listen, point and say.**

● Pupils look at the picture. Ask *Where are they?* (*In the
film studios*). Play the recording once and pupils point
to the person who is speaking. Play it a second time,
pausing after each line, and ask the class to say who
is speaking.
● Tell pupils to listen to the recording again and say the
sentences. The class looks at the picture carefully and
repeats the sentences.

3 **Work in pairs. Introduce yourselves.**

● Focus on the sentences in the bubble. Ask pupils
to read them and check that they understand the
meaning. Help them understand if necessary.
● Pupils work in pairs. They take it in turns to introduce
themselves using the model sentences as an example.
Practise with the whole class before they work
in pairs.

4 **Match the characters with the clothes.**

● Explain to the class that they have to read the words
for clothes and match each character with the clothes
he's/she's wearing. Revise vocabulary for clothes using
the flashcards if necessary. Check answers with
the class.

KEY **1** Sam, **2** John, **3** Jenny, **4** Ruby

5 **Work in pairs. Describe what you are
wearing.**

● Focus on the prompt in the bubble. Ask pupils to read it
and check that they understand the meaning. Help them
understand if necessary.
● Pupils work in pairs. They take it in turns to describe
what they are wearing using the prompt as an example.
Practise with the whole class before they work in pairs.

Practice

● Write the names of the characters on the board.
● Ask questions to help pupils remember the description
of each character, e.g. *What colour is Sam's hair? How
old is he?* Write the answers on the board under Sam's
name to make a written description. Repeat with the
other characters.
● Stick the character story cards of the four children on
the board. Describe one character, e.g. *She's got
white trainers and a pink T-shirt. What's her name?* Pupils
answer.
● Divide the class into pairs and have them ask and
answer about the characters in turn.

Activity Book page 2

1 **Write and match.**

● Focus pupils' attention on the pictures and descriptions.
They read the descriptions, write the correct names in
the spaces and draw lines matching the descriptions to
the pictures. Check as a class.

2 **Draw or stick a picture of yourself and a
friend. Then write.**

● Explain the activity (L1) and model your own description
first. Say, e.g. *My name's ... I am (age) years old.* If the
number is over 50, you may translate it. *I like (animals).*
Write it on the board if necessary.

Activity Book page 3

3 **Write.**

● Explain to the class that they have to look at the
characters and describe what they are wearing. They
complete the activity individually. Then ask a few pupils
to read out their descriptions.

4 **Write about yourself and your partner.**

● Explain the activity (L1) and model your own description
first. Say, e.g. *My name's (name). I've got (a blue skirt) and
(a white blouse).*
● Pupils complete the descriptions about themselves and
about their partners. Ask a few pupils to read
out their descriptions.

② 🔊 1:03 **Listen, point and say.**

Hello! My name's Ruby.

And my name's Sam. Do you like my skateboard?

I'm John. And this is my sister, Jenny. She likes films.

Look! It's Madley Kool.

LEGEND OF THE GOLDEN BANANA

I'm Cleopatra.

③ **Work in pairs. Introduce yourselves.**

Hi! My name's Ann. I'm **10** and I like football.

④ **Match the characters with the clothes.**

(Ruby)　(Sam)　(John)　(Jenny)

1　red hat, green shorts, white shirt, black and white trainers

2　black T-shirt, brown trousers, black trainers

3　purple trousers, pink T-shirt, white trainers

4　pink skirt, pink blouse, jacket, glasses, white trainers

⑤ **Work in pairs. Describe what you are wearing.**

I've got ...

8　Lesson 1 grammar (introductions and greetings)　　　*AB pp.2–3*

Ending the lesson

- Ask the children to say their favourite characters.
- (For AB Answer Key, see p. 46. For Audioscript, see p. 47.)

(For AB Answer Key, see p. 46. For Audioscript, see p. 47.)

OPTIONAL ACTIVITIES

Flashcard game
Play *Name it* see p. 299 with the flashcards (clothes).

Flashcard game
Play *Memory* see p. 299.

Photocopiable W.1 see Teacher's notes p. 286

39

Lesson 2

Lesson aims
To practise vocabulary: times of day

Revision
(in the) morning, afternoon, evening, (at) night
Do you like films? Yes, I do./No, I don't.
He/She likes films.

Materials
Audio CD

Starting the lesson

- Write *morning, afternoon, evening, night* on the board and ask pupils to say the words.

Pupil's Book page 9

Presentation

- Present the times of day vocabulary (*morning, afternoon, evening, night*) with sentences and mimes. Mime sleeping and waking up and ask (L1) what time of day this is (morning). Say *Yes, it's morning* and pupils repeat the English word. Repeat with the other times of day.
- Write the times of day as headings on the board and brainstorm (L1) some things that you do at those times. When pupils suggest target language, echo it in English and write it on the board under the correct heading.

6 **Listen and chant.**

- Tell pupils that they are going to listen to a chant. Play the recording a few times. Pupils chant and mime, e.g. yawn and stretch arms as if getting up, drink from a cup and eat toast.
- Divide the class into two groups. Each group chants four lines each.

7 Ask and answer.

- Divide the class into pairs. Tell them to take it in turns to ask and answer questions about the characters in the photos. Practise with the model sentences first and help pupils understand if necessary.
- Pupils talk in pairs. Walk around the class and help pupils when necessary.

Practice

8 Do a survey. Write in your notebook.

- Explain to the class that they are going to work in groups of four. Ask pupils to draw in their notebooks a table like the one in the book. Then they write the names of four film stars in the first column, and the names of the three other pupils in their group in the Friend 1–3 headings.
- Practise with the class the types of questions and answers pupils can use: *Do you like ...? Yes, I do. No, I don't. I don't know him/her.* They write the answers. Finally, ask each group to report to the class: *Three people in my group like ...,* etc.
- Revise new vocabulary. Say, e.g. *I have breakfast/go to school* and invite pupils to complete the sentence, e.g. *in the morning.*

Activity Book page 4

5 **Listen and match.**

- Ask pupils to listen and match the people to their favourite film stars. Play the recording.
- When they have finished, ask a few pupils to show their work to the class.

6 Write.

- Tell the pupils that they must complete the text with the name of their favourite film stars and what they can do.

Ending the lesson

- Ask the children to say the chant.
- (For AB Answer Key, see p. 46. For Audioscript, see p. 47.)

6  Listen and chant.

morning

I get up in the morning,
Have breakfast, go to school.
Home in the afternoon.
That's cool!
Have dinner in the evening,
Then we go and play.
I go to bed at night
And get up the next day ...

afternoon

evening

night

7 Ask and answer.

1

Daniel Radcliffe

2

Miranda Cosgrove

3

Ashton Kutcher

4

Robert Pattinson

5

Lea Michele

Do you like ...?

Yes, I do.

No, I don't.

Sorry, I don't know him/her.

8 Do a survey. Write in your notebook.

like = ☺   don't like = ☹   don't know him/her =

Film star	Me	_____ (Friend 1)	_____ (Friend 2)	_____ (Friend 3)
1				
2				
3				
4				

OPTIONAL ACTIVITIES

Team game
Play *Reading race* see p. 301 to revise questions and
answers: *Do you like ...? Yes, I do. No, I don't.
I don't know him/her.*

Flashcard game
Play *Pass the flashcards* see p. 298.

Lesson 3

Lesson aims
To learn and practise new vocabulary: numbers 50–100

Target language
What's your favourite number? My favourite number is fifty.

Materials
Audio CD

Optional materials
Number cards

Starting the lesson

- Play a chain game saying the numbers 1–49. One pupil starts with one number, e.g. *Thirteen* and the other pupils continue the chain.
- Start writing a number on the board and ask pupils to come and finish writing the word correctly.

Pupil's Book page 10

Presentation

- Write on the board: *My favourite number is sixty.* Revise the forms: *What's your favourite number? My favourite number is seventy.*
- Write some numbers between 1 and 50 on the board in random order and say them as you write them. Pupils repeat. Call individual pupils to the board in turn to write the numbers in the correct order and say them.
- Show homemade cards for numbers 50, 60, 70, 80, 90 and 100 in order. Say each number a few times for pupils to repeat after you. Show the cards again. Pupils say the numbers without help. Show the cards in random order and ask *Which number?* Pupils answer.
- Write numbers on the board, e.g. *51, 79, 62.* Say them and pupils repeat. Then continue writing numbers and ask pupils to say the words without help.

9 **Listen and say.**

- Direct pupils' attention to the numbers. Play the recording once. Pause after each number for pupils to repeat. Play it again, pausing if necessary after each number.

10 **Listen and point.**

- Direct pupils' attention to the numbers. Play the recording once, pointing at the numbers. Pause after each number for pupils to point. Play it again, pausing if necessary while pupils point.

11 **Listen and point. Then sing.**

- Tell the class that they are going to listen to a song. Play the recording once. Pupils follow in their books. Play it again a few times until pupils are confident enough to sing along. You can now play the karaoke song (Active Teach).

12 **Ask and answer.**

- Focus on the question and answer. Ask pupils to read them. Check that they understand the meaning of the question and answer. Help them understand if necessary.
- Pupils work in pairs. They take it in turns to ask and answer questions about their favourite numbers using the model dialogue as an example. Practise with the whole class before they work in pairs.

Practice

- Prepare series of numbers. Write them on the board and ask the pupils to write them in their notebooks. They complete the series. Then ask individual pupils to come to the board and complete them.

Activity Book page 5

7 **Listen and write the numbers.**

- Tell the class that they are going to listen to a series of numbers and they must write the missing numbers. Play the recording. Pupils write the numbers they hear. Play the recording a second time. Check answers with the class.

8 **Write.**

- Pupils read the numbers and write them. When they have finished, some pupils show their work to the class.

9 **Write your favourite numbers.**

- Pupils write their favourite numbers. Read out the sentences and check that pupils understand. When they have finished, they say their favourite numbers to the class.

Ending the lesson

- Divide the class into two groups. Play the numbers song CD1:08 again and the class sings along.
- (For AB Answer Key, see p. 46. For Audioscript, see p. 47.)

9 🔊 1:06 **Listen and say.**

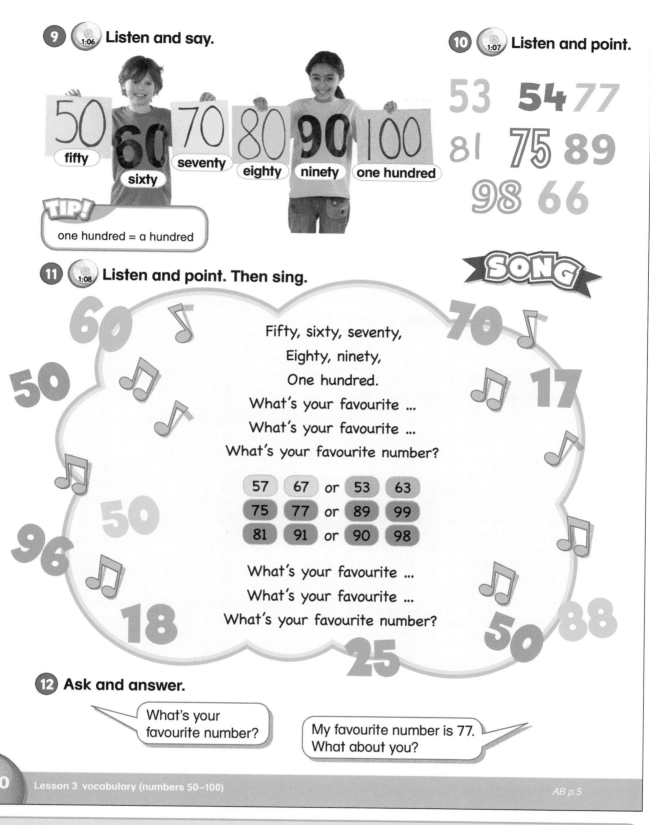

50 **fifty**
60 **sixty**
70 **seventy**
80 **eighty**
90 **ninety**
100 **one hundred**

TIP!
one hundred = a hundred

10 🔊 1:07 **Listen and point.**

53 54 77
81 75 89
98 66

11 🔊 1:08 **Listen and point. Then sing.**

SONG

Fifty, sixty, seventy,
Eighty, ninety,
One hundred.
What's your favourite ...
What's your favourite ...
What's your favourite number?

57	67	or	53	63
75	77	or	89	99
81	91	or	90	98

What's your favourite ...
What's your favourite ...
What's your favourite number?

60 50 70 17 50 96 18 25 50 88

12 **Ask and answer.**

What's your favourite number?

My favourite number is 77. What about you?

OPTIONAL ACTIVITIES

Team game
Play *Missing numbers* with numbers 50–100 see p. 300.

Maths sums
Divide the class into pairs. Each pupil writes a few addition and subtraction sums. Pupils dictate their sums to their partner, who writes them down and works out the answers. Invite some pupils to dictate their sums for another pupil to write on the board.

Lesson 4

Lesson aims
To learn and practise new vocabulary and structures: comparatives

Revision
I'm younger and faster than Madley.
bigger, smaller, older, younger, taller, shorter, faster, cleverer
Adjectives for physical description

Materials
Audio CD; Flashcards (Physical appearance)

Starting the lesson

- Hold up the flashcards describing physical appearance in turn and say the words. Pupils repeat the words.

Pupil's Book page 11

Presentation

- Focus on the adjectives in the Tip! box. Revise the forms: *tall, taller; short, shorter,* etc. Elicit more examples and write them on the board.

13 **Listen and say.**

- Present the adjectives that the pupils are going to listen to in the recording. Write them on the board. Tell pupils they are going to hear a recording. Ask them to look and listen. Play the recording.
- Focus on the Look! box. Go through the sentences with the class. Explain (L1) that all the sentences express comparisons.
- Read out the Look! box.
- Elicit more examples and write them on the board.

14 **Work in pairs. Compare and say.**

- Organise the class in pairs. Pupils look at the pictures and read the sentences. Then they write comparisons. Give an example: *I'm shorter than him.*

Practice

- Write sentences on the board about pupils in the class or characters in the book making comparisons, e.g. *Pedro is taller than Sara.* Pupils read the sentences and say *True* or *False*.

Activity Book page 6

10 **Look and circle.**

- Pupils look at the pictures and read the sentences. Then they circle the correct word. Check answers with the class.

11 **Look and write.**

- Pupils look at the pictures, read the information and complete the sentences. Check answers with the class.

Activity Book page 7

12 **Read and draw.**

- Pupils read the sentences and draw pictures accordingly. Read out the sentences and check that they understand. When they have finished, they show their work to the class.

Ending the lesson

- Invite pupils to come to the front and tell the class about their favourite film stars.
- (For AB Answer Key, see p. 46. For Audioscript, see p. 47.)

 **Listen and say.**

Sam is younger and faster than Madley Kool.

But Madley is taller and bigger than Sam.

And I'm cleverer.

TIP!

tall	taller
short	shorter
big	bigger
small	smaller
young	younger
old	older
fast	faster
clever	cleverer

LOOK!

I'm **taller than** Sam/you/him/her.

He's/She's **taller than** Sam/you/me.

You're **taller than** Sam/me/him/her.

My hands are **bigger**.

14 **Work in pairs. Compare and say.**

1

I'm … than him/her.

2

My hands are …

His/Her hands are …

3

My feet are …

His/Her feet are …

4

How old are you?

I'm 8 years and 3 months old.

I'm … than him/her.

OPTIONAL ACTIVITIES

Drawing activity
Give pupils pieces of card to compare themselves with a partner. Ask them to do a drawing. Write model sentences on the board that they can use for the description, e.g. *I'm taller than Luis.*

Team game
Pupils play *Stop!* see p. 301 in teams of three or four.

Activity Book Answer Key

p. 2, Activity 1
1 Ruby, 2 Jenny, 3 Sam, 4 John

p. 3, Activity 3
1 I've got
2 I've got, shorts
3 I've got, trainers
4 I've got, white

p. 4, Activity 5
1 c, 2 a, 3 d, 4 e, 5 b

p. 5, Activity 7
a 84, 100, 52, 95, 17
b 15, 70, 66, 19, 77
c 62, 49, 57, 88, 10
d 75, 93, 64, 31, 99

p. 5, Activity 8
fifty, sixty, seventy, eighty, ninety, one hundred
(accept 'a hundred')

p. 6, Activity 10
1 taller, 2 smaller, 3 faster, 4 smaller, 5 shorter

p. 6, Activity 11
1 older than, 2 younger than, 3 cleverer than,
4 younger than

Audioscript

Lesson 1 Activity 1 — CD1:02

J = JENNY   G = GUARD   S = SAM   R = RUBY   C = CLEO

J Wow!
G Welcome to Discovery Film Studios.
G Do you like jungles?
S Oops! Sorry!
S Hey! I like jungles! Look at me!
R Aarrgh! I don't like monsters!
C Miaooow!
J Look! It's Madley Kool! I love Madley Kool.
J He's tall ... and strong ... and he's really cool.
G He's making a film here.
J Madley Kool? Really? Here? He's my favourite film star.
G It's a film about ... SHARKS!

Lesson 1 Activity 2 — CD1:03

R = RUBY   S = SAM   JO = JOHN   JE = JENNY

R Hello! My name's Ruby.
S And my name's Sam. Do you like my skateboard?
JO I'm John. And this is my sister, Jenny. She likes films.
JE Look! It's Madley Kool.

Lesson 2 Activity 6 — CD1:04

I get up in the morning,
Have breakfast, go to school.
Home in the afternoon.
That's cool!
Have dinner in the evening,
Then we go and play.
I go to bed at night
And get up the next day ...

Lesson 2 Activity 5 (AB) — CD1:05

M = MATT   S = SIMON   C = CAROL   K = KIM   B = BEN

M I'm Matt. My favourite film star is Molly Vanilla. Look at her picture. She's wearing a pink sweater and blue jeans. She's a really cool actor and she's a great dancer, too.
S My name is Simon. My favourite film star is Jackson Black. He's an action star. He can do karate and he's very strong. Look at his picture. He's got broad shoulders!
C My name is Carol. My favourite film star is Shelley Baronski. She's in films about love. Sometimes the films are sad. Look at her picture. She's sitting in front of the mirror in her room.
K I'm Kim. My favourite film star is Walter Rascal. Walter is a detective in my favourite film. Look at his picture. He can run really fast to catch the bad guys.
B My name is Ben. I want to tell you about my favourite film star, Leah Leeds. She's beautiful. Look at her picture. She's got big eyes and long eyelashes. In my favourite film, she makes machines and does magic.

Lesson 3 Activity 9 — CD1:06

50, 60, 70, 80, 90, 100

Lesson 3 Activity 10 — CD1:07

89, 77, 98, 54, 66, 81, 75, 53

Lesson 3 Activity 11 — CD1:08

Fifty, sixty, seventy,
Eighty, ninety,
One hundred.
What's your favourite ...
What's your favourite ...
What's your favourite number?

57 67 or 53 63
75 77 or 89 99
81 91 or 90 98

What's your favourite ...
What's your favourite ...
What's your favourite number?

Lesson 3 Activity 7 (AB) — CD1:09

84, 100, 52, 95, 17, 15, 70, 66, 19, 77, 62, 49, 57, 88, 10, 75, 93, 64, 31, 99

Lesson 4 Activity 13 — CD1:10

S = SAM   J = JENNY   C = CLEO

S Sam is younger and faster than Madley.
J But Madley is taller and bigger than Sam.
C And I'm cleverer.

Objectives

- describe activities people like
- talk about activities at the weekend
- talk about unusual homes
- pronounce properly /ou/ and /ow/

Topics
- Leisure activities
- Types of homes

Phonics
/ou/ and /ow/

Values
- Set goals

Stories
- Unit opener: leisure activities characters practise
- Story episode: looking for Madley Kool

Language
Vocabulary
- Leisure activities: skiing, cooking, watching TV, playing the guitar, playing computer games, skateboarding, chatting online, reading the newspaper, skipping, painting, playing hockey, reading magazines, watching films, surfing the internet, walking the dog, riding a scooter

Structures
What do you/we/they like doing?
I/We/They like (skiing).
What does he/she like doing?
He/She likes (skiing).
He/She doesn't like (skiing)./I/We/They don't like (skiing).

Do you/they like (skipping)?
Yes, I/we/they do./No, I/we/they don't.
Does he/she like (skipping)?
Yes, he/she does./No, he/she doesn't.

CLIL language
Special houses: lighthouse, stairs, sea

Songs and chants
- Chant
- Song about leisure activities
- Karaoke song

Sociocultural aspects
- Finding out about leisure activities children practise at the weekends in other parts of the world
- Comparing activities
- Thinking about the influence of environment on leisure activities

Cross-curricular contents
- Science: the world around us
- Art & Music: chant, song
- Language Arts: reading a story, acting out, telling a story
- Language skills: describing special homes

Learning strategies
- Using previous knowledge
- Practising using words in sentences to memorise new words
- Identifying rules about the use of *like + -ing*
- Logical thinking: comparing and contrasting information
- Critical thinking: observing and comparing different types of homes
- Collaborative learning: project work, pair and group work
- Self assessment

Basic competences

- Linguistic communication: Use the language to ask for help in the classroom (L1 to L10)
- Knowledge and interaction with the physical world: Explore the world through leisure activities (L1 to L4); Identify different types of homes (L7)
- Mathematical competence: Identify singular and plural (L1 to L4)
- Processing information and digital competence: Use *Film Studio Island* online component
- Social and civic competence: Set goals (L5)
- Cultural and artistic competence: Know about leisure activities in other parts of the world (L8)
- Learning to learn: Reflect on what has been learnt and self-evaluate progress (L10)
- Autonomy and personal initiative: Develop one's own criteria and social skills (L1 to L10)

Skills

Listening
- Identifying leisure words in recordings
- Listening to words and sentences and repeating them
- Identifying information about leisure activities people like doing
- Understanding specific information in a song about leisure activities people like or don't like
- Understanding general and specific information in a story

Reading
- Understanding information in sentences (*like + -ing*)
- Using illustrations to anticipate the content of a text and interpret information
- Understanding general and specific information in short texts about leisure activities
- Understanding general and specific information in a cartoon strip story
- Understanding texts about places where people live in other parts of the world

Speaking
- Saying words and sentences about leisure activities
- Chanting and singing
- Pronouncing /ou/ and /ow/ correctly
- Saying sentences from the Look! boxes

Talking
- Asking and answering about activities people like doing
- Participating in a dialogue to talk about leisure activities
- Role playing a story
- Answering questions posed by the teacher and classmates

Writing
- Writing leisure words
- Completing sentences about leisure activities characters like doing
- Providing written answers to questions
- Reading and matching halves to make sentences
- Transferring information from a table and writing it
- Completing a crossword

Classroom ideas

- Display cross-curricular poster and projects about unusual homes in the classroom
- Display flashcards and wordcards in the classroom while exploiting this unit
- Decorate the class with photos and pictures of different leisure activities
- Use the internet to find information about special homes
- Play games with flashcards
- Photocopiables

Take-home English

- Home-School Link
- Notes for Parents
- A sample of work each week
- Portfolio

Self assessment

- Pupils can describe activities people like
- Pupils can talk about activities at the weekend
- Pupils can talk about unusual homes

Evaluation

- Pupil's Book page 21
- Activity Book page 17
- Picture Dictionary
- Photocopiable 1.7
- Test Booklet – Unit 1

Free time

Lesson 1

Lesson aims
To learn and practise new vocabulary: *like + -ing* verbs

Target language
skiing, cooking, watching TV, playing the guitar, playing computer games, skateboarding, reading the newspaper, chatting online

Materials
Audio CD; Flashcards and Wordcards (Leisure activities)

Optional materials
Pictures of people doing sports and activities; Active Teach; Digital Activity Book; Photocopiable 1.1

Starting the lesson

- Revise actions that pupils know with a game of *Pass the actions* see p. 298.

Pupil's Book pages 12–13

Presentation

- Hold up the flashcards and pictures for the lesson's vocabulary one at a time and say the words for pupils to repeat. Hold up the flashcards again and ask individual pupils to say the words.
- Mime a sport or an activity and say, e.g. *I like (playing the guitar)*. Give more examples. Then point to individual pupils and ask *What do you like doing?* Pupils mime and answer. Mime other activities and say grumpily *I don't like (swimming)*. Elicit similar mimes and sentences from pupils.
- Look at the main illustration. Point to the characters and ask *Who's this?* (*From left to right: John, Jenny, Ruby, Sam*). Ask *Where are the children?* Tell them to look at the picture for clues, e.g. the photographs on the wall. When you've heard their ideas (L1), explain/confirm (L1) that they are in Madley Kool's trailer at the film studio. Ask (L1) if they think Madley Kool is tidy or untidy.
- Brainstorm items pupils can say in English in the illustration, e.g. *books, photos, ball*. Ask questions, e.g. *How many books are there?*
- Ask pupils to find and point to the following in the picture: playing the guitar, books, cooking, football, swimming, skiing.

Listen.

- Tell pupils (L1) that you are going to play a recording, and that they have to find five activities in the Activity 1 picture when they are mentioned on the recording. (The five key words in the audio are: football, swimming, books, cook, clean.)
- Play the recording. Pupils point to the activities. Play the recording again.

Practice

2 Listen and repeat.

- Play the recording, pausing after each word. Pupils point to the pictures in Activity 1. Play the recording again. Pupils point and repeat each word. Ask *What's (a)?* Pupils look and answer.
- Display the flashcards (leisure activities) on one side of the board and write the corresponding words or put up wordcards on the other side. Pupils come to the front, read out the words and match them to the pictures.
- Shuffle the flashcards and pictures of actions pupils know and choose one. Hold it up and smile. Pupils say *I like (skiing)* and mime the action. If you frown, they say *I don't like (skiing)*. Pupils then take turns to choose a flashcard, show it to the class and make a sentence.

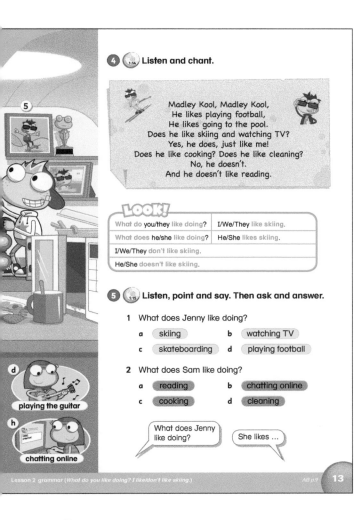

4 🔊 1:14 **Listen and chant.**

Madley Kool, Madley Kool,
He likes playing football,
He likes going to the pool.
Does he like skiing and watching TV?
Yes, he does, just like me!
Does he like cooking? Does he like cleaning?
No, he doesn't.
And he doesn't like reading.

LOOK!

What do **you/they** like doing?	**I/We/They** like skiing.
What does **he/she** like doing?	**He/She** likes skiing.
I/We/They don't like skiing.	
He/She doesn't like skiing.	

5 🔊 1:15 **Listen, point and say. Then ask and answer.**

1 What does Jenny like doing?
  a skiing   b watching TV
  c skateboarding d playing football

2 What does Sam like doing?
  a reading   b chatting online
  c cooking   d cleaning

What does Jenny like doing? — She likes …

playing the guitar

chatting online

Lesson 2 grammar (*What do you like doing? I like/don't like skiing.*)   AB p.9   **13**

Ending the lesson

- Explain (L1) that you are going to draw an object and the class has to guess the activity. Draw, e.g. a book. Pupils say *Reading.* After a couple of examples, invite individual pupils to take your role. You can turn this into a competition by dividing the class into two teams.
- (For AB Answer Key, see p. 70. For Audioscript, see p. 71.)

OPTIONAL ACTIVITIES
Make a poster
Give pupils paper and tell them (L1) to draw themselves and things they like doing. They can draw themselves doing activities, or draw objects that they need for the activities. Then they write a few sentences describing the picture, e.g. they draw a guitar and write *I like playing the guitar.* Display the mini posters around the classroom.
Drawing game
Play *Bingo.* Pupils draw a grid of six squares. In each square, they draw or write an activity and a tick or cross, depending on whether they like the activity. Make sentences with *I like/don't like …ing,* and pupils cross out any squares that correspond to your sentences. The first to cross out all his/her squares shouts *Bingo!*
Photocopiable 1.1 see Teacher's notes p. 286.

3 🔊 1:13 **Listen and say *True* or *False*.**

- Ask the class to look at the main illustration and find the numbers 1–5. Explain that they are going to listen to a recording and they have to say if the sentences are true or false: there is one sentence for each numbered part of the picture. Play the recording, pausing after each sentence. Play the recording again. Check answers with the class.

KEY 1 False, **2** True, **3** False, **4** True, **5** True

Activity Book page 8

1 Match.

- Pupils read the words and match them to the correct picture.

2 Look and write.

- Pupils look at the pictures. Ask (L1) which picture shows the activities Madley Kool likes and which shows the activities he doesn't like. What activities do the pictures show?
- Pupils read the example. Then they complete the sentences.

NOTES

Lesson 2

Lesson aims
To revise the vocabulary; to learn and practise a new structure

Target language
What do you like doing? I like (skiing).
We don't like (skiing). What does he/she like doing?
He/She likes (skiing). He/She doesn't like (skiing).

Materials
Audio CD; Flashcards and Wordcards (Leisure activities)

Optional materials
Active Teach; Digital Activity Book; Grammar Booklet; pictures of famous people

Starting the lesson

- Hold up the flashcards (leisure activities) in turn, and smile or frown. Pupils say the correct sentence, e.g. *I like (cooking).*

Pupil's Book page 13

- Direct pupils' attention to the main illustration. Ask questions about Madley Kool: *Does he like (cooking)?* Pupils answer *Yes* or *No*.

Presentation

- Pupils read the examples in the Look! box. Explain (L1) that we use an action ending in *-ing* after *like*. Ask what extra word we use in questions (*do/does*).
- Read out the Look! box.
- Pupils look at the main illustration in Lesson 1 and make more example sentences, questions and answers. Write them on the board for pupils to copy into their notebooks.
- Ask pupils to think of an activity that they like doing. They draw an object that represents this activity.
- When they have finished their picture, divide the class into pairs to play a guessing game. Pupil 1 asks questions to guess what the person likes: *What do you like doing?* Pupil 2 answers, only saying *I like (playing the guitar)* when Pupil 1 is asking about the activity in the picture. When Pupil 1 guesses correctly, they change roles.

4 🔊 **Listen and chant.**

- Pupils look at the chant. Play the recording for pupils to listen and follow the words. Play the chant again, pausing after each line for pupils to repeat. Play once more for pupils to say together. Use the flashcards to help prompt the words if necessary.
- Divide the class into two groups and practise the chant. One group says the questions and the other says the answers. Then swap roles so that all pupils have a chance to do the whole chant.

Practice

5 🔊 **Listen, point and say. Then ask and answer.**

- Ask the pupils to read the words in the activity. Help them understand if necessary.
- Play the recording once. Pupils point to the words as the activities are mentioned. Play the recording again, pausing after *watching TV*. Play this section a few times if necessary. Then ask *What does Jenny like doing?* Pupils answer. Then do the same with the second half of the recording and the words for Sam.
- Ask individual pupils to choose an activity and make affirmative and negative sentences about Jenny and Sam, e.g. *Jenny likes playing football. Jenny doesn't like skiing.*
- Divide the class into pairs. Pupils take turns to ask and answer questions about what Jenny and Sam like.

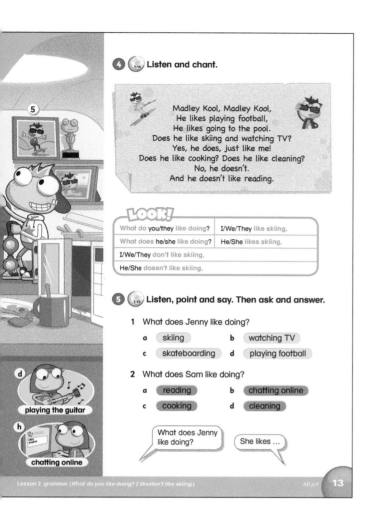

Ending the lesson

- Play *What's missing?* See p. 298 using the activities from Lesson 2.
- (For AB Answer Key, see p. 70. For Audioscript, see p. 71.)

OPTIONAL ACTIVITIES

Team game

Play *Miming competition* see p. 301.

Famous person chant

In small groups, pupils write a chant about a famous person, based on the one on page 13 of the Pupil's Book. It doesn't have to rhyme, but it should have sentences, questions and answers about the famous person's likes and dislikes. Give groups the opportunity to perform their chant for the class if they wish.

Grammar Booklet p. 1 see Answer Key p.284.

NOTES

Activity Book page 9

3 1:16 **Listen and write ✓ = likes or ✗ = doesn't like.**

- Pupils look at the pictures. Tell them that they are going to listen to a recording and must tick or cross the boxes accordingly. Play the recording. Pupils listen and put ticks and crosses to show what Ruby and John like and dislike.

4 Look at Activity 3 and write.

- Pupils look at the pictures and information in Activity 3. Then they write sentences describing Ruby and John's likes and dislikes. Point out the example. Check as a class.

5 Write.

- Pupils write the answer to the question *What do you like doing?* If necessary, give examples beginning with *I like ... / I don't like ...* . Ask some pupils to read out their texts.

Lesson 3

Lesson aims
To extend the unit vocabulary set about leisure activities; to practise the unit language with a song

Target language
skipping, painting, playing hockey, reading magazines, watching films, surfing the internet, walking the dog, riding a scooter

Materials
Audio CD; Flashcards and Wordcards (Leisure activities)

Optional materials
Pictures of someone riding a scooter and playing computer games; Active Teach; Digital Activity Book; Photocopiables 1.2–1.3; Reading and Writing Booklet

Starting the lesson

- Play the chant from Lesson 2 CD1:14. Pupils chant along, and smile and frown to show what Madley likes and doesn't like doing.

Pupil's Book page 14

Presentation

  Listen and repeat.

- Introduce the new words (*skipping, painting,* etc.) using the flashcards. Hold them up and say the words for pupils to repeat. Ask individual pupils to say the words. Play the recording for pupils to listen and repeat.
- Now put the flashcards on the board. Point to the different flashcards and ask the class to say the words.
- Point to a picture and ask pupils *Do you like (painting)?* They answer *Yes* or *No*. If they answer *No*, ask *What do you like doing?* Repeat with the other pictures.

Song

  Listen and point. Then sing.

- Play the recording with books closed. Lead the class in performing the actions while listening. Play the song again with books open. The class follows the lines and mimes. Play the song a few more times, until pupils can sing along.

- Divide the class into boys and girls. They sing alternate lines of the verses and sing the chorus all together. Then they swap lines. You can now play the karaoke song (Active Teach).

Practice

- Organise the class in pairs. Ask the pupils to take it in turns to ask and answer questions about leisure activities they like or dislike.
- Write the question *What do you like doing?* on the board. Explain (L1) that Pupil 1 asks *What do you like doing?* and Pupil 2 answers *I like …* and a leisure activity.

Activity Book page 10

  Listen and write *Y = Yes* or *N = No*.

- Explain to the class that they are going to listen to a recording and must write *Y* or *N* in each box according to the information they hear. Play the recording. Pupils listen and put *Y* for *Yes* and *N* for *No*. Check answers with the class.

7 **Look at Activity 6 and write.**

- Pupils look at the pictures and information in Activity 6. Then they complete the sentences. Point out the example. Check as a class.

8 **Write.**

- Pupils complete the questions based on the pictures, and write answers based on the leisure activities they like or dislike doing.
- Ask individual pupils to read his/her questions and answers to the class, and collect the information on the board.

Ending the lesson

- Play *Mime and guess.* Divide the class into two groups. They take it in turns to choose a picture. They mime what the character likes or doesn't like doing in that picture, e.g. playing the guitar. The other group guesses what it is, e.g. *He likes playing the guitar.*
- For the next lesson, ask pupils to bring in a photo of themselves doing leisure time activities with friends or pets.
- (For AB Answer Key, see p. 70. For Audioscript, see p. 71.)

6 🔊 1:17 **Listen and repeat.**

a
skipping

b
painting

c
playing hockey

d
reading magazines

e
watching films

f
surfing the Internet

g
walking the dog

h
riding a scooter

7 🔊 1:18 **Listen and point. Then sing.**

SONG

Do you like riding your (scooter) (bike) ?
Yes, I do. I like riding my (scooter) (bike) .

Do you like playing the (guitar) (piano) ?
Yes, I do. Look! Look! I'm a pop star.

What do you, do you like doing?
What do you, do you like doing?

Do you like playing (computer games) (football) ?
No, I don't. I like riding my (scooter) (bike) .

Do you like (skateboarding) (painting) too?
Yes, I like (skateboarding) (painting) ! How about you?

What do you, do you like doing?
What do you, do you like doing?

OPTIONAL ACTIVITIES

TPR (total physical response) game
Play *Grab it* see p. 299.
My favourite timetable
Write: *morning, afternoon, evening, night.* Pupils
write something they like doing for one heading. In
pairs, pupils ask and answer.

Photocopiable 1.2 see Teacher's notes p. 286.
Photocopiable 1.3 see Teacher's notes p. 286.
Reading and Writing Booklet p. 1 see Answer Key
p.282.

Lesson 4

Lesson aims
To develop reading, writing, listening and speaking skills; new structures: talking about likes and dislikes

Target language
skipping; use of *he* and *she* for pets

Materials
Audio CD; Flashcards (Leisure activities)

Optional materials
Active Teach; Digital Activity Book; Grammar Booklet

Starting the lesson

- Sing the song from Lesson 3 CD1:18 in two groups: boys and girls if you have a mixed class.

Pupil's Book page 15

Presentation

- Focus on the illustrations that go with the texts. Ask the class to listen to your descriptions and point to the corresponding photo: *He is skiing. They are singing*, etc. Elicit more sentences and write them on the board.

Skills

- Direct pupils' attention to the Look! box. Look at the questions and short answers and focus on the use and position of *Do* in the questions. Elicit more examples from the class and write a few on the board. Pupils copy in their notebooks.

8 **Listen, read and find. Then ask and answer.**

- Pupils read the descriptions and match them to the correct picture.
- Explain (L1) that in English they can use *he/she* to refer to their pets because they are special animals for them.
- Ask the pupils to read the texts again. Read out the question and answer and check that the pupils understand. Allow them time to ask and answer questions based on the text.

KEY 1 b, 2 c, 3 a

Practice

9 **Write in your notebook. Then ask and answer.**

- Pupils write the table and complete it in their notebooks. They work in pairs. Ask them to take it in turns to ask and answer questions.

Activity Book page 11

9 **Listen and write ✓ = likes or ✗ = doesn't like.**

- Play the recording. Pupils put ticks in the table for the activities that the people like, and crosses for the activities they don't like.

10 **Look at Activity 9 and write.**

- Pupils complete the sentences using the table.

11 **Write questions and answers.**

- Pupils look at the pictures and write questions and answers about them. Ask a few pupils to read out their questions and answers.

Ending the lesson

- Pupils work in pairs. Ask them to write a sentence on a piece of paper describing some leisure activity they like doing. Ask them to put the paper with the sentence on their forehead. Ask *Does (he) like (running)?* The partner answers *Yes, (he) does* or *No, (he) doesn't. He likes (swimming).*
- (For AB Answer Key, see p. 70. For Audioscript, see pp. 71–2.)

Pupils can now go online to *Film Studio Island* and find the prop that Cleo is holding. It is shaped like a horse and can be found between the first and second buildings immediately inside Discovery Studios. Once pupils click on the prop they are taken to a supplementary language game based on the vocabulary in this unit.

LOOK!

Do you/they like skipping?	Yes, I/we/they do.
	No, I/we/they don't.
Does he/she like skipping?	Yes, he/she does.
	No, he/she doesn't.

8 1:20 **Listen, read and find. Then ask and answer.** SKILLS

1

a
This is my dog Timmy. He doesn't like running and he doesn't like catching a ball. But he likes skateboarding. Look! He's cool.

2

b
Hi, I'm Anna. I'm 9 years old. I like singing with my friends. I don't like chatting online but I like surfing the Internet.

3

c
I'm Charlie. I don't like watching TV and I don't like cooking. I like skiing. My sister doesn't like watching TV either. She likes skiing with me. It's fun!

> Does Timmy like running?

> No, he doesn't. He likes skateboarding.

9 **Write in your notebook. Then ask and answer.**

I like …

I don't like …

My … likes …
(mother, father, brother, sister or friend)

He/She doesn't like …

> Do you like chatting online?

> Yes, I do.

> Does your mum like watching TV?

> No, she doesn't. She likes reading.

Lesson 4 grammar (*Do you like skipping? Yes, I do. / No, I don't.*)   AB p.11   **15**

OPTIONAL ACTIVITIES

Flashcard game
Play *What's missing?* see p. 298

Make a mini poster
Pupils make a mini poster of the activities they like doing with their family and friends. Pupils write a few sentences, e.g. *I like going to the park with my mum.*
Grammar Booklet p. 2 see Answer Key p. 284.

Lesson 5

Lesson aims
To consolidate the unit language with a story

Values
To set goals

Receptive language
find, actually, lying, help, detective

Materials
Audio CD; Story cards

Optional materials
Props for acting out the story, e.g. glasses for Ruby, baseball cap and/or skateboard for Sam, baseball cap for crew member, black T-shirt for John, grey jumper for Cleo; Active Teach; Digital Activity Book; Photocopiable 1.4; Reading and Writing Booklet

Starting the lesson

- Ask pupils to look at the opening episode in the Welcome Unit on page 6. Ask questions, e.g. *Where are the children? (At a film studio.) Who likes Madley Kool? (Jenny.) Is Madley Kool at the studio? (Yes.) What is the film about? (Sharks.)*

Pupil's Book page 16

Presentation

10 **Listen and read. Then act out.**

- Show the story cards one at a time and ask the *Before listening to the story* questions. Pupils predict what happens in the story.
- Play the recording. Pupils listen as they follow the story in their books. Ask if their predictions were correct. Then ask the *After listening to the story* questions.
- Divide the class into five groups and assign a character to each. Pupils read their parts as a group from their seats.
- Invite volunteers to the front of the class to act out the story. Encourage tone of voice and expressions to match those in the pictures. Use props that you've brought to class if you wish.

Practice

- Shuffle the story cards and put them in random order on the board. With books closed, pupils put them in the correct order. Point to each story card in turn and ask pupils to call out its number in the story sequence. At the end, pupils open their books and check.

- Hold up the story cards in order and retell the story, making some deliberate mistakes. Every time the pupils spot a mistake, they stand up and correct it. Alternatively, retell the story, pausing at certain points so pupils can complete your sentences, e.g. *The children are in ...* Pupils say *the film studio.*

Values

Read out the Values box and help the pupils understand if necessary. Say a few goals, e.g. *I want to learn a new sport. I want to make new friends.* Write some examples on the board and ask pupils to give similar examples.

- Organise the class in pairs. Pupils take it in turns to ask and answer about their goals. Discuss (L1) the importance of setting goals.

Activity Book page 12

12 **Read the story again. What does Cleo like doing? Write.**

- Pupils can look back at the story on PB p. 16, and/ or listen again to the recording of the story, before taking turns to ask and answer. Then they write the answer on the line.

13 **Number the pictures in order.**

- Pupils look at the pictures and they number them in order. Once they have finished, check answers with the whole class.

14 **Write.**

- Direct pupils' attention to the poster of Madley Kool. Ask *Who's this?* Pupils answer. Explain (L1) that posters like these are used to find people who have gone missing.
- Tell pupils to complete the sentences using the words in the word bank to make the profile of Madley Kool. Ask individual pupils to read the sentences to the class.

Home-School Link

- Ask pupils to create a list with three goals to show to their family. As follow-up, discuss with the class what their families have said about the goals.

Ending the lesson

- Play *Hot seat* with the character story cards. Pupils make sentences about the character, e.g. *He likes skateboarding,* so that the pupil in the hot seat can guess his/her identity.
- (For AB Answer Key, see p. 70.)

1

Where's Madley?

I don't know – but **we** can find him.

2

Hello, cat. What's your name?

She's Cleo.

Cleopatra, actually.

3

She likes sleeping and eating and sleeping!

And lying in the sun.

4

Goodbye, Cleo. We're looking for Madley Kool.

5

You're looking for Madley Kool! I can help.

I like watching and looking and listening. I'm Cleopatra, the detective cat!

6

 **VALUES**

Set goals.

 HOME-SCHOOL LINK

Think of three goals and make a list. Show your family.

16 Lesson 5 story and values (Set goals.)

AB p.12

OPTIONAL ACTIVITIES

Story writing
Pupils rewrite some of the speech bubbles in the story. Pupils practise reading their new stories and then perform them for the class.

Flashcard game
Play *Pass the wordcards* see p. 298.
Photocopiable 1.4 see Teacher's notes p. 286.
Reading and Writing Booklet p. 2 see Answer Key p. 282.

Lesson 6

Lesson aims
To learn the sounds and letters /ou/ and /ow/

Materials
Audio CD; Flashcards and Wordcards (Phonics);
Phonics poster

Optional materials
Active Teach; Digital Activity Book;
Photocopiable 1.5

Starting the lesson

- Show pupils the flashcards (phonics).
- Read the words aloud and ask pupils to find a common pattern.

Pupil's Book page 17

Presentation

11 **Listen and repeat.**

- Write on the board the phonemes /ou/ and /ow/. Play the recording for pupils to listen. Play it a second time for pupils to listen and repeat.

12 **Listen, point and say.**

- Tell the pupils that they must point to the sound (/ou/ or /ow/) that they hear. Play the recording for pupils to listen and point. Play it a second time for pupils to listen, point and say.

13 **Listen and blend the sounds.**

- Demonstrate the blending of the first sound. Pupils repeat what they hear. Then tell the pupils that they must listen and blend the sounds. Play the recording for pupils to listen and say the words that contain the corresponding sounds.

Practice

14 **Read the sentences aloud. Then find /ou/ and /ow/.**

- Ask different pupils to read the sentences aloud. Pupils then find the sounds /ou/ and /ow/. Ask them to read out the words containing these sounds.

Activity Book page 13

15 **Read the words. Circle the pictures.**

- The pupils read the words and circle the corresponding parts of the picture.

16 **Listen and connect the letters. Then write.**

- Play the recording and give the pupils time to draw the lines to connect the letters. Play the recording again, and give pupils time to write the words.

17 **Listen and write the words.**

- Play the recording, pausing if necessary to give pupils time to write the words. Play it again for them to check what they have written. Check answers.

18 **Read aloud. Then listen and check.**

- Ask different pupils to read the text aloud, one sentence each. Then play the recording. They listen and check.

Ending the lesson

- Divide the class into two groups. Give each group a sound from this lesson: /ou/ and /ow/. Say words, some with and some without the new sounds. Pupils stand when they hear their sound.
- (For AB Answer Key, see p. 70. For Audioscript, see p. 72.)

11 (1:23) **Listen and repeat.**

1 **ou**   2 **ow**

12 (1:24) **Listen, point and say.**

13 (1:25) **Listen and blend the sounds.**

1 ou – t   out   2 l – ou – d   loud
3 sh – ou – t   shout   4 c – l – ou – d   cloud
5 l – ow   low   6 s – n – ow   snow
7 b – l – ow   blow   8 y – e – ll – ow   yellow

14 **Read the sentences aloud. Then find** *ou* **and** *ow*.

1 I can see a big rain cloud.

2 The yellow sun is low.

3 Blow the snow from the path.

4 Shout out loud!

OPTIONAL ACTIVITIES

Phonics game
Play *Pass the parcel* see p. 302 with words
containing the sounds /ou/ and /ow/.

Phonics game
Play *Words in the air* see p. 302.
Photocopiable 1.5 see Teacher's notes p. 286.

Lesson 7

Lesson aims
To connect other areas of the curriculum with English learning; to develop the cross-curricular topic through a short project

Cross-curricular focus
Social science (Unusual homes)

Target language
lighthouse, stairs, sea

Materials
Audio CD

Optional materials
Old home magazines, pictures of houses; reference books or internet; A3 paper; Active Teach; Digital Activity Book; CLIL poster; Photocopiable 1.6

Starting the lesson

- Play *Name it* see p. 299 to revise home vocabulary: *living room, kitchen, bedroom, bathroom, garden.*

Pupil's Book page 18

Presentation

- Draw a boat slowly on the board and ask the class to guess. Introduce *boat*. Repeat with *lighthouse*. Ask the class (L1) what a lighthouse is for and if they would like to live in one.

15 **Listen and read. Then say the name.**

- Tell the class that they are going to listen to a recording and follow in their books. Ask them to think about the question *Where does she live?* Play the recording, stopping at the end of Rosa's text. Pupils answer *(In a boat).*
- Play Rosa's text again. Ask a few more questions: *Does she like living in a boat? What does she like doing there?*
- Before playing Will's part, ask: *Does Will like climbing stairs?* Mime to show the meaning of *stairs*. Play the second half of the recording. Pupils answer *(No, he doesn't).*
- Play the recording again. Ask a few comprehension questions: *Does Rosa like her boat? Does she like watching TV?* etc.
- Pupils read the sentences and decide if they refer to Will or Rosa. Do the first sentence with the class. Then ask individual pupils to read out the sentences and the class says the correct name.

- Point out the speech bubble (*Rosa likes ... Will doesn't like ...*). Ask pupils to give you sentences based on these prompts.

KEY 1 Rosa, **2** Will, **3** Will, **4** Will, **5** Rosa

Mini-project

- Pupils read the Think! box and the Mini-project instructions. They could work individually or in pairs to design an unusual house. Bring a collection of old magazines or cut outs that they can use. They can also draw. They write a description of the house and things they like and don't like doing in it. Display the projects around the class.

Activity Book page 14

19 **Listen and read. Then write.**

- Ask (L1) what type of house is in the picture and teach the word in English *(a castle)*. Check meaning of the words in the table and teach *description* if necessary. Pupils read about Megan and complete the table.
- Copy the table on the board and ask individual pupils to fill it in with the correct information.

20 **Listen and tick (✓).**

- Play the recording. Pupils look at each picture carefully, listen and decide which is Rosa's bedroom.

21 **Draw or stick a photo of a special house.**

- Explain (L1) that pupils can draw a picture, or stick a photo into the space.

Ending the lesson

- Ask some pupils to show the houses they designed in AB Activity 21 and describe them. Ask the class to choose their favourite design and say why they like it.
- (For AB Answer Key, see p. 70. For Audioscript, see p. 72.)

15 **Listen and read. Then say the name.**

lighthouse   stairs   sea

Special houses

This is Rosa. Look at her house. It's a boat. Rosa likes her boat. She doesn't like watching TV. She likes reading and playing the guitar. She also likes riding her bike but not on the boat! She's got a cat. He likes sleeping on the boat.

This is Will. This is his house. It's a lighthouse by the sea! There are a lot of stairs. Will likes living in the lighthouse but he doesn't like climbing the stairs. He likes playing computer games and watching TV. He likes cooking too. His favourite food is fish.

Rosa or Will

1 ... likes reading.

2 ... likes cooking.

3 ... likes playing computer games.

4 ... doesn't like climbing the stairs.

5 ... doesn't like watching TV.

Rosa likes ...
Will doesn't like ...

THINK!

Houses come in different shapes and sizes. What other kinds of houses are there?

MINI-
PROJECT

Design an unusual house. Write about things you can do in it.

18   Lesson 7 social sciences (special houses)

AB p.14

OPTIONAL ACTIVITIES

Research
Write on the board: *igloo, tipi, tree house, caravan, cave house.* Pupils find information about these unusual types of home. They draw pictures and label them.

TPR game
Play *Teacher says* see p. 299.
Photocopiable 1.6 see Teacher's notes p. 287.

Lesson 8

Lesson aims
To learn about other cultures and respect
cultural differences

Cross-cultural focus
To learn about free time activities in other countries

Receptive language
stadium, floating

Materials
Audio CD

Optional materials
World map or globe; reference books, pictures
of free time activities; CLIL poster; Active Teach;
Digital Activity Book; Photocopiable 1.7

Starting the lesson

- Ask (L1) for pupils to name a country, and ask what
  they think of when they think about that country,
  e.g. *Canada – snow*. Ask them what kind of activities
  children might like doing in those countries.
- Play *Teacher says* see p. 299. Instead of saying e.g.
  Teacher says: Sleep! Say *Teacher says: I like …ing*.

Pupil's Book page 19

Presentation

- Ask pupils to look at the texts and say where the
  children come from. Write the names of the countries
  on the board *(France, Mexico)*. Then ask the class to
  help you locate them on the map or globe.

16 **Listen and read.**

- Point to the photographs of the children. Ask *Where
  are they?* or *What are they doing?*
- Ask *What's her/his name?* Pupils look for the answers
  in the texts.
- Tell the class that you are going to play a recording
  and they have to follow in their books. Play the
  recording once. Play it again, stopping after each
  description. Ask a few comprehension questions, e.g.
  What does Anne like doing? Where is the water park?

Practice

17 **Read and say *True* or *False*.**

- Pupils read the sentences. They reread the
  information about the children and decide if the
  sentences are true or false.
- Explain any new or difficult vocabulary. Ask them to
  correct the false sentences.
- Divide the class into pairs. Pupils take turns to ask and
  answer about his/her hobbies. Help with additional
  vocabulary if necessary.

KEY 1 False, **2** False, **3** True, **4** True.

Portfolio project

- Ask the pupils to think about what they like doing at
  the weekend.
- Pupils can write in their notebooks, using the texts on
  p. 19 as a model.

Activity Book page 15

22 **Read and write *T = True* or *F = False*.**

- Ask the pupils to find the names of the places on the
  world map. Explain any new or difficult vocabulary.
  Pupils read the texts and decide if the sentences are
  true or false. They correct the false ones.

Ending the lesson

- Play *Hangman* to revise the spelling of the leisure
  activities learnt in this lesson and in the rest of Unit 1.
- (For AB Answer Key, see p. 70. For Audioscript,
  see p. 73.)

OPTIONAL ACTIVITIES

Make a sentence
Show photos of people doing leisure activities that
pupils have learnt. Divide the class into two teams.
One pupil from each team in turn chooses a picture
and says a sentence, e.g. *He likes skiing*. Give a
point for each correct sentence. Teams can repeat
pictures but not sentences, so Team B can say, e.g.
The man doesn't like skiing.

Vote with your feet
Give the class choices while pointing to opposite
sides of the classroom. Point left and say *Skiing
… and then point right and say … or swimming?*
Pupils choose the activity they prefer, run to the
correct part of the classroom and mime the activity.
Continue with other pairs of activities, and then
allow individual pupils to take over your role.
Photocopiable 1.7 see Teacher's notes p. 287.

Wider World
At the weekend

16 🔘 1:32 **Listen and read.**

Anne's blog ⊗

Hi, I'm Anne. I'm from France. I like riding my bike with my mum and dad. It's good exercise. I like riding my bike on sunny days. My little brother likes riding too!

Anne, 9, France

Carlos's blog ⊗

Hi, I'm Carlos. I'm from Mexico. Look! I'm at a beautiful water park in Cancun. I like swimming and floating down the stream with my friends. It's great!

Carlos, 10, Mexico

17 **Read and say** *True* **or** *False*.

1 Anne lives in Spain.

2 Carlos doesn't like swimming.

3 Anne likes riding her bike with her family.

4 Carlos goes to a water park.

PORTFOLIO

Think and write.

What do you like doing at the weekend?

Lesson 9

Lesson aims
To review the unit language with a game and the Picture Dictionary

Materials
Audio CD; Flashcards (Leisure activities)

Optional materials
Active Teach; Digital Activity Book; CLIL poster; Reading and Writing Booklet

Starting the lesson

- Write on the board: *leisure activities*. Divide the class into pairs. Ask them to write as many words as they can think of for this category. For stronger classes, you may set a time limit. Check which pair has written more words.

Pupil's Book page 20

18 Write in your notebook. Then play.

- Focus on the game board. Read out the instructions. Check that pupils understand them. Revise the vocabulary using the flashcards (leisure activities). Practise with the pupils the language to be used: *Does he like skateboarding? Yes, he does./No, he doesn't.*
- Pupils write the table in their notebooks and complete the information about themselves and family members. Then they take turns to ask and answer and complete the information for their partners under the 'Friend 1', 'Friend 2' headings.
- Pupils can use the Picture Dictionary (AB p. 104.)

Activity Book page 16

23 Look and write.

- Ask pupils (L1) if they have ever done a crossword and elicit/explain how to do one if necessary. Pupils solve the puzzle individually or in pairs. Check as a class, asking, e.g. *What's number 2?* Pupils answer.

24 Look and write.

- Direct the pupils' attention to the lists of likes and dislikes for the boy and the girl. Tell them to use this information to complete the sentences.
- When they have finished, ask individual pupils to read the sentences to the class.

Ending the lesson

- Say and mime, e.g. *I like reading.* Ask a pupil to repeat the sentence, adding another activity and mime, e.g. *I like reading and drinking.* Continue in the same way and after three turns say *But I don't … .* The next pupil has to say a negative sentence about an action that hasn't been mentioned before, e.g. *I like reading and drinking and eating but I don't like playing tennis.* The pupil after that starts a new round.
- (For AB Answer Key, see p. 70.)

18 **Write in your notebook. Then play.**

HAVE FUN!

	Family member 1 (man)	Family member 2 (woman)	Friend 1 (boy)	Friend 2 (girl)
Me				
My friend				

Friend 1. Does he like skateboarding?

No, he doesn't.

Does he like cooking?

No, he doesn't.

Does he like watching films?

No, he doesn't. My turn.

Guess!

Picture Dictionary

AB p.104

20 Lesson 9 review and consolidation

AB p.16

OPTIONAL ACTIVITIES

Flashcard game
Play *Hit the card* see p. 299.

Draw a picture
Pupils draw their favourite activity in their notebooks. Ask one pupil to show his/her picture to the class. Elicit a description of it using the words

from the word bank. Then ask pupils to write a description of his/her own picture. Divide the class into pairs. Pupils ask and answer questions about their pictures.

Reading and Writing Booklet p. 3 see Answer Key p. 282.

67

Lesson 10

Lesson aims
To personalise and assess efforts
To revise language from the unit

Materials
Audio CD

Optional materials
Digital Activity Book; CLIL poster; Online material – *Film Studio Island*; Active Teach; Grammar reference and Review for Unit 1 (PB p. 112 and AB p. 96); Test Booklet; Grammar Booklet

Starting the lesson

- This is a self assessment activity. Tell the pupils that the activities on this page will show what they have learnt in this unit.

Pupil's Book page 21

19   **Listen and point.**

- Tell the pupils that they must choose the correct picture, a or b, for each question. Play the recording more than once if necessary.
- Pupils listen, look at the pictures and choose the correct answer.

> **KEY** 1 a, 2 b, 3 b, 4 a, 5 b, 6 a, 7 a, 8 a

20 Look, read and answer.

- Pupils answer the questions, based on the pictures.

> **KEY** 1 She likes cooking. 2 He likes painting.

Activity Book page 17

- Focus on the *I can* sentences at the bottom of the page. Tell the pupils that they have to tick the boxes, depending on whether they think they can do the *I can* points.

25 What do or don't you like doing? Write ✓ or X.

- Pupils look at the pictures and decide what they like or don't like doing. They write ticks or crosses accordingly. Check answers asking a few pupils to tell the class.

26 Look at Activity 25 and write.

- Pupils write a short description based on the opinions they expressed in the previous activity. They write what they like and what they don't like. Ask a few pupils to read their texts to the class.

27 Write about your friends or family.

- Pupils read the gapped sentences. Ask (L1) what words can go in the sentences (*leisure activities*). Pupils then complete the sentences about their friends or family.

Ending the lesson

- Play *Last man standing* see p. 301 to revise questions, e.g. *Do you like (cleaning)? Does (Madley Kool) like (skateboarding)? What does (Madley Kool) like doing?*
- (For Audioscript, see p. 73.)

19 **1:33** Listen and point.

20 Look, read and answer.

1   What does she like doing?

2   What does he like doing?

OPTIONAL ACTIVITIES

Drawing game
Play *Alternative bingo* see p. 299 with free time activities.

Flashcard game
Play *Correct order* see p. 298.

Activity Book Review see p. 96.
Grammar Booklet p. 3 see Answer Key p. 284.
Test Booklet Unit 1 see Answer Key p. 294.
Online World
Pupils can now go online to *Film Studio Island* and enjoy the fun and games.

Activity Book Answer Key

p. 8, Activity 1
1 playing the guitar, 2 reading the newspaper,
3 cooking, 4 watching TV, 5 skateboarding,
6 playing computer games, 7 skiing, 8 chatting online

p. 8, Activity 2
1 He doesn't like playing computer games. 2 He likes playing the guitar. 3 He doesn't like cooking. 4 He likes skiing.

p. 9, Activity 3
a ✓, b ✗, c ✓ d ✗, e ✓, f ✓, g ✗, h ✗

p. 9, Activity 4
1 skiing, playing computer games, cooking, reading the newspaper
2 cooking, reading the newspaper, skateboarding, skiing

p. 10, Activity 6
1 Y, 2 Y, 3 N, 4 N

p. 10, Activity 7
1 playing hockey, Yes, does
2 riding a scooter, Yes, does
3 walking the dog, No, don't
4 painting, No, doesn't

p. 10, Activity 8
1 skipping, 2 reading, 3 watching TV, 4 surfing the internet

p. 11, Activity 9

	playing computer games	surfing the internet	watching TV	walking the dog	chatting online
Me	✓	✓	✗	✓	✓
My mum	✗	✗	✓	✓	✓
My dad	✗	✓	✓	✗	✓

p. 11, Activity 10
1 Yes, she does.
2 No, she doesn't.
3 chatting online, watching TV, walking the dog
4 watching TV, surfing the internet, chatting online
(For questions 3 and 4, the activities can be mentioned in any order.)

p. 11, Activity 11
1 Does he like skiing? No, he doesn't.
2 Does he like cooking? Yes, he does.

p.12, Activity 12
Cleo likes watching and looking and listening.

p. 12, Activity 13
a 5, b 3, c 2, d 1, e 4

p. 12, Activity 14
1 looking, 2 sleeping, eating, 3 lying, 4 watching, listening

p. 13, Activity 16
boy, chair, day, year

p. 13, Activity 17
1 out, 2 loud, 3 low, 4 yellow

p. 14, Activity 19
House: castle, **Description:** 21 rooms and a big garden, **Animals:** swans, **Likes:** playing in the garden, reading outside, **Doesn't like:** cleaning the castle

p. 14, Activity 20
Picture 1

p. 15, Activity 22
1 T, 2 F, 3 T, 4 T, 5 F, 6 T

p. 16, Activity 23

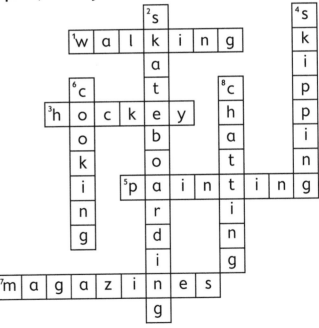

p. 16, Activity 24
1 playing computer games and reading the newspaper
2 Does she like playing the guitar?
3 He likes skiing and watching TV.
4 like riding a scooter

Audioscript

Lesson 1 Activity 1 CD1:11
JE = JENNY   JO = JOHN   S = SAM   R = RUBY

JE   Where's Madley Kool? Is he here?
JO   No, he isn't.
JE   Look at his room!
JO   He likes playing football.
S   Look at the photos! He likes skiing. Hmm, does he like swimming?
JO   He likes watching TV.
R   Look at the books! He doesn't like reading.
JE   And he doesn't like cooking.
R   Eeeuw! He doesn't like cleaning!

Lesson 1 Activity 2 CD1:12
a skiing
b cooking
c watching TV
d playing the guitar
e playing computer games
f skateboarding
g reading the newspaper
h chatting online

Lesson 1 Activity 3 CD1:13
1 He's watching TV.
2 He's playing the guitar.
3 She's reading the newspaper.
4 He's skiing.
5 He's skateboarding.

Lesson 2 Activity 4 CD1:14
Madley Kool, Madley Kool,
He likes playing football,
He likes going to the pool.
Does he like skiing and watching TV?
Yes, he does, just like me!
Does he like cooking? Does he like cleaning?
No, he doesn't.
And he doesn't like reading.

Lesson 2 Activity 5 CD1:15
R = RUBY   J = JOHN

R   What does Jenny like? Does Jenny like skiing?
J   No, she doesn't.
R   Does she like playing football?
J   Yes, she likes playing football. And she likes watching TV.
R   How about Sam? Does he like cooking?
J   Yes, he does. But he doesn't like cleaning.
R   Does he like reading?
J   No, he doesn't.

Lesson 2 Activity 3 (AB) CD1:16
Ruby likes skiing and playing computer games. She doesn't like cooking. She doesn't like reading the newspaper.

John likes cooking and reading the newspaper. He doesn't like skateboarding. He doesn't like skiing.

Lesson 3 Activity 6 CD1:17
a skipping
b painting
c playing hockey
d reading magazines
e watching films
f surfing the internet
g walking the dog
h riding a scooter

Lesson 3 Activity 7 CD1:18
Do you like riding your bike?
Yes, I do. I like riding my bike.
Do you like playing the guitar?
Yes, I do. Look! Look! I'm a pop star.

What do you, do you like doing?
What do you, do you like doing?

Do you like playing computer games?
No, I don't. I like riding my scooter.
Do you like skateboarding too?
Yes, I like skateboarding! How about you?

What do you, do you like doing?
What do you, do you like doing?

Lesson 3 Activity 6 (AB) CD1:19
1 Do you like playing hockey?
   Yes, I do.
2 Do you like riding a scooter?
   Yes, I do. I love it.
3 Do you like walking the dog?
   No, we don't. We love our dog, but he is too big!
4 Do you like painting?
   No, I don't.

Lesson 4 Activity 8 CD1:20
a This is my dog, Timmy. He doesn't like running and he doesn't like catching a ball. But he likes skateboarding. Look! He's cool.
b Hi, I'm Anna. I'm 9 years old. I like singing with my friends. I don't like chatting online but I like surfing the Internet.
c I'm Charlie. I don't like watching TV and I don't like cooking. I like skiing. My sister doesn't like watching TV either. She likes skiing with me. It's fun!

Lesson 4 Activity 9 (AB) CD:21

I'm Fiona. I like playing computer games and I like surfing the Internet. I don't like watching TV. I like walking the dog and chatting online.

My mum doesn't like playing computer games and she doesn't like surfing the Internet. But she likes chatting online. She likes walking the dog and watching TV too.

My dad also likes watching TV and he likes surfing the Internet. He doesn't like playing computer games but he likes chatting online. He doesn't like walking the dog.

Lesson 6 Activity 11 CD:23

o u
/ou/ /ou/ /ou/
o w
/ow/ /ow/ /ow/

Lesson 6 Activity 12 CD:24

/ow/ /ow/
/ou/ /ou/
/ow/ /ow/
/ou/ /ou/
/ou/ /ou/
/ow/ /ow/

Lesson 6 Activity 13 CD:25

1 /ou/ /t/
   out
2 /l/ /ou/ d/
   loud
3 /sh/ /ou/ /t/
   shout
4 /k/ /l/ ou/ /d/
   cloud
5 /l/ /ow/
   low
6 /s/ /n/ /ow/
   snow
7 /b/ /l/ /ow/
   blow
8 /y/ /e/ /l/ /ow/
   yellow

Lesson 6 Activity 16 (AB) CD:26

1 /b/   /oy/
2 /ch/   /air/
3 /d/   /ay/
4 /y/   /ear/

Lesson 6 Activity 17 (AB) CD:27

1 out
2 loud
3 low
4 yellow

Lesson 6 Activity 18 (AB) CD:28

It's wintertime. The wind blows and black clouds are low. There is a lot of snow. Wear a coat, a hat and a scarf when you go out.

Lesson 7 Activity 15 CD:29

This is Rosa. Look at her house. It's a boat. Rosa likes her boat. She doesn't like watching TV. She likes reading and playing the guitar. She also likes riding her bike but not on the boat! She's got a cat. He likes sleeping on the boat.

This is Will. This is his house. It's a lighthouse by the sea! There are a lot of stairs. Will likes living in the lighthouse but he doesn't like climbing the stairs. He likes playing computer games and watching TV. He likes cooking too. His favourite food is fish.

Lesson 7 Activity 19 (AB) CD:30

This is Megan. She lives in a special house. It's a castle. It's got 21 rooms and a big garden. She likes playing in the garden and reading outside. In the morning she can hear the swans but at night it's very quiet. She doesn't like cleaning the castle, it's too big!

Lesson 7 Activity 20 (AB) CD:31

I'm Brandon. I like skateboarding. I don't like watching TV. I like reading and I like playing the guitar. I don't like cleaning.

Lesson 8 Activity 16

1 Anne's blog: Hi, I'm Anne. I'm from France. I like riding my bike with my mum and dad. It's good exercise. I like riding my bike on sunny days. My little brother likes riding too! Anne, 9, France.

2 Carlos's blog: Hi, I'm Carlos. I'm from Mexico. Look! I'm at a beautiful water park in Cancun. I like swimming and floating down the stream with my friends. It's great! Carlos, 10, Mexico.

Lesson 10 Activity 19

1 She likes surfing the Internet.
2 I like walking the dog.
3 What do you like doing?
   I like playing the guitar.
4 What do they like doing?
   They like playing football?
5 What does she like doing?
   She likes painting.
6 Does he like riding a scooter?
   No, he doesn't. He likes skateboarding.
7 Does he like cooking?
   Yes, he does.
8 Do they like playing computer games?
   Yes, they do.

Objectives

- describe animals
- talk about what animals eat and where they live
- describe manner
- pronounce properly /all/ and /aw/

Topics
- Wild animals and their food
- Wild animals and their habitats
- Types of animals

Phonics
/all/ and /aw/.

Values
- Protect wildlife

Stories
- Unit opener: characters with wild animals
- Story episode: seeing crocodiles and other animals

Language
Vocabulary
- Wild animals: giraffe, elephant, lion, monkey, hippo, crocodile, leaves, grass
- Food: leaves, grass, fruit, meat
- Habitats: river, desert, grassland, forest, rainforest
- Types of animals: herbivores, omnivores, carnivores
- Other animals: crab, camel, zebra, panda, gorilla
- Other words: wildlife park, energy

Revision
meat, fruit, bird, insects, frog, worm, horse, cow, bees, cat, mouse, rabbit, claws, eat, sleep, run, zoo, rock, tree

Structures
(Giraffes) eat (leaves).
Do (giraffes) eat (leaves)? Yes, they do.
Do (giraffes) eat (meat)? No, they don't.
What do (crabs) eat? They eat (worms).
Where do (crabs) live? They live in (rivers).
How many (teeth) have (gorillas) got? They've got (32 teeth).
How much (fish) do they (eat)? They (eat) a lot of (fruit and leaves).
They walk slowly but they can run fast.
They can swim very well.

CLIL language
The food chain: herbivores, carnivores, omnivores

Songs and chants
- Chant
- Song about physical description of people
- Karaoke song

Sociocultural aspects
- Finding out about wildlife parks in other parts of the world
- Comparing types of wildlife parks
- Identifying characteristics of wildlife parks

Cross-curricular contents
- Science: the food chain
- Language Arts: reading a story, acting out, telling a story
- Language skills: reading and understanding information provided through diagrams

Learning strategies
- Using illustrations to infer the meaning of words
- Classifying words to remember them better
- Identifying rules about the use of *Have got*
- Logical thinking: using graphic organisers
- Critical thinking: comparing and contrasting information
- Collaborative learning: project work and pair work
- Self assessment

Basic competences

- Linguistic communication: Observe regularities in language use to infer rules (L1 to L10)
- Knowledge and interaction with the physical world: Know about animals, what they eat and where they live (L1 to L4): Know about the food chain (L7)
- Mathematical competence: Interpret a diagram (L7)
- Processing information and digital competence: Use *Film Studio Island* online component
- Social and civic competence: Protect wildlife (L5)
- Cultural and artistic competence: To identify wildlife parks in the world (L8)
- Learning to learn: Reflect on what has been learnt and self-evaluate progress (L10)
- Autonomy and personal initiative: Develop one's own criteria and social skills (L1 to L10)

Skills

Listening
- Identifying wild animals, their food and habitats in recordings
- Understanding information to identify wild animals
- Understanding specific information in a song about wild animals
- Understanding general and specific information in a story

Reading
- Understanding information in sentences (wild animals)
- Understanding general and specific information in a cartoon strip story
- Reading a text about crocodiles; understanding general and specific information
- Showing understanding of texts about wildlife parks through answering questions

Speaking
- Chanting and singing
- Pronouncing /all/ and /aw/ correctly
- Saying where animals live and what they eat
- Describing a food chain

Writing
- Writing words for wild animals, what they eat and their habitats
- Transferring information from a table to questions and answers
- Unscramble words and write them
- Completing short texts with words provided
- Complete a crossword
- Write information in a table
- Writing descriptions of wild animals

Talking
- Exchanging information about what animals eat
- Asking and answering about animals in an animal park
- Role playing a story
- Asking and answering questions about wild animals and their characteristics
- Talking about a food chain

Classroom ideas

- Play memory games with flashcards
- Decorate the class with the cross-curricular poster
- Use the internet to find information about wild animals, what they eat and their habitats
- Find other examples of food chains on the internet
- Bring to the classroom library books that include wild animals
- Photocopiables

Take-home English

- Home-School Link
- Notes for Parents
- A sample of work each week
- Portfolio

Self assessment

- Pupils can describe animals
- Pupils can talk about what animals eat and where they live
- Pupils can describe manner

Evaluation

- Pupil's Book page 31
- Activity Book page 27
- Photocopiable 2.7
- Picture Dictionary
- Test Booklet – Unit 2

2 Wild animals

Lesson 1

Lesson aims
To learn and practise new vocabulary (Wild animals)

Target language
giraffe, elephant, lion, monkey, hippo, crocodile, leaves, grass, fruit, meat

Materials
Audio CD; Flashcards and Wordcards (Wild animals)

Optional materials
Active Teach; Digital Activity Book; Photocopiable 2.1

Starting the lesson

- Elicit all the animals pupils have learnt so far. Write them on the board.
- Write headings *Pets*, *Farm*, *Forest*, *Insects* and check meaning (L1). Point to one of the category headings. Pupils say the animals from the list on the board that go in that category.

> Pupil's Book pages 22–23

Presentation

- Hold up the wild animal flashcards for the lesson's animals one at a time and say the words for pupils to repeat. Hold up the flashcards again and ask individual pupils to say the words.
- Direct pupils' attention to the main illustration. Point to the characters and ask *Who's this? (From left to right: Sam, Cleo the cat, Jenny, John and Ruby)*. Ask (L1) what they can remember about the characters' adventures so far. (*The children are at a film studio and are looking for the film star Madley Kool. Cleo the cat is helping them.*) Ask *Where are they now?* Elicit (L1) that they are on a film set.

  Listen.

- Point to the animals in the main illustration and ask *What's this?* Pupils answer.
- Tell pupils (L1) they are going to listen to a recording describing what they can see in the main illustration. (If possible, explain that Cleo the cat and the two birds aren't relevant in this activity.)
- Tell pupils that two of the wild animals in the picture are not mentioned in the recording. Play the recording again. Pupils decide what's missing. Pupils check if they were right.

KEY Wild animals not mentioned: frog, crocodile
Also not mentioned: Cleo the cat (not wild), the two birds (not animals)

 Listen and repeat.

- Direct pupils' attention to the labelled food pictures g–j: *leaves, grass, fruit, meat.* Check the meaning. Say the words and pupils repeat.
- Play the recording, pausing after each word. Pupils point to the pictures in Activity 1. Play the recording again. Pupils point and repeat each word. Ask *What's (a)?* Pupils look and answer.
- Display the relevant wild animal flashcards on one side of the board and write the corresponding words or put up wordcards on the other side. Pupils come to the front, read out the words and match them to the pictures.
- Shuffle the flashcards of the wild animals from this lesson and choose one. Do not show it to the class. Describe it: *It's (big) and (grey). It's got (four legs) and a (long nose).* Pupils call out the correct word.

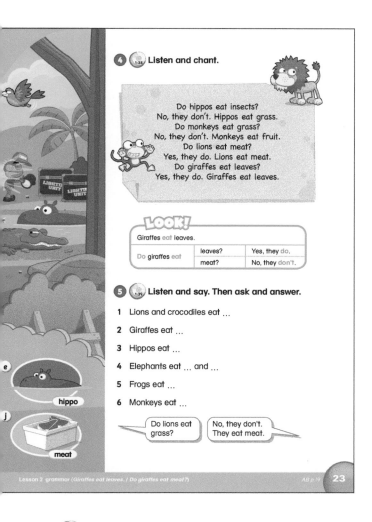

4 🔊 **Listen and chant.**

Do hippos eat insects?
No, they don't. Hippos eat grass.
Do monkeys eat grass?
No, they don't. Monkeys eat fruit.
Do lions eat meat?
Yes, they do. Lions eat meat.
Do giraffes eat leaves?
Yes, they do. Giraffes eat leaves.

LOOK!

Giraffes eat leaves.

Do giraffes eat	leaves?	Yes, they do.
	meat?	No, they don't.

5 🔊 **Listen and say. Then ask and answer.**

1 Lions and crocodiles eat …

2 Giraffes eat …

3 Hippos eat …

4 Elephants eat … and …

5 Frogs eat …

6 Monkeys eat …

Do lions eat grass?

No, they don't. They eat meat.

 hippo

 meat

Lesson 2 grammar (*Giraffes eat leaves. / Do giraffes eat meat?*)   AB p.19 **23**

3 🔊 **Listen and find.**

- Point to the lion and the meat and say *Lions like meat.* Point to the elephant and the grass. Ask *And elephants? Do elephants like meat?* Pupils answer *yes* or *no*. Say *No, elephants like grass.* Repeat with the other animals.
- Play the recording, pausing after each word. Pupils point to the animal and food pictures. Play the recording again. Pupils point and repeat each word. Ask *What's (a)?* Pupils look and answer.

Activity Book page 18

1 🔊 **Listen and number.**

- Tell pupils to listen to the recording and number the pictures following the information they hear. Play the recording. Ask pupils to write the numbers. Play the recording a second time. Check answers with the class.

2 **Look and write.**

- Explain (L1) that pupils have to work out what animal is in each picture and then write the answers in complete sentences, as in the example. Check answers with the class.

Ending the lesson

- Play a guessing game. Ask pupils to think of an animal. Ask questions to guess what animal it is, e.g. *Is it (big)? Has it got (four legs)? Is it (brown)? Can it (swim)?* When pupils have grasped the idea, think of an animal and tell pupils to ask the questions.
- (For AB Answer Key, see p. 96. For Audioscript, see p. 97.)

OPTIONAL ACTIVITIES

Perform a scene
Play CD1:34 again, pausing after each line, and ask pupils to help you write it on the board. Read it as a class. Divide the class into groups of four and assign a character to each group member. Groups rehearse their parts. Ask groups to come to the front of the class in turn to act out the dialogue.

Flashcard game
Play *Animal farm* see p. 299.

Photocopiable 2.1 see Teacher's notes p. 287.

NOTES

Lesson 2

Lesson aims
To revise the vocabulary of Lesson 1; to learn and practise the new structures (asking and answering about food)

Target language
(Giraffes) eat (leaves). Do (giraffes) eat (leaves)? Yes, they do. Do (giraffes) eat (meat)? No, they don't.

Materials
Audio CD; Flashcards and Wordcards (Wild animals)

Optional materials
Active Teach; Digital Activity Book; Grammar Booklet; paper for posters; pictures of animals, e.g. from magazines

Starting the lesson

- Use the wild animal flashcards to revise the new vocabulary from the previous lesson. Hold up the flashcards in turn and elicit the words. Then hold up the animal wordcards and pupils read out the words. Alternatively, with stronger classes, ask individual pupils to come to the front and write the words on the board.
- Play *Picture charades* see p. 298 with animal words.

Pupil's Book page 23

- Direct pupils' attention to the main illustration. Ask questions about the animals: *Do giraffes eat leaves?* Pupils answer *Yes* or *No*.

Presentation

- Pupils read the sentences in the Look! box. Explain (L1) that they use *do* in questions and short answers about more than one person, animal or thing. Ask pupils to give more example questions, e.g. *Do cats eat insects?* Write them on the board. Pupils copy in their notebooks.
- Read the Look! box.

4 **Listen and chant.**

- Play the recording. Pupils listen to the chant and follow the words. Play the chant again. Pause after each line for pupils to repeat. Play the chant once more for pupils to join in and say together. Use the flashcards to help prompt the words if necessary.
- Divide the class into two groups. One group chants the questions and the other chants the answers. They then swap roles.

Practice

5 **Listen and say. Then ask and answer.**

- Ask pupils (L1) to read the sentences and check that they understand the meaning.
- Ask two pupils to read out the speech bubbles. Say the question and ask pupils to repeat a few times.
- Divide the class into pairs. Play the recording. Pupils take turns to ask and answer questions about what animals eat. Tell the class to ask about a variety of animals and not just the ones that appear in the lesson.
- Write on the board: *meat, fruit, leaves* and *grass*. Elicit from pupils the animals they know that like to eat these, e.g. *Dogs eat meat. Hippos eat grass.*
- You may wish to explain (L1) that animals that like meat are *carnivores*, those that eat fruit, grass and vegetables are *herbivores*, and the ones that eat both are *omnivores*, e.g. bears and people.

KEY 1 meat, **2** leaves, **3** grass, **4** leaves, grass, **5** insects, **6** fruit

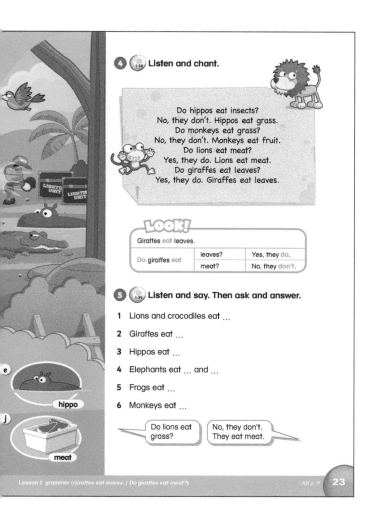

4 Listen and chant.

Do hippos eat insects?
No, they don't. Hippos eat grass.
Do monkeys eat grass?
No, they don't. Monkeys eat fruit.
Do lions eat meat?
Yes, they do. Lions eat meat.
Do giraffes eat leaves?
Yes, they do. Giraffes eat leaves.

LOOK!

Giraffes eat leaves.

| Do giraffes eat | leaves? | Yes, they do. |
| | meat? | No, they don't. |

5 Listen and say. Then ask and answer.

1 Lions and crocodiles eat …

2 Giraffes eat …

3 Hippos eat …

4 Elephants eat … and …

5 Frogs eat …

6 Monkeys eat …

Do lions eat grass?

No, they don't. They eat meat.

hippo

meat

Lesson 2 grammar (Giraffes eat leaves. / Do giraffes eat meat?)   AB p.19   **23**

Ending the lesson

- Display the wild animal flashcards around the room and play *Guess the card* see p. 299.
- (For AB Answer Key, see p. 96. For Audioscript, see p. 97.)

OPTIONAL ACTIVITIES

Question and answer

Pupils ask and answer questions about animals and food, e.g. *Do giraffes eat meat? What do cats eat?*

Animal poster

Make a poster with the class. Give pupils magazines to cut out pictures of animals. Alternatively, bring the cut outs yourself. Write three headings on top of a sheet of poster paper: *They eat meat. / They eat grass, leaves or fruit. / They eat insects.* Ask pupils to stick in the corresponding pictures and label them.

Grammar Booklet p.4 aee Answer key 284.

NOTES

Activity Book page 19

3 What do the animals eat? Write.

- Direct pupils' attention to the pictures. Point to the animals in turn and ask *What's this?* Pupils answer.
- Now turn their attention to the words in the word bank and the example sentence. They make sentences about what each animal eats.
- When they have finished, have pairs of pupils ask *What do (monkeys) eat?* and answer by reading out their sentences to the class.

4 Look and write.

- Make sure pupils know how to use the table. Ask yes/no questions about what monkeys eat, miming the drawing of a tick with a nod for yes, and the drawing of a cross with a head shake for no.
- Focus on the questions and answers. Read the example and tell pupils (L1) to complete the others in a similar way. Ask individual pupils to read a question and answer in turn.

2

Lesson 3

Lesson aims
To extend the unit vocabulary set about wild animals and their habitats; to practise the unit language with a song

Target language
crab, camel, zebra, panda, gorilla, river, desert, grassland, forest, rainforest

Materials
Audio CD; Flashcards and Wordcards (Wild animals)

Optional materials
World map or globe; Active Teach; Digital Activity Book; Photocopiables 2.2–2.3; Reading and Writing Booklet

Starting the lesson

- Play the chant from Lesson 2 CD1:38 and repeat it in two groups: Group A asks the questions and Group B answers. Then they swap over.

Pupil's Book page 24

Presentation

6 **Listen and repeat.**

- Introduce the new words using the flashcards. Hold them up and say the words for pupils to repeat. Ask individual pupils to say the words. Play the recording for pupils to listen and repeat.
- Now put the flashcards on the board. Point to the different flashcards and ask the class to say the words.
- Point to a picture and ask pupils: *What's this?* They answer. Repeat with the other pictures.

Song

7 **Listen and point. Then sing.**

- Show a map or globe of the world and ask *Where's Africa?* Invite pupils to answer. If necessary, point to the map and say *Here, this is Africa.* Ask, e.g. *Are there monkeys/snakes, etc. in Africa?* Pupils answer.
- Play the recording. Pupils listen and follow in their books. Play the song again. Mime to make meaning clear. Explain (L1) the meaning of *all day long* and *catch.* Play the song again. Pupils join in and sing together. You can now play the karaoke song (Active Teach).

- Direct pupils' attention to the Look! box. Read the sentences with the class. Explain (L1) that we add /s/ to *live* with *he, she* and *it*, but we do not add /s/ with *they* or when we are speaking about more than one person, animal or thing. Ask pupils for more examples and write them on the board. Pupils copy in their notebooks.
- Read the Look! box.

Practice

8 **Ask and answer.**

- Organise the class in pairs. Ask the pupils to take it in turns to ask and answer questions about places where animals live.
- Write the question *What do gorillas eat?* on the board. Explain (L1) that Pupil 1 asks *What do gorillas eat?* and Pupil 2 answers *They eat fruit and leaves.* Then it's Pupil 2's turn to ask another question.

Activity Book page 20

5 **Match.**

- Pupils read the words and match them to the correct picture.

6 **Unscramble and write. Then number.**

- Pupils look at the words with jumbled letters. Ask them to unscramble and write them. Then they write the corresponding number in each picture.

7 **Listen and write.**

- Play the recording once. Pupils just listen. Play it again, pausing after each sentence for the pupils to complete the sentences. Play the recording again so pupils can check their answers.

Ending the lesson

- Divide the class into two groups. One pupil from Group A describes an animal, e.g. *It's got four legs. It eats grass. It's very tall.* Group B guesses what animal it is (*It's a giraffe*). Allow a limited number of guesses to make the game more challenging.
- (For AB Answer Key, see p. 96. For Audioscript, see p. 97.)

OPTIONAL ACTIVITIES
Endangered animal mini-project
Pupils draw an endangered animal and write a short description. Write an example on the board, e.g. *Pandas live in China. They're black and white and they're big. They eat bamboo.* Give help as necessary.

6 (1:40) **Listen and repeat.**

a crab
b camel
c zebra
d panda
e gorilla
f river
g desert
h grassland
i forest
j rainforest

7 (1:41) **Listen and point. Then sing.**

SONG

Zebras Lions live in forests grasslands .
They're big and strong.
They like sleeping all day long.
They run very fast to catch their lunch.
What do they eat? They eat meat leaves .
Crunch, crunch, munch!

Pandas Gorillas live in rainforests forests .
They're big and cute.
They like eating all day long.
They climb tall trees to find their lunch.
What do they eat? They eat fruit leaves .
Crunch, crunch, munch!

8 **Ask and answer.**

Where do zebras live?
They live in grasslands.
What do they eat?
They eat grass.

LOOK!

What do crabs eat?	They eat worms.
Where do crabs live?	They live in rivers.

Team game
Play *Hide and seek* see p. 301.
Photocopiable 2.2 see Teacher's notes p. 287.
Photocopiable 2.3 see Teacher's notes p. 287.

Reading and Writing Booklet p. 4 see Answer Key p. 282.

2

Lesson 4

Lesson aims
To develop reading, writing, listening and speaking skills; to learn and practise new structures: *How much/many ...?*, adverbs of manner

Target language
Keeper, How many teeth have they got? They've got 65 teeth. How much meat and fish do they eat every other day? About a kilo and a half/ Adverbs of manner: Crocodiles can swim very well. They can't run fast.

Materials
Audio CD; Flashcards (Wild animals)

Optional materials
Active Teach; Digital Activity Book; Grammar Booklet; a map of the world

Starting the lesson

● Describe animals that pupils know, making deliberate mistakes, e.g. *Elephants live in Africa. They eat meat. They can swim. They like playing tennis.* Pupils stand up and correct you when they hear a mistake.

Pupil's Book page 25

Presentation

● Direct pupils' attention to the Look! box. Read the questions and answers with the class. Explain (L1) that we use *How many?* to ask about countable nouns, and *How much?* to ask about uncountable nouns. Give some more examples from the language of the unit, e.g. *How much fruit? 2 kilos. How many bananas? Six. How many elephants? How much meat?* Ask pupils for more examples and write them on the board.
● Read the Look! box.

Skills

9 🔊 1:43 **Listen and read. Then answer.**

● Focus first on the illustrations that go with the text. Point to the animal park keeper and explain the meaning. Ask the class to say what they know about crocodiles (L1). Write the information on the board. Then play the recording.
● Tell pupils (L1) that this text is a blog entry.
● Pause after each sentence and ask a pupil to reread the sentence aloud.
● Read out the questions and check that pupils understand. Pupils read the text again and answer the questions. They can write their answers in their notebooks. Check answers with the class.
● Depending on your class, you may wish to explain the meaning of *every other day.*

KEY
1 They eat meat.
2 Yes, they do.
3 They live in Africa and Australia. They live in rivers.
4 They've got 65 teeth.
5 It's cleaning her teeth.
6 They eat about a kilo and a half of meat or fish (every other day).

10 🔊 1:44 **Listen and read. Then ask and answer.**

● Ask the class what they know about giraffes (L1). Write the information on the board.
● Play the recording. Read out the questions and check that pupils understand. Ask the pupils to read the model questions aloud. Organise the class in pairs. Tell the pupils to take it in turns to ask and answer questions about giraffes.

Practice

Activity Book page 21

8 **Look and write.**

● Tell the pupils that they have to complete the sentences about different animals. They try to insert the words in the word bank in the correct place. Check answers with the class.

9 **Look at Activity 8 and write.**

● Tell the class that now they have to complete the questions and answers about different animals following the example. Explain (L1) that most of the information is in Activity 8, but some they will have to remember or check in the PB.
● Pupils complete the questions and answers individually. Then they check answers in pairs. Check them with the class.

Ending the lesson

● Sing the song from Lesson 3 CD1:41.
● Pupils work in groups or pairs to compile a poster about their favourite animal, modelling the text in AB Activity 9 and illustrating it using their own drawings or pictures from magazines or the internet.
● (For AB Answer Key, see p. 96. For Audioscript, see p. 98.)

Pupils can now go online to *Film Studio Island* and find the light that Cleo is holding. It is inside the Wildlife Studio at the very top of the tree where Jungle Man's treehouse is. Once pupils click on the light they are taken to a supplementary language game based on the vocabulary in this unit.

82

LOOK!

| How many teeth have gorillas got? | They've got 32 teeth. |
| How much fish do crocodiles eat? | They eat a lot of fish. |

9 **Listen and read. Then answer.**

Discovery Island Animal Park: Crocodiles

Blog posted by: Paul, animal park keeper

Hi, I'm Paul. There are seven crocodiles here at Discovery Island Animal Park. This is Snapper. She's my favourite. Look at the bird in her mouth! It's cleaning her teeth.

Crocodiles live in Africa and Australia. They live in rivers. They are very big and strong. They like sleeping in the sun and swimming. They can swim very well. They can run but they can't run really fast. Crocodiles have got very big mouths with 65 teeth. When they are four years old, they eat about a kilo and a half of meat or fish every other day. They can eat you too so watch out!

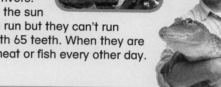

1 What do crocodiles eat?

2 Do crocodiles swim well?

3 Where do crocodiles live?

4 How many teeth have crocodiles got?

5 What's the bird doing?

6 How much meat or fish do they eat?

10 **Listen and read. Then ask and answer.**

Giraffes live in Africa. They live in grasslands. They have got very long necks and they are the tallest land animal. A giraffe has got 32 teeth and they eat a lot of leaves. They walk slowly but they can run fast.

Where do giraffes live?

Do they walk slowly?

How many teeth have they got?

How much food do they eat?

OPTIONAL ACTIVITIES

Flashcard game
Play *Snap* see p.298.

Flashcard game
Play *Who's got it?* see p. 298.
Grammar Booklet p. 5 see Answer Key p. 284.

Lesson 5

Lesson aims
To consolidate the unit language with a story

Values
Protect wildlife

Receptive language
Do they eat (grass)? Are they here?

Materials
Audio CD; Story cards

Optional materials
Active Teach; Digital Activity Book; Photocopiable 2.4; props for acting out the story, e.g. glasses for Ruby, baseball cap and/or skateboard for Sam, black T-shirt for John, necklace for Jenny, grey jumper for Cleo; Reading and Writing Booklet

Starting the lesson

- Pupils look back at the main illustration in Lesson 1. Ask *Where are the children? (In a film set.) What animals are there?* Pupils name the animals.
- Play a guessing game. Begin drawing a hippo, elephant or crocodile very slowly and pupils guess what it is. Invite a pupil to take over the drawing.

Pupil's Book page 26

Presentation

11   **Listen and read. Then act out.**

- Show the story cards one at a time and ask the *Before listening to the story* questions. Pupils predict what happens in the story.
- Play the recording for pupils to listen as they follow the story in their books. Ask if their predictions were correct, and then ask the *After listening to the story* questions.
- Divide the class into groups of five. Assign characters to different members of the group. Pupils act out the story.

Practice

- Talk about the story, making some deliberate mistakes, e.g. *Elephants are small. There are two elephants in picture 1.* Every time the pupils spot a mistake, they stand up and correct it.

Values

- Talk with pupils (L1) about the importance of respecting and protecting wildlife and about wildlife that is endangered. Introduce *endangered species, extinction, illegal hunting.* Discuss reasons why species become endangered. Ask their opinion about hunting animals for their fur or skin, like crocodiles, which are hunted to make bags and shoes.

Activity Book page 22

10 **Read the story again. Do elephants eat cats? Write.**

- Pupils think about what elephants eat. They read the story again to check whether they eat cats. They write their answer on the line.

11 **Number the pictures in order.**

- Pupils look at the pictures and they number them in order. Once they have finished, check answers with the whole class.

12 **Write.**

- Tell the pupils that they have to write the answers to the questions. Ask *Are elephants big?* Pupils answer. Pupils then answer all the questions. Ask individual pupils to read out their answers.

13 **Where do animals live? Write.**

- Pupils complete the sentences using the words in the word bank. When they have finished, ask individual pupils to read out their answers.

Home-School Link

- Tell the class to sing their parents the song from Lesson 3 and sing it at home together. They could also show them any poster or display they have made about their favourite wild animal (see Ending the lesson, Lesson 4).

Ending the lesson

- Play *Guess who*: say one or two words spoken by the characters in the story or mime his/her actions and the class guesses who said them.
- (For AB Answer Key, see p. 96.)

11 (1:45) **Listen and read. Then act out.**

Protect wildlife.

HOME-SCHOOL LINK
Make a poster on how to protect wild animals. Show your family.

OPTIONAL ACTIVITIES

Story writing
In small groups, pupils rewrite some of the speech bubbles in the story, e.g. they change the animals, what they like eating. Pupils practise reading their new stories and then perform for the class.

Flashcard game
Play *Bluff* see p 298.
Photocopiable 2.4 see Teacher's notes p. 287.
Reading and Writing Booklet p. 5 see Answer Key p. 282.

Lesson 6

Lesson aims
To learn the sounds and letters /all/ and /aw/

Target language
call, wall, tall, small, saw, draw, claw, yawn

Materials
Audio CD; Flashcards and Wordcards (Phonics); Phonics poster

Optional materials
Active Teach; Digital Activity Book; Photocopiable 2.5

Starting the lesson

- Show pupils the flashcards (phonics).
- Read the words aloud and ask pupils to find a common pattern.

Pupil's Book page 27

Presentation

12 **Listen and repeat.**

- Write on the board the sounds /all/ and /aw/. Play the recording for pupils to listen. Play it a second time for pupils to listen and repeat.

13 **Listen, point and say.**

- Tell the pupils that they must point to the sound that they hear. Play the recording for pupils to listen and point. Play it a second time for pupils to listen, point and say.

14 **Listen and blend the sounds.**

- Demonstrate the blending of the first sound; pupils repeat what they hear. Then tell pupils that they must listen and blend the sounds. Play the recording for pupils to listen and say the words that contain the corresponding sounds.

Practice

15 **Read the sentences aloud. Then find /all/ and /aw/.**

- Ask different pupils to read the sentences aloud. Pupils then find and point to the sounds /all/ and /aw/. Ask them to read out the words containing these sounds.

Activity Book page 23

14 **Read the words. Circle the pictures.**

- Give pupils time to read the words and circle the corresponding items in the picture.

15 **Listen and connect the letters. Then write.**

- Play the recording and give the pupils time to draw the lines to connect the letters. Play the recording again, and give pupils time to write the words.

16 **Listen and write the words.**

- Play the recording, pausing if necessary to give pupils time to write the words. Play it again for them to check what they have written. Check answers.

17 **Read aloud. Then listen and check.**

- Ask different pupils to read the text aloud, one sentence each. Then play the recording: they listen and check.

Ending the lesson

- Hand out sheets of paper, each showing one of the two sounds from this lesson: /all/ or /aw/. Say words, some with and some without the new sounds. Pupils stand and hold up their sheet when they hear their sound, or words beginning with their sound.
- (For AB Answer Key, see p. 96. For Audioscript, see p. 98.)

12 (1:46) **Listen and repeat.**

1 **all**

2 **aw**

13 (1:47) **Listen, point and say.**

14 (1:48) **Listen and blend the sounds.**

1	c – all	call	2	w – all	wall
3	t – all	tall	4	s – m – all	small
5	s – aw	saw	6	d – r – aw	draw
7	c – l – aw	claw	8	y – aw – n	yawn

15 **Read the sentences aloud. Then find *all* and *aw*.**

1 Don't yawn in class!

2 Draw a red car.

3 My cat has got a big claw.

4 The wall is tall and the boy is small.

Lesson 7

Lesson aims
To connect other areas of the curriculum with English learning; to develop the cross-curricular topic through a short project

Cross-curricular focus
Science (The food chain)

Target language
herbivores, carnivores, omnivores, food chain

Materials
Audio CD

Optional materials
Active Teach; Digital Activity Book; magazine cut outs; CLIL poster; Photocopiable 2.6

Starting the lesson

- Say a few sentences about animals, using *can/can't* and *have got*, e.g. *They've got two legs. They can fly.* Pupils guess what animals they are (*birds*). You may divide the class into two teams and turn the activity into a class competition.

Pupil's Book page 28

Presentation

- Read the headings (*Herbivores, Carnivores, Omnivores*) and ask pupils to point to the headings, and then repeat. Ask pupils if they know some animals that eat other animals and some animals that eat plants. Ask, e.g. *What do mice eat? Which animals eat plants?* Pupils answer, in L1 if necessary.
- Explain the meaning of *herbivores, carnivores, omnivores* using L1 if necessary. Ask a few comprehension questions: *Do lions eat meat? Are they carnivores? Do tigers eat plants?*

16 **Listen and read. Then ask and answer.**

- Ask pupils to read the texts on herbivores, carnivores and omnivores aloud (you could divide the class into three groups and lead each group reading one text each, in chorus). Play the recording for them to compare, pausing at the end of the omnivores text.
- Pupils read the heading: *The food chain*. Explain the meaning, asking the pupils to look at the diagram. Play the whole recording. Pupils listen with books closed. Ask *What animals are in this food chain?* Pupils answer: *Grasshopper, mouse, snake, eagle.* Tell the class that they are going to listen again and follow in their books. Play the recording again.

Practice

- Organise the class in pairs. Tell them to ask and answer questions about animals. Practise with the model dialogue first as an example. Ask the class to say with you this part of the text: *Grasshoppers eat grass, mice eat grasshoppers, snakes eat mice and eagles eat snakes.*

Think!

- Ask pupils if they know whether humans are omnivores. They could also find out about vegetarians. Ask them to look on the internet for information.

Mini-project

- In pairs or small groups, pupils make a food chain. They can find information in reference books or on the internet. They choose the elements of the food chain. They make a drawing or use magazine cut outs. Then they draw arrows to show the chain. Finally, they can write about it. When they have finished, they show their project to the class and describe their food chains.

Activity Book page 24

18 **Read and write.**

- Copy the diagram on the board if necessary. Tell the pupils that they have to read the classification of animals and complete the sentences. Help them understand some words if necessary. Pupils complete the sentences. When they have finished, check answers with the class.

19 **Look at the food chain. Write.**

- Pupils look at the food chain and complete the description. Check that they remember all the words used in the food chain. They complete the text.
- Divide the class into pairs. Pupils take turns to read out the information to his/her partner.

Ending the lesson

- Play *Reading race* see p. 301 using the language and vocabulary of the unit. Pupil A says, e.g. *Frogs eat insects.* Pupil B says, e.g. *Birds eat frogs,* etc.
- (For AB Answer Key, see p. 96. For Audioscript, see p. 98.)

Herbivores

These are animals that eat mainly plants. This includes leaves, grass, flowers, fruit and much more. Some herbivores are horses, rabbits and cows.

Carnivores

These are animals that eat mainly meat. This includes other animals and insects. Some carnivores are lions, tigers, cats, spiders and frogs.

Omnivores

These are animals that eat plants and animals. Some omnivores are bears and monkeys.

The food chain

When animals run or jump, they use energy. Animals get energy from the food they eat. A food chain shows that some animals eat plants, and some animals eat other animals. Look at the example.

grass   grasshopper   mouse   snake   eagle

Grasshoppers eat grass, mice eat grasshoppers, snakes eat mice and eagles eat snakes.

Do horses eat grass? — Yes, they do.

Are horses omnivores? — No, they aren't.

Are they herbivores? — Yes, they are.

THINK! Are humans omnivores?

MINI-PROJECT Make a poster showing a food chain.

OPTIONAL ACTIVITIES

Flashcard game
Play *Basketball* see p. 298 using animal names and foods.

Drawing activity
Play *Feed the monster* see p. 299). Pupils describe a food chain.
Photocopiable 2.6 see Teacher's notes p. 288.

Lesson 8

Lesson aims
To learn about other cultures and respect cultural differences

Cross-cultural focus
To learn about animals in other countries and their habits

Target language
orangutan, lion cub

Materials
Audio CD

Optional materials
World map or globe; Active Teach; Digital Activity Book; CLIL poster; Photocopiable 2.7; soft ball or small bean bag; pictures of animals

Starting the lesson

- Elicit the names of wild animals and write them on the board.
- Draw one very slowly. The class guesses the animal. Then they describe the animal, e.g. *It's big. It eats meat. It's got four legs.*

Pupil's Book page 29

Presentation

- Focus on the pictures. Ask pupils to name the animals: *lions, orangutans.* Explain *lion cub.* Say: *Look, these are baby lions. They're lion cubs.* Teach the word *zoo.*
- Pupils look at the texts, find the names of the countries/cities where the children live and locate them on the map or globe.

17 **Listen and read.**

- Play the recording. Pupils listen and follow the text in their books. Ask pupils to find the names of the children. Write them on the board. Ask some questions e.g. *Where does James live? What do orangutans eat? What is a baby lion called?*

Practice

18 Ask and answer.

- Divide the class into pairs. Pupils ask and answer the questions in the activity. Help with any additional vocabulary as necessary, e.g. names of animals or countries.
- When they have finished, ask individual pupils to demonstrate their questions and answers to the class.

Portfolio project

- Elicit names of wild animals that can be found in the pupils' country and write them on the board. Divide the class into pairs. Tell pupils to choose one or two wild animals and write a description. They can draw pictures or cut them out from magazines.
- Pupils can write in their notebooks, using the texts on p. 29 as a model.
- Display the projects around the room and give pupils time to admire each other's work.

Activity Book page 25

20 Read and answer.

- Focus on the pictures. Ask pupils to name the animal: *giraffe.* Pupils look at the text, find the name of the country where Akeyo lives and locate it on the map or globe.
- Pupils read the text and answer the questions. Check answers with the class.
- Explain (L1) what a *National Park* is (a large area of countryside where animal habitats are protected). Remind pupils of the word *zoo* and discuss (L1) the differences between National Parks and zoos.

Ending the lesson

- Play *Picture charades* see p. 298 with wild animal vocabulary.
- (For AB Answer Key, see p. 96. For Audioscript, see p. 98.)

Wider World
Wildlife parks

17 🔊 1:53 **Listen and read.**

orangutans

I'm Surian. I live in Borneo. There is an orangutan centre near my house. Baby orangutans are cute. They drink milk and eat bananas every day. Orangutans have got long red hair and long arms. They live in rainforests. They like climbing trees.

Surian, 10, Borneo

I'm James. I live in London. I like going to the zoo to see animals. My favourite animals are lions. There are some cute lion cubs too. They like playing but they've got sharp claws.

James, 10, England

lion cubs

18 **Ask and answer.**

1 Where does Surian live?
2 Is there an animal centre near his house?
3 What do orangutans drink and eat?
4 Where does James live?
5 What are his favourite animals?
6 What do they like to do?

PORTFOLIO

Think and write.

What animals live near your house?
Where do they live?

OPTIONAL ACTIVITIES

TPR game
Play *Ball throw* see p. 300 revising food, animals, activities, etc.

Zoo research
Divide the class into pairs. Tell pupils to look for information about zoos in their country or famous zoos around the world, e.g. the San Diego Zoo. They write sentences about what animals they can see there and draw pictures.

Photocopiable 2.7 see Teacher's notes p. 288.

Lesson 9

Lesson aims
To revise the unit language with a game and the Picture Dictionary

Materials
Audio CD; Flashcards (Wild animals)

Optional materials
Plastic bottle; spinners or dice; Active Teach; Digital Activity Book; CLIL poster; Reading and Writing Booklet

Starting the lesson

- Play *Spin the bottle* see p. 301 to revise the questions learnt in this unit and a variety of other questions related to animals, e.g. *Do (lions) eat (grass)? What do (giraffes) eat? Can elephants (swim)?*

 Pupil's Book page 30

19 Play.

- Focus on the game board. Read out the instructions. Check that pupils understand the colour code showing them which questions they must ask and answer. Revise the vocabulary using the flashcards (wild animals). Practise with the pupils the language to be used: *Where do crocodiles live? They live in rivers.*
- Organise the class in pairs. Pupils take it in turns to spin or throw the dice; they must ask and answer questions about the animals according to the colour code on the board.
- Pupils can use the Picture Dictionary AB p. 105.

Activity Book page 26

21 Write the animals' names. Then match.

- Ask pupils to look at the animals. They write the names under each animal. Check answers.
- Tell pupils (using L1 if necessary) that some habitats are correct for more than one animal, and some animals may have more than one habitat. Give them time to match the animals to the habitats. When they have finished, ask them to swap and check answers in pairs. Allow time for the checking, and then ask pairs to report answers to the class.

22 Write.

- Give pupils time to complete the answers to the questions. Check answers with the class.

Ending the class

- Put the flashcards (wild animals) in a bag or box. Begin to reveal one flashcard very slowly. The class guesses what picture it is. The first pupil to make a correct guess takes your role.
- (For AB Answer Key, see p. 96.)

OPTIONAL ACTIVITIES
Flashcard game
Play *Tick or cross* see p. 299.
Odd one out
Write on the board: *lion, crocodile, horse, cat.* Ask pupils (L1) to decide which is the odd one out and give a reason, e.g. *The horse. Lions, crocodiles and cats eat meat. Horses eat grass.* Accept more than one answer if pupils can think of a convincing reason for their choice. In pairs, pupils write down some more sets of four animals. Then they work with another pair. They look at the other pair's sets of animals and decide which animals are the odd ones out, giving reasons for their choices.
Reading and Writing Booklet p. 6 see Answer Key p. 282.

19 Play.

Where do ... live?　　What do ... eat?　　Do ... eat ...?

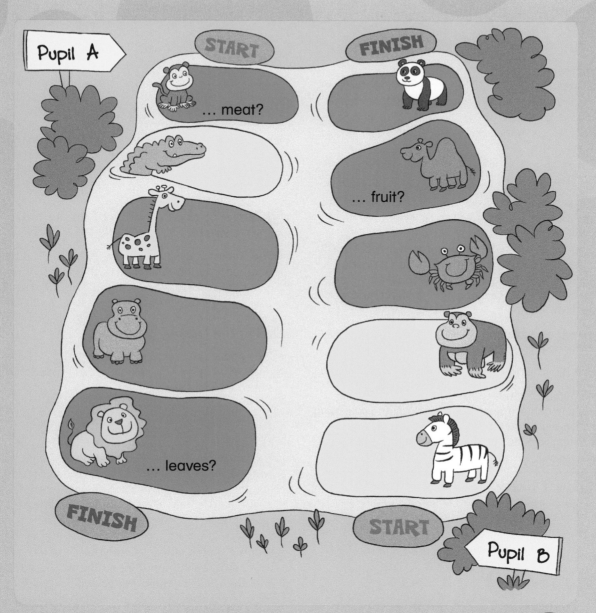

Pupil A

START　　FINISH

... meat?

... fruit?

... leaves?

FINISH　　START

Pupil B

Picture Dictionary
AB p.105

Lesson 10

Lesson aims
To personalise and assess efforts; to revise language from the unit

Materials
Audio CD

Optional materials
Digital Activity Book; CLIL poster; Online material – *Film Studio Island*; Active Teach; Grammar reference and Review for Unit 2 (PB p. 112 and AB p. 97); Test Booklet; Grammar Booklet

Starting the lesson

- This is a self assessment activity. Tell the pupils that the activities on this page will show what they have learnt in this unit.
- Write sequences of scrambled words, e.g. food words: *sevale, ssrga, ctienss*. Divide the class into pairs and ask pupils to unscramble them. You could make the activity a little more challenging by mixing food words and animals.

Pupil's Book page 31

20 **Listen and point.**

- Tell the pupils that they must choose the correct picture, a, b or c, for each question. Play the recording more than once if necessary.
- Pupils listen, look at the pictures and choose the correct answer.

> **KEY** 1 c, 2 c, 3 a, 4 b, 5 a, 6 b, 7 a, 8 a

21 **Read and answer.**

- Pupils read the two questions. Tell them to write the answers in their notebooks or on the board, or ask them to say the answers.

> **KEY**
> 1 Yes, they do.
> 2 They live in deserts.

Activity Book page 27

- Focus on the *I can* sentences at the bottom of the page. Tell the pupils that they have to tick the boxes, depending on whether they think they can do the *I can* points.

23 **Draw or stick a photo of an animal. Then write.**

- Pupils must draw a picture or stick a cut out photo of an appropriate animal in each habitat. Then they write the corresponding descriptions. Check answers asking a few pupils to tell the class.

Ending the lesson

- Play *Miming competition* see p. 301.
- (For AB Answer Key, see p. 96. For Audioscript, see p. 99.)

OPTIONAL ACTIVITIES
Flashcard game
Play *Flashcard relay*. Put all the Unit 1 and 2 wordcards face up at one end of the classroom and the Unit 1 and 2 flashcards at the other, all in jumbled order. Divide the class into two or four teams, depending on the size of your class (there should be no more than eight pupils in a team). Two teams stand in a line. When you say *Go*, the first member of each team runs to the wordcards, takes one, then runs to the other end of the room to find the corresponding flashcard. Then he/she runs back to his/her team, and the second member of the team does the same. The first team to collect eight pairs of cards is the winner. If you have two more teams, they then play the game. You could also have a final between the two winning teams to find a class champion.

20 (1:54) **Listen and point.**

1
 a
 b
 c

2
 a
 b
 c

3
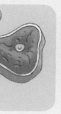 a
 b
 c

4
 a
 b
 c

5 **a** Yes, they do.

   b No, they don't.

6 **a** Yes, they do.

   b No, they don't.

7
 a
 b

8
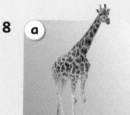 a
 b

21 **Read and answer.**

1 Do crocodiles swim well?

2 Where do camels live?

TPR game
Play *Pass the ball* see p. 300 to revise vocabulary, e.g. animals, food, actions and language of the unit, e.g. *(Lions) like (meat). (Giraffes) eat leaves. Monkeys (can) climb trees.*

Activity Book Review p. 97
Grammar Booklet p. 6 see Answer Key p. 284.
Test Booklet Unit 2 see Answer Key p. 294.
Online World
Pupils can now go online to *Film Studio Island* and enjoy the fun and games.

Activity Book Answer Key

p. 18, Activity 1
a 7, b 3, c 5, d 2, e 4, f 8, g 6, h 1

p. 18, Activity 2
1 It's a lion. 2 It's an elephant. 3 It's a monkey.
4 It's a hippo. 5 It's a crocodile. 6 It's a giraffe.

p. 19, Activity 3
1 Monkeys eat fruit.
2 Hippos eat grass.
3 Crocodiles eat meat.
4 Lions eat meat.
5 Elephants eat leaves and grass.
6 Giraffes eat leaves.

p.19, Activity 4
1 Yes, they do.
2 No, they don't.
3 Do, eat, Yes, they do.
4 Pupils' own answers
5 Pupils' own answers

p. 20, Activity 5
1 lion, 2 gorilla, 3 camel, 4 panda, 5 zebra, 6 crab

p. 20, Activity 6
1 a forest, 2 d desert, 3 e grassland, 4 c rainforest,
5 b river

p. 20, Activity 7
1 Zebras live in grasslands.
2 Pandas live in forests.
3 Camels live in deserts.

p. 21, Activity 8
1 Camels, slowly
2 Pandas, playing
3 Zebras, fast

p. 21, Activity 9
1 grass
  They don't drink much water.
  Yes, they can.
2 pandas eat
  bamboo, fruit and leaves
  They can eat 38 kilos of food (every day).
  Yes, they do.
3 zebras eat
  grass and leaves
  They eat a lot of grass.
  Yes, they can.

p. 22, Activity 10
No, they don't.

p. 22, Activity 11
a 2, b 4, c 3, d 5, e 1

p. 22, Activity 12
1 Yes, they are.
2 They eat grass and leaves.
3 John.
4 They are under John's feet.
5 tarzan

p. 22, Activity 13
1 grasslands, forests
2 Hippos live in rivers and grasslands.
3 Crocodiles live in rivers.

p. 23, Activity 15
thank, dinner, summer, cowboy

p. 23, Activity 16
1 all, 2 tall, 3 small, 4 saw

p. 24, Activity 18
1 Herbivores: plants rabbits, elephants, cows (Accept
  animals in any order.)
2 Carnivores: other animals (Accept '(mainly) meat'.)
  tigers, snakes (Accept animals in any order.)
3 Omnivores: plants, animals, pigs, mice (Accept
  animals in any order.)

p. 24, Activity 19
leaves, insects, birds

p. 25, Activity 20
1 Serengeti National Park in Tazania.
2 Yes, there are.
3 the giraffes
4 tall, long necks
5 They eat the leaves at the top of the trees.

p. 26, Activity 21
1 gorilla, d; 2 camel, b; 3 panda, c; 4 crocodile, e;
5 crab, e; 6 elephant, a, c; 7 hippo, a, e;
8 monkey, c, d; 9 lion, a; 10 giraffe, a, c; 11 zebra, a

p. 26, Activity 22
1 No, they don't.
  They live in rivers.
2 What do zebras eat
  They live in grasslands.

Audioscript

Lesson 1 Activity 1   CD1:34
S = SAM   JE = JENNY   JO = JOHN   R = RUBY
- **S**   Where's Madley Kool? Is he here?
- **JE**   No, he isn't. But look at all the animals. What's your favourite animal?
  I like the giraffe. Look at it's long neck!
- **JO**   I like the monkeys. They're funny.
- **R**   I like the elephant. It's big!
- **S**   And I like the hippo. It's cool.
- **JO**   Look! It's a lion!
- **S**   What do lions eat?
- **R**   They eat meat. Quick, run!

Lesson 1 Activity 2   CD1:35
- **a**   giraffe
- **b**   elephant
- **c**   lion
- **d**   monkey
- **e**   hippo
- **f**   crocodile
- **g**   leaves
- **h**   grass
- **i**   fruit
- **j**   meat

Lesson 1 Activity 3   CD1:36
1. Monkeys like fruit.
2. Lions like meat.
3. Crocodiles like meat.
4. Hippos like grass.
5. Elephants like grass.
6. Giraffes like leaves.

Lesson 1 Activity 1 (AB)   CD1:37
1. What's that?
   It's a giraffe.
2. I can see a lion.
3. It's grass.
4. What's that?
   It's a crocodile.
5. Where's the monkey?
   It's in the tree.
6. Are there any leaves?
   Yes, there are.
7. What's this?
   It's a hippo.
8. I can see an elephant.

Lesson 2 Activity 4   CD1:38
Do hippos eat insects?
No, they don't. Hippos eat grass.
Do monkeys eat grass?
No, they don't. Monkeys eat fruit.

Do lions eat meat?
Yes, they do. Lions eat meat.
Do giraffes eat leaves?
Yes, they do. Giraffes eat leaves

Lesson 2 Activity 5   CD1:39
1. Do Lions eat grass?
   No, they don't. They eat meat. Crocodiles eat meat.
2. Do giraffes eat leaves?
   Yes, they do.
3. Do hippos eat fruit?
   No, they don't. They eat grass.
4. Do elephants eat meat?
   No, they don't. They eat leaves and grass.
5. Do frogs eat insects?
   Yes, they do.
6. Do monkeys eat fruit?
   Yes, they do. They love bananas.

Lesson 3 Activity 6   CD1:40
- **a**   crab
- **b**   camel
- **c**   zebra
- **d**   panda
- **e**   gorilla
- **f**   river
- **g**   desert
- **h**   grassland
- **i**   forest
- **j**   rainforest

Lesson 3 Activity 7   CD1:41
Lions live in grasslands.
They're big and strong.
They like sleeping all day long.
They run very fast to catch their lunch.
What do they eat? They eat meat.
Crunch, crunch, munch!

Pandas live in rainforests.
They're big and cute.
They like eating all day long.
They climb tall trees to find their lunch.
What do they eat? They eat leaves.
Crunch, crunch, munch!

Lesson 3 Activity 7 (AB)   CD1:42
1. I like zebras. They're pretty.
   Where do they live?
   They live in grasslands.
2. I love pandas. They're cute.
   Where do they live?
   They live in forests.
3. I like camels. They're my favourite animal.
   Where do they live?
   They live in deserts.

Lesson 4 Activity 9 CD1:43

Discovery Island Animal Park: Crocodiles
Blog posted by Paul, animal park keeper
Hi, I'm Paul. There are seven crocodiles here at Discovery Island Animal Park. This is Snapper. She's my favourite. Look at the bird in her mouth! It's cleaning her teeth.
Crocodiles live in Africa and Australia. They live in rivers. They are very big and strong. They like sleeping in the sun and swimming. They can swim very well. They can run but they can't run really fast. Crocodiles have got very big mouths with 65 teeth. When they are four years old, they eat about a kilo and a half of meat or fish every other day. They can eat you too so watch out!

Lesson 4 Activity 10 CD1:44

Giraffes live in Africa. They live in grasslands. They have got very long necks and they are the tallest land animal. A giraffe has got 32 teeth and they eat a lot of leaves. They walk slowly but they can run fast.

Lesson 6 Activity 12 CD1:46

a double l
/all/ /all/ /all/
a w
/aw/ /aw/ /aw/

Lesson 6 Activity 13 CD1:47

/aw/ /aw/
/all/ /all/
/all/ /all/
/aw/ /aw/
/aw/ /aw/
/all/ /all/

Lesson 6 Activity 14 CD1:48

1 /k/ /all/
  call
2 /w/ /all/
  wall
3 /t/ /all/
  tall
4 /s/ /m/ /all/
  small
5 /s/ /aw/
  saw
6 /d/ /r/ /aw/
  draw
7 /k/ /l/ /aw/
  claw
8 /y/ /aw/ /n/
  yawn

Lesson 6 Activity 15 (AB) CD1:49

1 /th/ /a/ /n/ /k/
2 /d/ /i/ /n/ /er/
3 /s/ /u/ /m/ /er/
4 /k/ /ow/ /b/ /oy/

Lesson 6 Activity 16 (AB) CD1:50

1 all
2 tall
3 small
4 saw

Lesson 6 Activity 17 (AB) CD1:51

Welcome to the zoo. Look at the big cats! They've got sharp teeth and sharp claws. I'm glad the wall is tall. You cats can't eat me for dinner!

Lesson 7 Activity 16 CD1:52

Herbivores
These are animals that eat mainly plants. This includes leaves, grass, flowers, fruit and much more. Some herbivores are horses, rabbits and cows.

Carnivores
These are animals that eat mainly meat. This includes other animals and insects. Some carnivores are lions, tigers, cats, spiders and frogs.

Omnivores
These are animals that eat plants and animals. Some omnivores are bears and monkeys.

The food chain
When animals run or jump, they use energy. Animals get energy from the food they eat. A food chain shows that some animals eat plants, and some animals eat other animals. Look at the example.
grass → grasshopper → mouse → snake → eagle
Grasshoppers eat grass, mice eat grasshoppers, snakes eat mice and eagles eat snakes.

Lesson 8 Activity 17 CD1:53

1 I'm Surian. I live in Borneo. There is an orangutan centre near my house. Baby orangutans are cute. They drink milk and eat bananas every day. Orangutans have got long red hair and long arms. They live in rainforests. They like climbing trees.
  Surian, 10, Borneo
2 I'm James. I live in London. I like going to the zoo to see animals. My favourite animals are lions. There are some cute lion cubs too. They like playing but they've got sharp claws.
  James, 10, England

Lesson 10 Activity 20 CD1:54

1 Lions eat meat.
2 Monkeys eat fruit.
3 What do crocodiles eat?
4 What do elephants eat?
5 Do giraffes eat leaves?
6 Do lions eat leaves?
7 They live in rainforests. They eat fruit and leaves.
8 They live in grasslands and forests. They eat leaves, fruit and flowers.

3 The seasons

Objectives

- talk about weather conditions
- talk about seasonal activities
- talk about natural disasters
- pronounce properly /ew/ and /y/

Topics
- Weather conditions
- Seasonal activities
- Natural disasters

Phonics
/ew/ and /y/.

Values
- Be a good friend

Stories
- Unit opener: seasons
- Story episode: weather conditions while filming

Language
Vocabulary
- Weather conditions: stormy, wet, humid, warm, lightning, thunder, temperature, degrees
- Seasonal activities: go hiking, go camping, go water skiing, go snowboarding, go surfing, go cycling
- Seasons: spring, summer, autumn, winter

Revision
weather, sun, wind, rain, snow, storm, cloud, today, rainy, snowy, sunny, cloudy, go skiing, go swimming, kite, hot, cold

Structures
What's the weather like today?
It's (warm).
There's (thunder and lightning).
What's the temperature today?
It's (25) degrees.
I/We/They go (camping) in the (spring).
He/She goes (camping) in the (spring).
What was the weather like (last summer)? It was sunny.
What was the weather like (yesterday)? It was windy.

CLIL language
Natural disasters: hurricane, typhoon, cyclone, wave
Wide World: earthquake, tornado

Songs and chants
- Chant
- Song about pets
- Karaoke song

Sociocultural aspects
- Finding out about natural disasters in other parts of the world
- Comparing types of natural disasters

Cross-curricular contents
- Science: to know about hurricanes
- Language Arts: reading a story, acting out, telling a story
- Language skills: reading and understanding information to identify true/false sentences

Learning strategies
- Looking at the title and illustrations to create expectations about the text
- Relating new words to known words
- Identifying rules about the use of *go + -ing*
- Logical thinking: understanding cause and effect
- Critical thinking: giving personal opinions when writing
- Collaborative learning: dialogues and interactional activities
- Self assessment

Basic competences

- Linguistic communication: Use language as an instrument for communication (L1 to L10)
- Knowledge and interaction with the physical world: Talk about the weather (L1 to L4): Find out about hurricanes (L7)
- Mathematical competence: Identify number of degrees (L2)
- Processing information and digital competence: Use *Film Studio Island* online component
- Social and civic competence: Be a good friend (L5)
- Cultural and artistic competence: Find out about natural disasters in the world (L8)
- Learning to learn: Reflect on what has been learnt and self-evaluate progress (L10)
- Autonomy and personal initiative: Develop one's own criteria and social skills (L1 to L10)

Skills

Listening
- Identifying words for weather conditions in recordings
- Understanding information about weather conditions and seasonal activities
- Understanding specific information in a song about activities in different seasons
- Understanding general and specific information in a story
- Understanding information about hurricanes

Reading
- Understanding information in sentences (weather conditions and seasonal activities)
- Understanding specific data about hurricanes
- Reading a description of natural disasters and identifying true/false sentences

Speaking
- Saying words and expressions for weather conditions and seasonal activities
- Chanting and singing
- Pronouncing /ew/ and /y/ correctly

Talking
- Participating in conversations to talk about weather conditions
- Exchanging information about activities in the different seasons
- Role playing a story
- Exchanging information about natural disasters

Writing
- Completing a weather forecast
- Writing answers to questions
- Completing sentences with the words provided
- Completing a hurricane quiz
- Completing a crossword
- Completing short texts about seasonal activities

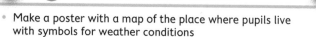

Classroom ideas

- Make a poster with a map of the place where pupils live with symbols for weather conditions
- Make a chart for weather conditions to be used daily in the classroom
- Decorate the class with the cross-curricular poster
- Ask the pupils to draw mind maps and vocabulary maps
- Use the internet to find information about natural disasters
- Use photos from the internet to show seasonal activities in other parts of the world
- Bring to the classroom library books that talk about seasons
- Photocopiables

Take-home English

- Home-School Link
- Notes for Parents
- A sample of work each week
- Portfolio

Self assessment

- Pupils can talk about weather conditions
- Pupils can talk about seasonal activities
- Pupils can talk about natural disasters

Evaluation

- Pupil's Book page 41
- Activity Book page 37
- Photocopiable 3.7
- Picture Dictionary
- Test Booklet – Unit 3

3 The seasons

Lesson 1

Lesson aims
To learn and practise new vocabulary (weather)

Target language
warm, humid, wet, stormy, lightning, thunder, temperature, degrees

Materials
Audio CD; Flashcards and Wordcards (Weather conditions)

Optional materials
Real clothes or pictures of clothes; map of the country; card; scissors; Active Teach; Digital Activity Book; Weather poster; Photocopiable 3.1

Starting the lesson

- Bring in some clothes (or, if that is not possible, display some pictures of clothes) that the class has learnt. You need a mix of summer and winter clothes, e.g. T-shirt, trousers, skirt, socks, shoes, dress, boots, jumper, hat, coat, trainers, shirt, shorts, scarf.
- Revise *hot* and teach *cold*, using mime. Show a garment and ask *Is it for hot weather or cold weather?* Pupils say *Hot* or *Cold*.

> **Pupil's Book pages 32–33**

Presentation

- Use the flashcards (weather conditions) to teach the vocabulary. Hold up the flashcards in turn and say the words for pupils to repeat. Hold up the flashcards again, this time asking individual pupils to say the words.
- Direct pupils' attention to the main illustration. Ask questions to help the class describe the picture. Pupils can answer in L1, e.g. *What's this? (A weather machine.) What's Sam doing? (He's playing with it./He's changing the weather.)*

1 Listen.

- Tell pupils (L1) they are going to listen to a recording describing what they can see in the main illustration. Play the recording: pupils point to the weather mentioned.
- Tell pupils that one of the weather conditions in the picture is not mentioned in the recording. Play the recording again: pupils decide what's missing.

> **KEY** Missing weather word: cloud/cloudy

Practice

2 Listen and repeat.

- Play the recording, pausing after each word. Pupils point to the small weather pictures a–h. Play the recording again. Pupils point and repeat each word.
- Hold up the flashcards in turn and ask individual pupils to say the words.
- Divide the class into pairs. Pupil A says the letter of one of the small pictures, e.g. *Picture a*, and Pupil B says the weather word, *warm*. They then swap roles.
- Display the relevant weather flashcards on one side of the board and write the corresponding words or put up wordcards on the other side. Pupils come to the front, read out the words and match them to the pictures.

3 Listen and say *True* or *False*.

- Ask the pupils to look at the main illustration.
- Play the recording. Pupils have to find the corresponding pictures and point to them. Then they say whether the statements are *True* or *False*.

> **KEY** 1 True, 2 True, 3 True, 4 True, 5 False

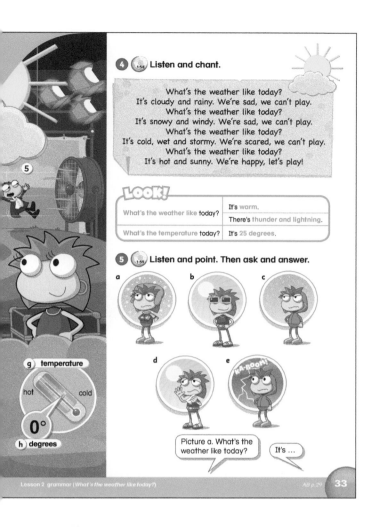

OPTIONAL ACTIVITIES

Drawing game
Play *Dice game* see p. 299 using weather vocabulary.

Weather map
Display a map of the country on the board. Divide the class into pairs and give them a piece of card. Pupils draw and cut out a picture of a weather word of their choice, e.g. *cloudy*, *rain*. Then they choose where to put it on the map. When all the pairs have done this, they say what there is in each region, e.g. *There's a lot of rain in (place). It's hot in (place).*
Photocopiable 3.1 see Teacher's notes p. 288.

NOTES

Activity Book page 28

❶ Match.

• Pupils look at the map and the pictures. Give them time to read the weather words and match them to the pictures.

❷ Look at Activity 1 and write.

• Pupils use the words in Activity 1 to complete the weather forecast according to the picture prompts. Make sure pupils understand the compass: can they find the words *north*, *south*, *east* and *west* in the text and point to the correct parts of the map?
• Tell the class to read the weather words and match them to the pictures. Point out the example and complete the description of the weather in the north as a whole-class activity.
• Check by asking individual pupils to read the completed sentences.

Ending the lesson

• Play *Who's the fastest?* see p. 298 using weather words.
• (For AB Answer Key, see p. 122. For Audioscript, see p. 123.)

Lesson 2

Lesson aims
To revise the vocabulary; to learn and practise the structure *What's the weather like today? It's humid.*

Target language
What's the weather like today? It's (warm).
What's the temperature today? It's 25 degrees.

Materials
Audio CD; Flashcards and Wordcards (Weather conditions)

Optional materials
Active Teach; Digital Activity Book; Grammar Booklet

Starting the lesson

- Use the flashcards (weather conditions) to revise the vocabulary from the previous lesson. Hold up the flashcards and elicit the words. Then ask individual pupils to hold up the flashcards at the front of the class. Hold up the wordcards or write the words on the board, and pupils point to the correct flashcards.
- With stronger classes, ask individual pupils to come to the front and write the words on the board.

Pupil's Book page 33

- Show a flashcard, e.g. rain, and ask *What's the weather like?* Say *It's wet.* Ask the class to repeat *It's wet* after you. Repeat with the other words.

Presentation

- Read out the questions and answers in the Look! box. Pupils read them. Focus on the first question and give more answers, e.g. *It's stormy.* Elicit more answers from the pupils and write them on the board. Focus on the second question and give more answers, e.g. *It's 30 degrees.* Elicit more answers from the pupils and write them on the board. Revise all the examples with the class. Pupils can copy them into their notebooks.

4 **Listen and chant.**

- Play the recording. Pupils listen and follow the words. Play the chant again. Pause after each line for pupils to repeat. Play the chant once more for pupils to join in and say together. Use the flashcards to help prompt the words if necessary.

Practice

5 **Listen and point. Then ask and answer.**

- Tell the class that they are going to listen to a recording and have to point to the corresponding numbers. Play the recording for pupils to listen and point.
- Organise the class into pairs and explain the second part of the activity. Pupil A says a letter from a to e and asks *What's the weather like?* Pupil B looks at the picture and answers. Then they swap.

KEY 1 d, 2 a, 3 e, 4 c, 5 b

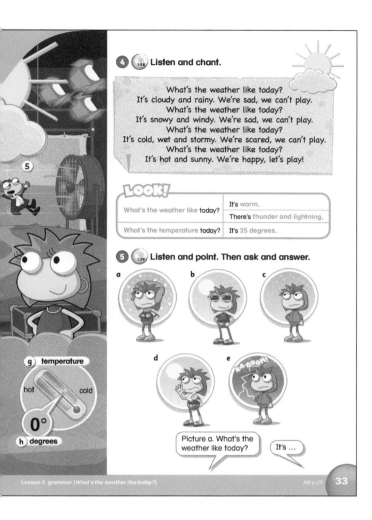

Ending the lesson

- Play *Spelling bee*, using words for weather conditions. Pupils listen to the words you say and, taking turns, they try to spell them correctly. You could also include other words, e.g. clothes, activities, animals.
- (For AB Answer Key, see p. 122. For Audioscript, see p. 123.)

OPTIONAL ACTIVITIES

Weather around the world

Revise the months and then divide the class into twelve groups, one for each month. Each group finds out about the weather in different places in their month, either in reference books or on the internet. They make a small poster with the month as a heading and sentences, e.g. *In Russia, it's cold and snowy.* They should add weather symbols for each sentence. Give help with country vocabulary as necessary. Combine all the month posters in the correct order to make a big display.

Weatherman

Explain (L1) what a weatherman/weatherwoman is. Tell the pupils to imagine they are the weatherman/weatherwoman on TV.

Write some expressions on the board: *Good morning / Good afternoon. The weather today is (hot and sunny). There is (wind) here. Goodbye.* They choose the expressions they like and write their forecast for the city/region and draw the weather symbols. Then they come to the front and act it out like a TV weather report.

Grammar Booklet p.7 see Answer Key p. 284.

NOTES

Activity Book page 29

3 Listen and number.

- Tell the class (L1) that they are going to listen to a recording and have to number the pictures in the order they hear them. Play the recording twice. Allow time for pupils to number the pictures. Play the recording again. They check their answers.

4 Look and write.

- Direct pupils' attention to the pictures. Explain that they have to look at the pictures and complete the sentences under each picture with the correct words. When they have finished, ask individual pupils to read their sentences to the class.
- Ask the pupils to give any more answers they can, that correspond to the actual weather, e.g. for picture 4: *It's snowy.*

Lesson 3

Lesson aims
To extend the unit vocabulary set to include seasons and activities; to practise the unit language with a song

Target language
go camping, go water skiing, go hiking, go snowboarding, spring, summer, autumn, winter

Materials
Audio CD; Flashcards and Wordcards (Weather conditions)

Optional materials
A calendar; Active Teach; Digital Activity Book; Photocopiables 3.2–3.3; Reading and Writing Booklet

Starting the lesson

- Show the flashcards (weather conditions) in turn and ask *What's the weather like?* Pupils answer, e.g. *It's wet.*

Pupil's Book page 34

Presentation

- Show a calendar to the class and revise the months. Then say *Twelve months is one … .* Elicit *year* in L1, and say *Yes, one year.* Pupils repeat *year.*
- Write, e.g. 21 June, 21 September, and ask (L1) what season it is. Teach *spring, summer, autumn* and *winter.* Then ask *Is it (cold) in (spring)? What's the weather like in (spring)?* Repeat with the other seasons.

6 🔘 1:61 **Listen and repeat.**

- Introduce the new words (*spring, summer, …*) using the flashcards. Hold them up and say the words for pupils to repeat. Ask individual pupils to say the words. Play the recording for pupils to listen and repeat.
- Now put the flashcards on the board. Point to the different flashcards and ask the class to say the words.

Song

7 🔘 1:62 **Listen and point. Then sing.**

- Play the recording with books closed. Lead the class in miming the actions while listening. Play the song again with books open. The class follows the lines and mimes. Play the song a few more times, until pupils can sing along as they mime. You can now play the karaoke song (Active Teach).

Practice

8 🔘 1:63 **Listen and say.**

- Direct pupils' attention to the Look! box. Look at the sentences and focus on the use of *go + -ing* form. Read the Look! box. Elicit more examples from the class and write a few on the board. Pupils can copy them into their notebooks.
- Organise the class in pairs. Play the recording. Ask the pupils to take it in turns to say sentences describing activities for the different seasons.

Activity Book page 30

5 **Look and write.**

- Pupils write the correct season from the word bank under each picture. Check as a class. Point to a picture and ask *What's the weather like?* Pupils answer. Then ask *What season is it?* Pupils answer.

6 **Look and write.**

- Direct pupils' attention to pictures 1 to 4. Explain (L1) that they have to choose the words from the word bank and write them under the corresponding pictures. Check answers with the class.

7 **Look at Activity 6 and write.**

- Explain to the pupils that they have to write sentences describing what the characters are doing in each season. Check answers with the class.

Ending the lesson

- Divide the class into two groups – if you have a mixed class, Group 1 could be boys and Group 2 girls. Play the song CD1:62. Group 1 sings along to the spring and autumn verses and Group 2 to the summer and winter ones. They sing the chorus together. Then swap groups and sing the song again so that all the class has a chance of singing the whole song.
- (For AB Answer Key, see p. 122. For Audioscript, see p. 123.)

6 **Listen and repeat.**

go camping

go water skiing

go hiking

go snowboarding

spring

summer

autumn

winter

7 **Listen and point. Then sing.**

SONG

Spring, summer, autumn, winter
Four seasons in the year.

It's spring autumn .
We go hiking go camping in spring.
We fish and swim in the river.

It's autumn summer .
I go swimming go water skiing
in summer.

I jump up high in the sea.

It's autumn summer .
She goes camping goes hiking
in autumn.

She walks and climbs in the mountains.

It's spring winter .
He goes water skiing
goes snowboarding in winter.

He rides and jumps in the snow.

LOOK!

| I/We/They go camping in spring. |
| He/She goes camping in spring. |

8 **Listen and say.**

1 spring
2 summer
3 winter
4 autumn

He goes …
in spring.

OPTIONAL ACTIVITIES

Flashcard game
Play *Guess the card* see p. 299 to revise months and weather words.

Question chain
Make a Question chain, asking questions about the activities pupils do in different seasons or weather conditions.

Photocopiable 3.2 see Teacher's notes p. 288.
Photocopiable 3.3 see Teacher's notes p. 288.
Reading and Writing Booklet p. 7 see Answer Key p. 282.

Lesson 4

Lesson aims
To develop reading, writing, listening and speaking skills; to learn and practise the new structure: *What was the weather like yesterday?*

Target language
What was the weather like last summer?
It was sunny.
What was the weather like yesterday? It was windy.

Materials
Audio CD; Flashcards (Weather conditions)

Optional materials
Active Teach; Digital Activity Book; Grammar Booklet

Starting the lesson

- Write the day on the board, e.g. *Monday*. Ask *What's the weather like today?* Draw the appropriate weather symbol. Pupils can copy it into their notebooks. Repeat this procedure every class, or when the weather is different from normal.

Pupil's Book page 35

Presentation

- Focus on the illustrations that go with the texts. Ask the class to listen to your descriptions and point to the corresponding picture: *They are flying a kite. They are playing*, etc. Elicit more sentences and write them on the board.

Skills

9 **Listen, read and match.**

- Look together at the pictures. Pupils say what they can see: *I can see flowers*, etc.
- Pupils read each text silently. Then ask a pupil to read the first text aloud. Ask *What season is it?* Pupils answer and say which season picture matches the text. They do the same with the other texts and pictures.
- Organise the class in pairs. Play the recording. Tell them to ask and answer about what they like doing in their favourite season. They work in pairs. Ask them to take it in turns to ask and answer questions.

KEY 1 a, 2 c, 3 d, 4 b

10 **Look and say.**

- Read out the questions and answers in the Look! box. Pupils read them. Focus on the first question and give true answers, e.g. *It was sunny*. Elicit more answers from the pupils and write them on the board. Focus on the second question and give true answers, e.g. *It was warm*. Write the answers on the board. Revise all the examples with the class. Pupils can copy them into their notebooks.
- The pupils look at the pictures and the prompts in bubbles. They write sentences describing the pictures in their notebooks. Ask a few pupils to read out their sentences. Write them on the board.

Activity Book page 31

8 **Read and number.**

- Ask pupils to look at the pictures carefully. Read out sentences 1–4 and check that pupils understand. Pupils number the pictures. Check answers with the class.

9 **Write.**

- Tell the class that they have to look at the pictures and then answer the questions below. Read out the questions and check that pupils understand. Give them time to answer the questions. Ask a few pupils to read out their answers and write the correct ones on the board.

Ending the lesson

- Play *Memory* see p. 299 with flashcards. Pupils say *It's (sunny)* when they turn over a card.
- (For AB Answer Key, see p. 122. For Audioscript, see p. 124.)

Pupils can now go online to *Film Studio Island* and find the computer that Cleo is holding. It is the computer screen to the extreme left on the top floor of the Special Effects Studio. Once pupils click on the computer they are taken to a supplementary language game based on the vocabulary in this unit.

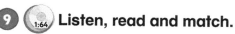
9 (1:64) **Listen, read and match.**

SKILLS

a It's windy and I can fly my kite. The weather is cool. There are a lot of apples on the tree in my garden. Yum!

b I like the flowers. The birds sing in the trees. I like listening to the birds and the rain. I love the weather. It's always mild and cool or warm.

c It's hot and humid and there's no school! Sometimes it's 35 degrees. I go swimming with my friends. I go to the park with my friends. I eat a lot of fruit. My favourites are strawberries and peaches.

d It snows and it's really cold. But it's beautiful. Some birds don't like the cold and they fly to hot places. Some animals sleep. I go skiing.

LOOK!

| What **was** the weather like last summer? | It **was** sunny. |
| What **was** the temperature yesterday? | It **was** 5 degrees. |

10 **Look and say.**

last summer

yesterday

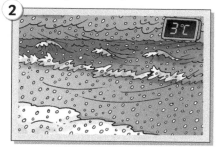

Last summer it was …

Yesterday it was …

OPTIONAL ACTIVITIES

Pairwork game
Play *Snap* see p. 300. Use weather, colours, food, clothes, activities, etc.

Song
Teach pupils the song *Singin' in the Rain.* Use mime and L1 translation to deal with difficult vocabulary. Keep to verse one initially and add verse two for stronger pupils.
Grammar Booklet p. 8 see Answer Key p. 284.

Lesson 5

Lesson aims
To consolidate the unit language with a story

Values
Be a good friend.

Receptive language
Action!, Quiet!, This way!, beach, lie, place

Materials
Audio CD; Story cards; Character story cards; Flashcards (Weather conditions)

Optional materials
Props for acting out the story, e.g. glasses for Ruby, baseball cap and/or skateboard for Sam, black T-shirt for John, necklace for Jenny, grey jumper for Cleo, cone of paper for director's megaphone; Active Teach; Digital Activity Book; Photocopiable 3.4; Reading and Writing Booklet

Starting the lesson

- Ask pupils (L1) what they can remember about the story from the previous episode. Show the Unit 2 story cards to help pupils remember. Ask a question about each frame. Ask (L1) what happens to John at the end of the story.

Pupil's Book page 36

Presentation

9 **Listen and read. Then act out.**

- Show the story cards one at a time and ask the *Before listening to the story* questions. Pupils predict what happens in the story.
- Play the recording. Pupils listen as they follow the story in their books. Ask if their predictions were correct, and then ask the *After listening to the story* questions.
- Divide the class into six groups and assign a character to each group. Pupils read their parts as a class. This may encourage quieter pupils to take part in the acting later on.
- Ask pupils who would like to take the parts of the different characters. Invite volunteers to the front of the class to act out the story. Encourage tone of voice and expressions to match those in the pictures. Use props that you've brought to class if you wish.

Practice

- Shuffle the story cards and put them in random order on the board. With books closed, ask *Which is number one?* Pupils answer. Continue until all the story cards are in order.
- Hold up the story cards in order and retell the story making some deliberate mistakes. Every time pupils spot a mistake, they put up their hands and correct it.

Values

- Say a few ways to be a good friend, e.g. *Help your friends. Listen to your friends.* Ask pupils to say what good friends do and what they do not do. Write some examples on the board of good things to do and ask pupils to give more examples.
- Organise the class in pairs. Pupils take it in turns to ask and answer about ways to be a good friend. Discuss (L1) the importance of being a good friend.

Activity Book page 32

10 **Read the story again. Why do they like the beach? Write.**

- Pupils work in pairs to discuss why the characters in the story like the beach. They then write the answer on the line.

11 **Look and write. Then number the pictures in order.**

- Direct pupils' attention to the pictures and speech bubbles. Ask them to complete the bubbles with sentences from the word bank. Point to picture 1 and do that with the class. Pupils write sentences for the other speech bubbles. Then they number the pictures in order. Check answers with the class.

12 **Look at Activity 11 and write.**

- Pupils look at the pictures again. They then read the questions and answer them. When they have finished, ask individual pupils to read an answer each.

Home-School Link

- Tell pupils to think about the actions they do to help their friends. Give pupils a sheet of paper and ask them to draw a picture of themselves helping a friend. When they have finished, they write a few sentences describing it.

Ending the lesson

- Play *Guess who*: ask individual children to mime the actions of one of the story characters and the class guesses what they are doing and who they are, e.g. *You're reading on the beach! You're Ruby!*
- (For AB Answer Key, see p. 122.)

11 🔊 1:65 **Listen and read. Then act out.**

STORY

 **VALUES**
Be a good friend.

HOME-SCHOOL LINK
Draw a picture of you helping a friend.
Show your family. Talk about it.

 PARENT

OPTIONAL ACTIVITIES

Flashcard game
Play *Mix-matched flashcards* see p. 298 using the
Unit 3 flashcards.

Make a weather chart
Each pupil writes a weather word and draws a
symbol for it on a card. Draw a weather chart,
with the days of the week at the top. Each lesson,
pupils say *Today's (Monday). It's (sunny)* and add the
weather card.

Photocopiable 3.4 see Teacher's notes p. 288.
Reading and Writing Booklet p. 8 see Answer
Key p. 282.

Lesson 6

Lesson aims
To learn the sounds and letters /ew/ and /y/

Target language
new, dew, chew, stew, my, try, fly, sky

Materials
Audio CD; Flashcards and Wordcards (Phonics); Phonics poster

Optional materials
Active Teach; Digital Activity Book; Photocopiable 3.5

Starting the lesson

- Show pupils the flashcards (phonics).
- Read the words aloud and ask pupils to find a common pattern.

Pupil's Book page 37

Presentation

12  **Listen and repeat.**

- Write on the board the sounds /ew/ and /y/. Play the recording for pupils to listen. Play it a second time for pupils to listen and repeat.

13 **Listen, point and say.**

- Tell the pupils that they must point to the sound that they hear. Play the recording for pupils to listen and point. Play it a second time for pupils to listen, point and say.

14 **Listen and blend the sounds.**

- Demonstrate the blending of the first sound; pupils repeat what they hear. Then tell the pupils that they must listen and blend the sounds. Play the recording for pupils to listen and say the words that contain the corresponding sounds.

Practice

15 **Read the sentences aloud. Then find /ew/ and /y/.**

- The pupils read the sentences aloud. Then they find and point to the sounds /ew/ and /y/. Ask them to read out the words containing these sounds.

Activity Book page 33

13 **Read the words. Circle the pictures.**

- Give pupils time to read the words and circle the corresponding parts of the picture.

14 **Listen and connect the letters. Then write.**

- Play the recording and give the pupils time to draw the lines to connect the letters. Play the recording again, and give pupils time to write the words.

15 **Listen and write the words.**

- Play the recording, pausing if necessary to give pupils time to write the words. Play it again for them to check what they have written. Check answers.

16 **Read aloud. Then listen and check.**

- Ask different pupils to read the text aloud, one sentence each. Then play the recording: they listen and check.

Ending the lesson

- Divide the class into two groups. Give each group a sound from this lesson: /ew/ or /y/. Say words, some with and some without the new sounds. Pupils stand when they hear their sound, or words containing their sound.
- (For AB Answer Key, see p. 122. For Audioscript, see p. 124)

12 Listen and repeat.

1 ew   **2** y

13 Listen, point and say.

14 Listen and blend the sounds.

1 n - ew   new   **2** d - ew   dew

3 ch - ew   chew   **4** s - t - ew   stew

5 m - y   my   **6** t - r - y   try

7 f - l - y   fly   **8** s - k - y   sky

15 Read the sentences aloud. Then find *ew* and *y*.

1 There's dew on the grass.

2 I am trying to fly!

3 Chew the stew.

4 My new jet can fly in the sky.

OPTIONAL ACTIVITIES

Phonics game
Play *Words in the air* see p. 302.

Phonics game
Play *Slow motion game* see p. 302.
Photocopiable 3.5 see Teacher's notes p. 288.

Lesson 7

Lesson aims
To connect other areas of the curriculum with English learning; to develop the cross-curricular topic through a short project

Cross-curricular focus
Science (Extreme weather)

Target language
hurricane, typhoon, cyclone, wave

Materials
Audio CD

Optional materials
World map or globe; Active Teach; Digital Activity Book; CLIL poster; Photocopiable 3.6; pieces of card

Starting the lesson

- Use a globe or put a world map on the board. Point to places on the map and ask questions about the weather there that pupils should be able to answer from general knowledge: *Is it (cold) in (Canada) in (winter)? What's the weather like in (the Sahara Desert)?*

> Pupil's Book page 38

Presentation

- Ask (L1) what extreme weather pupils can think of. Prompt ideas by saying, e.g. *It's very snowy and windy.* Pupils say (L1) *a blizzard. It's very, very windy (a hurricane). There's water in houses (a flood)*, etc. Discuss (L1) what makes these weather conditions dangerous.

16 **Listen and read. Then say *True* or *False*.**

- Focus on the pictures and ask *What's this?* Pupils predict. Look together at the title of the article and say *Hurricane!* Ask *Do you like storms?* Pupils answer.
- Play the recording. Pupils listen and read. Play the recording again. Use the photos and mime to check meaning of *camera, circle, knock down* and *waves*. Pupils read the sentences about the text and decide if they are true or false. You may want to play the recording again while the class is reading the text.
- Allow pupils time to think about the answers. Then ask individual pupils to read out a sentence and the class says *True* or *False.* Correct the false sentences.

> KEY 1 True, 2 False, 3 False, 4 False

Practice

17   **Listen and say.**

- Focus on the sentences and tell the class that they have to listen and say the missing words. Pupils should use their notebooks. Revise the meanings of words in the sentences if necessary. Play the recording. Pupils listen and say the words. Play the recording again. Check answers with the class.

> KEY 1 storm, 2 weather, 3 lightning, 4 temperature

Think!

- Focus pupils' attention on the Think! box and ask them to read the information. They write the correct words for 1–3. Tell them to use a world map if necessary.

Mini-project

- Ask pupils (L1) to suggest other extreme weather conditions. Write their ideas on the board, e.g. *heat/cold waves, blizzards, floods, cyclones, hailstorms.*
- Divide the class into pairs. They choose one situation of extreme weather and look for information about it in reference books or on the internet. Give each pair a sheet of A4 paper. They write a few sentences about their choice. They can illustrate their text with drawings or printed pictures. Display the projects around the room and give pupils time to read each other's work.

> Activity Book page 34

17 **Read and circle.**

- Pupils read the quiz items carefully and circle the correct answer, A or B. When they have finished, check answers with the class, referring to the information on PB p. 38.

18 **Write *hurricane, typhoon* or *cyclone*.**

- Focus pupils' attention on the words in the word banks. Tell them to read the Think! information on PB p. 38. They write the correct words. Tell them to use a world map if necessary.

Ending the lesson

- Play *Pass the wordcards* see p. 298 using language and vocabulary of this unit, e.g. *I swim in the sea in summer.*
- (For AB Answer Key, see p. 122. For Audioscript, see p. 124.)

3

16 (1:72) **Listen and read. Then say *True* or *False*.**

HURRICANE!

Do you like hurricanes?
This man likes hurricanes. He's flying into a hurricane with his camera.

What is a hurricane?
A hurricane is a big storm. There's a lot of wind and a lot of rain. The hurricane goes round in a big circle. It can knock down trees and houses. There are big waves on the sea too.

wave

What is the eye of a hurricane?
The eye is the centre of the hurricane. It isn't windy and rainy there. Can you see the eye of the hurricane in the picture?

hurricane

When are there hurricanes?
There are hurricanes in the summer and the autumn.

1 The man with the camera likes storms.

2 A hurricane is a small storm.

3 It's sunny when a hurricane comes.

4 It's windy and rainy in the eye of a hurricane.

THINK!

Big storms have got different names in different places.
• hurricane = North/Central America
• typhoon = Asia
• cyclone = Australia

Hurricane, typhoon or cyclone?
1 Mexico
2 China
3 the United States

17 (1:73) **Listen and say.**

storm   lightning   temperature   weather

1 This is a … warning.

2 The … today is very windy and rainy.

3 There's thunder and …

4 The … is 18 degrees.

MINI-PROJECT   Write about storms in your country.

38   Lesson 7 science (hurricanes)   *AB p.34*

OPTIONAL ACTIVITIES

Hurricane danger zones
In pairs, pupils use reference books or the internet to find out where hurricanes often occur. They write the places on pieces of card. Stick up a world map or use a globe, and ask pupils to stick their cards in the correct places.

Team game
Play *Spin the bottle* see p. 301 with weather and other vocabulary.
Photocopiable 3.6 see Teacher's notes p. 289.

115

Lesson 8

Lesson aims
To learn about other cultures and respect cultural differences

Cross-cultural focus
To learn about world natural disasters

Target language
tornado, earthquake

Materials
Audio CD

Optional materials
World map or globe; Active Teach; Digital Activity Book; CLIL poster; Photocopiable 3.7

Starting the lesson

- Write the words *earthquake*, *tsunami* and *tornado* on the board. Explain the meaning or show pictures to show the meaning. Brainstorm other words for world natural disasters and write them on the board.

Pupil's Book page 39

Presentation

- Focus on the photos and the texts. Ask pupils to name the natural disasters mentioned: *earthquake*, *tsunami* and *tornado*.
- Pupils look at the texts, find the names of the countries/cities where the children live and locate them on the map or globe.

  Listen and read.

- Play the recording. Pupils listen and follow the texts in their books. Ask pupils to find the names of the children. Write them on the board.
- Ask a few comprehension questions: *Are there earthquakes in Texas? Is 'tsunami' a Spanish word? Are there tsunamis in Japan?*

Practice

19 Ask and answer.

- Direct pupils' attention to the questions. Check that they understand. Organise the class in pairs. They take it in turns to ask and answer the questions.
- When they have finished, ask individual pupils to demonstrate their questions and answers to the class.

> **KEY 1** Yes, there are. **2** No, it isn't. (It's a Japanese word.) **3** Build strong buildings. **4** Yes, there are. **5** Yes, there are. **6** Stay calm and look for a safe place.

Portfolio project

- Ask pupils what natural disasters there are in their country and what they can do to protect themselves.
- Pupils can write in their notebooks, using the texts on p. 39 as a model.

Activity Book page 35

19 Read and match.

- Ask the pupils to look at the pictures and match each sentence to the correct picture. Check answers with the class.

20 Answer.

- Ask the class about natural disasters in their country. Read out the questions and check that pupils understand. They read the questions and answer them. Check answers with the class.

Ending the lesson

- Play *Picture charades* see p. 298 with vocabulary for natural disasters.
- (For AB Answer Key, see p. 122. For Audioscript, see p. 125.)

Wider World
Natural disasters

18 (1:74) **Listen and read.**

earthquake

1 Aiko's blog

My name's Aiko and I live in Japan. Sometimes there are earthquakes in Japan. Some earthquakes are dangerous and others are not. We build strong buildings to protect ourselves. We also have tsunamis. These are big waves made by an earthquake under the water. 'Tsunami' is a Japanese word. I love my country.

Aiko, 10, Japan

2 Dan's blog

I'm Dan and I live in Texas. There are tornadoes in the town where I live. Some people like watching tornadoes but it can be dangerous. A tornado is a storm with air that goes round very quickly. It looks like a giant snake in the sky. The US gets about one thousand tornadoes every year. When there is a tornado, we stay calm and look for a safe place.

Dan, 11, United States

tornado

19 Ask and answer.

1 Are there earthquakes in Japan?
2 Is 'tsunami' a Chinese word?
3 What can we do to protect ourselves from earthquakes?
4 Are there tornadoes in Texas?
5 Are there tornado watchers?
6 What can we do to protect ourselves from tornadoes?

PORTFOLIO

Think and write.

What natural disasters are there in your country? What can you do to protect yourself?

OPTIONAL ACTIVITIES

Team game
Play *Board game* see p. 301 revising weather, natural disasters, etc.

Research
Divide the class into pairs. Tell pupils to look for information about natural disasters in their country. They write sentences about them and draw pictures.
Photocopiable 3.7 see Teacher's notes p. 289.

Lesson 9

Lesson aims
To review the unit language with a game and the Picture Dictionary

Materials
Audio CD; Flashcards (Weather conditions, Seasons, Seasonal activities)

Optional materials
Active Teach; Digital Activity Book; CLIL poster; Reading and Writing Booklet

Starting the lesson

- Divide the class into two teams. Ask the pupils to stand up and show them flashcards of weather words and say a sentence, e.g. *It's wet.* Make some mistakes. If the sentence is correct, pupils say *Yes* and turn around. If you make a mistake, they say *No* and sit down.

Pupil's Book page 40

20 Write in your notebook. Then play.

- Focus on the game board. Revise the vocabulary using the flashcards (weather conditions, seasons, seasonal activities). Read out the instructions. Check that pupils understand them. Practise with the pupils the language to be used in the bubbles: *Summer. You go swimming. No, my turn,* etc.
- Pupils write the table in their notebooks and complete the information about themselves. Then they take turns to ask and answer and complete the information for their partners. The winner is the one who guesses all the seasons correctly; if neither partner does this, the winner is the one with more correct guesses.
- Pupils can use the Picture Dictionary AB p. 106.

Activity Book page 36

21 Look and write.

- Ask pupils (L1) if they have ever done a crossword and elicit/explain how to do one if necessary. Pupils solve the puzzle individually or in pairs. Check as a class, asking, e.g. *What's number (2)?* Pupils answer.

22 Write.

- Direct the pupils' attention to the words in the word bank. Tell them to use this information to complete the sentences.
- When they have finished, ask individual pupils to read the sentences to the class.

23 Think and write.

- Pupils write sentences describing what the weather was like yesterday. When they have finished, ask individual pupils to read the sentences to the class.

Ending the lesson

- Say and mime, e.g. *I go swimming.* Ask a pupil to repeat the sentence, adding another activity and mime, e.g. *I go swimming and surfing.* Continue in the same way to make a chain.
- (For AB Answer Key, see p. 122.)

20 **Write in your notebook. Then play.**

	Spring	Summer	Autumn	Winter
Me				
My friend				

> Summer. You go swimming.

> No. My turn. Winter. You go skiing.

> Yes. My turn.

AB p.106

OPTIONAL ACTIVITIES

Team game
Play *Yes or no?* see p. 301.

Flashcard game
Play *Sponge throw* see see p. 299.
Reading and Writing Booklet p. 9 see Answer Key p. 282.

Lesson 10

Lesson aims
To personalise and assess efforts

Materials
Audio CD

Optional materials
Digital Activity Book; CLIL poster; Online material – *Film Studio Island*; Active Teach; Grammar reference and Review for Unit 3 (PB p. 113 AB p. 98); Test Booklet; Grammar Booklet; a bag or box

Starting the lesson

- This is a self assessment activity. Tell the pupils that the activities on this page will show what they have learnt in this unit.

Pupil's Book page 41

21 Listen and point.

- Tell the pupils that they must choose the correct picture for each question. Play the recording more than once if necessary.
- Pupils listen, look at the pictures and choose the correct answer.

KEY **1** b, **2** a, **3** b, **4** a, **5** a, **6** b, **7** a, **8** b

22 Look, read and say.

- Pupils look at the pictures and read the two gapped sentences. Tell them to write the complete sentences in their notebooks or on the board, or ask them to say the answers.

Activity Book page 37

- Focus on the *I can* sentences at the bottom of the page. Tell the pupils that they have to tick the boxes, depending on whether they think they can do the *I can* points.

24 Draw or stick a picture of your favourite season.

- Direct pupils' attention to the frame. Explain that they are going to draw or stick a picture and write in the frame. Ask them to choose a season that they like very much, and draw and colour a scene related to this season or find a picture that they can stick in. Ask volunteers to show their picture and describe it to the class.
- Divide the class into pairs. Pupils ask and answer questions about their pictures.

25 Write an email to your friend about your favourite season.

- Ask one pupil to show his/her picture from Activity 24 to the class. Elicit a description of it by answering questions: *Do you go swimming? What do you like doing?* Then ask pupils to write an email to a friend describing their favourite season. Work with the class to compile on the board a diagram of vocabulary and expressions to be used. Ask a few pupils to read their emails to the class.

Ending the lesson

- Put the weather and season flashcards in the bag or the box. Invite a pupil to take one card and, without showing it to the class, they mime the weather/season or an activity they would do in that weather/season. The class guesses what weather/season it is. The first pupil to make a correct guess takes the next turn.
- (For AB Answer Key, see p. 122. For Audioscript, see p. 125.)

21 (1:75) **Listen and point.**

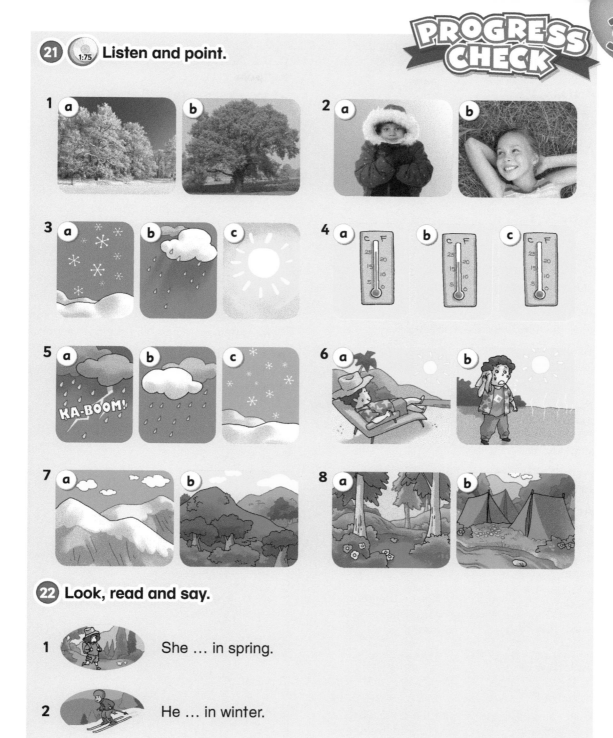

22 **Look, read and say.**

1   She ... in spring.

2   He ... in winter.

OPTIONAL ACTIVITIES

Make a chain
Say a sentence, e.g. *I swim in the sea in summer.* Ask a pupil to repeat the sentence and then add another element, e.g. *I swim in the sea in summer. I go hiking in the rain in autumn.* Continue in the same way until someone makes a mistake or forgets part of the sentence.

Team game
Play *Reading race* see p. 301.
Activity Book Review see p. 98.
Grammar Booklet p. 9 see Answer Key p. 284.
Test Booklet Unit 3 see Answer Key p. 295.
Online World
Pupils can now go online to *Film Studio Island* and enjoy the fun and games

Activity Book Answer Key

p. 28, Activity 1
humid – east; lightning, stormy, thunder – south; warm – north; wet – west

p. 28, Activity 2
1 warm, 2 29 degrees, 3 humid, 4 27 degrees, 5 wet, 6 19 degrees, 7 stormy, 8 thunder, 9 lightning, 10 23 degrees

p. 29, Activity 3
a 3, b 6, c 1, d 5, e 2, f 4

p. 29, Activity 4
1 thunder, lightning, 2 humid, 3 warm/hot/sunny, 4 wet/cold, 5 34 degrees, 6 2 degrees

p. 30, Activity 5
1 autumn, 2 summer, 3 winter, 4 spring

p. 30, Activity 6
1 go snowboarding, 2 go camping, 3 go water skiing, 4 go hiking

p. 30, Activity 7
1 goes snowboarding, winter, 2 goes camping, spring (accept 'summer'), 3 goes water skiing, summer, 4 go hiking, autumn

p. 31, Activity 8
1 d, 2 a, 3 c, 4 b

p. 31, Activity 9
1 It was warm.
2 It was 30 degrees.
3 She goes water skiing.
4 It was cold.
5 It was 1 degree.
6 He goes skiing.

p. 32, Activity 10
Because it's hot.

p. 32, Activity 11
a Action! 1
b We can climb. 5
c It's hot. 4
d There's a beach! 3
e It's wet! 2
f I can sleep! 6

p. 32, Activity 12
a No, he isn't.
b He can climb.
c On the beach.
d Yes, it is.
e Yes, it is.

p. 33, Activity 14
leaf, coin, mail, week

p. 33, Activity 15
1 stew, 2 dew, 3 my, 4 try

p. 34, Activity 17
1 B, 2 B, 3 A

p. 34, Activity 18
Korea: typhoon, the United States: hurricane, Australia: cyclone, China: typhoon

p. 35, Activity 19
Picture 1: earthquake, big waves, Japan
Picture 2: tornado, strong storm, One thousand a year, Texas

p. 36, Activity 21
Across: 1 wet, 3 humid, 5 temperature, 7 degrees
Down: 2 thunder, 4 lightning, 6 warm, 8 stormy

p. 36, Activity 22
1 winter, 2 go snowboarding, 3 goes camping, 4 spring, 5 summer, 6 go water skiing

Audioscript

Lesson 1 Activity 1 CD1:55
S = SAM J = JENNY R = RUBY
S Wow! Look at this.
J Don't touch, Sam! ... Where's Madley Kool?
S Look at this big, red button.
R Sam! Don't touch!
S What does this do?
S Oh! Wow! ... Rain!
S Wind!
S A storm!
S Snow!
R Quick, Sam! It's cold. We want the sun. We want to be hot! P-Press the button again!

Lesson 1 Activity 2 CD1:56
a warm
b humid
c wet
d stormy
e lightning
f thunder
g temperature
h degrees

Lesson 1 Activity 3 CD1:57
1 It's stormy.
2 It's snowy.
3 It's wet.
4 It's hot.
5 There's lightning.

Lesson 2 Activity 4 CD1:58
What's the weather like today?
It's cloudy and rainy. We're sad, we can't play.
What's the weather like today?
It's snowy and windy. We're sad, we can't play.
What's the weather like today?
It's cold, wet and stormy. We're scared,
we can't play.
What's the weather like today?
It's hot and sunny. We're happy. Let's play!

Lesson 2 Activity 5 CD1:59
1 What's the weather like today?
   It's humid.
2 What's the weather like today?
   It's cold.
3 What's the weather like today?
   There's thunder and lightning.
4 What's the weather like today?
   It's wet.
5 What's the weather like today?
   It's warm.

Lesson 3 Activity 3 (AB) CD1:60
1 What's the weather like today?
   It's wet.
2 What's the weather like today?
   It's 5 degrees. It's cold.
3 What's the weather like today?
   It's warm.
4 What's the weather like today?
   It's humid.
5 What's the weather like today?
   It's stormy. There's thunder and lightning.
6 What's the weather like today?
   It's 32 degrees. It's hot.

Lesson 3 Activity 6 CD1:61
a go camping
b go water skiing
c go hiking
d go snowboarding
e spring
f summer
g autumn
h winter

Lesson 3 Activity 7 CD1:62
Spring, summer, autumn, winter
Four seasons in the year.
It's spring.
We go camping in spring.
We fish and swim in the river.

It's summer.
I go water skiing in summer.
I jump up high in the sea.

It's autumn.
She goes hiking in autumn.
She walks and climbs in the mountains.

It's winter.
He goes snowboarding in winter.
He rides and jumps in the snow.

Lesson 3 Activity 8 CD1:63
1 He goes camping in spring.
2 He goes water skiing in summer.
3 He goes snowboarding in winter.
4 He goes hiking in autumn.

Lesson 4 Activity 9 CD1:64

a It's windy and I can fly my kite. The weather is
cool. There are a lot of apples on the tree in my
garden. Yum!
b I like the flowers. The birds sing in the trees. I
like listening to the birds and the rain. I love the
weather. It's always mild and cool or warm.
c It's hot and humid and there's no school!
Sometimes it's 35 degrees. I go swimming with my
friends. I go to the park with my friends.
I eat a lot of fruit. My favourites are strawberries
and peaches.
d It snows and it's really cold. But it's beautiful.
Some birds don't like the cold and they fly to hot
places. Some animals sleep. I go skiing.

Lesson 6 Activity 12 CD1:66

e   w
/ew/   /ew/   /ew/
y
/iy/   /iy/   /iy/

Lesson 6 Activity 13 CD1:67

/iy/   /iy/
/ew/   /ew/
/ew/   /ew/
/ew/   /ew/
/iy/   /iy/
/iy/   /iy/

Lesson 6 Activity 14 CD1:68

1 /n/ /ew/
  new
2 /d/ /ew/
  dew
3 /ch/ /ew/
  chew
4 /s/ t/ /ew/
  stew
5 /m/ /y/
  my
6 /t/ /r/ /y/
  try
7 /f/ /l/ /y/
  fly
8 /s/ /k/ /y/
  sky

Lesson 6 Activity 14 (AB) CD1:69

1 /l/ /ea/   /f/
2 /k/   /oi/   /n/
3 /m/   /ai/   /l/
4 /w/   /ee/   /k/

Lesson 6 Activity 15 (AB) CD1:70

1 stew
2 dew
3 my
4 try

Lesson 6 Activity 16 (AB) CD1:71

In my new jet I fly up and down, high and low. I see
the clouds and the sun, the rain and the snow. I like
to be up in the sky.

Lesson 7 Activity 16 CD1:72

Hurricane!
Do you like hurricanes?
This man likes hurricanes. He's flying into a hurricane
with his camera.

What is a hurricane?
A hurricane is a big storm. There's a lot of wind and
a lot of rain. The hurricane goes round in a big circle.
It can knock down trees and houses. There are big
waves on the sea too.

What is the eye of a hurricane?
The eye is the centre of the hurricane. It isn't windy
and rainy there. Can you see the eye of the hurricane
in the picture?

When are there hurricanes?
There are hurricanes in the summer and the autumn.

Lesson 7 Activity 17 CD1:73

Hello, everybody! Please listen carefully. This is a
storm warning. The weather today is very windy
and rainy. There's thunder and lightning. The
temperature is 18 degrees.
Please be careful! The eye of the hurricane is coming.

Lesson 8 Activity 18 CD1:74

1 Aiko's blog
My name's Aiko and I live in Japan. Sometimes there are earthquakes in Japan. Some earthquakes are dangerous and others are not. We build strong buildings to protect ourselves. We also have tsunamis. These are big waves made by an earthquake under the water. 'Tsunami' is a Japanese word. I love my country.
Aiko, 10, Japan

2 Dan's blog
I'm Dan and I live in Texas. There are tornadoes in the town where I live. Some people like watching tornadoes but it can be dangerous. A tornado is a storm with air that goes round very quickly. It looks like a giant snake in the sky. The US gets about one thousand tornadoes every year. When there is a tornado, we stay calm and look for a safe place.
Dan, 11, United States

Lesson 10 Activity 21 CD1:75

1 What's the weather like today?
It's warm.
2 What's the weather like today?
It's cold.
3 What's the weather like today?
It's wet.
4 What's the temperature today?
It's 25 degrees.
5 What's the weather like today?
There's lightning and thunder.
6 What's the weather like today?
It's humid.
7 I go skiing and snowboarding in winter.
8 I go camping in spring. There are many beautiful flowers.

Objectives

- talk about routines during the week
- say the time for activities
- express means of transport
- pronounce properly /ie/ and /ue/.

Phonics
/ie/ and /ue/

Values
- Develop new interests

Topics
- Routines
- Time
- Frequency

Stories
- Unit opener: activities during the week
- Story episode: about Madley not being able to swim

Language
Vocabulary
- Activities: have music lessons, have ballet lessons, do karate, do gymnastics, practice the piano, practice the violin, learn to cook, learn to draw, study English, study Maths
- Parts of the day: morning, midday, afternoon, evening
- Time: a quarter past, half past, a quarter to, minute, hour, second

Revision
Days of the week: Sunday, Monday, Tuesday, Wednesday, Thursday, Friday, Saturday
Activities: go (skateboarding), go (swimming)
Others: thirty, rivers

Structures
What do you do on (Saturdays)?
I (have music lessons) on (Saturdays).
What does he/she do on (Saturdays)?
She/He (has music lessons) at (2 o'clock).
When do you (have music lessons)?
I have (music lessons) in the (morning).
I have (music lessons) at (2.15).
When does he/she (have music lessons)?
He/She (has music lessons) at (quarter past) 2.
She always (has ballet lessons) in the (morning).
She never (walks).
She often (goes to parties).
How do you go to school?
He goes to school (by car).

CLIL language
How do you go to school?: road, river, radio, internet, plane, snowmobile

Songs and chants
- Chant
- Song about where pets are
- Karaoke song

Sociocultural aspects
- Finding out about timetables for shop opening and closing in different parts of the world
- Comparing types of shops
- Finding out about school routines in other countries

Cross-curricular contents
- Social Science: reading information about different types of schools for children
- Language Arts: reading a story, acting out, telling a story
- Language skills: reading and understanding information about routines

Learning strategies
- Using the Picture Dictionary to remember the meaning of words
- Revise the Look! boxes as a reference for structures
- Identifying rules about the use of adverbs of frequency
- Logical thinking: developing skills for using the dictionary
- Critical thinking: selecting and using techniques that help to learn
- Collaborative learning: checking answers in pairs and small groups
- Self assessment

Basic competences

- Linguistic communication: To use linguistic resources to describe routines (L1 to L4)
- Knowledge and interaction with the physical world: Talk about means of transport to go to school (L7)
- Mathematical competence: Express time (L1 to L4, and L8)
- Processing information and digital competence: Use *Film Studio Island* online component
- Social and civic competence: Develop new interests (L5)
- Cultural and artistic competence: To compare shops and timetables for shops in different countries (L8)
- Learning to learn: Reflect on what has been learnt and self-evaluate progress (L10)
- Autonomy and personal initiative: Develop one's own criteria and social skills (L1 to L10)

Skills

Listening
- Identifying routines in recordings
- Understanding people describing their routines
- Listening to an interview and saying the time
- Understanding specific information in a song about activities and times to do them
- Understanding general and specific information in a story
- Identifying true/false information

Reading
- Reading sentences and short texts to grasp specific information (routines)
- Reading a text about week routines to identify true/false information
- Understanding general and specific information in a cartoon strip story
- Reading a text about how to go to school and understand general and specific information
- Showing understanding of texts about shop timetables

Speaking
- Repeating words and sentences
- Saying the time
- Saying the sentences from Grammar boxes
- Chanting and singing
- Pronouncing /ie/ and /ue/ correctly
- Describing a bedroom

Writing
- Completing sentences with words provided
- Completing questions and answers about routines
- Writing times
- Writing sentences about means of transport and extracting information from a table
- Describing time and days of the week to do certain activities

Talking
- Participating in dialogues to talk about routines
- Role playing a story
- Asking and answering questions about the time

Classroom ideas
- Use the cross-curricular poster of the unit and put it on the wall
- Find out about famous people's routines
- Bring pictures and photos of different types of schools
- Bring to the classroom library books that include activities and times
- Photocopiables

Take-home English
- Home-School Link
- Notes for Parents
- A sample of work each week
- Portfolio

Self assessment
- Pupils can talk about routines during the week
- Pupils can say the time for activities
- Pupils can express means of transport

Evaluation
- Pupil's Book page 51
- Activity Book page 47
- Photocopiable 4.7
- Picture Dictionary
- Test Booklet – Unit 4

127

Lesson 1

Lesson aims
To learn and practise new vocabulary (activities)

Target language
have music lessons, have ballet lessons, do karate, do gymnastics, practise the piano, practise the violin, learn to draw, learn to cook, study English, study Maths

Materials
Audio CD; Flashcards and Wordcards (Activities)

Optional materials
Active Teach; Digital Activity Book; Photocopiable 4.1

Starting the lesson

- Revise sports and actions. Tell pupils that you are going to give some orders and they have to follow them. Say, e.g. *Move your legs. Shake your body. Play tennis.* You might want to do this to music.

Pupil's Book pages 42–43

Presentation

- Use the flashcards to teach the vocabulary. Hold up the flashcards in turn and say the words for pupils to repeat. Hold up the flashcards again, this time asking individual pupils to say the words.
- Ask or remind pupils (L1) where the story characters were in Unit 2 (a jungle film set) and Unit 3 (a film set with a weather machine). Direct pupils' attention to the main illustration. Point to the karate clothes. Ask (L1) what kind of film set this is (a set for a karate or martial arts scene). Ask *Can you see Madley Kool? Where is he?* Pupils answer *In the picture.*

① Listen.

- Tell pupils (L1) they are going to hear a recording describing what they can see in the main illustration but that one of the activities in the main illustration won't be mentioned. Play the recording. Give pupils time to find the activities mentioned. Play the recording again. Pupils decide what's missing. Pupils check if they were right.

KEY Missing activity: (doing) gymnastics

Practice

② Listen and repeat.

- Play the recording, pausing after each activity. Pupils point to the activity pictures. Play the recording again. Pupils point and repeat each word.
- Divide the class into pairs. Pupil A says the letter of one of the pictures, e.g. *Letter d*, and Pupil B says the activity, *do gymnastics*. They then swap roles.
- Focus on the main illustration. Point to the thought bubbles and pupils say the actions.
- Shuffle the flashcards (activities). Choose one. Hold it up and pupils say and mime the action, e.g. *go skateboarding*. Pupils take turns to choose a flashcard and say the action to the class.
- Display the relevant flashcards on one side of the board and write the corresponding words or put up wordcards on the other side. Pupils come to the front, read out the words and match them to the pictures.

③ Listen and find.

- Play the recording, pausing after each activity. This time pupils point to the activity pictures in the main illustration. Play the recording again with books closed. Pupils can mime after each word.

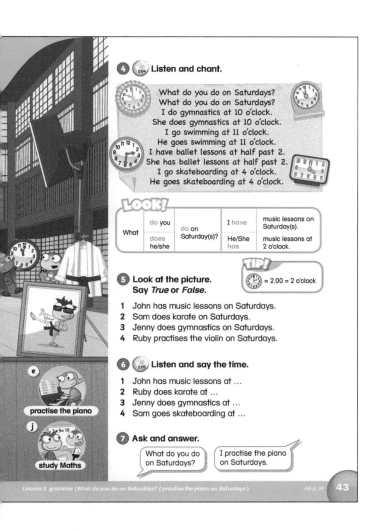

Ending the lesson

- Compile a word map with the class: draw a circle and write *Things we do* in it. Elicit words for activities they have learnt in this lesson, in Unit 1 and in previous years. Write them on the board. Pupils could copy into their notebooks.
- (For AB Answer Key, see p. 148. For Audioscript, see p. 149.)

OPTIONAL ACTIVITIES

Flashcard game

Draw an object e.g. a musical note, and the class has to guess the activity (*have music lessons*). Ask individual pupils to take a turn drawing. You can turn this into a competition by dividing the class into two teams.

Make a chain

Start a sentence chain by saying *On Saturdays I (do karate)*. Pupil A says *On Saturdays I (do karate) and (go skateboarding)*. Continue going round the class, with each pupil adding an activity to the list. They can use any activities they can remember. When a pupil makes a mistake or can't think of another activity, start a new chain.

Photocopiable 4.1 see Teacher's notes p. 289.

NOTES

Activity Book page 38

1 Match.

- Direct pupils' attention to the pictures and the word bank. Tell the class to match the phrases to the pictures.
- Check as a class. Ask *What's number (1)?* Pupils answer.

2 Write.

- Direct pupils' attention to the question in the speech bubble and the answers 1–10. Tell them to complete the sentences with the correct word from the word bank.
- When they have finished, ask individual pupils to read the answers.

Lesson 2

Lesson aims
To revise the vocabulary with a chant; to learn and practise the new structure *What do you do on Saturdays? I have music lessons on Saturdays.*

Target language
What do you do on (Saturdays)? I have (music lessons) on (Saturdays).
What does he/she do on (Saturdays)? He/She has (music lessons) at 2 o'clock.

Materials
Audio CD; Flashcards and Wordcards (Activities)

Optional materials
(Analogue) clock; Active Teach; Digital Activity Book; Grammar Booklet

Starting the lesson

- Play *Pass the actions* see p. 298 to practise hobbies and actions, including the vocabulary of Lesson 1.

Pupil's Book page 43

Presentation

- Show a flashcard, e.g. do karate, and ask *What do you do on Saturdays?* Say *I do karate.* Ask the class to repeat the question and answer after you. Repeat with other activities.
- Bring an analogue clock to the class. Show ten o'clock and say *It's ten o'clock.* Pupils repeat. Give more examples. Encourage pupils to say the time without help.
- Show half past ten. Say *It's half past ten.* Practise *half past* as for *o'clock* above.
- Ask individual pupils *Do you (play tennis)?* If the answer is yes, ask *What time do you (play tennis)?* Pupils answer. Repeat with other activities.
- Pupils read the sentences in the Look! box. Explain (L1) that they should use *have* with *I* and *has* with *he, she* and *it*. Also explain that they should use *at* before times.
- Read the Look! box.
- Pupils give more examples. Write them on the board. Pupils could copy them into their notebooks.
- Ask pupils to look at the Tip! box. Explain that we say, e.g. *2 o'clock* and that we can write *2.00* or *2 o'clock*.

4 Listen and chant.

- Play the recording. Pupils listen and follow the words. Play the chant again. Pause after each line for pupils to repeat. Play it a few more times. Pupils chant together. Use the flashcards and the clocks on the page to help prompt the words if necessary.

5 Look at the picture. Say *True* or *False*.

- Ask pupils to look at the main illustration. Point to the journalist with purple hair and ask *Who is she?* Elicit/Explain (L1) that she is a journalist who is interviewing the children.
- Focus on the four sentences and ask the pupils to decide if they are true or false. Check answers with the class.

> **KEY** 1 False, 2 False, 3 True, 4 False

Practice

6 Listen and say the time.

- Explain that pupils have to listen to a recording and say a time for each activity. Play the recording once. Pupils listen. Play it again and pupils note their answers. Play it a third time, pausing after each of Tina's sentences giving the time of the characters' activities. Pupils say their answer and correct the false sentences.
- Play the recording again. Ask (L1) *What lesson don't the children have?* (acting lessons). Explain (L1) the meaning of *acting* lessons.

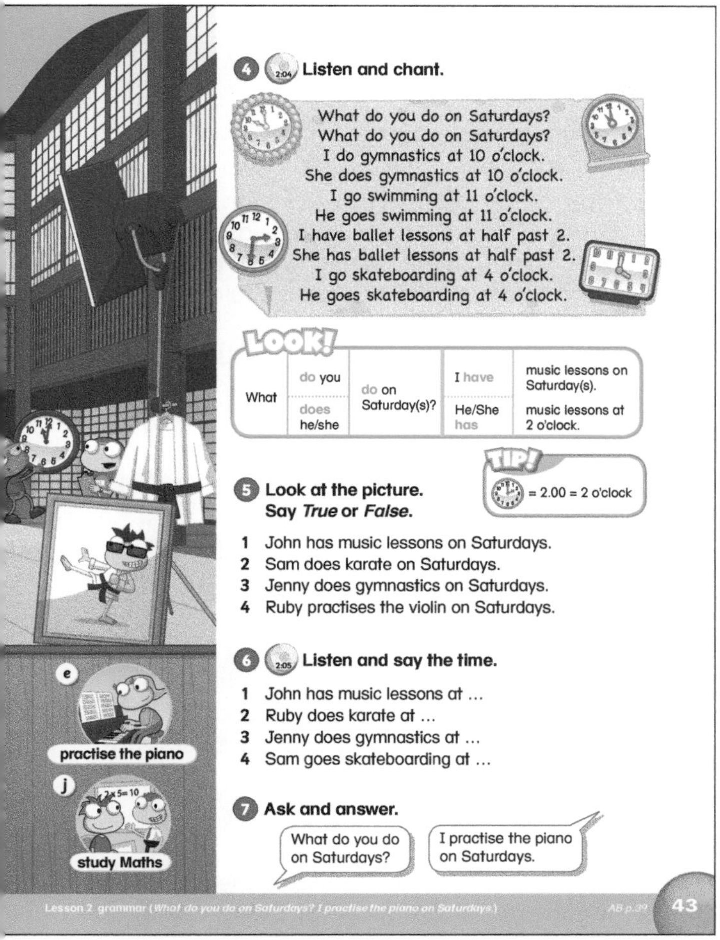
4 Listen and chant.

What do you do on Saturdays?
What do you do on Saturdays?
I do gymnastics at 10 o'clock.
She does gymnastics at 10 o'clock.
I go swimming at 11 o'clock.
He goes swimming at 11 o'clock.
I have ballet lessons at half past 2.
She has ballet lessons at half past 2.
I go skateboarding at 4 o'clock.
He goes skateboarding at 4 o'clock.

LOOK!

What	do you	do on Saturday(s)?	I have	music lessons on Saturday(s).
	does he/she		He/She has	music lessons at 2 o'clock.

5 Look at the picture. Say *True* or *False*.

TIP! = 2.00 = 2 o'clock

1 John has music lessons on Saturdays.
2 Sam does karate on Saturdays.
3 Jenny does gymnastics on Saturdays.
4 Ruby practises the violin on Saturdays.

6 Listen and say the time.

1 John has music lessons at …
2 Ruby does karate at …
3 Jenny does gymnastics at …
4 Sam goes skateboarding at …

7 Ask and answer.

What do you do on Saturdays?
I practise the piano on Saturdays.

e practise the piano
j study Maths

Lesson 2 grammar (*What do you do on Saturdays? I practise the piano on Saturdays.*) AB p.39 43

KEY **1** 3 o'clock, **2** 9 o'clock, **3** 10 o'clock, **4** 4 o'clock

7 Ask and answer.

- Focus the pupils' attention on the model dialogue. Organise the class in pairs. Pupils take it in turns to ask and answer about the activities they do on different days of the week.

Activity Book page 39

3 Look and write.

- Focus on the example and explain (L1) that pupils must complete the questions and answer them. Ask them to look at the pictures and write. Make sure they understand they are only writing about the activities and the days (not the times). Check answers with the class.

4 Look at Activity 3 and write.

- Pupils look at the previous activity and write sentences with the activities and times. Check as a class.

Ending the lesson

- Divide the class into teams. Use the clock. A pupil from Team A says an activity and time, e.g. *I do karate at half past three*, and a pupil from Team B must come to the front and put the clock to the correct time and say a sentence, e.g. *He does karate at half past three.* The teams take turns. They get a point for each correct time and another one for each correct sentence. The first team to score 10 points wins.
- (For AB Answer Key, see p. 148. For Audioscript, see p. 149.)

OPTIONAL ACTIVITIES

TPR game
Play *Number groups* see p. 300 with sports and actions.

Flashcard game
Play *Picture charades* see p. 298 to revise the actions learnt in this lesson (*do gymnastics, practise the piano*, etc.) and in previous years.

Grammar Booklet p. 10 see Answer Key p. 284.

NOTES

Lesson 3

Lesson aims
To extend the unit vocabulary set and structures; to practise the unit language with a song

Target language
morning, midday, afternoon, evening, a quarter past, half past, a quarter to

Materials
Audio CD; Flashcards and Wordcards (Activities)

Optional materials
(Analogue) clock; Active Teach; Digital Activity Book; Photocopiables 4.2–4.3; Reading and Writing Booklet

Starting the lesson

- Play the chant from Lesson 2 CD2:04. Divide the class into two groups. They all chant the first two lines, and then the two groups chant alternate lines.

  Pupil's Book page 44

Presentation

- Bring an analogue clock to the class. Show half past ten and say *It's half past ten.* Pupils repeat. Give more examples. Encourage pupils to say the time without help.
- Follow the same procedure with *It's a quarter to ten.*
- Ask individual pupils *Do you (play tennis)?* If the answer is yes, ask *What time do you (play tennis)?* Pupils answer. Repeat with other activities.

8 **Listen and repeat.**

- Introduce the new words (*morning, midday,* etc.) using the flashcards. Hold them up and say the words for pupils to repeat. Ask individual pupils to say the words. Play the recording for pupils to listen and repeat.
- Now put the flashcards on the board. Point to the different flashcards and ask the class to say the words.

Song

9 **Listen and point. Then sing.**

- Play the recording with books closed. Mime the actions to make meaning clear. Play the song again. The class mimes with you as they listen. Then play the song again, with books open. Pupils point to the correct coloured words. Play the song again: the class sings along with the recording. You can now play the karaoke song (Active Teach).

Practice

10 **Ask and answer.**

- Direct pupils' attention to the Look! box. Look at the questions and answers and focus on the use of *do* and *does.* Focus on the use of *When* and information about time provided in answers. Read the Look! box; pupils listen and repeat. Elicit more examples from the class and write a few on the board. Pupils could copy them into their notebooks.
- Organise the class in pairs. Ask the pupils to take it in turns to ask and answer questions following the model dialogue.
- Divide the class into pairs. Pupil A asks a question. Pupils B answers and asks another question to Pupil A. The dialogue continues like this.

Activity Book page 40

5 **Look and write.**

- Focus on the pictures and the words in the word bank. Pupils have to write the corresponding time expression below each picture. Check answers with the class.

6   **Listen and match.**

- Explain (L1) that pupils have to match the activities with the corresponding times. Play the recording. Pupils match. Play the recording again for pupils to check. Check answers with the class.

Ending the lesson

- Pupils sing the song. Divide the class into two groups. With books closed, one group sings while the other mimes; then they swap roles.
- (For AB Answer Key, see p. 148. For Audioscript, see p. 149.)

> **OPTIONAL ACTIVITIES**
> **Drawing activity**
> Divide the class into pairs. Pupil A says a sentence giving an activity and a time (clock time or time of day). Pupil B makes the drawing and writes the sentence. They continue taking turns. Model the game with a confident pupil.

8  **Listen and repeat.**

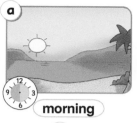
morning

midday

afternoon

evening

2.15
a quarter past 2

2.30
half past 2

2.45
a quarter to 3

9 **Listen and point. Then sing.**

When does she study Maths?

Does she start at ?

Does she study Maths in the
morning afternoon ?

Please tell me when. (x2)

She studies Maths at 9.00 10.00 .

Yes, she studies Maths at 9.00 10.00 .

She doesn't study at 10.00 11.00 .

She studies Maths at 9.00 in the morning.

When do you learn to cook?

Do you start at ?

Do you start to cook in the
afternoon evening ?

Please tell me when. (x2)

I start to cook at 5.00 6.00 .

Yes, I learn to cook at 5.00 6.00 .

No, I don't start at 5.30 5.45 .

I learn to cook at 5.00 in the afternoon.

When	do you	have music lessons?	I have music lessons	in the morning. at 2.15.
	does he/she		He/She has music lessons	at a quarter past 2.

10 **Ask and answer.**

When do you study Maths?

I study Maths in the afternoon.

Sentence building chain
Pupils build sentences by adding one word each. Pupil A says, e.g. *I*, Pupil B says *I practise*, Pupil C says *I practise the*, etc. They should make the sentences as long as they can.

Photocopiable 4.2 see Teacher's notes p. 289.
Photocopiable 4.3 see Teacher's notes p. 289.
Reading and Writing Booklet p. 10 see Answer Key p. 282.

Lesson 4

Lesson aims
To develop reading, writing, listening and speaking skills; to learn and practise the new structure: expressing frequency

Target language
She always has (ballet lessons) in the morning. She never (walks). She often goes to a party.

Materials
Audio CD

Optional materials
(Analogue) clock; Active Teach; Digital Activity Book; Grammar Booklet

Starting the lesson

- Bring an analogue clock to the class. Show different times and say *It's (half past six)*; include some false statements where the time you say does not match the time you show. Pupils say *Yes* or *No* and correct the false sentences.
- Ask *What do you do in the (afternoon)? What time do you (play tennis)?*

Pupil's Book page 45

Presentation

- Focus on the illustrations that go with the texts. Ask the class to listen to your descriptions and point to the corresponding picture: *Fifi is dancing. Fifi is at the party*, etc. Elicit more sentences and write them on the board.

Skills

11 **Listen and read. Then say *True* or *False*.**

- Focus on the four pictures. Ask *Where is Fifi?* Teach/revise the word *party*.
- Pupils read about Fifi's busy day. Ask a few comprehension questions. Tell pupils to listen to some sentences about the text. Play the recording once. Pupils listen. Then play each sentence in turn, pausing to allow time for pupils to decide whether they are True or False and correct the false sentences.

KEY 1 True, **2** True, **3** False (She has ballet lessons in the morning), **4** False (She goes skateboarding at 2 o'clock)

Practice

12 **Ask and answer.**

- Pupils read the sentences in the Look! box. Explain (L1) that *always, never* and *often* are used to express frequency. Read the Look! box. Pupils give more examples. Write them on the board. Pupils could copy them into their notebooks.
- Organise the class in pairs. Focus the pupils' attention on the sample dialogues. Tell them to ask and answer about what they do, when and how often. They work in pairs. Ask them to take it in turns to ask and answer questions.

Activity Book page 41

7 **Listen and draw the time. Then write.**

- Focus on the pictures and the times. Play the recording once while pupils listen. Play it again, pausing for them to draw the times on the clocks.
- Play the recording again for pupils to check the information they now have about activities and times.
- Focus on the sentences and point out the example. Allow pupils time to complete the sentences.
- Check answers.

8 **Look and write.**

- Tell pupils that they must write the questions and the answers. Work through question 1 as a whole class. Allow pupils time to complete the questions and answers. Check answers, asking different pupils to read out what they have written.

9 **Write about you.**

- Pupils write about their personal routine. Tell them to write complete sentences, and to give a time with each activity that they mention. Give them time to write and then ask volunteers to read their sentences to the class.

Ending the lesson

- Pupils look at the flashcards. Then they play a game in pairs. Pupil A looks at a card but does not show it to Pupil B. Pupil B asks *What do you do on Saturdays?* Pupil A mimes the activity on the card and Pupil B guesses.
- (For AB Answer Key, see p. 148. For Audioscript, see p. 150.)

Pupils can now go online to *Film Studio Island* and find the umbrella that Cleo is holding. It is the red and yellow striped umbrella to the left of the swimming pool in the recreation area. Once pupils click on the umbrella they are taken to a supplementary language game based on the vocabulary in this unit.

She **always** has ballet lessons in the morning.

She **often** goes to parties.

She **never** walks.

11 (2:09) **Listen and read. Then say *True* or *False*.**

 SKILLS

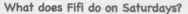

What does Fifi do on Saturdays?

She has a busy day! She always has ballet lessons in the morning. She loves dancing very much!

When does she have ballet lessons?

She always has ballet lessons at 10 o'clock.

How does she go to her ballet lesson? Does she walk?

No, she never walks. She goes by car! She doesn't like walking. Her mum drives her there at a quarter to 10.

What does she do in the afternoon?

She goes skateboarding in the park at 2 o'clock. Then she often goes to a party with her friends. She has a lot of fun on Saturdays!

1 Fifi always has ballet lessons at 10 o'clock.

2 She never walks to her ballet lesson.

3 She often has ballet lessons in the afternoon.

4 She never goes skateboarding in the afternoon.

TIP!

	M	T	W	T	F
always	✓	✓	✓	✓	✓
often	✓		✓		✓
never					

12 Ask and answer.

What do you do on Saturdays?

I study English.

When do you study English?

I study English at 2.30.

Do you always practise the violin on Sundays?

No, I never practise the violin on Sundays. I often practise the violin on Mondays.

Lesson 4 grammar (*always, often, never*)　　　AB p.41　**45**

OPTIONAL ACTIVITIES

My diary
On A4 paper, pupils write his/her diary for one day of the week. They write the time of each of their activities and add pictures. They show it to the class.

Pairwork game
Play *Snap* with actions see p. 300.
Grammar Booklet p. 11 see Answer Key p.284.

Lesson 5

Lesson aims
To consolidate the unit language with a story

Values
Develop new interests

Receptive language
work (n), have singing lessons, feed, Does he walk to work?, On ... he ...

Materials
Audio CD; Story cards; Character story cards

Optional materials
Active Teach; Digital Activity Book; Photocopiable 4.4; Reading and Writing Booklet

Starting the lesson

- Ask pupils (in L1) what they can remember about the story from the previous episode. Use the Unit 3 story cards as prompts.

Pupil's Book page 46

Prestentation

13 **Listen and read. Then act out.**

- Tell pupils (L1) they are going to find out about Madley Kool's week. They predict some of the activities he does.
- Show the Unit 4 story cards one at a time and ask the *Before listening to the story* questions. Pupils predict what happens in the story.
- Play the recording. Pupils listen as they follow the story in their books. Ask if their predictions were correct and then ask the *After listening to the story* questions.

Practice

- Divide the class into eight groups and assign a speech bubble to each. Pupils read the story as a class.
- Tell pupils (L1) to act being Madley Kool. Play or say the relevant lines from Frames 2 to 6. Pupils act out Madley's activities.
- Retell the story, making some deliberate mistakes. Every time pupils spot a mistake, they put up their hands and correct it.

Values

- Talk (L1) about how children develop new interests, e.g. learn a new language, learn about a topic, write stories, etc. Focus on the importance of developing new interests and talk (L1) about the role of education in their lives. Highlight the importance of developing new interests to create a better future for them.

Activity Book page 42

10 **Read the story again. Can Madley sing and do karate? Write.**

- Pupils read the story in the PB again to work out the answer to the question. Then they write their answer on the line.

11 **Number the pictures in order.**

- Direct pupils' attention to the pictures and speech bubbles. Explain that they must look at the story on PB p. 46 for the information. Ask them to number the pictures in order. Check answers with the class.

12 **Look at Activity 11 and write.**

- Explain that the pupils have to answer the questions. They can look at the story again if necessary. Ask individual pupils to read out their answers for the class.

13 **Write.**

- Explain that pupils have to answer the two questions. They can look at the story again if necessary. Ask individual pupils to read out their answers for the class.

Home-School Link

- Ask the class to research an article or story they find interesting and show it to their family, talking about it. You could provide printed or appropriate internet sources.

Ending the lesson

- Revise what happens in the story. Write some incomplete sentences about Madley Kool on the board, e.g. *He goes to work ... On Mondays he ... .* Ask pupils to complete them. You could turn this activity into a competition by dividing the class into two teams and asking one pupil from each team to complete each sentence.
- (For AB Answer Key, see p. 148.)

Listen and read. Then act out.

 Develop new interests.

HOME-SCHOOL LINK
Find an interesting article or story.
Show your family and talk about it.

OPTIONAL ACTIVITIES

TPR game
Play *Memory* see p. 300 using the vocabulary of this unit, days of the week, activities and transport.

Drawing game
Play *Dice Game* see p. 299 using activities and time.

Photocopiable 4.4 see Teacher's notes p. 289.
Reading and Writing Booklet p. 11 see Answer Key p.282.

Lesson 6

Lesson aims
To learn the sounds and letters /ie/ and /ue/

Target language
pie, tie, lie, fried, blue, glue, true, tissue

Materials
Audio CD; Flashcards and Wordcards (phonics);
Phonics poster

Optional materials
Active Teach; Digital Activity Book;
Photocopiable 4.5

Starting the lesson

- Show pupils the flashcards (phonics).
- Read the words aloud and ask pupils to find a common pattern.

 Pupil's Book page 47

Presentation

14 🔊 2:12 **Listen and repeat.**

- Write on the board the sounds /ie/ and /ue/. Play the recording for pupils to listen. Play it a second time for pupils to listen and repeat.

15 🔊 2:13 **Listen, point and say.**

- Tell the pupils that they must point to the sound that they hear. Play the recording for pupils to listen and point. Play it a second time for pupils to listen, point and say.

16 🔊 2:14 **Listen and blend the sounds.**

- Demonstrate the blending of the first sound; pupils repeat what they hear. Then tell the pupils that they must listen and blend the sounds. Play the recording for pupils to listen and say the words that contain the corresponding sounds.

Practice

17 **Read the sentences aloud. Then find /ie/ and /ue/.**

- The pupils read the sentences aloud. Then they find and point to the sounds /ie/ and /ue/. Ask them to read out the words containing these sounds.

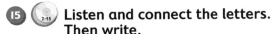 **Activity Book page 43**

14 **Read the words. Circle the pictures.**

- Give pupils time to read the words and circle the corresponding parts of the picture.

15 🔊 2:15 **Listen and connect the letters. Then write.**

- Play the recording and give the pupils time to draw the lines to connect the letters. Play the recording again, and give pupils time to write the words.

16 🔊 2:16 **Listen and write the words.**

- Play the recording, pausing if necessary to give pupils time to write the words. Play it again for them to check what they have written. Check answers.

17 🔊 2:17 **Read aloud. Then listen and check.**

- Ask different pupils to read the text aloud, one sentence each. Then play the recording: they listen and check.

Ending the lesson

- Divide the class into two groups. Give each group a sound from this lesson: /ie/ and /ue/. Say words, some with and some without the new sounds. Pupils stand when they hear their sound, or words containing their sound.
- (For AB Answer Key, see p. 148. For Audioscript, see p. 150.)

14 (2:12) **Listen and repeat.**

¹ ie

² ue

15 (2:13) **Listen, point and say.**

16 (2:14) **Listen and blend the sounds.**

1 p – ie pie	2 t – ie tie
3 l – ie lie	4 f – r – ie – d fried
5 b – l – ue blue	6 g – l – ue glue
7 t – r – ue true	8 t – i – ss – ue tissue

17 **Read the sentences aloud. Then find *ie* and *ue*.**

1 Do you like fried fish?

2 My dad has got a blue tie.

3 Is it true that trees are blue?

4 Let's lie on the picnic blanket and eat plum pie.

OPTIONAL ACTIVITIES

Phonics game
Play *Scrambled words* see p. 301.

Phonics game
Play *Build the word* see p. 301.
Photocopiable 4.5 see Teacher's notes p. 289.

Lesson 7

Lesson aims
To connect other areas of the curriculum with English learning; to develop the cross-curricular topic through a short project

Cross-curricular focus
Social science (Transport/access to school)

Target language
road, river, radio, internet, plane, snowmobile
How do you go to school?

Materials
Audio CD

Optional materials
World map or globe, Active Teach; Digital Activity Book; CLIL poster; Photocopiable 4.6

Starting the lesson

- Divide the class into two groups. Group A writes a means of transport on a piece of paper and gives it to one pupil from Group B. This pupil comes to the board and draws it, e.g. a car. Group B guesses what it is, as quickly as possible.

Pupil's Book page 48

Presentation

- Ask (L1) what means of transport pupils can think of to go to school. Encourage a wide range of ideas by saying e.g. *by plane, by bus.* Pupils say (L1) means of transport. Write them on the board.
- Point out the Tip! box as a reminder to pupils to use *by* with forms of transport.

  Listen, read and find.

- With books closed, tell pupils (L1) they are going to read an article called *How do you go to school?* They answer the question for themselves and then predict what pictures they will see in the article.
- Tell the class to read and find the texts that correspond to the pictures. Play the recording. Pupils follow in their books. Check as a class.
- Ask a few comprehension questions.

 Listen and point to *T = True* or *F = False.*

- Ask the pupils to look at the three texts in Activity 18 again. Play the recording.
- Ask the pupils to listen to the sentences again and decide if they are true or false. Allow pupils time to think about the answers, pausing the recording as necessary.

- To check answers, play the recording again and ask individual pupils to say *True* or *False*. Ask volunteers to correct the false sentences.
- Ask the pupils to look at the Tip! box.

> **KEY** **1** True, **2** False (He goes by boat), **3** True, **4** True, **5** True, **6** False (She rides her snowmobile)

Mini-project

- Pupils conduct a survey to find out how their classmates come to school. Ask them to look at the Think! box and follow the instructions. Organise the class in small groups. They ask each other, within the groups, how they come to school. Then collect the answers from the different groups. Pupils write a few sentences about the findings. They may illustrate their text with drawings or printed pictures.

Activity Book page 44

  Listen and write. Then number.

- Explain (L1) that pupils are going to listen to the children in the pictures talking about how they go to school. Play the recording once. Pupils just listen.
- Play it again. Pupils complete the sentences.
- Play it once more and ask pupils to number the transport pictures in the correct order. Check as a class.

How do you and your friends go to school? Tick (✓) and write.

- First, pupils tick the means of transport they use to go to school. Then they write the names of two friends in the spaces 2 and 3 and ask them *How do you go to school?* They tick the correct means of transport. Finally, they write the sentences using the information in their chart. Remind them to use *walk/go* for themselves and *walks/goes* for their friends.
- Ask volunteers to read their sentences aloud to the class.

Ending the lesson

- Write words in three columns on the board: *I, He* and *She* in the first column, *school* and *park* in the second column, and *train, bike, boat, bus, car, walk* in the last column. Point to a word from each column to prompt a sentence. Pupils say, e.g. *He goes to the park by bike.* Repeat and speed up until pupils are confident making the sentences.
- (For AB Answer Key, see p. 148. For Audioscript, see pp. 150–1.)

18 (2:18) **Listen, read and find.**

road   radio   plane   snowmobile

How do you go to school?

1
Lanau doesn't go to school by car. His family hasn't got a car. There aren't many roads where he lives but there are a lot of rivers. So Lanau and his friends go to school by boat. Their school is on the water too!

2
Ricky doesn't go to a school! It's too far away. He has lessons at home — on the radio and on the Internet. On Fridays his teacher goes to his house by plane.

3
Susanna lives in a cold place. She doesn't walk to school. She goes to school by snowmobile. She likes riding her snowmobile. It's cool!

a

b

c

19 (2:19) **Listen and point to *T = True* or *F = False*.**

1 T / F   **2** T / F   **3** T / F

4 T / F   **5** T / F   **6** T / F

I go to school **by** boat. She goes to school **by** snowmobile.

THINK!
Make a list of different ways of going to school.

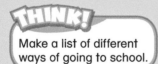
MINI-PROJECT
Find out how your classmates go to school. Do a survey.

48   Lesson 7 social sciences (going to school)   AB p. 44

OPTIONAL ACTIVITIES

Make a bar chart
Pupils create a bar chart showing the data from the Mini-project survey.

Team game
Play *Reading race* see p. 301, with questions like *Do you walk to school? Do you have swimming lessons?*
Photocopiable 4.6 see Teacher's notes p. 289.

Lesson 8

Lesson aims
To learn about other cultures and respect cultural differences

Cross-cultural focus
Daily routines and timetables in other parts of the world

Target language
open, close, a.m., p.m.

Materials
Audio CD

Optional materials
World map or globe; Active Teach; Digital Activity Book; CLIL poster; Photocopiable 4.7

Starting the lesson
- Write the words *open, close, a.m., p.m.* on the board. Explain the meaning. Elicit other words about daily routines and write them on the board.

Pupil's Book page 49

Presentation
- Focus on the photos. Pupils look at the texts, find the names of the countries where the children live and locate them on the map or globe.

20 **Listen and read.**
- Play the recording. Pupils listen and follow the text in their books. Ask pupils to find the names of the children. Write them on the board.
- Ask a few comprehension questions, e.g. *What time do shops usually open in the UK? What time do shops usually open in Spain?*

Practice

21 **Read and say *True* or *False*.**
- Direct pupils' attention to the sentences. Check that they understand. Allow pupils time to reread the text and decide if the sentences are true or false. When they have finished, check answers with the class.
- Divide the class into pairs. Pupils ask and answer questions about the texts.

> **KEY** **1** False, **2** False, **3** True, **4** True

Portfolio project
- Ask pupils to write about their daily routines. Pupils can write in their notebooks, using the texts on p. 49 as a model.

Activity Book page 45

20 **Read and write.**
- Ask the pupils to read the word bank and the text. They must complete the text with the words from the word bank as in the example. Check answers with the class.

21 **Look at Activity 20 and answer.**
- Pupils read the text from the previous activity and answer the questions. Read out the questions and check that pupils understand. They read the questions and answer them. Check answers with the class.

Ending the lesson
- Play *Picture charades* see p. 298 with vocabulary for shops.
- (For AB Answer Key, see p. 148. For Audioscript, see p. 151.)

Wider World
Daily routines and timetables

20 2:21 **Listen and read.**

I'm Kate and I live in the United Kingdom. Here the shops often open at 9.00 in the morning and close at 5.00 in the evening. Most shops don't close for lunch. Children start school at 9.00 and finish at 3.00. I have lunch at school and dinner at home. Dinner is between 6.00 and 7.00 in the evening.

Kate, 10, United Kingdom

I live in Spain and I'm 9. My name's Diego. In Spain shops usually open at 10.00 in the morning and close at 8.30 in the evening. Many shops close for lunch between 1.30 and 4.30. We start school at 9.00 and finish at 3.00 in the afternoon, after lunch. Other schools finish later. I have dinner at home at 8.00 in the evening.

Diego, 9, Spain

21 **Read and say *True* or *False*.**

1 In Britain shops often open at 11.00 in the morning.
2 In Britain most shops close for lunch.
3 In Spain many shops close for lunch.
4 In Spain school starts at 9.00 in the morning.

PORTFOLIO

Think and write.

Write about your daily routine.

OPTIONAL ACTIVITIES

TPR game
Play *Pass the ball* see p. 300 revising daily routines, shops, etc.

Research
Divide the class into pairs. Tell pupils to look for information about shopping in their country. They write sentences about it and draw pictures.
Photocopiable 4.7 see Teacher's notes p. 290.

Lesson 9

Lesson aims
To review the unit language with a game and the Picture Dictionary

Materials
Audio CD; Flashcards (Activities)

Optional materials
Active Teach; Digital Activity Book; CLIL poster; Reading and Writing Booklet; a bag or box

Starting the lesson

- Divide the class into two teams and play *Spelling bee* to revise spelling of days of the week, activities and means of transport. Pupils listen to the words you say and, in turn, they try to spell them correctly.

Pupil's Book page 50

22 Write in your notebook. Then play.

- Focus on the pictures. Tell pupils that they will be playing a guessing game with their partners. Revise the vocabulary using the flashcards. Practise with the pupils the language to be used: *You practise the piano on Mondays. Yes! My turn.* Encourage pupils to use activities from earlier units, e,g. *watching TV,* as well as the activities shown on the page.
- Pupils copy the table into their notebooks and complete the information about themselves. They write and guess about their partner for each day, and write these in the 'My friend' column.
- Then they take turns to ask and answer and complete the information about their partners. For a correct guess, they tick the box; for a wrong one, they put a cross in the box. The winner is the one with more correct guesses.
- Pupils can use the Picture Dictionary AB p. 107.

Activity Book page 46

22   Listen, number and tick (✓).

- Direct pupils' attention to the pictures and tell them to number the pairs of pictures 1–4. Show that the first one is done as an example. Play the recording once, pausing if necessary to allow pupils time to number the pairs of pictures. Check answers with the class.
- Play the recording again. This time pupils choose and tick the correct picture in each pair. Pause after the first one, to make sure they understand what to do. Allow time, pausing if necessary, for pupils to find and tick the correct pictures. Check answers with the class.

23 What does Julie do on Saturdays? Write.

- Pupils look at the schedule and write sentences. Read out the example. Check answers with the class. Pupils can refer back to PB p. 42 for the required phrases.

Ending the lesson

- Put the flashcards (activities) in a bag or box. Ask a pupil to take out one of the flashcards and look at it without showing it to anyone. He/She then mimes the activity. The class guesses what picture it is. The first pupil to make a correct guess takes a turn. You may want to demonstrate with the first card.
- (For AB Answer Key, see p. 148. For Audioscript, see p. 151.)

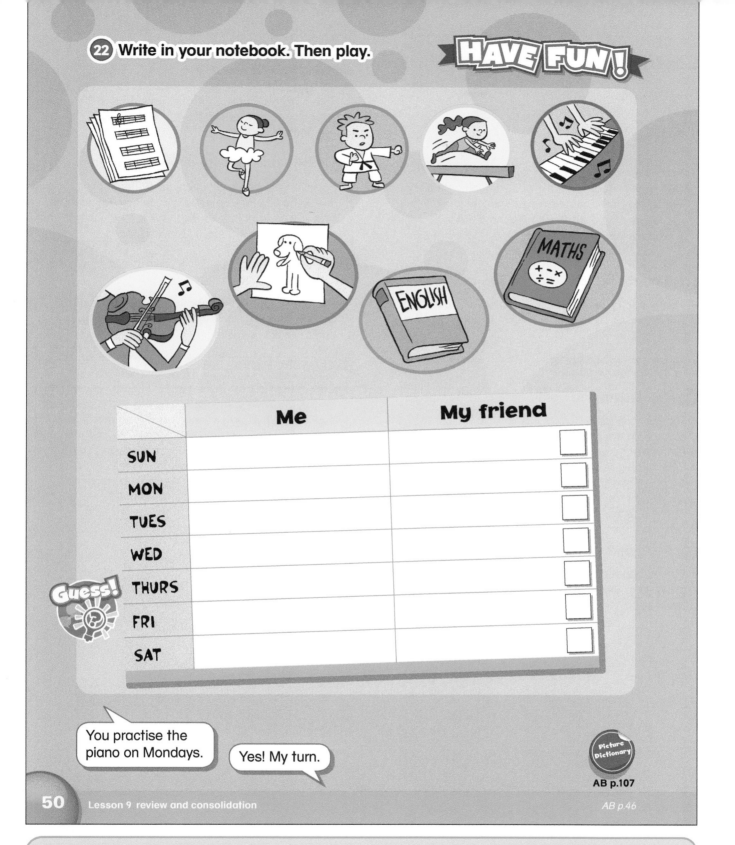

22 Write in your notebook. Then play.

HAVE FUN!

	Me	My friend	
SUN			☐
MON			☐
TUES			☐
WED			☐
THURS			☐
FRI			☐
SAT			☐

Guess!

You practise the piano on Mondays.

Yes! My turn.

Picture Dictionary
AB p.107

OPTIONAL ACTIVITIES

Make a poster
Divide the class into pairs and ask them to look for pictures of different ways of going to school in their country. They make a poster by sticking their pictures onto A3 or A4 paper and writing a short description under each one.

Team game
Play *Anagrams* see p. 301 with activities, transport, days of the week, times of day.
Reading and Writing Booklet p. 12 see Answer Key p. 282.

Lesson 10

Lesson aims
To personalise and assess efforts

Materials
Audio CD

Optional materials
Digital Activity Book; CLIL poster; Online material – *Film Studio Island*, Active Teach; Grammar reference and Review for Unit 4 (PB p. 113 and AB p. 99); Test Booklet; Grammar Booklet

Starting the lesson

- This is a self assessment activity. Tell the pupils that the activities on this page will show what they have learnt in this unit.

Pupil's Book page 51

23 **Listen and point.**

- Tell the pupils that they must choose the correct picture for each question. Play the recording more than once if necessary.
- Pupils listen, look at the pictures and choose the correct answer.

> **KEY** 1 a, 2 b, 3 a, 4 b, 5 a, 6 b, 7 b, 8 b

24 **Read and answer.**

- Pupils read the questions. Tell them to write the answers in their notebooks or on the board, or ask them to say their answers.

Activity Book page 47

- Focus on the *I can* sentences at the bottom of the page. Tell the pupils that they have to tick the boxes, depending on whether they think they can do the *I can* points.

24 **Write one activity and time for each day.**

- Focus on the timetable/diary grid. Tell pupils that they are going to write an activity for each day and the time. They work individually. Ask a few pupils to show their completed timetable to the class.

25 **Look at Activity 24. Write your own questions and answers.**

- Pupils write questions about their activities and answer them. Ask volunteers to read their questions and answers to the class.

Ending the lesson

- Copy the grid from AB Activity 24 on p. 47 onto the board, allowing plenty of space within the grid. Ask pupils to tell you their ideas for a fun timetable. Start them off by telling them some ideas of your own, e.g. *I go to the beach, morning.* Encourage/elicit the use of language from previous units.
- (For AB Answer Key, see p. 148. For Audioscript, see p. 151.)

23 **2:23** **Listen and point.**

1
a
b

2
a
b

3
a
b

4
a
b

5
a
b
c

6
a
b
c

7
a
b

8
a
b

24 **Read and answer.**

1 How do you go to school?

2 Does your friend go to school by bus?

OPTIONAL ACTIVITIES

Flashcard game
Play *Noughts and crosses* see p. 298 with flashcards (weather conditions and activities) or the Unit 3 and 4 wordcards. Pupils have to make sentences using the words on the cards.

Drawing game
Play *Dice game* see p. 299.
Activity Book Review see p. 99.
Grammar Booklet p. 12 see Answer Key p. 284.
Test Booklet Unit 4 see Answer Key p. 295.
Online World
Pupils can now go online to *Film Studio Island* and enjoy the fun and games.

Activity Book Answer Key

p. 38, Activity 1
1 learn to draw, 2 practise the violin, 3 do gymnastics, 4 have ballet lessons, 5 study English, 6 practise the piano, 7 have music lessons, 8 do karate, 9 learn to cook, 10 study Maths

p. 38, Activity 2
1 do, 2 have, 3 practise, 4 do, 5 practise, 6 have, 7 study, 8 learn to, 9 study, 10 learn to

p. 39, Activity 3
1 She has music lessons on Saturdays.
2 He does karate on Wednesdays.
3 What does he do on Sundays? He practises the piano on Sundays.
4 What does she do on Mondays? She learns to draw on Mondays.
5 What does he do on Fridays? He studies English on Fridays.

p. 39, Activity 4
1 She has music lessons at 7 o'clock.
2 He does karate at 8 o'clock.
3 He practises the piano at 5 o'clock.
4 She learns to draw at 4 o'clock.
5 He studies English at 2 o'clock.

p. 40, Activity 5
1 morning
2 evening
3 afternoon
4 midday
5 a quarter to nine
6 a quarter past eight
7 half past three

p. 40, Activity 6
1 b, 2 e, 3 a, 4 d, 5 c

p. 41, Activity 7
1 10 o'clock, 2 does gymnastics, half past eleven, 3 does karate, a quarter to 3, 4 She practises the piano at a quarter past 4.

p. 41, Activity 8
1 in the morning.
2 practise the violin, He practises the violin in the evening.
3 When does he learn to draw? He learns to draw at midday.
4 When does she study Maths? She studies Maths in the afternoon.

p. 42, Activity 10
He can do karate but he can't sing.

p. 42, Activity 11
a 4, b 3, c 5, d 1, e 2

p. 42, Activity 12
1 On Mondays he does karate.
2 He has singing lessons on Fridays.
3 He goes swimming on Saturdays.
4 No, he can't.

p. 42, Activity 13
1 No, he doesn't.
2 Yes, he has. He goes to work by car.
(Accept linguistically correct answers with the same information.)

p. 43, Activity 15
cake, home, dive, shape

p. 43, Activity 16
1 fried, 2 blue, 3 true, 4 tissue

p. 44, Activity 18
2 bike, 3 bus, 4 train
a 4, b 2, c 1, d 3

p. 45, Activity 20
1 there are, 2 on Sundays, 3 toys, 4 cinemas, 5 the bus

p. 45, Activity 21
1 12 hours.
2 Yes, they do.
3 Food, drink, toys, games and more.
4 Yes, there are.
5 Yes, they are.

p. 46, Activity 22
Order of pictures: 1 practising the violin, 2 doing karate, 3 learning to draw, 4 studying English
Correct pictures to tick: 1 b, 2 b, 3 b, 4 a

p. 46, Activity 23
She studies Maths at 8 o'clock.
She has a music lesson at a quarter past 9.
She has a ballet lesson at 11 o'clock.
She practises the piano at half past 1.
She does gymnastics at a quarter to 3.
She learns to cook at 4 o'clock.

Audioscript

Lesson 1 Activity 1   CD2:01
RE = REPORTER   JO = JOHN   RU = RUBY
S = SAM   JE = JENNY
RE Hi. I'm Tina from Star magazine. I'm here to talk to Madley. Madley Kool. Where is he?
JO I don't know. You can talk to me.
RE You? Erm ... What's your name?
JO I'm John Smith.
RE John, what do you do on Saturdays?
JO I go swimming in the morning and I have Music lessons in the afternoon.
RU Hello, I'm Ruby. I do karate in the morning and have ballet lessons in the afternoon.
S I'm Sam. I go skateboarding in the afternoon.
JE And I ...
RE What's that?

Lesson 1 Activity 2   CD2:02
a have music lessons
b have ballet lessons
c do karate
d do gymnastics
e practise the piano
f practise the violin
g learn to draw
h learn to cook
i study English
j study Maths

Lesson 1 Activity 3   CD2:03
1 go swimming
2 have music lessons
3 have ballet lessons
4 do gymnastics
5 do karate
6 go skateboarding

Lesson 2 Activity 4   CD2:04
What do you do on Saturdays?
What do you do on Saturdays?
I do gymnastics at 10 o'clock.
She does gymnastics at 10 o'clock.
I go swimming at 11 o'clock.
He goes swimming at 11 o'clock.
I have ballet lessons at half past 2.
She has ballet lessons at half past 2.
I go skateboarding at 4 o'clock.
He goes skateboarding at 4 o'clock.

Lesson 2 Activity 6   CD2:05
1 What does John do on Saturdays?
  He has music lessons at 3 o'clock.
2 What does Ruby do on Saturdays?
  Ruby does karate at 9 o'clock on Saturdays.
3 What does Jenny do on Saturdays?
  She does gymnastics at 10 o'clock.
4 What does Sam do on Saturdays?
  He goes skateboarding at 4 o'clock on Saturdays.

Lesson 3 Activity 8   CD2:06
a morning
b midday
c afternoon
d evening
e 2.15
  a quarter past 2
f 2.30
  half past 2
g 2.45
  a quarter to 3

Lesson 3 Activity 9   CD2:07
When does she study Maths?
Does she start at 10 o'clock?
Does she study Maths in the morning?
Please tell me when.

She studies Maths at 9.00.
Yes, she studies Maths at 9.00.
She doesn't study at 10.00.
She studies Maths at 9.00 in the morning.

When do you learn to cook?
Do you start at half past 5?
Do you start to cook in the afternoon?
Please tell me when.

I start to cook at 5.00.
Yes, I learn to cook at 5.00.
No, I don't start at half past 5.
I learn to cook at 5.00 in the afternoon.

Lesson 3 Activity 6 (AB)   CD2:08
1 When does she have ballet lessons?
  She has ballet lessons at half past 7.
2 When does he do gymnastics?
  He does gymnastics in the evening.
3 When does she practise the violin?
  She practises the violin at a quarter past 6.
4 When does he learn to cook?
  He learns to cook at midday.
5 When does she study Maths?
  She studies Maths at a quarter to 5.

Lesson 4 Activity 11   CD2:09
What does Fifi do on Saturdays?
She has a busy day!
She always has ballet lessons in the morning.
She loves dancing very much!
When does she have ballet lessons?
She always has ballet lessons at 10 o'clock.
How does she go to her ballet lesson? Does she walk?
No, she never walks. She goes by car! She doesn't like walking. Her mum drives her there at a quarter to 10.
What does she do in the afternoon?
She goes skateboarding in the park at 2 o'clock. The she often goes to a party with her friends. She has a lot of fun on Saturdays!

Lesson 4 Activity 7 (AB)   CD2:10
This is my cat, Midge.
She's cute. What does she do on Saturdays?
At 10 o'clock she goes swimming.
At half past eleven she does gymnastics.
In the afternoon, she does karate at a quarter to 3.
Then, she practises the piano at a quarter past 4.

Lesson 6 Activity 14   CD2:12
i   e
/ie/ /ie/ /ie/
u   e
/ue/ /ue/ /ue/

Lesson 6 Activity 15   CD2:13
/ie/ /ie/
/ie/ /ie/
/ue/ /ue/
/ue/ /ue/
/ie/ /ie/
/ue/ /ue/

Lesson 6 Activity 16   CD2:14
1 /p/ /ie/
   pie
2 /t/ /ie/
   tie
3 /l/ /ie/
   lie
4 /f/ /r/ /ie/ /d/
   fried
5 /b/ /l/ /ue/
   blue
6 /g/ /l/ /ue/
   glue
7 /t/ /r/ /ue/
   true
8 /t/ /i/ /sh/ /ue/
   tissue

Lesson 6 Activity 15 (AB)   CD2:15
1 /k/   /ay/   /k/
2 /h/   /oh/   /m/
3 /d/   /iy/   /v/
4 /sh/   /ay/   /p/

Lesson 6 Activity 16 (AB)   CD2:16
1 fried
2 blue
3 true
4 tissue

Lesson 6 Activity 17 (AB)   CD2:17
Ha-ha-ha! The man with the tie has got glue on his boots. He can't run. He is stuck with the pie in his hand.

Lesson 7 Activity 18   CD2:18
How do you go to school?
1 Lanau doesn't go to school by car. His family hasn't got a car. There aren't many roads where he lives but there are a lot of rivers. So Lanau and his friends go to school by boat. Their school is on the water too!
2 Ricky doesn't go to a school! It's too far away. He has lessons at home – on the radio and on the internet. On Fridays his teacher goes to his house by plane.
3 Susanna lives in a cold place. She doesn't walk to school. She goes to school by snowmobile. She likes riding her snowmobile. It's cool!

Lesson 7 Activity 19 CD2:19

1 Lanau lives near a river.
2 Lanau goes to school by car.
3 Ricky gets his lessons on the internet.
4 Ricky's teacher lives far away.
5 Susanna has got a snowmobile.
6 Susanna rides a bike to school.

Lesson 7 Activity 18 (AB) CD2:20

1 Alex, how do you go to school?
I walk to school. I like keeping fit.
2 Meiling, how do you go to school?
I go to school by bike. I like riding my bike. I don't like going to school by bus.
3 Jodie, how do you go to school?
I can't walk to school. The school is far away from my house, so I go to school by bus. I like going in the bus with my friends.
4 Kabir, how do you go to school?
I go to school by train. There are a lot of people on the train!

Lesson 8 Activity 20 CD2:21

1 I'm Kate and I live in the United Kingdom. Here the shops often open at 9.00 in the morning and close at 5.00 in the evening. Most shops don't close for lunch. Children start school at 9.00 and finish at 3.00. I have lunch at school and dinner at home. Dinner is between 6.00 and 7.00 in the evening. Kate, 10, United Kingdom.
2 I live in Spain and I'm 9. My name's Diego. In Spain shops usually open at 10.00 in the morning and close at 8.30 in the evening. Many shops close for lunch between 1.30 and 4.30. We start school at 9.00 and finish at 3.00 in the afternoon, after lunch. Other schools finish later. I have dinner at home at 8.00 in the evening. Diego, 9, Spain.

Lesson 9 Activity 22 (AB) CD2:22

1 What does she do on Fridays?
She practises the violin on Fridays.
When does she practise the violin?
She practises the violin at half past six.
2 What does he do on Wednesdays?
He does karate on Wednesdays.
When does he do karate?
He does karate at a quarter past 10.
3 What does he do on Tuesdays?
He learns to draw on Tuesdays.
When does he learn to draw?
He learns to draw in the evening.
4 What does she do on Saturdays?
She studies English on Saturdays.
When does she study English?
She studies English in the morning.

Lesson 10 Activity 23 CD2:23

1 I learn to cook on Sundays.
2 She always practises the violin on Wednesdays.
3 What does he do on Thursdays?
He studies Maths on Thursdays.
4 What do you do on Saturdays?
I have ballet lessons on Saturdays.
5 She always does gymnastics at half past six.
6 When does he have music lessons?
He has music lessons at a quarter to five.
7 I learn to draw on Mondays and Wednesdays. I practise the piano on Fridays.
8 I practise the violin and study English on Thursdays. I do karate on Sundays.

Objectives

- talk about jobs
- say what you want to be
- give reasons
- pronounce properly /le/ and /y/

Topics
- Jobs
- Personal heroes

Phonics
/le/ and /y/

Values
- Study hard, work hard, and play hard

Stories
- Unit opener: favourite jobs
- Story episode: John wants to be Madley Kool

Songs and chants
- Chant
- Song about clothes
- Karaoke song

Language

Vocabulary
- Jobs: builder, firefighter, police officer, basketball player, film star, ballet dancer, astronaut, singer, model, journalist, photographer, carpenter, mechanic, lawyer, athlete

Revision
doctor, farmer, teacher, artist, nurse

Structures
What do you want to be?
I want to be an (astronaut).
What does he/she want to be?
He/She wants to be a (builder).
I don't want to be an (astronaut).
I don't want to be a (builder.)
Do you want to be a (singer)?
Yes, I do./No, I don't.
Does he/she want to be a (singer)?
Yes, he/she does./No, he/she doesn't.
Why do you want to be a (singer)?
I want to be a (singer) because I (am good a singing).

CLIL language
Future jobs: Olympic Games, champion, coach, train, famous, brave

Sociocultural aspects
- Finding out about personal heroes
- Getting information about heroes around the world
- Identifying heroes in our country

Cross-curricular contents
- Social Science: understanding entries in a forum where people express their opinions
- Arts: making drawings and describing them
- Language Arts: reading a story, acting out, telling a story
- Language skills: reading and understanding information from an internet forum

Learning strategies
- Using previous knowledge to learn new words
- Identifying rules about the use of 'want to be'
- Logical thinking: examining patterns and reaching conclusions
- Creative thinking: doing activities based on visual memory
- Critical thinking: comparing and contrasting reasons
- Collaborative learning: asking for help when necessary
- Self assessment

Basic competences

- Linguistic communication: Use the language to communicate in the classroom (L1 to L10)
- Knowledge and interaction with the physical world: Think about future jobs (L7)
- Mathematical competence: Express singular number (L1 to L4)
- Processing information and digital competence: Use *Film Studio Island* online component
- Social and civic competence: Understand the social value of having a job or profession (L1 to L4): Study hard, work hard, and play hard (L5)
- Cultural and artistic competence: Talk about heroes (L8)
- Learning to learn: Reflect on what has been learnt and self-evaluate progress (L10)
- Autonomy and personal initiative: Develop one's own criteria and social skills (L1 to L10)

Skills

Listening
- Identifying jobs in recordings
- Understanding people describing what they want to be and why
- Understanding specific information in a song about future jobs
- Understanding general and specific information in a story

Reading
- Understanding information in sentences and short texts (jobs)
- Reading short texts about future jobs and finding the corresponding photos
- Answering comprehension questions to show understanding of a text
- Reading entries to a forum and identifying true/false information
- Understanding general and specific information in a cartoon strip story

Speaking
- Repeating words and sentences
- Chanting and singing
- Pronouncing /le/ and /y/ correctly
- Saying what we want to be in the future

Writing
- Writing missing letters to make words
- Completing questions and answers
- Ordering words to write sentences
- Writing a short text about themselves
- Completing sentences

Talking
- Taking part in dialogues about future jobs
- Role playing a story
- Asking and responding to questions about jobs
- Giving reasons to choose a job and asking others about their reasons
- Talking about a famous person they admire

Classroom ideas

- Bring to the class prompts associated with jobs and ask the pupils to use them to do some activities
- Find out about famous people in their jobs on the internet
- Find pictures and photos of jobs and bring them to the class
- Bring to the classroom library books that include jobs
- Photocopiables

Take-home English

- Home-School Link
- Notes for Parents
- A sample of work each week
- Portfolio

Self assessment

- Pupils can talk about jobs
- Pupils can say what they want to be
- Pupils can give reasons

Evaluation

- Pupil's Book page 61
- Activity Book page 57
- Photocopiable 5.7
- Picture Dictionary
- Test Booklet – Unit 5

5 Jobs

Lesson 1

Lesson aims
To learn and practise new vocabulary (Jobs)

Target language
builder, firefighter, police officer, basketball player, film star, ballet dancer, astronaut

Materials
Audio CD; Flashcards and Wordcards (Jobs)

Optional materials
Active Teach; Digital Activity Book; Photocopiable 5.1; soft ball, waste paper bin or basket

Starting the lesson

- Elicit the clothes words that pupils know and write them on the board. Then say *I'm wearing (e.g. a red T-shirt and black trousers)*. Ask *What are you wearing?* Listen to individual pupils' answers.
- Focus on the picture. Ask *Where are the children now?* Pupils answer (L1) (the canteen at the film studio). Pupils describe what the characters (anyone in the picture) are wearing.

> Pupil's Book pages 52–53

Presentation

- Use the flashcards to teach this lesson's vocabulary. Hold them up in turn and say the words. Pupils repeat. Hold up the flashcards again, asking individual pupils to say the words.
- Pupils open their books. Focus on the main illustration. Point to the characters and say the words. Pupils repeat.

  Listen.

- Tell pupils (L1) they are going to hear a recording describing the people numbered 1–7 in the main illustration. Make sure they have found the numbered people. Tell them that two of the people won't be mentioned. Play the recording. Give pupils time to find the people mentioned. Play the recording again. Pupils decide who's missing. Pupils check if they were right.

> **KEY** People not mentioned: **3** (builder), **6** (police officer)

Practice

  Listen and repeat.

- Play the recording, pausing after each word. Pupils point to the pictures. Play the recording again. Pupils point and repeat each word.
- Shuffle the flashcards (jobs) and choose one. Hold it up. Pupils say and mime the job, e.g. they say *basketball player* and pretend to bounce a ball.
- Display the relevant flashcards (jobs) on one side of the board and write the corresponding words or put up wordcards on the other side. Pupils come to the front, read out the words and match them to the pictures.

  Listen and say *True* or *False*.

- Pupils look at the numbered people in the main illustration again. They will hear one sentence for each number. They must decide if the sentences they hear are true or false about that person. Play the recording, pausing after each sentence. Pupils say if it's true or false.

> **KEY** **1** True, **2** True, **3** False, **4** True, **5** True, **6** False, **7** False

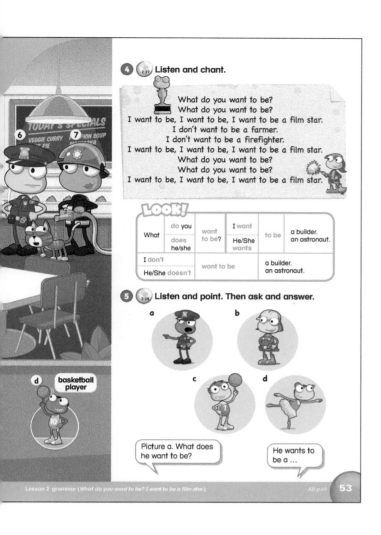

OPTIONAL ACTIVITIES

Flashcard game
Play *Basketball* see p. 298. Show pupils a flashcard (jobs) and pupils say the word.

Make a mini poster
Give pupils an A4 sheet. They draw a picture of the job they like and write a caption. When they have finished, they show their picture to the class.

Photocopiable 5.1 see Teacher's notes p. 290.

NOTES

Activity Book page 48

1 Look and write.

- Focus on the pictures and the incomplete words. Pupils complete the words with the missing letters. Do number 1 as an example and ask the pupils to do the others in the same way.
- Check as a class. Ask pairs of pupils to come to the board. Pupil A spells the word and Pupil B writes it.

2 Look and write.

- Focus on the picture. Tell pupils (L1) to complete the speech bubbles with the correct job. Check as a class.

Ending the lesson

- Draw a word map with the class. Draw a circle and write *Jobs* in it. Elicit words for jobs the pupils have learnt in this lesson, plus any others they remember from previous lessons, e.g. *nurse, chef, pilot, detective, director, teacher.* Write them on the board. Pupils can copy them into their notebooks.
- Play *Mime and guess*: divide the class into pairs. Pupil A mimes a job. Pupil B guesses what it is.
- (For AB Answer Key, see p. 174. For Audioscript, see p. 175.)

Lesson 2

Lesson aims
To learn and practise the new structure

Target language
What do you want to be? I want to be (an astronaut).
What does he/she want to be? He/She wants to be (a film star).
I don't want to be (an astronaut). I don't want to be (a film star).

Materials
Audio CD; Flashcards and Wordcards (Jobs)

Optional materials
Active Teach; Digital Activity Book; Grammar Booklet

Starting the lesson

• Play *Spelling bee* to revise jobs from Lesson 1. Pupils listen to the words you say and, in turn, they try to spell them correctly.

Pupil's Book page 53

• Show a flashcard, e.g. ballet dancer, and ask *What's her job?* Say *She's a ballet dancer.* Ask the class to repeat the answer after you. Repeat with the other words.

Presentation

• Pupils read the sentences in the Look! box. Check meaning. Explain (L1) that they use *want to be* to talk about future jobs. Focus on affirmative and negative answers.
• Read the Look! box.
• Ask pupils to copy the examples from the Look! box into their notebooks, changing the jobs so the sentences are true for them. They should write one affirmative and one negative sentence.

4 🔊 **Listen and chant.**

• Play the recording. Pupils listen and follow the words. Play it again. Pause after each line for pupils to repeat. Play it once more. Pupils join in and say it together.
• Divide the class into two groups. One group says the questions *What do you want to be?* and the other says the rest of the chant. Then they swap parts.

Practice

5 🔊 **Listen and point. Then ask and answer.**

• Focus the pupils' attention on the pictures. Tell them that they have to listen to the recording and point to the corresponding picture. Play the recording.
• Organise the class in pairs. Explain the second part of the activity. Pupil A says a number from 1 to 4 and asks *What does she want to be?* Pupil B looks at the pictures and answers. Then they swap.

KEY 1 c, **2** d, **3** a, **4** b

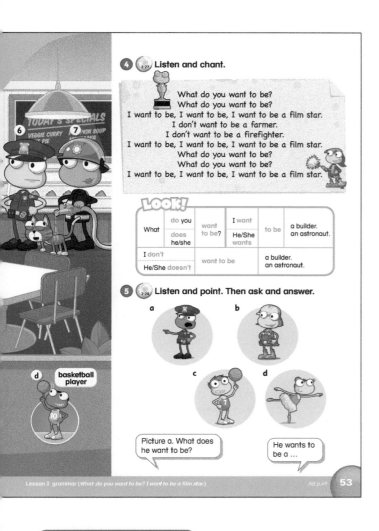

4 **2:27** Listen and chant.

What do you want to be?
What do you want to be?
I want to be, I want to be, I want to be a film star.
I don't want to be a farmer.
I don't want to be a firefighter.
I want to be, I want to be, I want to be a film star.
What do you want to be?
What do you want to be?
I want to be, I want to be, I want to be a film star.

LOOK!

What	do you	want to be?	I want	to be	a builder.
	does he/she		He/She wants		an astronaut.
I don't		want to be			a builder.
He/She doesn't					an astronaut.

5 Listen and point. Then ask and answer.

a   b
c   d

d basketball player

Picture a. What does he want to be?

He wants to be a …

Lesson 2 grammar (What do you want to be? I want to be a film star.)   AB p.49   **53**

Ending the lesson

- Play *Pass the flashcards* see p. 298 with jobs flashcards.
- Focus on the jobs in Activity 1. Ask a pupil *What do you want to be, number (6)?* The pupil answers *I want to be a (police officer).* This pupil then chooses another pupil and asks them *What do you want to be, number (2)?* Continue until all the class has asked and answered.
- (For AB Answer Key, see p. 174. For Audioscript, see p. 175.)

OPTIONAL ACTIVITIES

Team game
Play *Miming competition* see p. 301 using the vocabulary of the unit.

Flashcard game
Play *Collect the cards* see p. 298 using the target structure, e.g. *I want to be a film star.*

Grammar Booklet p. 13 see Answer Key p. 284.

NOTES

Activity Book page 49

3 **2:29** **Listen and number.**

- Point to each object. Pupils say the jobs. Tell the class that they are going to listen to a recording. They number the jobs that people want to do, in the order they are mentioned. Play the recording once. Pupils listen. Play it again. Pupils number the items. Play it a third time for pupils to check their answers.

4 **Look at Activity 3 and write.**

- Direct pupils' attention to the characters. Pupils complete/write the seven questions and answers using the numbered job information 1–7 in Activity 3. Work through the example with the class to make sure they understand how to find the information they need. To check answers, ask volunteers to read their completed questions and answers.

Lesson 3

Lesson aims
To extend the unit vocabulary set to include more jobs; to practise the unit language with a song

Target language
singer, model, journalist, photographer, carpenter, mechanic, lawyer, athlete

Materials
Audio CD; Flashcards and Wordcards (Jobs)

Optional materials
Active Teach; Digital Activity Book; Photocopiables 5.2–5.3; Reading and Writing Booklet; dice (one for each group)

Starting the lesson

- Show the firefighter flashcard and say an incorrect sentence, e.g. *I want to be a ballet dancer.* Pupils say *No.* Ask them to make a correct sentence about the picture: *I want to be a firefighter.* Repeat with other jobs, sometimes saying the right sentence for the flashcard, sometimes the wrong sentence.

Pupil's Book page 54

Presentation

- Direct pupils' attention to the pictures of jobs. Introduce the new vocabulary. Point to each picture in turn and say *He's a (singer). Do you want to be a singer?* Pupils answer *Yes, I do* or *No, I don't.*

 Listen and repeat.

- Introduce the new words (*singer, model,* etc.) using the flashcards. Hold them up and say the words for pupils to repeat. Ask individual pupils to say the words. Play the recording for pupils to listen and repeat.
- Now put the flashcards on the board. Point to the different flashcards and ask the class to say the words.

Song

 Listen and point. Then sing.

- Play the recording. Pupils follow the words. Play the song again. Pupils point to the correct picture when they hear a job mentioned. Play it a third time. Pupils join in and sing. You can now play the karaoke song (Active Teach).

Activity Book page 50

5 Look and write.

- Direct pupils' attention to the words in the word bank. Tell the class to write the words below the corresponding pictures. Check as a class by asking individual pupils to come to the board and write the words.

6 Unscramble and write.

- Focus on the example. Explain that pupils have to rearrange the words to make correct questions. They must then write short answers – affirmative if there is a tick, or negative if there is a cross. Work through the example with the class. In pairs or individually, pupils write the questions and answers. Check as a class by asking volunteers to read aloud what they have written.

Ending the lesson

- Work together as a class to write some new words for the song (you could include jobs such as *dancer, film star, pilot*).
- (For AB Answer Key, see p. 174. For Audioscript, see p. 175)

OPTIONAL ACTIVITIES
Flashcard game
Play *Mix-matched flashcards* see p. 298 to practise jobs vocabulary.

6  **Listen and repeat.**

a
singer

b
model

c
journalist

d
photographer

e
carpenter

f
mechanic

g
lawyer

h
athlete

7 **Listen and point. Then sing.**

SONG

Teacher, farmer, builder, doctor
What does he want to be?
Teacher, farmer, builder, doctor
Just a minute! Let me see.

Does he want to be a teacher   lawyer ?
No, no, no, he doesn't.
Does he want to be a builder   farmer ?
No, no, no, he doesn't.
Does he want to be a singer   builder ?
No, no, no, he doesn't.
Does he want to be a doctor   model ?
Yes, yes, yes, he does.
He wants to be a doctor   model .

Dice game
Divide the class into groups. Stick six occupations flashcards on the board. Number them 1–6. Pupils throw a die (without showing the rest of the group) and mime the corresponding flashcard. The group guesses *He/She wants to be a (doctor)*.

Photocopiable 5.2 see Teacher's notes p. 290.
Photocopiable 5.3 see Teacher's notes p. 290.
Reading and Writing Booklet p. 13 see Answer Key p. 282.

Lesson 4

Lesson aims
To develop reading, writing, listening and speaking skills; to learn and practise the new structure (talking about future jobs)

Target language
Do you want to be a singer? Yes, I do. No, I don't. Does he/she want to be a singer? Yes, he/she does. No, he/she doesn't.

Materials
Audio CD, Flashcards (Jobs)

Optional materials
Active Teach; Digital Activity Book; Grammar Booklet; pictures of jobs, activities and sports

Starting the lesson

- Play *Teacher says* see p. 299. Give instructions: pupils mime, but only if your instructions are preceded by *Teacher says*.

Pupil's Book page 55

Presentation

- Direct pupils' attention to the Look! box. Read the question and answers. Explain (L1) that they always use *want to be* in the question, but that with *he* and *she* they use *does/doesn't* instead of *do/don't*.
- Read the Look! box. Elicit more questions and answers and write them on the board. Pupils can copy them into their notebooks.

Skills

8 **Listen, read and find the photos. Then ask and answer.**

- Focus on the photos that go with the texts. Ask the class to listen to your descriptions and point to the corresponding picture: *She's got long hair. She's got dark hair*, etc. Elicit more sentences and write them on the board.
- Pupils read each text silently. Then ask a pupil to read the first text aloud. Ask *What's the matching picture?* Pupils answer. Pupils read the texts and match each child to the correct photo (1–4). Check as a class. Play the recording.
- In pairs, pupils take turns to ask and answer each other about what the four children want to be. Model the questions *What does ...? / Does Emma ...? / Does he ...?* with a confident pupil.

KEY a 4, b 3, c 1, d 2

Practice

9 **Look at Activity 8 and answer.**

- Pupils read questions 1–8. Check that they understand. Ask them to read the texts again and answer the questions in their notebooks. Pupils give short answers. Check answers with the class.

KEY 1 She wants to be a film star. **2** She can sing and dance and (she can) act very well. **3** No, she doesn't. **4** She can dance and (she can) jump. **5** Yes, he does. **6** He likes climbing and (he likes) helping people. **7** Because he's very tall. **8** He can jump and (he can) catch a ball.

Activity Book page 51

7 **Listen and tick (✓) or cross (✗).**

- Play the recording. Pupils listen and tick the correct picture in each pair. Then check as a class.

8 **Listen again. Then write.**

- Play the recording again (the audio for Activity 7).
- Focus on the example, and the /s/ at the end of *wants*. Revise the meaning of *because*. Pupils write three similar sentences about the other children. You might want to do the activity orally first to help weaker pupils.

9 **Write the questions. Then write your own answers.**

- Pupils complete question number one and write their personal answer. They have to write the other questions and the answers. Ask a few pupils to read out their questions and answers.

Ending the lesson

- Demonstrate a pairwork guessing game: ask a pupil to choose one of the Unit 5 flashcards but not to show it to you or to the class. Ask him/her questions, e.g. *Is it a man? Is he wearing a uniform?* etc. He/She can only answer *Yes* or *No*. When you guess correctly, you have a turn. Give out the flashcards, face down. Pupils then play in pairs.
- (For AB Answer Key, see p. 174. For Audioscript, see pp. 175–6)

 Pupils can now go online to *Film Studio Island* and find the coat hanger that Cleo is holding. It is the coat hanger on the sign on the front of the Costume Studio. Once pupils click on the coat hanger they are taken to a supplementary language game based on the vocabulary in this unit.

LOOK!

Do you **want to be** a lawyer?	Yes, I **do**.
	No, I **don't**.
Does he/she **want to be** a carpenter?	Yes, he/she **does**.
	No, he/she **doesn't**.

Why does he/she want to be an athlete? He/She wants to be an athlete **because** he/she can run fast.

8 (2:32) **Listen, read and find the photos. Then ask and answer.**

①
Martina

②
Emma

③
Tim

④
Bobby

a Hello, I'm Bobby. I like running. I can jump and I can catch a ball. I want to be a basketball player because I'm very tall.

b I'm Tim. I'm strong. I like climbing. I don't want to be an athlete. I want to be a firefighter because I like helping people.

c Hi! I'm Martina. I can sing and dance. I don't want to be a ballet dancer. I want to be a film star because I can act very well.

d I'm Emma. I like music. I don't want to be a singer. I want to be a ballet dancer because I can dance and I can jump.

Does Martina want to be a ballet dancer?

No, she doesn't. She wants to be …

9 **Look at Activity 8 and answer.**

1 What does Martina want to be?

2 What can she do?

3 Does Emma want to be a singer?

4 What can she do?

5 Does Tim want to be a firefighter?

6 What does he like doing?

7 Why does Bobby want to be a basketball player?

8 What can he do?

OPTIONAL ACTIVITIES

Flashcard game
Play *Mix-matched flashcards* see p. 298.

Flashcard game
Play *Odd one out* see p. 302 with jobs, clothes, sports, words with the /ə/ sound, etc.
Grammar Booklet p. 14 see Answer Key p. 284–5.

Lesson 5

Lesson aims
To consolidate the unit language with a story

Values
Study hard, work hard and play hard

Receptive language
I love dancing/animals, a lot of, difficult

Materials
Audio CD; Story cards

Optional materials
Props for acting out the story, e.g. glasses for Ruby, baseball cap and/or skateboard for Sam, necklace for Jenny, grey jumper and magnifying glass for Cleo; Active Teach; Digital Activity Book; Photocopiable 5.4; Reading and Writing Booklet

Starting the lesson

- Ask pupils (L1) what they remember about the story so far. Show the Unit 4 story cards and retell the story, making some deliberate mistakes. Every time pupils spot a mistake, they put up their hands and correct it.

Pupil's Book page 56

Presentation

10 **Listen and read. Then act out.**

- Show the story cards of Unit 5 one at a time and ask the *Before listening to the story* questions. Pupils predict what happens in the story.
- Play the recording. Pupils listen as they follow the story in their books. Ask if their predictions were correct, and then ask the *After listening to the story* questions.
- Divide the class into three groups and assign a character to each (Ruby, Jenny, Sam). Pupils read their parts as a class.
- Ask pupils who would like to take the parts of the different characters. Invite volunteers to the front of the class to act out the story. Encourage tone of voice and expressions to match those in the pictures. Use props that you've brought to class if you wish.

Practice

- Shuffle the story cards and put them in random order on the board. With books closed, ask *Which is number one?* Pupils answer. Continue until all the story cards are in order.

Values

- Ask the pupils what they think about studying hard, working hard and playing hard. Pupils draw a table in their notebooks. Organise the class in pairs. Pupils take it in turns to ask and answer about the time they spend in studying, working and playing following the model dialogue in the Pupil's Book. Discuss (L1) the importance of studying hard.

Activity Book page 52

10 **Read the story again. Why does John want to be a film star? Write.**

- Pupils discuss John's reasons for wanting to be a film star. Explain that they should look at picture 5 of the main illustration on PB p. 56. They write their answer on the line.

11 **Look and write.**

- Direct pupils' attention to the pictures and to the word bank. Ask them to complete the text below each picture, using one word from the word bank for each picture. Complete the text for picture 1 as a whole-class activity. Pupils write the other texts. Check answers with the class.

12 **What do you want to be? Write.**

- Make sure pupils understand that they have to complete the bubble for Cleo (not for themselves). Check by asking individual pupils to read their sentences.

Home-School Link

- Pupils make a poster showing their favourite subject, chore or game, to take home and show to their family.

Ending the lesson

- Play *Guess who*: say some words spoken by the characters in the story. Pupils guess who you are.
- (For AB Answer Key, see p. 174.)

Listen and read. Then act out.

VALUES

Study hard, work hard and play hard.

HOME-SCHOOL LINK

Make a poster showing your favourite subject, chore or game. Show your family.

56 Lesson 5 story and values (Study, work and play hard.) *AB p.52*

OPTIONAL ACTIVITIES

Story writing
Pupils rewrite the story in pairs, changing some words in the speech bubbles, e.g. the *-ing* words and the jobs. Ask pairs to read their new stories to the class.

Flashcard game
Divide the class into pairs to play *What's missing?* see p. 298.
Photocopiable 5.4 see Teacher's notes p. 290.
Reading and Writing Booklet p. 14 see Answer Key p. 282.

163

Lesson 6

Lesson aims
To learn the sounds and letters /le/ and /y/

Target language
jungle, tickle, little, paddle, happy, funny, sunny, rainy

Materials
Audio CD; Flashcards and Wordcards (phonics);
Phonics poster

Optional materials
Active Teach; Digital Activity Book;
Photocopiable 5.5

Starting the lesson

- Show pupils the flashcards (phonics).
- Read the words aloud and ask pupils to find a common pattern.

Pupil's Book page 57

Presentation

11 **Listen and repeat.**

- Write on the board the words /le/ and /y/. Play the recording for pupils to listen. Play it a second time for pupils to listen and repeat.

12 **Listen, point and say.**

- Tell the pupils that they must point to the sound that they hear. Play the recording for pupils to listen and point. Play it a second time for pupils to listen, point and say.

13 **Listen and blend the sounds.**

- Demonstrate the blending of the first sound; pupils repeat what they hear. Then tell them that they must listen and blend the sounds. Play the recording for pupils to listen and say the words that contain the corresponding sounds.

Practice

14 **Read the sentences aloud. Then find /le/ and /y/.**

- The pupils read the sentences aloud. Then they find and point to the sounds /le/ and /y/. Ask them to read out the words containing these sounds.

Activity Book page 53

13 **Read the words. Circle the pictures.**

- Give pupils time to read the words and circle the corresponding parts of the picture.

14 **Listen and connect the letters. Then write.**

- Play the recording and give the pupils time to draw the lines to connect the letters. Play the recording again, and give pupils time to write the words.

15 **Listen and write the words.**

- Play the recording, pausing if necessary to give pupils time to write the words. Play it again for them to check what they have written. Check answers.

16 **Read aloud. Then listen and check.**

- Ask different pupils to read the text aloud, one sentence each. Then play the recording: pupils listen and check.

Ending the lesson

- Give out sheets of paper, some with /le/ and some with /y/ written on them. Say words, some with and some without the new sounds. Pupils stand and hold up their sheet when they hear their sound, or words containing their sound.
- (For AB Answer Key, see p. 174. For Audioscript, see p. 176.)

11 (2:36) **Listen and repeat.**

¹ **le**   ² **y**

12 (2:37) **Listen, point and say.**

13 (2:38) **Listen and blend the sounds.**

1 j - u - n - g - le jungle   2 t - i - ck - le tickle

3 l - i - tt - le little   4 p - a - dd - le paddle

5 h - a - pp - y happy   6 f - u - nn - y funny

7 s - u - nn - y sunny   8 r - ai - n - y rainy

14 **Read the sentences aloud. Then find *le* and *y*.**

1 When it's rainy, I feel sad.   2 When it's sunny, I feel happy.

3 We paddle into the jungle.   4 It's funny to tickle the little baby!

OPTIONAL ACTIVITIES
Phonics game
Play *Sound trail* see p. 301.

Phonics game
Play *Sound hunt* see p. 302.
Photocopiable 5.5 see Teacher's notes p. 290.

Lesson 7

Lesson aims
To connect other areas of the curriculum with English learning; to develop the cross-curricular topic through a short project

Cross-curricular focus
Social science (Jobs)

Target language
Olympic Games, champion, coach, train

Materials
Audio CD

Optional materials
Active Teach; Digital Activity Book; CLIL poster; Photocopiable 5.6; white and coloured card

Starting the lesson

- Play a guessing game. Divide the class into two groups. Group A writes a job, e.g. *a doctor*, on a piece of paper and gives it to one pupil from Group B. This pupil comes to the board and mimes it or draws it on the board. Group B guesses what it is. The groups take turns.

Pupil's Book page 58

Presentation

- Write some names of sports champions on the board. Ask (L1) what these people have in common (*They're sports champions*). Explain the word *champion.* Ask *What sports do they do?*
- Introduce *Olympic Games.* Ask (L1) the location of the next, or the most recent, Games.
- Introduce famous journalists and firefighters.

15 **Listen and read. Then say *True* or *False.***

- Ask the pupils the name of the website the texts are from (*Kids' Forum*) and focus their attention on the nicknames of the kids.
- Before pupils attempt the questions, play the recording while the class looks at the text.
- Pupils must now listen to the sentences again and decide if they are true or false. Explain that just one false fact in a sentence means that the answer is *False.* Allow pupils time to think about the answers, pausing the recording as necessary.

- To check answers, play the recording again and ask individual pupils to say *True* or *False.* Ask volunteers to correct the false sentences.
- Ask pupils to read the instructions in the Think! box.
- Pupils practise asking and answering in pairs.

KEY **1** True, **2** False, **3** True, **4** False, **5** False, **6** True

Practice

16 **Listen and answer.**

- Focus on the questions and tell the class that they have to listen and choose the correct answers. Play the recording. Pupils listen and answer in their notebooks. Play the recording again. Check answers with the class.

KEY
1 No, she doesn't.
2 She wants to be a teacher because she likes helping people and she's good at speaking.
3 She reads a lot and studies hard. She's learning from all her teachers.

Mini-project

- Explain (L1) that pupils are going to do a class survey about what people want to be. Give each pupil a sheet of paper. Draw a two-column grid on the board. Write *Names* on top of the first column and *Job* on top of the second. Pupils copy this grid onto their sheets. Pupils write the names of five classmates under *Names.* They ask these pupils *What do you want to be?* and write the answer. You could collect the results on your grid and then discuss them as a whole-class activity.

Activity Book page 54

17 **Listen and circle.**

- Focus on the questions and the pictures. Play the recording once. Pupils just listen and read. Play it again. Pupils circle the correct pictures. Play it once more; pupils check their answers.

18 **Draw your dream job. Then write.**

- Pupils complete the text describing what they want to be and why. Ask volunteers to read out their texts.

Ending the lesson

- Play *Make a sentence* using the occupations flashcards. The sentences can be descriptive or express what pupils want/don't want to be, e.g. Pupil 1: *Astronaut. I don't want to be an astronaut.* Pupil 2: *Doctor. Doctors wear white coats.*
- (For AB Answer Key, see p. 174. For Audioscript, see pp. 176–7.)

15   **Listen and read. Then say *True* or *False*.**

| famous | champion | Olympic Games | train | coach | brave |

Kids' Forum

| Post a reply | Log in | FAQ |

What do you want to be and why? How can you make your dream come true?

Olympian

I want to be an athlete because I want to be famous. I want to be a champion at the Olympic Games. I train very hard and listen to my coach. I eat good food. And I go to bed early every night.

Newsgirl

I want to be a journalist because I like telling stories and I like talking to people. I want to be famous. I read a lot and write in my diary every day. I practise speaking aloud every day.

Flamefighter

I want to be a firefighter because I'm brave and strong. I like helping people. I take care of my body. I'm learning karate to make my body strong.

1   Olympian wants to be an athlete at the Olympic Games.

2   Olympian eats bad food and goes to bed late.

3   Newsgirl likes telling stories and talking to people.

4   Newsgirl writes in her diary every month.

THINK!
Your friend wants to be a doctor. What should he/she study?

5   Flamefighter is learning taekwondo.

6   Flamefighter is brave and strong. He likes helping people.

16 **Listen and answer.**

1   Does Julie want to be a lawyer?

2   What does she want to be and why?

3   How can she make her dream come true?

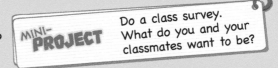
MINI-PROJECT
Do a class survey. What do you and your classmates want to be?

OPTIONAL ACTIVITIES

Olympic champion
In pairs, pupils use reference books or the internet to find out about an Olympic champion. On A4 paper, they write information about him/her: *He/She's from …*, etc. They can add a photo printed from the internet or cut from a magazine.

Communication
Match sportspeople (written on white card) with their sports (written on coloured card).
Photocopiable 5.6 see Teacher's notes p. 290.

Lesson 8

Lesson aims
To learn about other cultures and respect cultural differences

Cross-cultural focus
To learn about famous people

Materials
Audio CD

Optional materials
Pictures of famous people; world map or globe; Active Teach; Digital Activity Book; CLIL poster; Photocopiable 5.7

Starting the lesson

- Write on the board: TTRNSAAOU, OORCTD, FFGHTRREEII, AERRMF, UEIRDLB, AELLTB DERACN. Divide the class into pairs and ask pupils to unscramble these words for jobs (*astronaut, doctor, firefighter, farmer, builder, ballet dancer*).

Pupil's Book page 59

Presentation

- Focus on the photos. Ask pupils to name the jobs: *basketball player, ballet dancer.*
- Pupils look at the texts, find the names of the countries where the children live and locate them on the map or globe.

17 **Listen and read.**

- Focus on the large photos of famous people. Ask (L1) what pupils know about these people.
- Play the recording. Pupils read and listen to the children in the smaller photos speaking about their heroes. Ask a few comprehension questions, e.g. *Does Alejandro play basketball? Where is Elena from?*

Practice

18 **Ask and answer.**

- Elicit names of famous sportspeople, film stars, singers, etc. that pupils admire. Write the names of the famous people on the board.
- Direct pupils' attention to the questions. Check that they understand. Organise the class in pairs. They take it in turns to ask and answer questions. Tell them they can talk about a famous person or someone they know.
- Describe yourself as if you were a famous person, and pupils guess who you are, e.g. *I'm from the USA. I'm famous. I've got long hair. I'm a good actor. I have got six children. I am the star of (film).*

- Stronger classes can write about themselves in the first person in the same way. The rest of the class guesses who they are.

> **KEY**
> **1** He wants to be a basketball player.
> **2** His favourite basketball player is Pau Gasol.
> **3** She wants to be a ballet dancer.
> **4** Alina Somova is a famous ballet dancer from Russia.

Portfolio project

- Ask pupils to write about their hero.
- Pupils can write in their notebooks, using the texts on p. 59 as a model.

Activity Book page 55

19 **Read and write.**

- Pupils look at the texts, find the names of the countries where the children live and locate them on the map or globe. Focus on the questions. Pupils read the texts and answer. Check answers with the class.

20 **Read and write *T = True* or *F = False*.**

- Pupils read the sentences. Check that they understand. Ask them to read the texts again and decide if the sentences are true or false. Check answers with the class.

Ending the lesson

- Divide the class into two teams. Team A mimes a sport or showbusiness job from the unit and Team B has to give the name of a famous person who does that job. Teams take turns.
- (For AB Answer Key, see p. 174. For Audioscript, see p. 177.)

OPTIONAL ACTIVITIES
Famous people poster
Make a famous people poster. Ask pupils to cut out pictures of famous people they like and write about where the people are from and what they do. Collect the pictures and make a big poster.
Flashcard relay
Put all the Unit 4 and 5 wordcards face up at one end of the classroom and the Unit 4 and 5 flashcards at the other, all in jumbled order. Divide the class into two or four teams, depending on the size of your class (no more than eight pupils in a team). The teams stand in line. When you say *Go*, the first member of each team runs to the wordcards, takes one, then runs to the other end of the room to find the corresponding flashcard.

Wider World
My hero

17 (2·45) **Listen and read.**

Pau Gasol

① Alejandro's blog ✕

Hi! I'm Alejandro. I'm from Spain and I love playing basketball. I play every week. I want to be a famous basketball player one day. My favourite basketball player is Pau Gasol. He's cool! He's from Spain but he plays in the United States.

Alejandro, 10, Spain

② Elena's blog ✕

My name is Elena. I'm from Russia and I want to be a ballet dancer. I love dancing. I go to ballet school and I have ballet lessons every day. My favourite ballet dancer is Alina Somova. She's from Russia and she's a great dancer.

Elena, 9, Russia

Alina Somova

18 **Ask and answer.**

1 What does Alejandro want to be?
2 Who's his favourite basketball player?
3 What does Elana what to be?
4 Who's Alina Somova?

PORTFOLIO

Think and write.

Write about your hero.

Then he/she runs back to the second member of the team, who does the same. The first team to collect eight pairs of cards is the winner. If you have two more teams, they then play the game. You could also have a final between the two winning teams to find a class champion.
Photocopiable 5.7 see Teacher's notes p. 291.

Lesson 9

Lesson aims
To review the unit language with a game and the Picture Dictionary

Materials
Audio CD; Flashcards (Jobs)

Optional materials
Active Teach; Digital Activity Book; CLIL poster; Reading and Writing Booklet; pictures of jobs

Starting the lesson

- Ask questions starting with *Can*, related to the jobs in the unit, e.g. *Can you swim? Can you sing? Can you play basketball?* Pupils mime these actions when you say *OK. Go!*

Pupil's Book page 60

19 Draw and write in your notebook. Then play.

- Revise jobs vocabulary using the flashcards and elicit any other jobs that pupils know, writing these on the board. Practise with the pupils the language to be used: *Do you want to be a singer? No, I don't. Does he/she want to be a writer? No, he/she doesn't.*
- Pupils draw a picture of their chosen job in their notebooks, and write *I want to be a(n) ... .* For Round 1, they work in pairs, taking turns to ask and answer questions.
- For Round 2, organise the class into groups of four. They ask each other about other members of the group; the person asked may need to ask the person being asked about.
- Pupils can use the Picture Dictionary (AB p. 108.)

Activity Book page 56

21 Look and write the jobs.

- Direct pupils' attention to the pictures and point out the example. Tell the class to write the jobs associated with these objects next to each picture. Check as a class.

22 **Listen, number and tick (✓). Then write.**

- Direct pupils' attention to the pictures and tell them to number the pairs of pictures 1–4. Show that the first one is done as an example. Play the recording once, pausing if necessary to allow pupils time to number the pairs of pictures. Check answers with the class.
- Play the recording again. This time pupils choose and tick the correct picture in each pair. Pause after the first one, to make sure they understand what to do. Allow time, pausing if necessary, for pupils to find and tick the correct pictures. Check answers with the class.

Ending the lesson

- Say and mime, e.g. *singer.* Ask a pupil to repeat the sentence *I want to be a singer*, adding another activity and mime, e.g. *I want to be a singer and a film star.* Continue in the same way to make a chain.
- (For AB Answer Key, see p. 174. For Audioscript, see p. 177.)

19 **Draw and write in your notebook. Then play.** **HAVE FUN !**

Round 1

My dream job

I want to be …

Round 2

My …'s dream job
(brother, sister or friend)

He/She wants to be …

Guess!

Round 1 Do you want to be a …? Yes, I do.

Round 2 Does he/she want to be a …? No, he/she doesn't.

Picture Dictionary

AB p.108

OPTIONAL ACTIVITIES

Flashcard game
Play *Who's the fastest?* (see p. 298).

Draw a picture
Pupils draw their favourite job in their notebooks. Ask volunteers to show his/her picture to the class, for them to identify. Divide the class into pairs. Pupils ask and answer questions about their pictures.

Reading and Writing Booklet p. 15 see Answer Key p.282.

Lesson 10

Lesson aims
To personalise and assess efforts

Materials
Audio CD ; Flashcards (Jobs)

Optional materials
Digital Activity Book; CLIL poster; Online material – *Film Studio Island*; Active Teach; Grammar reference and Review for Unit 5 (PB p. 114 and AB p.100); Test Booklet; Grammar Booklet; a bag or box

Starting the lesson

● This is a self assessment activity. Tell the pupils that the activities on this page will show what they have learnt in this unit.

Pupil's Book page 61

20 **Listen and point.**

● Tell pupils that they must choose the correct answer for each question. Play the recording more than once if necessary.
● Pupils listen, look at the pictures and choose the correct answer.

> **KEY** **1** a, **2** a, **3** b, **4** b, **5** a, **6** b, **7** Yes, she does.
> **8** No, he doesn't. (He wants to be an athlete.)

21 **Read and say.**

● Pupils read the sentences. Tell them to write the questions in their notebooks or on the board, or ask them to say the questions.

> **KEY**
> **1** What does he want to be?
> **2** Does she want to be a mechanic?

Activity Book page 57

● Focus on the *I can* sentences at the bottom of the page. Tell the pupils that they have to tick the boxes, depending on whether they think they can do the *I can* points.

23 **Draw and write two things you want to be and two things you don't want to be.**

● Ask pupils to think about what they want to be and what they don't want to be. They draw the corresponding pictures and write the sentences. Ask volunteers to show their pictures and read out their sentences.

Ending the lesson

● Put the flashcards (jobs) in a bag or box. Take out one flashcard and look at it without showing the class. Then say *I want to be a …* and give clues without saying the word (mime or draw on the board). The class guesses what picture it is, e.g. *You want to be a pilot*. The first pupil to make a correct guess takes a turn.
● (For AB Answer Key, see p. 174. For Audioscript, see p. 177.)

> **OPTIONAL ACTIVITIES**
> **Jobs parade**
> Bring a collection of old clothes and accessories related to the jobs learnt in this unit. Pupils can also help by bringing things from home. Pupils dress up and organise a fashion show of jobs. One pupil introduces the others as they walk, one by one, down the catwalk, by reading out a short description that they have written about themselves in advance.

20 (2:47) **Listen and point.**

1
 a
 b

2
 a
 b

3
a
b

4
a
b

5
a
b

6
a
b

7

a Yes, she does.
b No, she doesn't.

8

a Yes, he does.
b No, he doesn't.

21 **Read and say.**

1 What ...? He wants to be a film star.

2 Does ...? Yes, she does. She wants to be a mechanic.

Important jobs
In pairs, pupils write down all the jobs they can think of. Collect all their ideas on the board. Ask pupils (L1) to choose the six most important jobs on the board. They give each job a number depending on how important they think it is (1 = the most important). As a class, discuss (L1) the reasons for their choices.

Activity Book Review see p. 100.
Grammar Booklet p. 15 see Answer Key p. 284–5.
Test Booklet Unit 5 see Answer Key p. 295.
Online World
Pupils can now go online to *Film Studio Island* and enjoy the fun and games.

Activity Book Answer Key

p. 48, Activity 1
1 firefighter, 2 basketball player, 3 ballet dancer,
4 police officer, 5 builder, 6 film star, 7 astronaut

p. 48, Activity 2
1 astronaut, 2 firefighter, 3 basketball player,
4 builder, 5 police officer

p. 49, Activity 3
a 5, b 3, c 1, d 7, e 4, f 2, g 6

p. 49, Activity 4
1 She wants to be a police officer.
2 He wants to be a film star.
3 What does she want to be? She wants to be a
   ballet dancer.
4 What does she want to be? She wants to be a
   builder.
5 What does he want to be? He wants to be a
   firefighter.
6 What does she want to be? She wants to be an
   astronaut.
7 What does he want to be? He wants to be a
   basketball player.

p. 50, Activity 5
1 journalist, 2 carpenter, 3 lawyer, 4 model,
5 mechanic, 6 athlete, 7 singer, 8 photographer

p. 50, Activity 6
1 Does he want to be a model? No, he doesn't.
2 Does she want to be a lawyer? Yes, she does.
3 Do you want to be a photographer? Yes, I do.
4 Does he want to be a singer? No, he doesn't.

p. 51, Activity 7
1 a ✓, b ✗, 2 a ✓, b ✗, 3 a ✗, b ✓, 4 a ✗, b ✓

p. 51, Activity 8
1 journalist, tell stories, model
2 wants to be a lawyer because she wants to help
   people, doesn't want to be a ballet dancer
3 a carpenter, wants to be a carpenter, she wants to
   make tables and chairs
4 does he want to be a police officer, wants to be a
   police officer because he can run very fast

p. 51, Activity 9
1 want to be an astronaut
2 Do you want to be a basketball player?
3 Do you want to be a ballet dancer?

p. 52, Activity 10
Because he wants to be Madley Kool.

p. 52, Activity 11
1 dancing, dancer
2 He loves acting. He wants to be a film star.
3 He loves jumping. He wants to be a basketball
   player.
4 She loves animals. She wants to be a farmer.

p. 52, Activity 12
I want to be a detective.

p. 53, Activity 14
swim, yellow, smell, scarf

p. 53, Activity 15
1 little, 2 tickle, 3 funny, 4 happy

p. 54, Activity 17
1 football, 2 7 o'clock, fruit and pasta, football,
3 do karate

p. 55, Activity 19
1 Kate, 2 Santiago

p. 55, Activity 20
1 T, 2 F, 3 T, 4 F

p. 56, Activity 21
1 police officer, 2 ballet dancer, 3 basketball player,
4 firefighter, 5 photographer, 6 builder, 7 singer,
8 mechanic

p. 56, Activity 22
Order of pictures: 1 firefighter / astronaut, 2 athlete /
model, 3 lawyer / journalist, 4 carpenter / builder
Correct pictures to tick: 1 a, 2 a, 3 a, 4 a
1 Does he want to be a firefighter?
2 Does she want to be a model? No, she doesn't.
3 She wants to be a lawyer.
4 He wants to be a carpenter.

Audioscript

Lesson 1 Activity 1 CD2:24
S = SAM   JE = JENNY   RU = RUBY   JO = JOHN

S   Wow! Look! Where's Madley Kool? Is he here?
JE No, I can't see him. But look at her. She's very pretty. She's a film star!
S   Look! She's got long legs. She's a ballet dancer.
R   Look! He's a farmer. He's got a hen!
JO Look! A basketball player! Wow, cool ball.
R   Look at him, at the table. He's wearing big boots. He's an astronaut.
JE Oh! A firefighter! Cleo – watch out!

Lesson 1 Activity 2 CD2:25
a builder
b firefighter
c police officer
d basketball player
e film star
f ballet dancer
g astronaut

Lesson 1 Activity 3 CD2:26
1 He's an astronaut.
2 She's a film star.
3 He's a police officer.
4 He's a basketball player.
5 She's a ballet dancer.
6 He's a farmer.
7 She's a builder.

Lesson 2 Activity 4 CD2:27
What do you want to be?
What do you want to be?
I want to be, I want to be, I want to be a film star.
I don't want to be a farmer.
I don't want to be a firefighter.
I want to be, I want to be, I want to be a film star.
What do you want to be?
What do you want to be?
I want to be, I want to be, I want to be a film star.

Lesson 2 Activity 5 CD2:28
1 What does he want to be?
   He wants to be a basketball player.
2 What does she want to be?
   She wants to be a ballet dancer.
3 What does he want to be?
   He wants to be a police officer.
4 What does she want to be?
   She wants to be a builder.

Lesson 2 Activity 3 (AB) CD2:29
1 What do you want to be? I want to be a police officer.
2 I don't want to be a farmer. I want to be a film star.
3 What do you want to be? I want to be a ballet dancer.
4 What do you want to be? I want to be a builder.
5 What do you want to be? I want to be a firefighter.
6 I don't want to be a ballet dancer. I want to be an astronaut.
7 I don't want to be a firefighter. I want to be a basketball player.

Lesson 3 Activity 6 CD2:30
a singer
b model
c journalist
d photographer
e carpenter
f mechanic
g lawyer
h athlete

Lesson 3 Activity 7 CD2:31
Teacher, farmer, builder, doctor
What does he want to be?
Teacher, farmer, builder, doctor
Just a minute! Let me see.
Does he want to be a teacher?
No, no, no, he doesn't.
Does he want to be a farmer?
No, no, no, he doesn't.
Does he want to be a builder?
No, no, no, he doesn't.
Does he want to be a doctor?
Yes, yes, yes, he does.
He wants to be a doctor.

Lesson 4 Activity 8 CD2:32
a Hello, I'm Bobby. I like running. I can jump and I can catch a ball. I want to be a basketball player because I'm very tall.
b I'm Tim. I'm strong. I like climbing. I don't want to be an athlete. I want to be a firefighter because I like helping people.
c Hi! I'm Martina. I can sing and dance. I don't want to be a ballet dancer. I want to be a film star because I can act very well.
d I'm Emma. I like music. I don't want to be a singer. I want to be a ballet dancer because I can dance and I can jump.

Lesson 4 Activity 7 (AB)　　　　CD2:33

1　Do you want to be a model?
　　No, I don't. I want to be a journalist. I want to tell stories.
2　What do you want to be?
　　I want to be a lawyer. I want to help people.
　　But you're a good dancer. You can be a ballet dancer.
　　I don't want to be a ballet dancer.
3　Do you want to be a doctor?
　　No, I don't. I want to be a carpenter. I want to make tables and chairs.
4　What do you want to be?
　　I want to be a police officer. I can run very fast.
　　Really? You can be an athlete.
　　I don't want to be an athlete.

Lesson 6 Activity 11　　　　CD2:36

l　　　　　　e
/le/ /le/　　/le/
y
/y/ /y/　　　/y/

Lesson 6 Activity 12　　　　CD2:37

/le/ /le/
/y/ /y/
/y/ /y/
/le/ /le/
/le/ /le/
/y/ /y/

Lesson 6 Activity 13　　　　CD2:38

1　/j/ /u/ /n/ /g/ /le/
　　jungle
2　t/ /i/ /k/ /le/
　　tickle
3　/l/ /i/ t/ /le/
　　little
4　/p/ /a/ /d/ /le/
　　paddle
5　/h/ /a/ /p/ /y/
　　happy
6　/f/ /u/ /n/ /y/
　　funny
7　/s/ /u/ /n/ /y/
　　sunny
8　/r/ /ai/ /n/ /y/
　　rainy

Lesson 6 Activity 14 (AB)　　　　CD2:39

1　/s/　　　/w/　　　/i/　　　/m/
2　/y/　　　/e/　　　/l/　　　/ow/
3　/s/　　　/m/　　　/e/　　　/l/
4　/s/　　　/k/　　　/ar/　　　/f/

Lesson 6 Activity 15 (AB)　　　　CD2:40

1　little
2　tickle
3　funny
4　happy

Lesson 6 Activity 16 (AB)　　　　CD2:41

We paddle down the river in our boat. The jungle is loud and the sun is hot. Look at that yellow snake! Look at that red and blue bird!

Lesson 7 Activity 15　　　　CD2:42

What do you want to be and why? How can you make your dream come true?

I want to be an athlete because I want to be famous. I want to be a champion at the Olympic Games. I train very hard and listen to my coach. I eat good food. And I go to bed early every night.

I want to be a journalist because I like telling stories and I like talking to people. I want to be famous. I read a lot and write in my diary every day. I practise speaking aloud every day.

I want to be a firefighter because I'm brave and strong. I like helping people. I take care of my body. I'm learning karate to make my body strong.

Lesson 7 Activity 16　　　　CD2:43

W = WOMAN　J = JULIE
W　Hi, Julie. What do you want to be when you finish school?
J　I want to be a teacher.
W　Why do you want to be a teacher?
J　Because I like helping people. Also, I'm good at speaking.
W　I see! That sounds great! How can you make this come true?
J　I read a lot and study hard at school. I'm learning from all my teachers.
W　That's great, Julie.
J　Thanks.

Lesson 7 Activity 17 (AB)　　CD2:44
1 Hello, Matthew. What do you want to be and why?
   I want to be a basketball player because I love sports.
2 What do you do to make your dreams come true?
   I go running at 7 o'clock in the morning. I eat only healthy food like pasta and fruit. In the afternoon I practise basketball with the team.
3 What other things do you do?
   I do karate on Sundays. I want to make my body strong.

Lesson 8 Activity 17　　CD2:45
1 Alejandro's blog: Hi! I'm Alejandro. I'm from Spain and I love playing basketball. I play every week. I want to be a famous basketball player one day. My favourite basketball player is Pau Gasol. He's cool! He's from Spain but he plays in the United States. Alejandro, 10, Spain
2 Elena's blog: My name is Elena. I'm from Russia and I want to be a ballet dancer. I love dancing. I go to ballet school and I have ballet lessons every day. My favourite ballet dancer is Alina Somova. She's from Russia and she's a great dancer. Elena, 9, Russia

Lesson 9 Activity 22 (AB)　　CD2:46
1 What does he want to be?
   He doesn't want to be an astronaut. He wants to be a firefighter.
2 What does she want to be?
   She doesn't want to be a model. She wants to be an athlete.
3 What does she want to be?
   She doesn't want to be a journalist. She wants to be a lawyer.
4 What does he want to be?
   He doesn't want to be a builder. He wants to be a carpenter.

Lesson 10 Activity 20　　CD2:47
1 What do you want to be?
   I want to be a ballet dancer.
2 I don't want to be a builder. I want to be a photographer.
3 She doesn't want to be a cook. She wants to be a police officer.
4 What does he want to be?
   He wants to be an astronaut.
5 Do you want to be a lawyer?
   Yes, I do.
6 Does she want to be a dancer?
   No, she doesn't. She wants to be a singer.
7 Does she want to be a doctor?
8 Does he want to be a pilot?

Objectives

- describe where things are
- could do
- talk about the past
- pronounce properly /ce/, /ci/ and /cir/.

Topics
- Places and elements in a rainforest
- Prepositions
- Activities in the past

Phonics
/ce/, /ci/ and /cir/

Values
- Be prepared

Stories
- Unit opener: in the rainforest
- Story episode: Cleo as a star

Language
Vocabulary
- Nature: hut, bridge, nest, waterfall, valley, mountain, vines
- Prepositions: around, through, towards, past
- Nature: lake, sea, coast, hills

Revision
Prepositions: behind, next to, in front of
Action verbs

Structures
Where's the (hut)?
It's (over) the (mountain).
It's (across) the (bridge).
Where are the (huts)?
They're (near) the (waterfall).
They're (between) the (waterfall) and the (mountain).
Could you (walk) around the lake?
Yes, I could./No, I couldn't
I could (walk) (around) the (lake), but I couldn't (swim) (across) it.
I walk through the hills.
Yesterday I walked through the hills.
He/She talks to the teacher.
Yesterday he/she talked to the teacher.
climb = climbed, hike = hiked, jump = jumped, listen = listened, look = looked, play = played, stay = stayed, walk = walked
I can go for a (run).

CLIL language
The Amazon Rainforest: nectar, hummingbird, tarantula, tapir, parrot

Songs and chants
- Chant
- Song about abilities and leisure facilities
- Karaoke song

Sociocultural aspects
- Finding out about forests in the world
- Identifying activities that can be done in a forest
- Being aware of forests in the country where pupils live

Cross-curricular contents
- Knowledge and interaction with the physical world: living in the rainforest
- Geography: getting information about the Amazon Rainforest
- Language Arts: reading a story, acting out, telling a story
- Language skills: reading and understanding texts in the past

Learning strategies
- Using previous knowledge to interpret information in a text
- Identifying rules about the use of the Past simple
- Logical thinking: problem solving
- Critical thinking: thinking critically about one's own abilities
- Collaborative learning: project work and pair work
- Self assessment

Basic competences

- Linguistic communication: Have interest in using new words (L1 to L10)
- Knowledge and interaction with the physical world: Value life in rainforests and forests (L7)
- Mathematical competence: Locate in space (L1 to L4)
- Processing information and digital competence: Use *Film Studio Island* online component
- Social and civic competence: Be prepared (L5)
- Cultural and artistic competence: Appreciate forests in our country as part of the cultural heritage (L8)
- Learning to learn: Reflect on what has been learnt and self-evaluate progress (L10)
- Autonomy and personal initiative: Develop one's own criteria and social skills (L1 to L10)

Skills

Listening
- Identifying places and elements in rainforests in recordings
- Understanding what others could or couldn't do
- Understanding specific information in a song about gorillas and where they are
- Understanding information about what people did
- Understanding general and specific information in a story

Reading
- Understanding information in sentences and short texts (rainforest and the past)
- Understanding general and specific information in a cartoon strip story
- Understanding general and specific information about forests in the world
- Answering questions to show comprehension of a text about forests.

Speaking
- Repeating words and sentences
- Chanting and singing
- Giving information about the rainforest
- Saying what they did in the past
- Pronouncing /ce/, /ci/ and /cir/ correctly

Writing
- Completing sentences with prepositions
- Completing questions and answers
- Looking at pictures and writing answers to questions
- Completing a crossword
- Describing a picture using prepositions

Talking
- Asking and answering about where things are
- Taking part in dialogues about what they could do
- Exchanging information about forests in other parts of the world
- Role playing a story

Classroom ideas

- Bring photos of the rainforest
- Use the unit flashcards to play games
- Decorate the class with flashcards and the cross-curricular poster
- Ask pupils in the class from other countries to talk about forests in their countries
- Use the internet to find out about rainforests
- Bring to the classroom library books about the forest
- Photocopiables

Take-home English

- Home-School Link
- Notes for Parents
- A sample of work each week
- Portfolio

Self assessment

- Pupils can describe where things are
- Pupils can express what others could do
- Pupils can talk about the past

Evaluation

- Pupil's Book page 71
- Activity Book page 67
- Photocopiable 6.7
- Picture Dictionary
- Test Booklet – Unit 6

Lesson I

Lesson aims
To learn and practise new vocabulary
(The natural world)

Target language
hut, bridge, nest, waterfall, valley, mountain, vines,
river, over, across, near, between

Materials
Audio CD; Flashcards and Wordcards (Nature)

Optional materials
Active Teach; Digital Activity Book; Photocopiable
6.1; world map or globe

Starting the lesson

- Elicit the names of wild animals pupils have learnt
  so far.
- Direct pupils' attention to the title of the unit. Ask
  What's a rainforest? What can you see in a rainforest?
  Pupils answer (L1). Ask if any of the animals from the
  brainstorm live in the rainforest.

> Pupil's Book pages 62–63

Presentation

- Use the flashcards to teach the vocabulary. Hold up
  the flashcards in turn and say the words for pupils to
  repeat. Hold up the flashcards again, asking individual
  pupils to say the words. Show the cards in random
  order and ask *What is it?*
- Pupils open their books. Focus on the main illustration.
  Ask *Where are the children now?* Pupils answer (L1). To
  make it clear that they're not in a real rainforest, ask
  them to look for clues that it's a film set (lights
  top right, steam machine bottom right, remote
  controlled crocodile).

1 Listen.

- Tell pupils (L1) they are going to listen to a recording
  describing the picture. Play the recording while pupils
  look at the main illustration. Now tell them they will
  listen again and they should point to the relevant
  parts of the picture as they listen. Play the recording
  again while they point.

Practice

2 Listen and repeat.

- Play the recording, pausing after each word. Pupils
  point to the pictures. Play the recording again. Pupils
  point and repeat each word.
- Display the relevant flashcards on one side of the
  board and write the corresponding words or put up
  wordcards on the other side. Pupils come to the front,
  read out the words and match them to the pictures.

3 Listen and say *True* or *False*.

- Ask the pupils to look at the main illustration.
- Play the recording. Pupils have to find the
  corresponding pictures and point to them. Then they
  say whether the statements are *True* or *False*.

> **KEY** **1** False, **2** True, **3** True, **4** True, **5** False

Ending the lesson

- Play *Spelling bee* to practise the spelling of the new words. Pupils listen to the words you say and, in turn, they try to spell them correctly.
- (For AB Answer Key, see p. 200. For Audioscript, see p. 201.)

NOTES

Activity Book page 58

1 Match.

- Direct pupils' attention to the picture. Tell them to look at the different parts of the picture carefully and label it using the words in the word bank.
- Check as a class.

2 Look and write.

- Direct pupils' attention to the pictures and the prepositions. Tell the class to complete the sentences. Check as a class by asking individual pupils to read one sentence each.
- Personalise by asking a few questions, e.g. *Do you like swimming in a river?*

Lesson 2

Lesson aims
To learn and practise the new structure

Target language
Where is/are the (hut/huts)? It's/They're (over) the mountain/(across) the bridge/(near) the lake/(between) the mountain and the lake.

Materials
Audio CD; Flashcards and Wordcards (Nature)

Optional materials
A cardboard box, toy animals; Active Teach; Digital Activity Book; Grammar Booklet

Starting the lesson

- Revise the Lesson 1 vocabulary. Hold up the flashcards. Pupils come to the front and write the words on the board.
- Bring a large box and put it where it is visible to all the class. Take different toy animals for which pupils know the names in English and revise prepositions *in*, *on* and *under*. Ask *Where's the (monkey)?* Pupils answer *It's (under) the box.*

> **Pupil's Book page 63**

Presentation

- Show a flashcard, e.g. *nest*, and ask *What's this?* Say *It's a nest.* Ask the class to repeat *It's a nest* after you. Repeat with the other words.
- Point to a pupil and say *(Name) is near (name).* Repeat with a few more pupils. Pupils repeat each sentence after you to practise pronunciation. Ask *Where's (name)?* Pupils answer *He/She's near … .*
- Use the toy animals to present the other prepositions. Pupils come to your table and place the toys in different positions. They ask the class, e.g. *Where's the (cat)?* The class answers.
- Read the Look! box. Pupils draw pictures and write sentences in their notebooks to illustrate the prepositions, e.g. *The cat is in front of the house.* Then they show their pictures to the class and say the sentences.

4 **Listen and chant.**

- Play the recording. Pupils listen and follow the words. Play it again, pausing after each line. Pupils repeat. Play it a third time. Pupils say it together. Use the picture to help prompt the words.
- Divide the class into two groups. One group chants the questions and the other group answers.
- Draw pupils' attention to the prepositions in the Tip! box.

5 **Listen and point. Then ask and answer.**

- Focus on the pictures. Play the recording. Pupils listen and find the illustrations. Play it again, pausing after each of the sentences.
- Divide the class into pairs. Focus on the pictures. Pupils ask and answer questions. Tell them to look at the model dialogue. You could ask pupils to write the answers in their notebook for extra practice. Pupils could invent more questions and answers, based on the main illustration.

> **KEY** **1** c, **2** d, **3** b, **4** a

Practice

- Divide the class into two teams for a memory game. Pupils look at the main illustration in PB p. 62 carefully for a minute and then close their books. Pupils from each team take turns to say what there is in the picture, e.g. *There's a crocodile under the bridge.* Ask them to give as many details as possible. Give a point for each correct sentence.

Ending the lesson

- Play *Teacher says* see p. 299 practising the prepositions from this lesson: *Stand near the chair. Girls stand behind boys. Put your bag between the chair and the desk,* etc.
- (For AB Answer Key, see p. 200. For Audioscript, see p. 201.)

OPTIONAL ACTIVITY

Drawing activity
Do a Picture dictation using the prepositions from this lesson with animal, furniture and natural world vocabulary.
Pairwork game
Play *Matching pairs* see p. 300.
Grammar Booklet p. 16 see Answer Key p. 285.

NOTES

Activity Book page 59

3 Look and write.

- Direct pupils' attention to the pictures and tell them to complete the sentences. Work on the example as a whole class. Allow pupils time to complete the sentences and then check as a class.

4 Listen and number. Then write.

- Pupils look at the pictures. Play the recording. They number the pictures.
- Play the recording again, pausing after numbers 2, 3 and 4 to allow pupils time to find the correct pictures and write the sentences. When they have finished, ask volunteers to read the sentences to the class.

Lesson 3

Lesson aims
To extend the vocabulary set (Natural world, Prepositions); to practise the unit language with a song

Target language
around, through, towards, past
lake, sea, coast, hills

Materials
Audio CD; Flashcards and Wordcards (Nature)

Optional materials
Active Teach; Digital Activity Book; Photocopiables 6.2–6.3; Reading and Writing Booklet

Starting the lesson

- Play *Guess the card* see p. 299 to revise landscape and animal words.

Pupil's Book page 64

Presentation

- Introduce the prepositions and make the meaning clear, pointing to the pictures. Then point to the pictures below and say *It's a lake. It's the sea,* etc.

6 **Listen and repeat.**

- Introduce the new words (*sea, lake, coast,* etc.) using the flashcards. Hold them up and say the words for pupils to repeat. Ask individual pupils to say the words. Play the recording for pupils to listen and repeat.
- Now put the flashcards on the board. Point to the different flashcards and ask the class to say the words.

Song

7 **Listen and point. Then sing.**

- Play the recording for pupils to listen and follow the text. Play the song again. Pupils point to the correct coloured words when they hear them. Use gesture to help show the meaning of *through, around, towards* and *past.* Pupils repeat. Play the song again for pupils to join in and sing together. You can now play the karaoke song (Active Teach).

Practice

- Read the Look! box. Pupils use the sentences as a model to ask and answer questions in pairs, based on the pictures. Ask volunteers to demonstrate questions and answers for each picture.

8 **Look, ask and answer.**

- Draw pupils' attention to the pictures and the ticks and crosses.
- Organise the class into pairs. Explain that they have to look at the pictures and ask and answer questions as in the example dialogue. Pupil A asks the question and Pupil B answers. Then they swap.

Activity Book page 60

5 **Unscramble and write. Then match.**

- Pupils unscramble the words and write them on the lines provided.
- Give pupils time to match the words to the pictures.

6 **Read and tick (✓).**

- Pupils look at the pictures and read the sentences. Then they tick the correct pictures. Check as a class. Ask *Which is number (one)?*

Ending the lesson

- Each group works together to write a song verse about a different animal. Circulate to help with ideas and vocabulary. Write the new verses on the board.
- (For AB Answer Key, see p. 200. For Audioscript, see p. 201.)

OPTIONAL ACTIVITIES
Flashcard game
Play *Pass the flashcards* see p. 298 using flashcards or magazine cut outs.

6  **Listen and repeat.**

a — around
b — through
c — towards
d — past
e — lake
f — sea
g — coast
h — hills

7 (2:55) **Listen and point. Then sing.**

SONG

Where are all the gorillas?
Let's watch them eat and play.
They're (around   past) the hills,
across the bridge,
Around the (lake   sea) and the trees.

We could walk through the valley,
Climb the (bridge   tree) and watch them play.
Could I go (past   near) the gorillas?
Yes, you could but not so near.

Where are all the gorillas?
Let's watch them eat and play.
They're (over   past) the hill, next to the huts,
Across the (sea   waterfall) .

Could I walk (towards   around) the valley,
Climb the (hill   mountain) and watch them play?
Yes, you could but be careful.
You could fall down the hill.

LOOK!

| Could you walk around the lake? | Yes, I could. |
| | No, I couldn't. |

I could walk around the lake but I couldn't swim across it.

Picture 1. Could you swim towards the coast?

No, I couldn't.

8 **Look, ask and answer.**

 1 ✗
 2 ✓
 3 ✓
 4 ✗

Draw a rainforest
In small groups, pupils draw a rainforest using the new words. Groups describe it to the class, e.g. *There are hills across the river. The river is under the bridge.*

Photocopiable 6.2 See Teacher's notes p. 291.
Photocopiable 6.3 See Teacher's notes p. 291.
Reading and Writing Booklet p. 16 see Answer Key p. 282.

Lesson 4

Lesson aims
To develop reading, writing, listening and speaking skills; to learn and practise the new structure (Past simple regular forms)

Target language
Yesterday I/he/she walked, talked, climbed, jumped, hiked, looked, listened, played, stayed

Materials
Audio CD

Optional materials
World map or globe; Active Teach; Digital Activity Book; Grammar Booklet

Starting the lesson

- Sing the song from Lesson 3 CD2:55 as a whole class.

Pupil's Book page 65

Presentation

- Direct pupils' attention to the Look! box. Look at the sentences and focus on the forms of the verbs in the present and the past. Read the Look! box. Elicit more examples from the class and write a few on the board. Pupils could copy them into their notebooks.

Skills

9 **Listen, read and find the photos.**

- Focus on the picture of the lake. Ask *What's this?* Point to the hippo. Ask *What's this? Where do hippos live? Are there hippos in (pupils' country)?* Do not confirm answers yet. Play the recording.
- Explain (L1) that the text is a diary someone has written while on holiday. Pupils scan the first text for names of places (*Lake Victoria, Uganda*). Help pupils to locate these places on a map or globe. Pupils scan the texts for the names of three animals (*hippos, monkeys, gorillas*). Ask a few comprehension questions: *What did they see? Did they go hiking?* Check answers with the class.

10 **Look at Activity 9 and say *True* or *False*.**

- Pupils read the sentences. Check that they understand them. They read the text again and decide if the sentences are true or false. You could ask confident pupils to correct the false sentences.

> **KEY** 1 True, 2 False, 3 True, 4 True, 5 False, 6 True

Activity Book page 61

7 **Listen and number. Then write.**

- Ask the pupils to look at the pictures. Play the recording and ask pupils to just listen. Play it again. Pupils number the pictures. Give pupils time to answer the questions. Play the recording again for pupils to check their answers. Check with the class.

8 **Listen and write ✓ = could or ✗ = couldn't. Then write.**

- Focus on the pictures. Pupils listen and tick the correct picture in each case. Then they complete the sentences. Check answers with the class.

9 **Write.**

- Pupils must write the verbs in the *-ed* past form. Check that they understand what they must do, by looking at the example as a whole class and referring to the Look! box on PB p. 65. Check answers with the class.

Ending the lesson

- Tell the class to say sentences about the text as fast as they can.
- (For AB Answer Key, see p. 200. For Audioscript, see p. 202.)

> Pupils can now go online to *Film Studio Island* and find the guitar that Cleo is holding. It is the guitar case leaning against the cupboard inside the Dino Park Studio. Once pupils click on the guitar they are taken to a supplementary language game based on the vocabulary in this unit.

LOOK!

Yesterday I **walked** through the hills.

Last week he/she **talked** to the teacher.

climb – climb**ed**, hike – hik**ed**, jump – jump**ed**, listen – listen**ed**,
look – look**ed**, play – play**ed**, stay – stay**ed**, walk – walk**ed**

9 (2:56) **Listen, read and find the photos.**

Wednesday, August 20ᵗʰ
Hippos in the lake!
We are on holiday in Uganda. Yesterday my family and I visited Lake Victoria. We stayed in a hut near the lake. It was amazing. We looked at many hippos. They were in the lake. That's why we couldn't swim.

Thursday, August 21ˢᵗ
The Ugandan rainforest
Now we're visiting the rainforest in Uganda. It's great! Yesterday we hiked in the rainforest. There were many different animals and plants but my favourites were the monkeys. They climbed and played in the trees. We wanted to see some gorillas but we couldn't find any.

Saturday, August 23ʳᵈ
Awesome gorillas!
They're big, black and beautiful but there are only 600 mountain gorillas left in the world. Yesterday we walked through the forest and listened for them. We were very quiet. We could hear them and smell them but we couldn't see them. Suddenly the gorillas were there! They were behind the trees. It was awesome!

a  **b**  **c**

10 **Look at Activity 9 and say *True* or *False*.**

1 They stayed inear Lake Victoria.

2 The hippos jumped really high.

3 They hiked in the rainforest.

4 The monkeys climbed in the trees.

5 The gorillas were in the grasslands.

6 They could hear the gorillas.

Lesson 4 grammar (past simple regular)   AB p.61   **65**

OPTIONAL ACTIVITES

Flashcard game
Play *Noughts and crosses* see p. 298.

Team game
Play *Drawing race* see p. 300.
Grammar Booklet p. 17 see Answer Key p. 285.

Lesson 5

Lesson aims
To consolidate the unit language with a story

Values
Be prepared.

Receptive Language
Behind you, star, big, real

Materials
Audio CD; Story cards

Optional materials
Props for acting out the story, e.g. glasses for Ruby, baseball cap and/or skateboard for Sam, black T-shirt for John, leopard mask for Jenny, toy snake, toy spider; Active Teach; Digital Activity Book; Photocopiable 6.4; image of King Kong; Reading and Writing Booklet

Starting the lesson

- Ask pupils (L1) what they can remember about the story from the previous episodes. Use the Unit 4 and 5 story cards as prompts.

 Pupil's Book page 66

Presentation

11 🔊 **Listen and read. Then act out.**

- Show the Unit 6 story cards one at a time and ask the *Before listening to the story* questions. Pupils predict what happens in the story.
- Play the recording. Pupils listen as they follow the story in their books. Ask if their predictions were correct and then ask the *After listening to the story* questions.
- Divide the class into four groups and assign a character to each. Pupils read their parts as a class.
- Ask pupils who would like to take the parts of the different characters. Invite volunteers to the front of the class to act out the story. Encourage tone of voice and expressions to match those in the pictures. Use props that you've brought to class if you wish.

Practice

- Shuffle the story cards and put them in random order on the board. With books closed, ask *Which is number one?* Pupils answer. Continue until all the story cards are in order.
- Show the story cards and retell the story, making some deliberate mistakes. Every time pupils spot a mistake, they put up their hands and correct it.

Values

- Say a few things you need for a hike in the hills, e.g. *a compass, water.* Read out the words in the Pupil's Book and help the pupils understand if necessary. Ask them to name as many things as they can remember.
- Organise the class in pairs. Pupils take it in turns to ask and answer about things they need for a hike in the hills. Discuss with the class the importance of being prepared.

Activity Book page 62

10 **Read the story again. Who's in a film? Write.**

- Elicit whether some pupils know the film *King Kong*. Show any images you have of the film, ideally the final scenes on the Empire State Building. Help them to describe the end of the film to other pupils: *It's about a gorilla. He climbed a building*, etc. They read the story again and write the answer to the question on the line.

11 **Number the pictures in order.**

- Direct pupils' attention to the pictures. Ask them to number the pictures in order. If they need to, they can refer to the main story illustration on PB p.66. Check answers with the class.

12 **Look at Activity 11 and write.**

- Pupils look at the pictures again. Allow them time to read the questions and answer them. When they have finished, ask individual pupils to read an answer each.

13 **Choose a picture from Activity 11 and write.**

- Direct pupils' attention to the pictures. Explain that they must choose one and write about it. They must say why they like (or don't like) it. Ask volunteers to read their texts.

Home-School Link

- Pupils make a list of things they do to prepare for a test, to show to their families. This could be done as a whole-class activity.

Ending the lesson

- Play *Guess who*: say some words spoken by the characters in the story or mime his/her actions, e.g. pretend to be pulling a snake away from you and say *It's really big!* Pupils guess who you are (*Sam*). Ask more confident pupils to act out another character for the class to guess.
- (For AB Answer Key, see p. 200.)

188

Be prepared.

HOME-SCHOOL LINK
Make a list of things you do to prepare for a test. Show your family.

OPTIONAL ACTIVITIES

Team game
Play *Spin the bottle* see p. 301.

My favourite film
Pupils draw a poster of their favourite film. Write on the board *My favourite film is ….* *It's got … in it.*

I like the … in it. Elicit ideas for completing the sentences. Then ask pupils to write similar sentences about the film they have drawn. Give help with extra vocabulary if necessary.
Photocopiable 6.4 see Teacher's notes p. 291.
Reading and Writing Booklet p. 17 see Answer Key p.282.

Lesson 6

Lesson aims
To learn the sounds and letters /ce/, /ci/ and /cir/

Target language
centre, princess, ice, rice, prince, city, circus, circle

Materials
Audio CD; Flashcards and Wordcards (Phonics); Phonics poster

Optional materials
Active Teach; Digital Activity Book; Photocopiable 6.5

Starting the lesson

- Show pupils the flashcards (phonics).
- Read the words aloud and ask pupils to find a common pattern.

Pupil's Book page 67

Presentation

12  **Listen and repeat.**

- Write on the board the sounds /ce/, /ci/ and /cir/. Play the recording for pupils to listen. Play it a second time for pupils to listen and repeat.

13 **Listen, point and say.**

- Tell the pupils that they must point to the sound that they hear. Play the recording for pupils to listen and point. Play it a second time for pupils to listen, point and say.

14 **Listen and blend the sounds.**

- Demonstrate the blending of the first sound; pupils repeat what they hear. Then tell them that they must listen and blend the sounds. Play the recording for pupils to listen and say the words that contain the corresponding sounds.

Practice

15 **Read the sentences aloud. Then find /ce/, /ci/ and /cir/.**

- The pupils read the sentences aloud. Then they find and point to the sounds /ce/, /ci/ and /cir/. Ask them to read out the words containing these sounds.

Activity Book page 63

14 **Read the words. Circle the pictures.**

- Give pupils time to read the words and circle the corresponding parts of the picture.

15 **Listen and connect the letters. Then write.**

- Play the recording and give the pupils time to draw the lines to connect the letters. Play the recording again, and give pupils time to write the words.

16 **Listen and write the words.**

- Play the recording, pausing if necessary to give pupils time to write the words. Play it again for them to check what they have written. Check answers.

17 **Read aloud. Then listen and check.**

- Ask different pupils to read the text aloud, one sentence each. Then play the recording: pupils listen and check.

Ending the lesson

- Give each pupil a piece of paper on which you have written one of the sounds from this lesson: /ce/, /ci/ and /cir/. Say words, some with and some without the new sounds. Pupils stand and hold up their piece of paper when they hear their sound, or words containing their sound.
- (For AB Answer Key, see p. 200. For Audioscript, see pp. 202–03.)

6

12 (2:60) **Listen and repeat.**

¹ **ce**   ² **ce**   ³ **ci**   ⁴ **cir**

13 (2:61) **Listen, point and say.**

14 (2:62) **Listen and blend the sounds.**

1 c - e - n - t - re   centre   2 p - r - i - n - c - e - ss   princess

3 i - ce   ice   4 r - i - ce   rice

5 p - r - i - n - ce   prince   6 c - i - t - y   city

7 c - ir - c - u - s   circus   8 c - ir - c - le   circle

15 **Read the sentences aloud. Then find *ce*, *ci* and *cir*.**

1 The prince is eating rice.   2 The princess likes ice in her drink.

3 This is the centre of the circle.   4 The circus is playing in the city for five nights.

CIRCUS

OPTIONAL ACTIVITES
Phonics game
Play *Odd one out* see p. 302.

Phonics game
Play *Snap* see p. 302.
Photocopiable 6.5 see Teacher's notes p. 291.

Lesson 7

Lesson aims
To connect other areas of the curriculum with English learning; to develop the cross-curricular topic through a short project

Cross-curricular focus
Geography (The Amazon Rainforest)

Target language
tapir, hummingbird, nectar, giant tarantula, parrot

Materials
Audio CD

Optional materials
World map or globe; pictures of animals; Active Teach; Digital Activity Book; CLIL poster; Photocopiable 6.6

Starting the lesson

- Play a guessing game. Divide the class into two teams. Call one pupil from Group A to the board. Whisper an animal word. He/She mimes the animal. His/Her group guesses what animal it is. If they guess correctly, they get a point.

 Pupil's Book page 68

Presentation

- Use a world map or globe. Ask *Where's the Amazon Rainforest?* Pupils guess (L1). Locate the Amazon Rainforest on the map. Say *It's in South America.*
- Focus on the pictures. Introduce *tapir* and *hummingbird* and revise the other animal words. Ask pupils (L1) what they know about the animals.

16 **Listen and read. Then say *True* or *False*.**

- Before pupils attempt sentences 1–5, play the recording while they follow in their books.
- Play it again. Ask comprehension questions, e.g. *Is the Amazon long or short? Have tapirs got long necks? What do hummingbirds drink? Where do tarantulas live?*
- Pupils must now listen to the text again and decide if the sentences are true or false. Allow pupils time to think about the answers, pausing the recording as necessary.
- To check answers, play the recording again and ask individual pupils to say *True* or *False*. Ask volunteers to correct the false sentences.
- Ask pupils to look at the Think! box and to talk about why the Amazon Rainforest is so important and special.

KEY 1 True, **2** False (They've got long tails), **3** False (They eat leaves and fruit), **4** True, **5** True

Mini-project

- Bring reference books to the class or, if conditions permit, use the internet. Divide the class into pairs and ask pupils to find names of other animals that live in the rainforest. Write the names on the board. Pairs choose two animals and work together looking for information about them. Then they make a mini poster with pictures and a written description, e.g. *(Animals) live in … They eat … They've got … They can … .*

Activity Book page 64

18 **Read and write.**

- Check meaning of the words in the word bank. Pupils then read the descriptions of the animals and write the name of each animal. Check as a class.

19 **Write about your favourite rainforest animal.**

- Focus pupils' attention on the description of the piranha. Help them understand some words if necessary. Then they follow the model to write their own descriptions. Ask a few pupils to read out their descriptions to the class. Pupils could do their own research using internet sites or reference sources that you recommend.

Ending the lesson

- Play *Odd one out*: write four animals on the board, e.g. parrot, hummingbird, swan, tarantula. Pupils decide which is the odd one out and give his/her reason, e.g. swan, because it doesn't live in the rainforest, or tarantula, because it hasn't got wings. There might be several correct answers.
- (For AB Answer Key, see p. 200. For Audioscript, see p. 203.)

16 **Listen and read. Then say *True* or *False*.**

The Amazon Rainforest

It's hot and wet in the Amazon Rainforest and there are a lot of tall trees. The Amazon River runs through the rainforest. It's very long. A lot of animals live in the rainforest and the river.

Hummingbirds
These birds are very small. They drink nectar from flowers. They like red, orange and yellow flowers.

nectar

Parrots
These birds have got very long tails. They're pretty colours.

Tapirs
These animals have got short necks and big ears. They live next to the river. They eat leaves and fruit. They love bananas.

Giant tarantulas
These big spiders have got long legs. They live under the leaves in the rainforest. They can eat a bird or a mouse.

1 It's hot and wet in the Amazon.

2 Parrots have got short tails.

3 Tapirs eat meat.

4 Hummingbirds like red, yellow and orange flowers.

5 Giant tarantulas live under leaves in the rainforest.

Why is the Amazon Rainforest special?

 **PROJECT** Find out about other animals that live in the Amazon Rainforest. Tell the class.

OPTIONAL ACTIVITIES

Imaginary animals
Pupils imagine a new animal for the rainforest. They draw the animal and write a description. Pupils ask each other questions about the animals, e.g. *Is it big or small? What colour is it?*

Team game
Play *Hide and seek* see p. 301.
Photocopiable 6.6 see Teacher's notes p. 292.

Lesson 8

Lesson aims
To learn about other cultures and respect cultural differences

Cross-cultural focus
To learn about world forests

Target language
Environment, pine tree

Materials
Audio CD

Optional materials
World map or globe; Active Teach; Digital Activity Book; CLIL poster; Photocopiable 6.7

Starting the lesson

- Write *world forest* on the board. Explain the meaning or show pictures to show the meaning. Elicit other words to do with forests and write them on the board.

Pupil's Book page 69

Presentation

- Focus on the photos. Say the names of the forests: *Irati Forest, Black Forest.* Ask pupils to repeat them.
- Pupils look at the texts, find the names of the countries where the children live and locate them on the map or globe.

17 **Listen and read.**

- Play the recording. Pupils listen and follow the texts in their books. Ask pupils to find the names of the children and the forests. Write them on the board.
- Ask a few comprehension questions: *Where's the Irati Forest? What can you do there? Where's the Black Forest? Is there a playground there?*

Practice

18 **Ask and answer.**

- Direct pupils' attention to the questions. Check that they understand. Organise the class in pairs. They take it in turns to ask and answer the questions. When they have finished, check answers with the class and accept the correct ones. Write them on the board.

> **KEY**
> 1 It's in the north of Spain.
> 2 It's in Germany.
> 3 You can go for a run or sit down and enjoy the natural environment. You can listen to the birds.
> 4 Yes, you can.

Portfolio project

- Ask pupils to think about the forests in their country.
- Pupils can write in their notebooks, using the texts on p. 69 as a model.

Activity Book page 65

20 **Look and write.**

- Ask the pupils to look at the pictures and the words in the word bank. They should write the words on the correct lines below the pictures. Check answers with the class.

21 **Look at Activity 20 and write.**

- Give the class time to complete the descriptions looking at the information in the previous activity. Check answers with the class: ask volunteers to read out their completed text.

Ending the class

- Play *Picture charades* see p. 298 with vocabulary for forests.
- (For AB Answer Key, see p. 200. For Audioscript, see p. 203.)

Wider World
World forests

17 **2:67** **Listen and read.**

> Hi! I'm Fernando and I live in Spain. There is a fantastic forest in the north of Spain called the Irati Forest. There are very tall trees and grass. There, you can go for a run or sit down and enjoy the natural environment. I go there every summer and I like listening to the birds.
>
> Fernando, 9, Spain

The Irati Forest

The Black Forest

> My name's Anka and I live near the Black Forest in Germany. There are many pine trees. It's a wonderful place to go walking or camping. There is a playground for children to do leisure activities. You can also do sports and climb trees.
>
> Anka, 10, Germany

18 **Ask and answer.**

1 Where's the Irati Forest?
2 Where's the Black Forest?
3 What can you do in the Irati Forest?
4 Can you do leisure activities in the Black Forest?

PORTFOLIO

Think and write.

Write about a forest near your house.

OPTIONAL ACTIVITIES

Pairwork game
Play *Snap* see p. 300 revising rainforests, weather and natural disasters.

Research
Divide the class into pairs. Tell pupils to look for information about forests in their country. They write sentences about them and draw pictures.
Photocopiable 6.7 see Teacher's notes p. 292.

Lesson 9

Lesson aims
To review the unit language with a game and the Picture Dictionary

Materials
Audio CD; Flashcards (Natural World, Prepositions)

Optional materials
Dice or spinners; Active Teach; Digital Activity Book; CLIL poster; Reading and Writing Booklet

Starting the lesson

- Divide the class into small groups. Say an animal from the vocabulary of this unit or one that is known to the class, and a verb, e.g. *tapir, walk*. Each group has to confer and come up with a sentence using the animal and the verb, e.g. *The tapir walked across the bridge.* Award points for correct sentences.

Pupil's Book page 70

19 Play.

- Revise the vocabulary using the flashcards (natural world, prepositions).
- Focus on the game board. Point out the colour code in the word bank and the coloured borders of the squares. Explain (L1) that when pupils land on a square they must say a sentence using words for that colour. Practise with the pupils the language to be used: *Where is/are ...? Could you/he/she/it/they ...? He/She/It/They could ... .*
- Pupils play in pairs or small groups.
- Pupils can use the Picture Dictionary (AB p. 109.)

Activity Book page 66

22 Look and write.

- Point out the sample answer in the crossword puzzle and make sure pupils understand how to use the sentence and picture clues. Ask, e.g. *What's number (two)?* Pupils answer. Pupils solve it individually or in pairs. Check as a class.

23 Listen and tick (✓).

- Direct pupils' attention to the pictures. Tell the class to listen and tick the correct picture in each case. When they have finished, check answers with the class.

Ending the lesson

- Play *Guess the card* see p. 299 using the vocabulary of this unit.
- (For AB Answer Key, see p. 200. For Audioscript, see p. 203.)

Play.

- ■ Where is/are …?
- ■ He/She/It/They could … the …
- □ Could he/she/it/they … the …?
- ■ Yesterday he/she/it/they …

 Start

1 	**2**	**3** he / hike	**4**
8 it / climb / Yes	**7** Loser misses a turn.	**6**	**5** fly
9 run	**10**	**11** he / swim / No	**12** Winner moves 1 space forward.
16	**15** it / walk	**14**	**13**

Finish

 Picture Dictionary

AB p.109

70 Lesson 9 review and consolidation

AB p.66

OPTIONAL ACTIVITIES

TPR
Display flashcards around the classroom, on walls and tables, and include instructions such as *Run to the mountains. Swim to the crocodile. Girls stand under the bridge. Boys sit next to the river*, etc.

Poster activity
See the notes on CLIL poster on p. 27.
Reading and Writing Booklet p. 18 see Answer Key p. 282.

Lesson 10

Lesson aims
To personalise and assess efforts

Materials
Audio CD

Optional materials
Digital Activity Book; CLIL poster; Online material – *Film Studio Island*; Active Teach; Grammar reference and Review for Unit 6 (PB p. 114 and AB p. 101); Test Booklet; Grammar Booklet

Starting the lesson

- This is a self assessment activity. Tell the pupils that the activities on this page will show what they have learnt in this unit.

Pupil's Book page 71

20 **Listen and point.**

- Tell the pupils that they must choose the correct picture for each question. Play the recording more than once if necessary.
- Pupils listen, look at the pictures and choose the correct picture.

> **KEY 1** a, **2** b, **3** b, **4** b, **5** b, **6** b, **7** a, **8** a

21 **Look, read and say.**

- Pupils read the gapped sentences. Point out the word *Yesterday* and ask them what form the verbs should have. Tell them to write the complete sentences in their notebooks or on the board, or ask them to say the sentences aloud.

> **KEY 1** played, **2** looked

Activity Book page 67

- Focus on the *I can* sentences at the bottom of the page. Tell the pupils that they have to tick the boxes, depending on whether they think they can do the *I can* points.

24 **Look and write.**

- Direct pupils' attention to the picture. Tell the class to look at it very carefully, and then read the sentences and questions. Tell pupils to find information in the picture to write the two questions and answer the two questions. Check the answers as a whole class.

25 **Imagine you were on the island in Activity 24. Write about what you could and couldn't do.**

- Direct pupils' attention to the picture in Activity 24.
- They write one sentence about what they could do on the island and one sentence about what they couldn't do.
- Ask volunteers to read out their sentences.

26 **Look and write. Then draw and write about you.**

- Focus pupils' attention on pictures 1 and 2 and gapped sentences 1 and 2. They must complete these sentences to describe pictures 1 and 2.
- Tell pupils to think of something they have done, e.g. last weekend, on holiday, last summer. They draw the activity in the space for picture 3 and complete sentence 3 to describe it. Allow pupils time to complete the activity and then ask volunteers to show their pictures and read their sentences. Vote for the best one.

Ending the lesson

- Play *Pass the wordcards* see p. 298 using the language of this unit, e.g. *The crocodile is under the bridge. Hippos have got short legs and big feet.*
- (For AB Answer Key, see p. 200. For Audioscript, see p. 203.)

> **OPTIONAL ACTIVITIES**
>
> **Team game**
> Play *Twenty seconds* see p. 300.
>
> **Prepositions race**
> Divide the class into two teams and tell them to stand in lines at one end of the room. Put two desks or large upturned boxes on the floor at the other end. Put some toys and flashcards relating to the vocabulary from Unit 6 on the floor in front of the first pupil of each row. Say, e.g. *Put the hill near the sea.* Blow a whistle or clap your hands to start. Pupils get the correct flashcards/toys and run to the other end of the room to place them as instructed, on their team's table/box, and run back to their lines. The first pupil to get back to the line gets a point for the team. If he/she gets the wrong item or puts it in the wrong place, the team gets no points. The game can be used to practise the prepositions *under, on, between, around, near*.

20 **2:69** **Listen and point.**

1  a  b   2  a  b

3  a  b   4  a  b

5  a  b   6  a  b

7  a  b   8  a  b

21 **Look, read and say.**

1  Yesterday the monkeys … (play) on the vines.

2  Yesterday I … (look) at a waterfall.

Prepositions challenge
Arrange some toys or flashcards at the front of the class, so that each thing is next to, under, on, in front of or behind something else. Pupils describe what they can see. Then divide the class into two teams. Ask Team 1 to face the opposite wall and close their eyes. Team 2 change the position of three things at the front of the class. Team 1 look at the things again and try to identify the three differences. Teams then swap roles.
Activity Book Review see p. 101.
Grammar Booklet p. 18 see Answer Key p. 285.
Test Booklet Unit 6 see Answer Key p. 295–6.
Online World
Pupils can now go online to *Film Studio Island* and enjoy the fun and games.

Activity Book Answer Key

p. 58, Activity 1

p. 58, Activity 2
1 across, river
2 over, mountain
3 near, river (Accept 'near the bridge'.)
4 hut, between, and

p. 59, Activity 3
1 near the vines
2 Where's the, across the bridge
3 Where's the, between the hut and the river
4 Where's the lion? It's over the mountain.

p. 59, Activity 4
Numbered order of pictures: a 1, b 3, c 4, d 2
a elephants, over the mountain
b Where are the crocodiles? They're near the waterfall.
c Where are the hippos? They're between the waterfall and the bridge.
d Where are the monkeys? They're across the bridge.

p. 60, Activity 5
1 lake / d, 2 sea / c, 3 hills / a, 4 coast / b, 5 past / g, 6 towards / e, 7 through / h, 8 around / f

p. 60, Activity 6
1 a, 2 a, 3 b, 4 a

p. 61, Activity 7
a 1 Yes, she could.
b 3 No, he couldn't.
c 4 No, they couldn't.
d 2 Yes, he could.

p. 61, Activity 8
1 ✗, 2 ✗, 3 ✓, 4 ✓
1 couldn't, could
2 couldn't, through
3 near, waterfall
4 could, around

p. 61, Activity 9
1 walked, 2 stayed, 3 climbed, 4 played

p. 62, Activity 10
Cleo is in the film *King Kong*.

p. 62, Activity 11
a 2, b 5, c 1, d 4, e 3

p. 62, Activity 12
1 Jenny, 2 Yes, she is. 3 behind, 4 It's near Ruby. (Accept 'It's behind Ruby'.) 5 No, it isn't. 6 Yes, he is.

p. 63, Activity 15
flag, glass, letter, sleep

p. 63, Activity 16
1 centre, 2 rice, 3 prince, 4 city

p. 64, Activity 18
1 tapir, 2 parrot, 3 hummingbird, 4 giant tarantula

p. 65, Activity 20
1 Forest: the Irati Forest; Country: Spain; Plants: tall trees and grass
2 Forest: the Black Forest; Country: Germany; Place: playground

p. 65, Activity 21
1 is the Irati, Spain, tall trees and grass
2 is the Black, Germany, playground

p. 66, Activity 22
Across: 1 coast, 3 lake, 5 waterfall, 7 vines
Down: 2 hut, 4 mountain, 6 nest, 8 bridge

p. 66, Activity 23
1 b, 2 a, 3 b, 4 b

p. 67, Activity 24
1 Where's the river?
2 Where are the elephants?
3 No, it isn't.
4 Yes, it is.

p. 67, Activity 26
1 walked
2 climbed a tree

Audioscript

Lesson 1 Activity 1   CD2:48

J = JENNY   S = SAM   R = RUBY   C = CLEO

J   Where are we?
S   Wow! It's a rainforest. Phew! It's hot.
J   Where's Madley Kool? Is he here?
S   Hey! That monkey has my baseball cap! ... Wait, where's Ruby?
J   There she is! On the bridge! She's scared.
R   Help! I don't want to fall in the river.
C   Mmm! What a pretty bird!
S   Come on, everybody. Let's go. I'm sure Madley is in the hut.
J   Yoohoo! Madley? Where are you?

Lesson 1 Activity 2   CD2:49

a   hut
b   bridge
c   nest
d   waterfall
e   valley
f   mountain
g   vines

Lesson 1 Activity 3   CD2:50

1   What's that?
    It's a hut.
2   Is it a mountain?
    Yes, it is.
3   I can see a bridge.
4   There's a waterfall.
5   There's one nest.

Lesson 2 Activity 4   CD2:51

Where's the gorilla?
It's over the mountain.
Where's the monkey?
It's across the river.
Where's the crocodile?
It's near the river.
Where is Madley Kool?
He's between you and the hut.
No, he isn't. Who are you trying to fool?

Lesson 2 Activity 5   CD2:52

1   Where's Ruby?
    She's between the crocodile and the monkey.
2   Where's the monkey?
    It's across the river.
3   Where's the hut?
    It's near the waterfall.
4   Where are the monkeys?
    They're over the mountain.

Lesson 2 Activity 4 (AB)   CD2:53

1   Where are the elephants?
    They're over the mountain.
2   Where are the monkeys?
    They're across the bridge.
3   Where are the crocodiles?
    They're near the waterfall.
4   Where are the hippos?
    They're between the waterfall and the bridge.

Lesson 3 Activity 6   CD2:54

a   around
b   through
c   towards
d   past
e   lake
f   sea
g   coast
h   hills

Lesson 3 Activity 7   CD2:55

Where are all the gorillas?
Let's watch them eat and play.
They're past the hills, across the bridge,
Around the lake and the trees.

We could walk through the valley,
Climb the bridge and watch them play.
Could I go near the gorillas?
Yes, you could but not so near.

Where are all the gorillas?
Let's watch them eat and play.
They're over the hill, next to the huts,
Across the waterfall.

Could I walk towards the valley,
Climb the hill and watch them play?
Yes, you could but be careful.
You could fall down the hill.

Lesson 4 Activity 9

CD2:56

Wednesday, August 20th

Hippos in the lake!

We are on holiday in Uganda. Yesterday my family and I visited Lake Victoria. We stayed in a hut near the lake. It was amazing. We looked at many hippos. They were in the lake. That's why we couldn't swim.

Thursday, August 21st

The Ugandan rainforest

Now we're visiting the rainforest in Uganda. It's great! Yesterday we hiked in the rainforest.

There were many different animals and plants but my favourites were the monkeys. They climbed and played in the trees. We wanted to see some gorillas but we couldn't find any.

Saturday, August 23rd

Awesome gorillas!

They're big, black and beautiful but there are only 600 mountain gorillas left in the world. Yesterday we walked through the forest and listened for them. We were very quiet. We could hear them and smell them, but we couldn't see them. Suddenly the gorillas were there! They were behind the trees. It was awesome!

Lesson 4 Activity 7 (AB)

CD2:57

1 I could run past the lions but I couldn't run through them.

2 I could walk towards the coast but I couldn't go over it.

3 I could walk around the lake but I couldn't swim through it.

4 We could walk over the hills but we couldn't go around them.

Lesson 4 Activity 8 (AB)

CD2:58

My family and I wanted to go to North Lake. We couldn't go by bus because it is very far but we could go by plane.

I loved North Park. It was beautiful. We couldn't swim through the lake because there were always so many people.

We stayed in one of the huts in the park. The huts were near the waterfall. We could walk through the waterfall. It was fun!

There were also wild animals in North Park. There were elephants, giraffes and hippos. We watched the lions. They were awesome. The lions were in the middle of the park. We could walk around them.

Lesson 6 Activity 12

CD2:60

c		e	
/s/		/s/	
c		e	
/s/	/e/	/s/	/e/
c		i	
/s/	/i/	/s/	/i/
c		i	r
/s/	/ir/	/s/	/ir/

Lesson 6 Activity 13

CD2:61

/s/	/e/	/s/	/e/
/s/	/ir/	/s/	/sir/
/s/	/i/	/s/	/i/
/s/	/e/	/s/	/e/
/s/	/ir/	/s/	/ir/
/s/	/s/		
/s/	/e/	/s/	/e/
/s/	/i/	/s/	/i/

Lesson 6 Activity 14

CD2:62

1 /s/ /e/ /n/ /t/ /er/
centre

2 /p/ /r/ /i/ /n/ /s/ /e/ /s/
princess

3 /i/ /s/
ice

4 /r/ /i/ /s/
rice

5 /p/ /r/ /i/ /n/ /s/
prince

6 /s/ /i/ /t/ /y/
city

7 /s/ /ir/ /k/ /u/ /s/
circus

8 /s/ /ir/ /k/ /l/
circle

Lesson 6 Activity 15 (AB)

CD2:63

1 /f//l/ /a/ /g/

2 /g/ /l/ /a/ /s/

3 /l//e/ /t/ /er/

4 /s/ /l/ ee/ /p/

Lesson 6 Activity 16 (AB)

CD2:64

1 centre

2 rice

3 prince

4 city

Lesson 6 Activity 17 (AB) CD2:65

The princess is at home and the circus is here. It's a sunny day and the circus is funny but the princess isn't happy. She wants to go to the city.

Lesson 7 Activity 16 CD2:66

The Amazon Rainforest

It's hot and wet in the Amazon Rainforest and there are a lot of tall trees. The Amazon River runs through the rainforest. It's very long. A lot of animals live in the rainforest and the river.

Parrots

These birds have got very long tails. They're pretty colours.

Tapirs

These animals have got short necks and big ears. They live next to the river. They eat leaves and fruit. They love bananas.

Hummingbirds

These birds are very small. They drink nectar from flowers. They like red, orange, and yellow flowers.

Giant tarantulas

These big spiders have got long legs. They live under the leaves in the rainforest. They can eat a bird or a mouse.

Lesson 8 Activity 17 CD2:67

Hi! I'm Fernando and I live in Spain. There is a fantastic forest in the north of Spain called the Irati Forest. There are very tall trees and grass. There, you can go for a run or sit down and enjoy the natural environment. I go there every summer and I like listening to the birds. Fernando, 9, Spain

My name's Anka and I live near the Black Forest in Germany. There are many pine trees. It's a wonderful place to go walking or camping. There is a playground for children to do leisure activities. You can also do sports and climb trees.Anka, 10, Germany

Lesson 9 Activity 23 (AB) CD2:68

1 Where are the monkeys?
They're near the valley.
2 Where are the monkeys?
They're between the hut and the river.
3 Where are the monkeys?
They're over the mountain.
4 Where are the monkeys?
They're under the bridge.

Lesson 10 Activity 20 CD2:69

1 Where's the bridge?
2 Where are the crocodiles?
3 Where are the hippos?
They're near the lake.
4 Where are the parrots?
Look! They're flying past the hill.
5 Where's the bus?
It's between the river and the hut.
6 Where's the bus?
It's going around the lake.
7 I could walk through the river.
8 I couldn't go over the hill.

7 Feelings

Objectives

- express actions connected to emotions
- talk about feelings
- talk about films
- talk about celebrations
- pronounce properly /ge/ and /dge/

Topics
- Actions
- Feelings and emotions
- Films

Phonics
/ge/ and /dge/

Values
- Help others in need

Stories
- Unit opener: emotions in films
- Story episode: feelings while filming

Language

Vocabulary
- Actions and emotions: crying, shouting, yawning, frowning, laughing, blushing, smiling, shaking
- Feelings: nervous, proud, relieved, surprised, relaxed, embarrassed, worried

Revision
hungry, thirsty, sad, happy, tired, angry, funny

Structures
Why is (he/she) (crying)?
(He's/She's) (crying) because (he's/she's) sad.
What's the matter?
I'm (nervous).
How do you feel?
I feel (nervous).
What makes you feel (nervous)?
(Tests) make me feel nervous.
Help me!
I can help you.
Put it in the box.
Give them a hug.
I = me, you = you, he = him, she = her, it = it, we = us, they = them

Wider World language
lantern, traditional dress, dragon dance

Songs and chants
- Chant
- Song about food likes and dislikes
- Karaoke song

Sociocultural aspects
- Finding out about celebrations around the world
- Being respectful with others' emotions and feelings
- Being aware of celebrations in the country where pupils live and the feelings they produce

Cross-curricular contents
- Social Science: understanding information about films
- Language Arts: reading a story, acting out, telling a story
- Language skills: reading and understanding a diagram

Learning strategies
- Using pictures to interpret information in a text
- Identifying rules about the use of adjectives to express feelings
- Understanding instructions
- Interpreting and organising information in a table
- Logical thinking: inferring ideas about feelings
- Critical thinking: thinking critically about one's own feelings
- Collaborative learning: project work and pair work
- Self assessment

Basic competences

- Linguistic communication: To use non-verbal language to express feelings and emotions (L1 to L4)
- Knowledge and interaction with the physical world: Observe the effect of music on feelings (L7)
- Mathematical competence: Identify other calendars (L8)
- Processing information and digital competence: Use *Film Studio Island* online component
- Social and civic competence: Help others when they need it (L5)
- Cultural and artistic competence: Express feelings that connect with popular activities in different parts of the world (L8)
- Learning to learn: Reflect on what has been learnt and self-evaluate progress (L10)
- Autonomy and personal initiative: Develop one's own criteria and social skills (L1 to L10)

Skills

Listening

- Identifying actions connected to emotions and feelings in recordings
- Understanding others talking about feelings
- Understanding specific information in a song about emotions
- Understanding general and specific information in a story
- Understanding specific information about celebrations in other countries

Reading

- Understanding information in sentences and short texts (feelings)
- Reading about Ricky and identifying true/false information
- Understanding general and specific information in a cartoon strip story
- Understanding specific information about films and matching text to pictures
- Answering questions about celebrations and feelings

Speaking

- Repeating words and sentences
- Chanting and singing
- Giving information about feelings and emotions
- Pronouncing /ge/ and /dge/ correctly

Writing

- Writing about feelings
- Making questions and answers from the words provided
- Describing pictures
- Transferring information from pictures to sentences
- Completing a table

Talking

- Asking and answering about feelings
- Taking part in dialogues about emotions and feelings
- Answering questions about feelings
- Role playing a story

Classroom ideas

- Decorate the class with flashcards and the cross-curricular poster
- Ask pupils to bring photos and pictures from the internet about feelings and emotions to decorate the classroom
- Display photos of popular celebrations in the country where pupils live
- Ask pupils in the class from other countries to talk about celebrations in their countries and their feelings
- Bring to the classroom library books about feelings
- Photocopiables

Take-home English

- Home-School Link
- Notes for Parents
- A sample of work each week
- Portfolio

Self assessment

- Pupils can express actions connected to emotions
- Pupils can talk about feelings
- Pupils can talk about films
- Pupils can talk about celebrations

Evaluation

- Pupil's Book page 81
- Activity Book page 77
- Photocopiable 7.7
- Picture Dictionary
- Test Booklet – Unit 7

7 Feelings

Lesson 1

Lesson aims
To present and practise new vocabulary

Target language
crying, shouting, yawning, frowning, laughing, blushing, smiling, shaking

Materials
Audio CD; Flashcards and Wordcards (Actions/Emotions)

Optional materials
Active Teach; Digital Activity Book; Photocopiable 7.1

Starting the lesson

- Write some previously learnt 'feelings' adjectives on the board: *happy, tired, sad, scared*. Then mime these feelings: smiling for *happy*, yawning for *tired*, crying for *sad*, pulling a scared face for *scared*. The class has to chorus *Aw, you're tired, Aw, you're sad, Aw, you're scared*, or *Hey, you're happy!* in response. Change from one to the other as quickly as possible. Add more adjectives, e.g. *hungry, angry*, if the game goes well.

> **Pupil's Book pages 72–73**

Presentation

- Hold up the flashcards in turn and say the words. Pupils repeat. Hold up the flashcards again, asking individual pupils to say the words.
- Pupils open their books. Focus on the main illustration. Ask questions: *Where are the children? Who's this? What's he/she doing?* Explain (L1) that the children are on a different film set, and the film is set in the countryside in the past.

Listen.

- Tell pupils (L1) they are going to listen to a recording describing the main illustration. Play the recording while pupils look at the illustration. Now tell them they will listen again and they should point to the relevant parts of the illustration as they listen. Play the recording again while they point.

Practice

2   Listen and repeat.

- Play the recording, pausing after each word. Pupils point to the pictures a–h. Play the recording again. Pupils point and repeat each word.
- Practise associating the feelings adjectives with the *-ing* verbs. Say, e.g. *She's scared.* Pupils respond *Picture h – she's shaking*. Demonstrate and then continue as a whole-class activity. (Exclude picture f unless you want to pre-teach *embarrassed*.)

3   Listen and say *True* or *False*.

- Ask pupils to look at the main illustration.
- Play the recording. Pupils have to find the corresponding pictures and point to them. Then they say whether the statements are *True* or *False*.

> **KEY 1** False, **2** False, **3** True, **4** True, **5** False

4 🔊 3.04 **Listen and chant.**

Why is she smiling?
Because she's happy.
Why is she crying?
Because she's sad.
Why is he drinking?
Because he's thirsty.
Why is he eating?
Because he's hungry.
Why is he shouting?
Because he's angry.
Why is she laughing?
Because it's funny!

LOOK!

| Why are you crying? | I'm crying because I'm sad. |
| Why is he/she smiling? | He's/She's smiling because he's/she's happy. |

5 🔊 3.05 **Listen and point. Then ask and answer.**

scared   happy   sad   tired   angry

a   b   c   d   e

frowning

shaking

Picture a. Why is she ...?

She's ... because she's ...

Lesson 2 grammar (Why are you crying?)   AB p.69   **73**

Ending the lesson

- Play *Mime and guess*: divide the class into pairs. They take it in turns to choose a character from the main illustration on PB p. 72. They mime what the characters are doing. The other pupil guesses who it is, what they are doing and how they are feeling, e.g. *You're Ruby. You're looking at Favolina Jolly. You're excited and you're shouting.*
- (For AB Answer Key, see p. 226. For Audioscript, see p. 227.)

(For AB Answer Key, see p. 226. For Audioscript, see p. 227.)

OPTIONAL ACTIVITIES

Pairwork game
Play *Matching pairs* see p. 300.

Word map
Draw a word map with the class. Draw a circle and write *Feelings* in it. Brainstorm with the class words for feelings they have learnt in this lesson. Then elicit situations when pupils have these feelings, and write them on the board too, e.g. for *scared*, write *There's a spider,* and for *tired*, write *It's eleven o'clock at night and I'm not sleeping.* Pupils can copy them into their notebooks.
Photocopiable 7.1 see Teacher's notes p. 292.

NOTES

Activity Book page 68

1 **Look and write.**

- Direct pupils' attention to the pictures and the word bank. Tell them to copy the correct word under each picture. Check as a class.

2 **Draw the correct faces.**

- Tell pupils to read the description for each picture. Check that they understand. They have to make drawings following each description. When they have finished, ask them to show their pictures to their partners.

Lesson 2

Lesson aims
To learn and practise the new structure

Target language
Why are you (crying)? I'm (crying) because I am (sad). Why is he/she (crying)? He's/She's (crying) because he's/she's (sad).

Materials
Audio CD; Flashcards and Wordcards (Actions/Emotions)

Optional materials
Props, e.g. glasses for Ruby, necklace for Jenny, handkerchief for Favolina, water jug and glass for John; Active Teach; Digital Activity Book; Grammar Booklet

Starting the lesson

• Use the flashcards to revise the vocabulary from the previous lesson.
• Elicit some feelings adjectives and -ing words from pupils; you could start them off by writing examples on the board. Then nominate a confident pupil to be the 'director', and you are the actor. Explain the game (L1): the director must say one of the feelings words to you, and you must mime the feeling/action. Pupils chorus *Yes!* if you get it right. Sometimes do the wrong action/expression, and pupils chorus *No!* Change the director after a few goes.

Pupil's Book page 73

Presentation

• Read the sentences in the Look! box. Explain that we use *why* for the question and *because* for the answer. Ask pupils to give a few more examples. Write them on the board. They could copy them into their notebooks.
• Tell pupils that they must ask you *Why* questions. Mime an action, e.g. crying. Turn to a confident pupil, who should ask *Why are you (crying)?* Answer: *Because I'm sad.* Write this exchange on the board and practise it with the class. Do this with another two or three feelings/expressions and then nominate a confident pupil to have a turn miming.
• Divide the class into pairs. Pupil A mimes an action from the chant: *crying, smiling, shouting* or *laughing*. Pupil B asks *Why are you ...?* Pupil A answers *Because I'm ... .* Then Pupil B mimes an action.

4 Listen and chant.

• Play the recording. Pupils listen and follow the words. Play it again, pausing after each line. Pupils repeat. Play it a third time. Pupils chant together. Use the pictures to help prompt the words if necessary.

Practice

5 Listen and point. Then ask and answer.

• Focus on the pictures of the characters and the feelings they express. Tell pupils to listen and point to the corresponding character in each case. Play the recording once. Pupils just listen. Play it again for the pupils to listen and point. Check as a class.
• Explain the second part of the activity. Focus their attention on the model dialogue. Organise the class in pairs. Pupil A ask a question: *Why is she crying?* Pupil B answers. Then they swap.

KEY **1** b happy, **2** d tired, **3** c angry, **4** e scared, **5** a sad

Act out

Play CD3:04 again and ask pupils to help you write it on the board. Read it as a class. Divide the class into groups of five pupils and assign a character to each group member. Groups rehearse their parts and then act out the dialogues. They could use props, e.g. glasses for Ruby, necklace for Jenny, loudspeaker (cone of paper), handkerchief for Favolina.

Team game

Play *Anagrams* see p. 301 to revise spelling of the unit vocabulary.

Grammar Booklet p. 19 see Answer Key p. 285.

NOTES

Activity Book page 69

3 **Listen and number.**

- Direct pupils' attention to the picture. Tell pupils to listen and number accordingly. Check by asking a pupil to say the numbers in order across the picture. Play the recording.

4 **Write.**

- Tell pupils to read the words carefully. Then focus on the example. Tell the class to write the other questions and the answers.
- Check as a class. Ask pairs of pupils to read the questions and the answers.

Ending the lesson

- Working in pairs, pupils take turns to ask and answer the questions from Activity 4 in AB p. 69.
- (For AB Answer Key, see p. 226. For Audioscript, see p. 227.)

Lesson 3

Lesson aims
To extend the vocabulary set (more feelings); to practise the unit language with a song

Target language
nervous, proud, relieved, surprised, relaxed, embarrassed, worried

Materials
Audio CD; Flashcards and Wordcards (Actions/Emotions)

Optional materials
Pictures of people with varying feelings; Active Teach; Digital Activity Book; Photocopiables 7.2–7.3; Reading and Writing Booklet

Starting the lesson

- Use photos, e.g. from TV magazines, of people looking happy/sad/angry, etc. Either hold them up and ask pupils to describe them (*She's smiling, she's happy*) or, if you have enough pictures, give one to each pupil or pair and they must describe it to the class.

Pupil's Book page 74

Presentation

- Bring a variety of pictures and/or flashcards from earlier units to illustrate things that make you feel happy/scared/excited/sad. Show an image of something you really like, e.g. the sea, look very happy and say *The sea makes me feel happy*. Show a picture of something scary, e.g. a big spider, and say *Spiders make me feel scared*. Repeat with *feel angry/sad*. Make appropriate gestures to make meaning clear.
- Personalise the language by showing the pictures again and saying to individual pupils, e.g. *Spiders make me feel scared. What about you?*

6 🔊 **Listen and repeat.**

- Introduce the new words (*nervous, proud*, etc.) using the flashcards. Hold them up and say the words for pupils to repeat. Ask individual pupils to say the words. Play the recording for pupils to listen and repeat.
- Now put the flashcards on the board. Point to the different flashcards and ask the class to say the words.

Song

7   **Listen and point. Then sing.**

- Pre-teach *naughty*. Play the recording once. Pupils listen and follow the words of the song in the book. Play the song again. Pupils point to the correct coloured words when they hear them.
- Play the song again a few times. Encourage pupils to join in and sing together. You can now play the karaoke song (Active Teach).

Practice

8 **Ask and answer.**

- Direct pupils' attention to the Look! box. Read the question and answers with the class. Explain that they use *make(s) you/me* with either *feel* + a feeling, e.g. *happy, sad, angry*, or with an action, e.g. *cry, laugh*. Read the Look! box to pupils.
- Look together at the words and phrases in the Look! box. Ask pupils for suggestions of places/people/events that make them feel these things. Then read out the question and answer in the speech bubbles and pupils repeat.
- Divide the class into pairs. Pupils ask and answer questions using the words and phrases in the Look! box.

Activity Book page 70

5 **Look and write.**

- Pupils write the correct feeling from the word bank under each picture. Check as a class. Point to a picture and ask *How does he/she feel?* Pupils answer.

6 **Look and write.**

- Direct pupils' attention to the pictures. Then focus on the questions and tell the class to write a sentence about each picture. Explain that there is more than one possible answer for each picture. Check as a class. Ask a few pupils to read the sentences to the class.

Ending the lesson

- Divide the class into four groups. All groups sing the questions, and each group sings the answers of one verse. Swap verses until all the groups have sung all the verses.
- (For AB Answer Key, see p. 226. For Audioscript, see p. 227.)

6 🔊 3:07 **Listen and repeat.**

nervous

proud

relieved

surprised

relaxed

embarrassed

worried

7 🔊 3:08 **Listen and point. Then sing.**

SONG

What makes you feel
proud happy ? (x2)
Sunny days.
Sunny days and holidays
Make me feel happy.

What makes you
nervous cry ? (x2)
Sad films.
Sad films and long goodbyes
Make me cry.

What makes you feel
scared worried ? (x2)
Big storms.
Big storms and green monsters
Make me feel scared.

What makes you
laugh smile ? (x2)
My friends.
My friends and
naughty monkeys
Make me laugh.

LOOK!

What's the matter?	I'm nervous.
How do you feel?	I feel ill/sick.
What makes you feel nervous?	Tests make me feel nervous.

8 **Ask and answer.**

What makes you feel ...?

... make me ...

OPTIONAL ACTIVITIES

Young songwriters
Pupils work in groups to write new verses for the song, similar to the original verses but with other things that make them happy/sad/scared, etc. Groups report their work and the class chooses the best three verses.

Flashcard game
Play *Echo* see p. 299 with feelings.
Photocopiable 7.2 see Teacher's notes p. 292.
Photocopiable 7.3 see Teacher's notes p. 292.
Reading and Writing Booklet p. 19 see Answer Key p. 282.

Lesson 4

Lesson aims
To develop reading, writing, listening and speaking skills; to learn and practise the new structure: 'I can help you' (object pronouns)

Target language
Tell me a story. Give him a present.

Materials
Audio CD

Optional materials
Active Teach; Digital Activity Book; Grammar Booklet

Starting the lesson
- Sing the song from Lesson 3 CD3:08 as a whole-class activity, miming the feelings.

Pupil's Book page 75

Presentation
- Focus on the photos of Ricky that go with the text. Ask the class to give you as much information as they can about Ricky: *Ricky is playing the guitar. He's got long hair*, etc. Write sentences on the board.

Skills

 Listen and read. Then say *True* **or** *False.*

- Focus on the article. Ask the class (L1) if they have visited any websites of their favourite singers or actors. Play the recording.
- Point to the picture of Ricky. Ask *Who makes Ricky laugh? What makes him feel relaxed?* Pupils read the text and find the answers.
- Focus the pupils' attention on sentences 1–4. Check that they understand. They read and decide if they are true or false. Change false sentences into true sentences.

> **KEY** **1** False (They make him feel relaxed.), **2** True **3** True, (It makes him feel relaxed.), **4** False (His friends make him feel relaxed.)

10 Read and say.

- Focus the pupils' attention on the Look! box. Pupils read the sentences. Help them understand if necessary. Explain that *me, you, her, him, it, us, them* are object pronouns. Help them to find the link with personal pronouns: *I, you, he, she, it, we, you, they.*

- Focus on the first sentence: *Help me!* and check the meaning. Do the same with the other sentences. Elicit more examples from the pupils and write them on the board. Pupils can copy them into their notebooks.
- Pupils choose the object pronouns to correct the sentences. Tell them they must use all the pronouns. Ask pupils to read the sentences aloud, including the pronoun. Demonstrate with the first one as an example.

> **KEY** **1** her, **2** us, **3** him, **4** them, **5** it, **6** me

Activity Book page 71

7 **Listen and tick (✓).**

- Play the recording once. Pupils listen while focusing on the pictures. Play it again. Pupils tick the correct picture. Play it a third time. Pupils check their answers.

8 Look at Activity 7 and write.

- Focus the pupils' attention on the word bank. Explain that they must look at the pictures they ticked in Activity 7, for each question. Then they must choose the correct words from the word bank to complete the questions and answers. Focus on the example. Give pupils time to complete the sentences. To check, ask individual pupils to read the questions and answers to the class.

9 Match and write.

- Pupils match the pairs of sentences by drawing linking lines, as in the example.
- Tell them to write the correct object pronouns in the spaces. They can look at the Look! box on PB p. 75 to revise object pronouns. Check answers with the class.

Ending the lesson

- As a whole-class activity, elicit eight things that make pupils feel happy. Show these at the foot of a bar chart grid on the board. Pupils work in groups to gather information about which ones make them feel happy. While they are working, add numbers at the side of the chart, depending on the size of your class. They report to you and you compile the information to create a class survey. What is most important to make you feel happy?
- (For AB Answer Key, see p. 226. For Audioscript, see p. 228.)

 Pupils can now go online to *Film Studio Island* and find the camera that Cleo is holding. It is the film camera just inside the Wild West Studio. Once pupils click on the camera they are taken to a supplementary language game based on the vocabulary in this unit.

9 🔊 3:09 **Listen and read. Then say** *True* **or** *False.*

Ricky Fansite!

Dear Ricky,
What makes you feel relaxed?
Sam

Hi Sam,
Dancing and singing make me feel relaxed. My family, my uncle, my aunt, my grandmother and grandfather make me feel relaxed because they make me laugh. My friends make me feel relaxed too. We go skateboarding and play computer games together. It's fun. What makes you feel relieved?
Ricky

Finishing all my homework makes me feel relieved. Passing a test makes me feel relieved and proud. But I feel surprised when I pass a Maths test. What makes you feel embarrassed?
Sam

Failing a test makes me feel embarrassed. Sometimes, my mother makes me feel embarrassed. She kisses me and hugs me in front of my friends. Does your mum do that too?
Ricky

1 Dancing and singing make Ricky feel embarrassed.

2 Finishing all his homework makes Sam feel relieved.

3 Passing a test makes Sam feel proud.

4 Ricky's friends don't make him feel relaxed.

LOOK!

Help me!	I can help you.
Put it in the box.	Give them a hug.

I – me, you – you, he – him, she – her, it – it, we – us, they – them

10 **Read and say.**

me   her   him   it   them   us

1 She's sad. Give … a hug.

2 We're bored. Tell … a story!

3 It's his birthday. Give … some cake

4 Tidy up the toys. Put … in a box.

5 The cat is hungry. Give … some food.

6 I can't do it. Can you help …?

OPTIONAL ACTIVITIES

Flashcard game
Play *Echo* see p. 299 to revise the feelings vocabulary of this unit.

Pairwork game
Play *Snap* see p. 300.
Grammar Booklet p. 20 see Answer Key p. 285.

Lesson 5

Lesson aims
To consolidate the unit language with a story

Value
Help others in need.

Receptive language
always, diver, seals, turtles, They're six metres long.

Materials
Audio CD; Story cards; Characters' Story cards

Optional materials
Pictures of scary animals and predators; Active Teach; Digital Activity Book; Photocopiable 7.4; Reading and Writing Booklet

Starting the lesson

- Ask pupils (L1) what they can remember about the story from the previous episode. Use the story cards from the previous unit as prompts.

Pupil's Book page 76

Presentation

11 3:11 **Listen and read. Then act out.**

- Show the Unit 7 story cards one at a time and ask the *Before listening to the story* questions. Pupils predict what happens in the story.
- Play the recording. Pupils listen as they follow the story in their books. Ask if their predictions were correct and then ask the *After listening to the story* questions.
- Divide the class into two groups and assign a character – John or Ruby – to each. The groups chorus their parts.
- Ask pupils who would like to take the parts of the different characters. Invite volunteers to the front of the class to act out the story. Encourage tone of voice and expressions to match those in the pictures. Use props that you've brought to class if you wish.

Practice

- Shuffle the story cards and put them in random order on the board. With books closed, ask *Which is number one?* Pupils answer. Continue until all the story cards are in order.
- Show the story cards and retell the story, making some deliberate mistakes. Every time pupils spot a mistake, they put up their hands and correct it.

Values

- Say a few ways to help others when they need it, e.g. *Help with Maths problems.* Ask them to say how they help others. Write some examples on the board.

- Organise the class in pairs. Pupils take it in turns to ask and answer about ways to help other people. Discuss (L1) the importance of helping others.

Activity Book page 72

10 **Read the story again. What is 'PLEH'? Write.**

- The pupils can read the story again, focusing on the last two frames, if they need support to work out that PLEH is HELP written backwards. They write the answer on the line.

11 **Look and write. Number the pictures in order.**

- Direct pupils' attention to the pictures. If they cannot number them from memory they can look back at the story on PB p. 76.
- Direct pupils' attention to the sentence bank. Point out the example answer under picture a and tell them to cross out this sentence in the sentence bank. Make sure they understand that they must copy the other sentences from the sentence bank under the correct pictures. Check answers with the class.

12 **Write about animals and how they make you feel.**

- Elicit animals that pupils are scared of, and why. Tell them the same information for yourself. Point out how to complete sentence 1, and tell them to complete all the sentences with their personal information. When they have finished, ask a few pupils to read their work to the class.

13 **Find out about one of the animals in Activity 12. Then write.**

- Pupils read the gapped sentences, think about an animal they are scared of and complete the description. Ask the pupils to tell their partners about their animals.

Home-School Link

- Tell pupils to think about the actions they do to help other people who need it. Give pupils a sheet of paper and ask them to draw a picture of themselves helping someone. When they have finished, they write a few sentences describing it. Then they make a list of five things they can do to help people in need. They show their family.

Ending the lesson

- Work with PB p. 76. Say the name of a character and the number of a frame, e.g. *Ruby, 4.* Pupils look at the corresponding frame in the book and read and act out the lines of the character. Encourage them to act scared or excited as necessary.
- (For AB Answer Key, see p. 226.)

Help others in need.

HOME-SCHOOL LINK
Make a list of five things you can do to help people in need. Show your family.

OPTIONAL ACTIVITIES

Predators
Explain the word *predator* and elicit some examples, giving the names in English if necessary. In small groups pupils make a mini poster about a predator, giving information from reference books or the internet and including pictures.

Pairwork game
Play *Matching pairs* see p. 300.
Photocopiable 7.4 see Teacher's notes p. 292.
Reading and Writing Booklet p. 20 see Answer Key p. 282.

Lesson 6

Lesson aims
To learn the sounds and letters /ge/ and /dge/

Target language
gem, gentleman, page, large, edge, badge, hedge, bridge

Materials
Audio CD; Flashcards and Wordcards (Phonics); Phonics poster

Optional materials
Active Teach; Digital Activity Book; Photocopiable 7.5

Starting the lesson

- Show pupils the flashcards (phonics).
- Read the words aloud and ask pupils to find a common pattern.

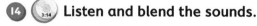

Presentation

 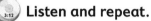 **Listen and repeat.**

- Write on the board the sounds /ge/ and /dge/. Play the recording for pupils to listen. Play it a second time for pupils to listen and repeat.

13 **Listen, point and say.**

- Tell the pupils that they must point to the sound that they hear. Play the recording for pupils to listen and point. Play it a second time for pupils to listen, point and say.

14 **Listen and blend the sounds.**

- Demonstrate the blending of the first sound; pupils repeat what they hear. Then tell them that they must listen and blend the sounds. Play the recording for pupils to listen and say the words that contain the corresponding sounds.

Practice

15 **Read the sentences aloud. Then find /ge/ and /dge/.**

- The pupils read the sentences aloud. Then they find and point to the sounds /ge/ and /dge/. Ask them to read out the words containing these sounds.

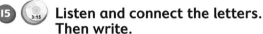

14 **Read the words. Circle the pictures.**

- Give pupils time to read the words and circle the corresponding parts of the picture.

15  **Listen and connect the letters. Then write.**

- Play the recording and give the pupils time to draw the lines to connect the letters. Play the audio again and give pupils time to write the words.

16 **Listen and write the words.**

- Play the recording, pausing if necessary to give pupils time to write the words. Play it again for them to check what they have written. Check answers.

17 **Read aloud. Then listen and check.**

- Ask different pupils to read the text aloud, one sentence each. Then play the recording: pupils listen and check.

Ending the lesson

- Divide the class into two groups. Give each group a sound from this lesson: /ge/ and /dge/. Say words, some with and some without the new sounds. Pupils stand when they hear their sound, or words containing their sound.
- (For AB Answer Key, see p. 226. For Audioscript, see p. 228.)

PHONICS

12 (3:12) **Listen and repeat.**

¹ **ge**   ² ge   ³ **dge**

13 (3:13) **Listen, point and say.**

14 (3:14) **Listen and blend the sounds.**

1 **g** – e – m   gem   2 **g** - e - n - t - le - m - a - n gentleman

3 p – a – ge   page   4 l – ar – ge   large

5 e – dge   edge   6 b – a – dge   badge

7 h – e – dge   hedge   8 b – r – i – dge   bridge

15 **Read the sentences aloud. Then find *ge* and *dge*.**

1 The large dog runs under the hedge …

2 … and over the bridge.

3 Then it runs along the edge of the lake.

4 The gentleman yells, 'Gem! Come back!'

OPTIONAL ACTIVITIES

Phonics game
Play *Hunting for letter sounds* see p. 302.

Phonics game
Play *Sound spy* see p. 302.
Photocopiable 7.5 see Teacher's notes pp. 292–3.

Lesson 7

Lesson aims
To connect other areas of the curriculum with English learning; to develop the cross-curricular topic through a short project

Cross-curricular focus
Music and feelings

Target language
How does (it/music) make you feel?

Materials
Audio CD; Flashcards

Optional materials
A recording of music suitable for a film; Active Teach; Digital Activity Book; CLIL poster; Photocopiable 7.6

Starting the lesson

- Show a flashcard (wild animals, weather conditions or leisure activities) to a pupil. The pupil mimes his/her feeling about it, e.g. show the *rain* flashcard and the pupil mimes *sad*. The rest of the class guesses the feeling, e.g. *Rainy days make (name) feel sad.* Repeat with other flashcards and other pupils.

Pupil's Book page 78

Presentation

- Ask pupils (L1) if they like music and what kind of music they like. Ask *Who's your favourite singer? What's your favourite group?*
- Ask (L1) if they ever notice the music in films. Do they have any favourite film music? Discuss (L1) how music in films can help to set the atmosphere.

 16 **Listen to the music. Then say how it makes you feel.**

- Play the recording. Stop after each piece of music and ask several pupils *How does it make you feel?* Pupils answer. Read the words for feelings and check that pupils understand all of them.
- Play the recording again, stopping after each piece of music. Pupils choose and say the word which represents how the music makes them feel. Help with other vocabulary if necessary. Pupils can compare in pairs to see if they chose the same words.

> **KEY** Pupils' personal answers, but most likely responses are as follows: **1** scared, **2** excited/happy, **3** sad, **4** happy

 17 **Listen, read and find.**

- Play the recording while pupils follow the text of the film descriptions.
- Direct pupil's attention to the posters and explain that they are posters of films. Pupils read the descriptions again and match them to the correct posters.

> **KEY 1** d, **2** b, **3** a, **4** c

Practice

Think!

- Focus pupils' attention on the Think! box and ask them to read the list. Ask them to list a song that makes them feel happy; a film that makes them laugh; and a film character that makes them feel scared.

Mini-project

- Give examples of what makes you feel happy, angry and scared: *(X) makes me feel (scared) because … .* Elicit (L1) ideas about what makes pupils feel those emotions. Give pupils some extra vocabulary to write their mini-projects. On A4 paper, pupils write about what makes them feel happy, scared or angry. They may illustrate their work. Display the mini-projects around the class and give pupils time to read each other's work.

Activity Book page 74

 18 **Circle. Then listen to the music and number.**

- Explain that the sentences describe the pictures, which are scenes from four films. The pupils look at the film scenes and circle the correct words in the sentences.
- Pupils then listen to the music and number the pictures in order. Check answers with the class.

19 **Write the name of a song, singer or band.**

- Elicit from the class the names of songs, singers or groups that they like. Write some of the names on the board. Ask for examples of music that make them feel relaxed, sad, etc.
- Tell the class to read the questions and write the name of a song, singer or band for each feeling. Read out the questions and check that the pupils understand. To check, ask pupils to read their answers. See if other pupils have the same choices.

Ending the lesson

- Play a game in pairs, using a selection of flashcards from Units 1–4. Pupil A turns over a card. Pupil B asks *How does it make you feel?* Pupil A answers *(Riding my bike) makes me feel (happy)* or *(Giraffes) make me (laugh).* Then they swap roles.
- (For AB Answer Key, see p. 226. For Audioscript, see pp. 228–9.)

16 3:18 **Listen to the music. Then say how it makes you feel.**

1 scared	nervous	worried	Other: …
2 relaxed	happy	excited	Other: …
3 nervous	angry	sad	Other: …
4 happy	relieved	relaxed	Other: …

17 3:19 **Listen, read and find.**

a
It's the end of the film. They're at the railway station. They're friends and they're saying goodbye. They're crying. It makes me feel sad. It makes me cry too.

b
There are a lot of people. They're laughing. They're learning to dance. The music is great. It makes me feel relaxed and happy. I want to sing and dance.

c
There are two boys. They're having a lot of fun. They're funny. They make me laugh.

d
There's a big, green monster. The monster has got big, sharp teeth. It makes me feel scared. That's why I'm shaking.

THINK!

Make a list:
• a song that makes you feel happy
• a film that makes you laugh
• a film character that makes you feel scared

MINI-PROJECT Write a blog post about what makes you feel proud.

OPTIONAL ACTIVITIES

Young film makers
Play a piece of music. Tell pupils (L1) to think of an idea for a film scene or story with this music in. Write on the board *Our film is about … It happens in … The film stars in it are … .* Pupils complete the sentences about their film.

Film posters
In groups, pupils invent a title for a film and create an A3 poster about it.
Photocopiable 7.6 see Teacher's notes p. 293.

Lesson 8

Lesson aims
To learn about other cultures and respect cultural differences

Cross-cultural focus
To learn about festivals

Target language
dragon dance, lantern, traditional dress

Materials
Audio CD

Optional materials
World map or globe; Active Teach; Digital Activity Book; CLIL poster; Photocopiable 7.7

Starting the lesson

- Write the word *Festivals* on the board and ask the pupils to suggest as many names of festivals as they can.

Pupil's Book page 79

Presentation

- Focus on the photos. Ask pupils to describe what they see in the photos. Ask them if they have a similar celebration in their country.
- Pupils look at the texts, find the names of the countries where the children live and locate them on the map or globe.

18 Listen and read.

- Direct pupils' attention to the pictures. Ask them to guess (L1) where these people are from. Then play the recording once. Pupils listen and follow in their books to find out the children's names and where they are from.
- Use the photos to present *lantern, dragon dance* and *traditional dress*. Play the recording again.

Practice

- Divide the class into pairs. Each pupil writes a sentence or sentences about the information they have heard and read in the texts (Activity 18). Provide some sentence starters, e.g. *He likes ... Lunar New Year makes her ...* . Then they read their sentences to their partner, who says which child it describes, Zhi or Diego.
- Ask some pupils to read out a sentence to the class. The class says who the sentence refers to, Zhi or Diego.

19 Ask and answer.

- Direct pupils' attention to the questions. Check that they understand. Organise the class in pairs. They take it in turns to ask and answer the questions. When they have finished, check answers with the class. Write some of them on the board.

KEY
1 Lunar New Year makes her feel happy because it's fun.
2 In January or February.
3 They clean their houses and visit family and friends.
4 Dancing makes him feel happy because it's good exercise.
5 They are wearing traditional dress and hats.

Portfolio project

- Ask the pupils to think about a festival or activity in their country that makes them feel happy.
- Pupils can write in their notebooks, using the texts on page 79 as a model.

Activity Book page 75

20 Read and match.

- Focus on the photos. Ask pupils to describe what they see in the photos. Ask them to read the blogs and match the blog texts to the photos. Check answers.
- Use the photo to present *choir*.

21 Read and write

- Focus on the questions. Pupils read the texts again to find the information. They write the answers. Check answers with the class.

Ending the lesson

- Play a guessing game. Say a sentence about one of the festivals in this lesson and pupils guess which one it is, e.g. *It's in January or February. It is the spring festival. You can see dragons and lanterns (Chinese New Year). It's in Canada. It's in winter (Winter Carnival). You can ice skate, eat pancakes and drink hot chocolate.*
- (For AB Answer Key, see p. 226. For Audioscript, see p. 229.)

Wider World
Cultural traditions

18 **Listen and read.**

1 Zhi's blog ✕

lantern

I'm Zhi. I'm from China. Lunar New Year makes me feel happy because it's fun. It's in January or February and it's called the Spring Festival. There are dragons and pretty lanterns. We clean our houses, then we visit family and friends.

Zhi, 10, China

dragon dance

2 Diego's blog ✕

traditional dress

I'm Diego. I'm from Peru. Dancing makes me feel happy because it's good exercise. I dance at a special dance club. Here I am with my friend. We're dancing and wearing traditional dress and hats. Do you like our clothes?

Diego, 10, Peru

19 Ask and answer.

1 What makes Zhi feel happy? Why?
2 When is Spring Festival?
3 What do people do during the festival?
4 What makes Diego feel happy? Why?
5 What are he and his friend wearing?

PORTFOLIO

Think and write.

Write about a festival or activity that makes you feel happy.

Lesson 8 wider world (cultural traditions) *AB p.75* **79**

OPTIONAL ACTIVITIES

TPR game
Play *Pass the ball* see p. 300 using the vocabulary of feelings, activities and months.

Drawing activity
Play *Alternative bingo* see p. 299. Pupil A describes a child at a festival, including the clothes that he/she is wearing, and Pupil B draws the scene. Then they swap roles.
Photocopiable 7.7 see Teacher's notes p. 293.

Lesson 9

Lesson aims
To review the unit language with a game and the Picture Dictionary

Materials
Audio CD; Flashcards (Actions/Emotions)

Optional materials
Game counters; Active Teach; Digital Activity Book; CLIL poster; Reading and Writing Booklet

Starting the lesson

- Play the chant from Lesson 2 CD3:04. Divide the class into two groups and do the chant. Group A chants the questions and Group B chants the answers. Then swap roles.

Pupil's Book page 80

20 Play.

- Revise the vocabulary using the flashcards (actions/emotions). Practise with the pupils the language to be used: *I'm happy/tired ... because ... .*
- Draw pupils' attention to the board. Explain that they take turns to move their counter one space. When it is Pupil A's turn, he/she moves on one and Student B asks questions which A must answer. They look at the model dialogue and the examples but make sure they understand they can invent their own answers.
- Pupils take turns to ask and answer the questions.
- Ask volunteers to demonstrate their favourite questions and answers.
- Pupils can use the Picture Dictionary AB p. 110.

Activity Book page 76

22 Look and write.

- Focus on the words in the word bank and the pictures. Ask a pupil to read the words. Explain (L1) that pupils have to write the sentences using *because* and the words in the word bank. Look at the example answer with the whole class, and tell them to cross out *smiling* and *relieved* in the word bank. Allow pupils time to write. Check answers with the class.

23 Write.

- Focus on the words in the word bank. Ask pupils to read the words. Explain (L1) that pupils have to classify the words and write them in the corresponding column. Make sure they understand they can make their own choices. Check answers with the class. If they have made choices that seem surprising, elicit an explanation or an example of a situation, to make sure they have not misunderstood the vocabulary.

24 Write.

- Pupils complete the sentences with object pronouns (if they need to, they could refer to the Look! box on PB p. 75). When they have finished, check answers with the class.

Ending the lesson

- Divide the class into groups of 4–6. Distribute the flashcards equally among the teams. The teams must make sentences about feelings, using the flashcard word, e.g. *Storms make me feel scared. I'm eating because I'm hungry.* Ask the groups to report their sentences. Award the group two points (one for each correct part) for each acceptable sentence.
- With weaker classes, you can begin the sentence and pupils complete it.
- (For AB Answer Key, see p. 226.)

OPTIONAL ACTIVITIES

Flashcard relay
Put all the Unit 6 and 7 wordcards face up at one end of the classroom and the Unit 6 and 7 flashcards at the other, all in jumbled order. Divide the class into two or four teams, depending on the size of your class (there should be no more than eight pupils in a team). Two teams stand in a line. When you say *Go*, the first member of each team runs to the wordcards, takes one, and then runs to the other end of the room to find the corresponding flashcard. Then he/she runs back to the second member of the team, who does the same. The first team to collect eight pairs of cards is the winner.

20 Play.

I'm feeling cold and ill. I'm happy because it's Friday.

I'm tired because it's Monday. I'm sad because my marks are bad.

I'm worried because I have a test. I'm bored because I can't watch the game.

I'm excited because it's Christmas. I'm angry because it's noisy.

I'm happy because the holidays are near. I'm nervous because I'm late for school.

Pupil A

Are you crying?

Yes.

Why are you crying?

I'm worried because I can't find my book.

Guess!

Pupil B

AB p.110

If you have two more teams, they then play the game. You could also have a final between the two winning teams to find a class champion.

Poster activity
See the notes on CLIL poster on p. 27.
Reading and Writing Booklet p. 21 see Answer Key p. 282

Lesson 10

Lesson aims
To personalise and assess efforts

Materials
Audio CD

Optional materials
Digital Activity Book; CLIL poster; Online material – *Film Studio Island*; Active Teach; Grammar reference and Review for Unit 7 (PB p. 115 and AB p. 102); Test Booklet; Grammar Booklet

Starting the lesson

- This is a self assessment activity. Tell the pupils that the activities on this page will show what they have learnt in this unit.

Pupil's Book page 81

21   **Listen and point.**

- Tell the pupils that they must choose the correct picture for each question. Play the recording more than once if necessary.
- Pupils listen, look at the pictures and choose the correct ones.

> **KEY** 1 b, 2 a, 3 a, 4 a, 5 b, 6 a, 7 b, 8 b

22 Read and say.

- Pupils read the gapped sentences. Ask them what kind of word is missing from the gaps. Ask them to say the sentences aloud.

> **KEY** 1 her, 2 me

Activity Book page 77

- Focus on the *I can* sentences at the bottom of the page. Tell the pupils that they have to tick the boxes, depending on whether they think they can do the *I can* points.

25 Look and circle.

- Ask the pupils to look at the picture and to circle the correct word describing the picture. Provide additional vocabulary as necessary. Ask a few pupils to read their descriptions to the class.

26 Draw or stick a picture of yourself. Then write.

- Ask the pupils to draw a picture of themselves or stick a photo into the space. Explain (L1) that the pictures can show an activity or situation (as in Mario's picture). Provide additional vocabulary as necessary. Then ask pupils to write about their own pictures.
- Allow pupils time to complete their descriptions. When they have finished, divide them into pairs and ask them to read their sentences to their partner. You could ask more confident pupils to read their sentences to the class.

Ending the lesson

- Describe feelings, putting flashcards on the board as prompts, e.g. *I'm sad. He's nervous.* Pupils say the sentences. Remove one of the flashcards and ask pupils to say all the sentences again. Continue in this way, removing one flashcard each time, until pupils are saying the whole sequence of sentences from memory.
- (For AB Answer Key, see p. 226. For Audioscript, see p. 229.)

21 🔊 3:22 **Listen and point.**

1 **a**  **b**    2 **a**  **b**

3 **a**  **b**    4 **a**  **b**

5 **a**  **b** 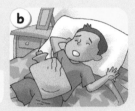   6 **a**  **b**

7 **a**  **b**    8 **a**  **b**

22 **Read and say.**

1 It's Jane's birthday. Give … a present.

2 I'm bored. Tell … a story, please.

OPTIONAL ACTIVITIES

Sentence chain
Say a sentence, e.g. *I'm happy because … .* Ask a pupil to repeat the sentence and then add another element, e.g. *I'm bored because … .* Continue in the same way until someone makes a mistake or forgets part of the sentence.

Flashcard game
Play *Memory* see p. 299.
Activity Book Review see p. 102.
Grammar Booklet p. 21 see Answer Key p. 285.
Test Booklet Unit 7 see Answer Key p. 285.
Online World
Pupils can now go online to *Film Studio Island* and enjoy the fun and games.

Activity Book Answer Key

p. 68, Activity 1
1 laughing, 2 yawning, 3 blushing, 4 smiling,
5 shouting, 6 frowning, 7 crying, 8 shaking

p. 68, Activity 2
1 shouting, 2 yawning, 3 crying, 4 smiling

p. 69, Activity 3
Numbers in order from left to right across the
picture: 1, 5, 4, 3, 2, 6

p. 69, Activity 4
1 shouting, shouting, angry
2 yawning, yawning, tired
3 Why is she smiling? She's smiling because she's
happy.
4 Why is he shaking? He's shaking because he's ill.
5 Why is she crying? She's crying because she's hurt.
6 Why is he frowning? He's frowning because he's
bored.
7 Why are you laughing? I'm laughing because I'm
excited.

p. 70, Activity 5
1 worried, 2 embarrassed, 3 nervous, 4 proud,
5 surprised, 6 relieved, 7 relaxed

p. 70, Activity 6
1 embarrassed, 2 relaxed (accept 'happy'), 3 I feel
nervous/worried/scared, 4 I feel proud
(accept 'excited', 'happy')

p. 71, Activity 7
1 a, 2 b, 3 a, 4 b

p. 71, Activity 8
1 Rainy days, sad
2 you feel nervous, Flying, nervous
3 makes you feel worried, Swimming, me feel worried
4 What makes you feel scared? Crocodiles, me feel
scared

p. 71, Activity 9
1 b him, 2 d me, 3 a her, 4 c them

p. 72, Activity 10
PLEH is HELP written backwards.

p. 72, Activity 11
a 1, b 2, c 5, d 3, e 4
a A film about Great Whites. b Have they got sharp
claws? c What's PLEH? d I feel scared now.
e There's a diver.

p. 73, Activity 15
green, cloud, train, spoon

p. 73, Activity 16
edge, hedge, bridge, badge

p. 74, Activity 18
Circle: a scared, b laughing, c surprised, d worried
Number: a 3, b 1, c 4, d 2

p. 75, Activity 20
1 b, 2 a

p. 75, Activity 21
1 She goes by bus and train.
2 She likes singing because she loves music/it makes
her feel happy.
3 Winter Carnival (makes him feel happy).
4 He goes skating, eats pancakes and drinks hot
chocolate with his family.

p. 76, Activity 22
1 smiling, relieved
2 He's frowning because he's nervous.
3 He's shouting because he's scared.
4 She's laughing because she's relaxed.

p. 76, Activity 23

crying	smiling	yawning	shaking
sad	happy	bored	angry
hurt	proud	tired	nervous

p. 76, Activity 24
1 her, 2 them, 3 us

p. 77, Activity 25
1 smiling, 2 happy, 3 basketball, 4 proud

Audioscript

Lesson 1 Activity 1   CD3:01
R = RUBY   JE = JENNY   S = SAM   JO = JOHN
D = DIRECTOR
R   Where are we?
JE   There's a house, and there are some horses. It's a farm. Ah, I'm happy. I like horses. You're a lovely horse.
S   And I like cake! Oh, mmm! I'm hungry.
R   Look, Sam!
S   Is it Madley Kool?
R   No, no! Look! It's Favolina Jolly! Oooh! I'm excited!
S   She's sad.
R   She's a film star! I love her films.
JO   I'm thirsty. Oh no!
JE   Cleo's scared! Oh dear!
D   Cut! Grrrr!
JO   Oops! He's angry.

Lesson 1 Activity 2   CD3:02
a   crying
b   shouting
c   yawning
d   frowning
e   laughing
f   blushing
g   smiling
h   shaking

Lesson 1 Activity 3   CD3:03
1   She's shouting.
2   She's blushing.
3   She's crying.
4   He's yawning.
5   He's shaking.

Lesson 2 Activity 4   CD3:04
Why is she smiling?
Because she's happy.
Why is she crying?
Because she's sad.
Why is he drinking?
Because he's thirsty.
Why is he eating?
Because he's hungry.
Why is he shouting?
Because he's angry.
Why is she laughing?
Because it's funny!

Lesson 2 Activity 5   CD3:05
1   She's smiling because she's happy.
2   He's yawning because he's tired.
3   He's frowning because he's angry.
4   She's shaking because she's scared.
5   She's crying because she's sad.

Lesson 2 Activity 3 (AB)   CD3:06
1   Why is she smiling?
2   Why is she laughing?
3   Why is he shouting?
4   Why is she yawning?
5   Why is he frowning?
6   Why is he crying?

Lesson 3 Activity 6   CD3:07
a   nervous
b   proud
c   relieved
d   surprised
e   relaxed
f   embarrassed
g   worried

Lesson 3 Activity 7   CD3:08
What makes you feel happy? What makes you feel happy?
Sunny days.
Sunny days and holidays
Make me feel happy.

What makes you cry? What makes you cry?
Sad films.
Sad films and long goodbyes
Make me cry.

What makes you feel scared? What makes you feel scared?
Big storms.
Big storms and green monsters
Make me feel scared.

What makes you laugh? What makes you laugh?
My friends.
My friends and naughty monkeys
Make me laugh.

Lesson 4 Activity 9 — CD3:09
S = SAM   R = RICKY

S Dear Ricky, What makes you feel relaxed? Sam

R Hi Sam, Dancing and singing make me feel relaxed. My family, my uncle, my aunt, my grandmother and grandfather make me feel relaxed because they make me laugh. My friends make me feel relaxed too. We go skateboarding and play computer games together. It's fun. What makes you feel relieved? Ricky

S Finishing all my homework makes me feel relieved. Passing a test makes me feel relieved and proud. But I feel surprised when I pass a Maths test. What makes you feel embarrassed? Sam

R Failing a test makes me feel embarrassed. Sometimes, my mother makes me feel embarrassed. She kisses me and hugs me in front of my friends. Does your mum do that too? Ricky

Lesson 4 Activity 7 (AB) — CD3:10
1 What makes you feel sad?
Rainy days make me feel sad because I can't go out.
2 What makes you feel nervous?
Flying makes me feel nervous because it's scary.
3 What makes you feel worried?
Swimming makes me feel worried because I swim terribly.
4 What makes you feel scared?
Crocodiles make me feel scared because they've got sharp teeth.

Lesson 6 Activity 12 — CD3:12
g e
/j/ /e/   /j//e/
g e
/j/ /j/
d g e
/j/ /j/

Lesson 6 Activity 13 — CD3:13
d g e
/j/ /j/
d g e
/j/ /j/
g e
/j/ /j/
g e
/j/ /e/   /j/ /e/
g e
/j/ /j/
g e
/j/ /e/   /j/ /e/

Lesson 6 Activity 14 — CD3:14
1 /j/ /e/ /m/
gem
2 /j/ /e/ /n/ /t/ /le/ /m/ /a/ /n/
gentleman
3 /p/ /ay/ /j/
page
4 /l/ /ar/ /j/
large
5 /e/ /j/
edge
6 /b/ /a/ /j/
badge
7 /h/ /e/ /j/
hedge
8 /b/ /r/ /i/ /j/
bridge

Lesson 6 Activity 15 (AB) — CD3:15
1 /g/   /r/   /ee/   /n/
2 /k/   /l/   /ou/   /d/
3 /t/   /r/   /ai/   /n/
4 /s/   /p/   /oo/   /n/

Lesson 6 Activity 16 (AB) — CD3:16
1 edge
2 hedge
3 bridge
4 badge

Lesson 6 Activity 17 (AB) — CD3:17
The gentleman looks at the gems. There are lots of small gems but he likes the large gem. 'How much is it?' he asks. Now he sighs, the price is too high.

Lesson 7 Activity 16 — CD3:18
1 [Scary music]
2 [Happy music]
3 [Sad music]
4 [Funny music]

Lesson 7 Activity 17　　　CD3:19

a　It's the end of the film. They're at the railway station. They're friends and they're saying goodbye. They're crying. It makes me feel sad. It makes me cry too.

b　There are a lot of people. They're laughing. They're learning to dance. The music is great. It makes me feel relaxed and happy. I want to sing and dance.

c　There are two boys. They're having a lot of fun. They're funny. They make me laugh.

d　There's a big, green monster. The monster has got big, sharp teeth. It makes me feel scared. That's why I'm shaking.

Lesson 7 Activity 18 (AB)　　　CD3:20

1　[Funny music]
2　[Sad music]
3　[Scary music]
4　[Happy music]

Lesson 8 Activity 18　　　CD3:21

1　Zhi's blog: I'm Zhi. I'm from China. Lunar New Year makes me feel happy because it's fun. It's in January or February and it's called the Spring Festival. There are dragons and pretty lanterns. We clean our houses, then we visit family and friends. Zhi, 10, China

2　Diego's blog: I'm Diego. I'm from Peru. Dancing makes me feel happy because it's good exercise. I dance at a special dance club. Here I am with my friend. We're dancing and wearing traditional dress and hats. Do you like our clothes?
Diego, 10, Peru

Lesson 10 Activity 21　　　CD3:22

1　Why are you shaking?
2　Why is she blushing?
3　Why is she crying?
　　She's crying because her friend is leaving.
4　Why are you frowning?
　　I'm frowning because I'm embarrassed.
5　What's the matter?
　　I'm sick.
6　How do you feel?
　　I feel worried. I can't find my book.
7　What makes you feel scared?
　　Spiders make me feel scared.
8　What makes you feel nervous?
　　Big games make me feel nervous.

8 Action!

Objectives

- talk about nature activities and extreme sports
- give suggestions and respond to them
- talk about future plans
- talk about summer camps
- pronounce properly /ph/ and /wh/

Topics
- Nature activities
- Extreme sports
- Summer camps

Phonics
/ph/ and /wh/

Values
- Enjoy all your activities

Stories
- Unit opener: filming nature activities
- Story episode: crazy about Madley Kool!

Language
Vocabulary
- Nature activities and equipment: snorkelling, snorkel, surfing, surfboard, sailing, life jacket, kayaking, paddle, fishing, fishing rod, horse-riding, riding boots
- Emotions: fond of, crazy about, bored with, scared of, terrified of
- Extreme sports: rafting, bungee jumping, rock climbing, scuba diving, hang gliding

Revision
climbing, water-skiing, surfing

Structures
Let's go (snorkelling)!
Great idea! I love (snorkelling).
Let's go (horse-riding)!
Sorry, I don't like (horse-riding).
Have you got (riding boots)?
Yes, I have./No, I haven't.
What are you going to do (tomorrow)?
I'm going (surfing)(tomorrow).
What is he/she going to do (this summer)?
He's/She's going (snorkelling) (this summer).

CLIL language
Save the reefs: save, coral reef, skeleton, seahorse, starfish, global warming, dead

Songs and chants
- Chant
- Song about actions at the moment of speaking
- Karaoke song

Sociocultural aspects
- Finding out about summer camp activities around the world
- Identifying activities that can be done in a summer camp in our country

Cross-curricular contents
- Science: saving the reefs
- Cultural and artistic competence: cultural activities in summer camps
- Language Arts: reading a story, acting out, telling a story
- Language skills: interpreting non verbal information accompanying written texts: pictures, layout, etc.

Learning strategies
- Using previous knowledge to interpret information in a text
- Interpreting and organising information
- Logical thinking: inferring the meaning of unknown words from the context
- Critical thinking: making predictions from information about saving nature
- Collaborative learning: project work and pair work
- Self assessment

Basic competences

- Linguistic communication: Have interest in using new words (L1 to L10)
- Knowledge and interaction with the physical world: Talk about nature activities and extreme sports (L1 to L4)
- Mathematical competence: Express time (U8)
- Processing information and digital competence: Use *Film Studio Island* online component
- Social and civic competence: Enjoy all your activities (L5)
- Cultural and artistic competence: Talk about summer camps in other parts of the world (L8)
- Learning to learn: Reflect on what has been learnt and self-evaluate progress (L10)
- Autonomy and personal initiative: Develop one's own criteria and social skills (L1 to L10)

Skills

Listening
- Identifying nature activities and extreme sports in recordings
- Understanding suggestions
- Understanding specific information in a song about activities
- Understanding information in a recorded conversation to ask and answer questions
- Understanding general and specific information in a story
- Understanding specific information about summer camps in other countries

Reading
- Understanding information in sentences and short texts (nature actions and extreme sports)
- Reading a postcard and identifying true/false information
- Looking at illustrations to anticipate the content of a text
- Understanding general and specific information in a cartoon strip story
- Understanding specific information about saving nature
- Understanding general and specific information about summer camps around the world

Speaking
- Repeating words and sentences
- Chanting and singing
- Giving information about future plans
- Pronouncing /ph/ and /wh/ correctly

Talking
- Giving suggestions and responding to them
- Asking and answering about future plans
- Talking about activities they are fond of or not
- Role playing a story

Writing
- Writing about the activities the characters are doing
- Answering questions about actions
- Giving suggestions and responding to them
- Writing personal information about feelings
- Completing a word map
- Completing a postcard

Classroom ideas

- Decorate the class with flashcards and the cross-curricular poster
- Ask pupils to bring photos and pictures from the internet about nature activities and extreme sports
- Display photos of summer camps in the country where pupils live
- Ask pupils to say the activities they enjoy and make a class survey
- Bring to the classroom library books about nature activities
- Photocopiables

Take-home English

- Home-School Link
- Notes for Parents
- A sample of work each week
- Portfolio

Self assessment

- Pupils can talk about nature activities and extreme sports
- Pupils can give suggestions and respond to them
- Pupils can talk about future plans
- Pupils can talk about summer camps

Evaluation

- Pupil's Book page 91
- Activity Book page 87
- Photocopiable 8.7
- Picture Dictionary
- Test Booklet – Unit 8

8 Action!

Lesson I

Lesson aims
To learn and practise new vocabulary (Nature activities and equipment)

Target language
snorkelling, snorkel, surfing, surfboard, sailing, life jacket, kayaking, paddle, fishing, fishing rod, horse-riding, riding boots

Materials
Audio CD; Flashcards and Wordcards (Nature activities, Sports equipment)

Optional materials
Active Teach; Digital Activity Book; Photocopiable 8.1

Starting the lesson

- Revise sports and actions. Tell the pupils that you are going to give some instructions and they have to mime the actions. Say, e.g. *play tennis, clean the floor, play basketball, skateboard.* Pupils mime.

Pupil's Book page 82

Presentation

- Hold up the flashcards in turn and say the words. Pupils repeat. Hold up the flashcards again, asking individual pupils to say the words.
- Focus on the main illustration. Ask *Where are the children?* Explain (L1) that the children are on a beach where a film is being made. Point to the person in the sailing boat and say *sailing.* Repeat with the other target words. Then ask *What's everyone doing?* Point to the speech bubble and check meaning. Then point to people in the picture and ask *What's he/she doing?* Pupils answer (e.g. *sailing*).

Listen.

- Tell pupils (L1) they are going to listen to a recording mentioning the sports in the main illustration, but that one of them won't be mentioned. Play the recording, while pupils point to the pictures mentioned. Play the recording again. Pupils decide which sport activity is not mentioned. Pupils check if they were right.

> **KEY** Missing word: surfing (Pupils may mention skateboarding as Sam is holding his skateboard.)

Listen and repeat.

- Play the recording, pausing after each word. Pupils point to the small sport pictures. Play the recording again. Pupils point and repeat each word.
- Hold up the flashcards in turn and ask individual pupils to say the words.
- Divide the class into pairs. Pupil A says the letter of one of the small pictures, e.g. *Picture b*, and Pupil B says the word, *surfing*. They then swap roles.
- Display the flashcards on one side of the board and write the corresponding words or put up wordcards on the other side. Pupils come to the front, read out the words and match them to the pictures.
- Shuffle the flashcards and choose one. Hold it up. Pupils say and mime the activity, e.g. *snorkelling.* Pupils then take turns to choose a flashcard and say and mime the action to the class.

Listen and find.

- Tell pupils (L1) they are going to listen to a recording describing items you use for different sports. They have to find the corresponding pictures and point to them. Play the recording. Pupils listen and point. Read the labels of the objects aloud in random order: pupils point and repeat.

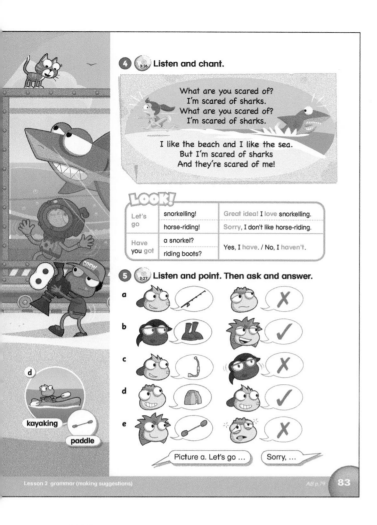

4 🔊 **Listen and chant.**

What are you scared of?
I'm scared of sharks.
What are you scared of?
I'm scared of sharks.

I like the beach and I like the sea.
But I'm scared of sharks
And they're scared of me!

LOOK!

Let's go	snorkelling!	Great idea! I love snorkelling.
	horse-riding!	Sorry, I don't like horse-riding.
Have you got	a snorkel?	Yes, I have. / No, I haven't.
	riding boots?	

5 🔊 **Listen and point. Then ask and answer.**

Picture a. Let's go ...   Sorry, ...

d kayaking / paddle

Lesson 2 grammar (making suggestions)   AB p.79   83

OPTIONAL ACTIVITIES

Word map

Draw a word map with the class. Draw two circles and write *Things we do in the sea* in one and *Things we do on the beach* in the other. Brainstorm with the class words for each category and write them on the board. They can be words learnt in this lesson or previously, e.g. *reading, swimming*, etc. Pupils copy into their notebooks.

Drawing activity

Do a picture dictation using the unit vocabulary and language. Dictate a picture for pupils to draw, e.g. *There's the sea and a beach. In the sea there's a shark. A man is snorkelling. He's scared of the shark.*

Photocopiable 8.1 see Teacher's notes p. 293.

NOTES

Activity Book page 78

➊ Match.

• Focus on the pictures and the words in the word bank. Pupils match the words to the pictures. To check, ask *What's number (one)?* Pupils answer.

➋ Unscramble the words. Then look and write.

• Focus on the scrambled letters. Ask the pupils to unscramble them and write the words. Then they complete the sentences with the correct words. Ask individual pupils to read the sentences.

Ending the lesson

• Play *Guess the action*: draw an object, e.g. a fishing rod, and the class has to guess the activity by saying, e.g. *Fishing.* Ask individual pupils to take your role. You can turn this into a competition by dividing the class into two teams. They draw for their own team to guess.

• (For AB Answer Key, see p. 252. For Audioscript, see p. 253.)

Lesson 2

Lesson aims
To learn and practise the new structure

Target language
Let's go horse-riding! Great idea! I love horse-riding.
Sorry, I don't like horse-riding.
Have you got riding boots? Yes, I have./
No, I haven't.

Materials
Audio CD; Flashcards and Wordcards (Nature activities, Sports equipment)

Optional materials
Active Teach; Digital Activity Book; Grammar Booklet

Starting the lesson

- Use the flashcards to revise the vocabulary from the previous lesson. Hold up the flashcards and elicit the words. Then ask individual pupils to hold up the flashcards at the front of the class. Hold up the wordcards or write the words on the board, and pupils point to the correct flashcards.
- With stronger classes, ask individual pupils to come to the front and write the words on the board.

> **Pupil's Book page 83**

- Play *Basketball* see p. 298 to revise the sport activities from Lesson 1.

Presentation

- Pupils read the sentences in the Look! box. Focus on how to give suggestions: *Let's go horse-riding!* Explain (L1) that *Let's* + infinitive is used to give suggestions. Ask the pupils to give more examples and write them on the board. Point out the positive and negative ways to respond to the suggestion: *Great idea! I love ...* or *I'm sorry, ...*
- Focus their attention on the second question. Revise the use of *Have got* and the short answer forms *Yes, I have/No, I haven't.* Point to a pupil and ask *Have you got brown eyes?* The pupil answers. Then practise with the target vocabulary, asking a few other pupils. Write some example questions on the board. Pupils can copy them into their notebooks.

4 🔊 Listen and chant.

- Focus on the pictures either side of the chant. Ask *How does the girl feel? (Scared). How does the shark feel? (Scared).*
- Play the recording. Pupils listen and follow the words. Play it again, pausing after each line. Pupils repeat. Play it a third time. Pupils chant together.

Practice

5 🔊 Listen and point. Then ask and answer.

- Focus on giving suggestions. Tell pupils to listen to the recording and point to the pictures in the Pupil's Book. Then they practise in pairs. Play the recording a few times. They listen and point. Organise the class in pairs. Pupils give suggestions and respond to them based on the pictures and symbols.
- Ask pupils if they have got something: *Have you got a life jacket?* They answer. Focus their attention on the model dialogue. Organise the class in pairs. Pupils take it in turns to ask and answer about the things they have got.

Ending the lesson

- Play *Spelling bee* with the sport activities from Lesson 1. Pupils listen to the words you say and, in turn, they try to spell them correctly.
- (For AB Answer Key, see p. 252. For Audioscript, see p. 253.)

OPTIONAL ACTIVITIES

Chant/Rap writers

With the class, write a new chant using different animals. To match the rhyme of the chant, animals have to be found in the sea. Alternatively, the fifth line could be *I like the forest and I like the trees* so pupils can choose animals from the rainforest, e.g. *But I'm scared of spiders*. Chant as a class. Pupils may copy the chant into their notebooks and illustrate it.

Class survey

Write eight activities on the board, e.g. the ones from this lesson, plus *reading*, *swimming*, *flying a kite*. Pupils copy them down. Divide the class into small groups. Pupils ask the other members of their group if they like each activity: *Do you like ...?* They work out the most popular in the group. Collect results from each group on the board to work out the class favourite.

Grammar Booklet p. 22 see Answer Key p. 285.

NOTES

Activity Book page 79

3 Listen, number and tick (✓).

- Focus on the pictures and tell the pupils that they must number the pictures according to the information from the recording. Play the recording for the pupils to listen and number. Check answers with the class.
- Play the recording again. This time pupils tick the correct picture in each case. Check answers with the class.

4 Write.

- Focus on the pictures. Pupils have to complete the suggestions and responses, based on the pictures. Pupils work individually. Then they check in pairs. Ask a few pupils to read their work to the class.

235

Lesson 3

Lesson aims
To extend the unit vocabulary set (extreme sports);
to practise the unit language with a song

Target language
Emotions: fond of, crazy about, bored with, scared
of, terrified of
Extreme sports: rafting, bungee jumping, rock
climbing, scuba diving, hang gliding

Materials
Audio CD; Flashcards and Wordcards (Emotions,
Extreme sports)

Optional materials
Soft ball or small beanbag; Active Teach; Digital
Activity Book; Photocopiables 8.2–8.3; Reading and
Writing Booklet

Starting the lesson

- Play *Guess the card* see p. 299 with flashcards from
  this unit and the previous two units displayed around
  the room.

Pupil's Book page 84

Presentation

- Look enthusiastic as you pretend to read a book, and
  say *I'm fond of reading.* Then look bored and fed up as
  you say *I'm bored with reading.* Then point to the floor
  with a horrified expression and say *Oh no! A spider.
  I'm very, very scared of spiders. I'm terrified of spiders!*

6 **Listen and repeat.**

- Introduce the new words (*rafting, bungee jumping*, etc.)
  using the flashcards. Hold them up and say the words
  for the pupils to repeat. Ask individual pupils to
  say the words. Play the recording for pupils to listen
  and repeat.
- Now put the flashcards on the board. Point to
  the different flashcards and ask the class to say
  the words.

7 **Listen and point. Then sing.**

- Play the recording. Pupils listen to the song and follow
  the words of the song in the book. Play the song
  again. Pupils point to the correct coloured words
  when they hear them. Play it again. Pupils join in
  and sing together.
- Divide the class into three groups. Each group sings
  a verse, and all groups sing the last two lines. Then
  swap verses until all the groups have sung the
  whole song. You can now play the karaoke song
  (Active Teach).

- Direct pupils' attention to the Look! box and focus
  on the question and answer. Read the Look! box. Ask
  pupils to give more examples. Write them on the
  board. Pupils can copy them into their notebooks.

Practice

- Prepare eight wordcards, each with one word on it:
  crazy, scared, fond, bored, terrified, about, of and *with.*
  Stick the three preposition cards on the board. Shuffle
  the adjective cards and place them face down on your
  table. Ask individual pupils to come to the table and
  pick one card. They put the adjective up on the board
  in front of the correct preposition.

8 **Look. Then ask and answer.**

- Ask pupils to look at the model dialogue and the
  labelled pictures. Model another question with a
  confident pupil. Divide the class into pairs. Pupil A
  asks a question and Pupil B answers. Then they
  swap roles.

Activity Book page 80

5 **Look and write**

- Direct pupils' attention to the words in the word bank.
  They have to write the correct answer below the
  corresponding picture. Check answers with the class.

6 **Write. Then listen and match.**

- Direct pupils' attention to the pictures. Allow them
  time to look at the pictures and write the words.
  When they have finished, play the recording. Pupils
  listen and match the opinions to the activities. Play
  the recording again. Pupils listen and check their
  answers. Then ask individual pupils to read out
  their answers.

Ending the lesson

- Play a True/False game based on the completed AB
  Activity 6. Say sentences, e.g. *I'm fond of diving. I'm
  bored with fishing.* The class tell you if they are true or
  false. Alternatively, write the sentences on the board.
  Divide the class into two groups. In turns, they decide
  if the sentences are true or false. If they are false,
  they correct them.
- (For AB Answer Key, see p. 252. For Audioscript,
  see pp. 253–4.)

OPTIONAL ACTIVITIES
TPR game
Play *Ball throw* see p. 300 asking questions, e.g.
What are you scared of? Do you like snakes?

6  **Listen and repeat.**

a (fond of)
b (crazy about)
c (bored with)
d (scared of)
e (terrified of)

f (rafting)
g (bungee jumping)
h 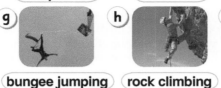 (rock climbing)
i  (scuba diving)
j (hang gliding)

7 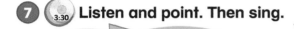 **Listen and point. Then sing.**

SONG

What are you fond of? I'm fond of these:
(Sailing) (Scuba diving) and climbing,
Big rocks, and the sea.

What are you bored with? I'm bored with these:
(Fishing) (Swimming) and sailing.
Not exciting, you see?

What are you scared of? Being up in the air.
(Bungee jumping) (Snorkelling), hang gliding. Not safe, you see?

Anything else, you ask? I'm terrified of sharks!

LOOK!

| What are you fond of? | I'm fond of rafting. |

What are you fond of?

I'm fond of rafting.

8 **Look. Then ask and answer.**

fond of	bored with	crazy about	scared of	terrified of
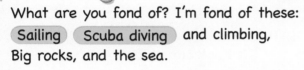				

Find out
In pairs, pupils take turns to tell his/her partner four things they're keen on, bored with, etc. Two are true and one is false, e.g. *I'm keen on football, swimming and ballet.* Partners guess the false one, e.g. *You aren't fond of ballet!* They get a point for each correct guess.

Photocopiable 8.2 see Teacher's notes p. 293.
Photocopiable 8.3 see Teacher's notes p. 293.
Reading and Writing Booklet p. 22 see Answer Key p.283.

Lesson 4

Lesson aims
To develop reading, writing, listening and speaking skills; to learn and practise the new structure

Target language
What are you going to do (tomorrow)? I'm going to (go surfing) (tomorrow).
What is he/she going to do (this summer)? He's/ She's going to (go snorkelling) (this summer).

Materials
Audio CD

Optional materials
Active Teach; Digital Activity Book; Grammar Booklet

Starting the lesson

- Ask pupils where they like to go on holidays, e.g. *to the sea*, *to the mountains*. Elicit things they can do in each place and write them on the board.

Pupil's Book page 85

Presentation

- Focus the pupils' attention on the Look! box. Pupils read the sentences. Explain that we use *going to* followed by a (bare infinitive) verb to talk about plans for the future. Talk about your plans for the weekend using *I'm going to ...* .

Skills

9 **Listen and read. Then answer.**

- Focus on the postcard layout and the illustration, asking the class to point to the elements you mention: *Point to the address. Point to the greeting*, etc. Focus on the address of the postcard. Explain how to write addresses. Pupils write their address in their notebooks.
- Pupils look at the photo and tell you what they can see, e.g. *I can see the sea. There are blue umbrellas on the beach*. Pupils read the postcard and find one thing Tara is crazy about.
- Play the recording while pupils follow the text.
- Tell pupils that they are going to answer questions about the postcard. Read out the questions and check pupils understand. Ask a few pupils to write the questions on the board. Ask individual pupils to write the answers.

KEY
1 They're at the beach.
2 She goes swimming with dolphins in the sea.
3 She's crazy about water sports.
4 She's going snorkelling.
5 They're going to go rafting on the river.
6 They're going to hike along the coast to the next town (and visit Tara's friend).

Practice

10 **Ask and answer.**

- Organise the class in pairs. Focus the pupils' attention on the dialogue. Tell them to ask and answer about what they are going to do this weekend.
- They work in pairs. Ask them to take it in turns to ask and answer questions. One pupil pretends to be Tara, and the other a friend who rings her while she is on holiday: they ask and answer, based on the postcard.

Activity Book page 81

7 **Look at Activity 6 and write.**

- Ask the pupils to look at AB Activity 6 and write the corresponding questions and answers. Do question 1 as an example and answer it. Tell pupils to do the others. Check as a class.

8 **Look and write.**

- Tell pupils to look at the pictures and complete the sentences. Check answers as a class.

9 **Write about yourself. Then draw or stick a picture.**

- Tell pupils to draw two pictures and write about their feelings. The first one has to be about something they are terrified of and the second has to be about something they are going to do tomorrow. Allow them time to write. Organise the class in small groups. Ask them to read out their sentences to the group. Check as a class, asking a few pupils.

Ending the lesson

- Divide the class into pairs. Pupil A plays an interviewer. Pupil B plays a film star. The interviewer asks questions about what Pupil B is scared of, fond of, etc. Pupil B makes up answers as he/she likes. Then they swap roles.
- (For AB Answer Key, see p. 252. For Audioscript, see p. 254.)

Pupils can now go online to *Film Studio Island* and find the crab that Cleo is holding. It is the little red crab moving about just in front of the Coconut Shack on the beach. Once pupils click on the crab they are taken to a supplementary language game based on the vocabulary in this unit.

What **are** you **going to do** next month?	I'm going to go surfing.
What's he/she **going to do** this summer?	He's/She's going to visit his/her grandparents.

9 (3:32) **Listen and read. Then answer.** SKILLS

Dear Grandma and Grandpa,

I'm having a great holiday at the beach. It's warm and sunny and there are a lot of exciting things to do. Every morning I go swimming with the dolphins in the sea. It makes me feel happy because dolphins are so intelligent! In the afternoon I go snorkelling. I love to see all the amazing animals in the sea.

Mum is bored with the beach. Today she's hang gliding!

I'm crazy about water sports, and next Monday I'm going to go scuba diving. I'm so excited! Then next Wednesday Sue and I are going to go rafting on the river. It's going to be so much fun! Finally, on Friday, we're all going to hike along the coast to the next town. My friend is going to be there and we're going to visit him.

I miss you.

Lots of love.

Tara

Mr and Mrs Jones
22 The Street
Greensboro, NC 27401
United States

1 Where are Tara and her family?

2 What does Tara do every morning?

3 What's Tara crazy about?

4 What's Tara going to do next Monday?

5 What are Tara and Sue going to do next Wednesday?

6 What are they going to do next Friday?

10 **Ask and answer.**

What are you going to do this summer?

I'm going to ...

OPTIONAL ACTIVITIES

Young writers
Elicit words about feelings and write them on the board. In pairs, pupils write a sentence using some of the words, and then read it out to the class.

Pairwork game
Play *Matching pairs* see p. 300. Pupils say *I'm (surfing)* as they turn over the cards.
Grammar Booklet p. 23 see Answer Key p. 285.

Lesson 5

Lesson aims
To consolidate the unit language with a story

Values
Enjoy all your activities

Receptive language
present (v), act (v), scene, Great! I'm not scared of ...

Materials
Audio CD; Story cards; Character Story cards

Optional materials
Props for acting out the story, e.g. glasses for Ruby, baseball cap for Sam, black T-shirt for John, necklace for Jenny, grey jumper for Cleo, sunglasses for Madley Kool (and extras for the others), waistcoat for director; Active Teach; Digital Activity Book; Photocopiable 8.4; Reading and Writing Booklet

Starting the lesson

- Ask pupils (L1) what they can remember about the story from the previous episodes. Use the Unit 6 and 7 story cards as prompts.

Pupil's Book page 86

Presentation

11 **Listen and read. Then act out.**

- Show the story cards one at a time and ask the *Before listening to the story* questions. Pupils predict what happens in the story.
- Play the recording. Pupils listen as they follow the story in their books. Ask if their predictions were correct, and then ask the *After listening to the story* questions.
- Divide the class into seven groups and assign a character to each. Pupils read their parts as a class.
- Ask pupils who would like to take the parts of the different characters. Invite volunteers to the front of the class to act out the story. Encourage tone of voice and expressions to match those in the pictures. Use props that you've brought to class if you wish.

Practice

- Shuffle the story cards and put them in random order on the board. With books closed, ask *Which is number (one)?* Pupils answer. Continue until all the story cards are in order.

Values

- Say a few activities pupils usually do in class, e.g. *reading books and magazines, going online.* Read out the activities in the Pupil's Book and help the pupils understand if necessary. Ask pupils to give more examples and write them on the board.
- Organise the class in pairs. Pupils take it in turns to ask and answer about ways to enjoy the activities. Discuss (L1) the importance of enjoying them.

Activity Book page 82

10 **Read the story again. How does Cleo help Madley Kool? Write.**

- The pupils can read the story again (PB p. 86), focusing on frames 2–4. Help them with the vocabulary if they need support. Then they write their answer on the line.

11 **Number the pictures in order.**

- Direct pupils' attention to the pictures and speech bubbles. Ask them to number the pictures in order. If they cannot number them from memory they can look back at the story on PB p. 86. Check answers with the class.

12 **Look and write.**

- Tell the class to complete the article about Madley Kool, using the words in the word bank. Explain any new words. Check as a class.

13 **Write.**

- Tell pupils to read the questions and answer them with information from the article in Activity 12. Check answers with the class.

Home-School Link

- Ask the pupils to make a poster of a school activity they enjoy, to show to their families. Give pupils a sheet of paper and ask them to draw a picture and write a sentence describing it.

Ending the lesson

- Play *Guess who*: say one or two words spoken by a character in the story on PB p. 86, or mime his/her actions, and the class guesses who you are.
- (For AB Answer Key, see p. 252.)

VALUES

Enjoy all your activities.

HOME-SCHOOL LINK

Make a poster of a school activity you enjoy doing. Show your family.

OPTIONAL ACTIVITIES

My favourite character
Pupils draw their favourite character and write a short description based on an outline on the board.

Vote for your favourite episode
Ask the class which is their favourite episode. Take a class vote.

Work out the class favourite and read and listen to it again.

Photocopiable 8.4 see Teacher's notes p. 293.
Reading and Writing Booklet p. 23 see Answer Key p. 282.

Lesson 6

Lesson aims
To learn the sounds and letters /ph/ and /wh/

Target language
phone, dolphin, elephant, alphabet, wheel, white, whale, whisper

Materials
Audio CD; Flashcards and Wordcards (Phonics); Phonics poster

Optional materials
Active Teach; Digital Activity Book; Photocopiable 8.5

Pupil's Book page 87

Presentation

12 🔊 **3:34 Listen and repeat.**

- Write on the board the sounds /ph/ and /wh/. Play the recording for pupils to listen. Play it a second time for pupils to listen and repeat.

13 🔊 **3:35 Listen, point and say.**

- Tell the pupils that they must point to the sound that they hear. Play the recording for pupils to listen and point. Play it a second time for pupils to listen, point and say.

14 🔊 **3:36 Listen and blend the sounds.**

- Demonstrate the blending of the first sound; pupils repeat what they hear. Then tell them that they must listen and blend the sounds. Play the recording for pupils to listen and say the words that contain the corresponding sounds.

Practice

15 Read the sentences aloud. Then find /ph/ and /wh/.

- The pupils read the sentences aloud. Then they find and point to the sounds /ph/ and /wh/. Ask them to read out the words containing these sounds.

Activity Book page 83

14 Read the words. Circle the pictures.

- Give pupils time to read the words and circle the corresponding parts of the picture.

15 🔊 **3:37 Listen and connect the letters. Then write.**

- Play the recording and give the pupils time to draw the lines to connect the letters. Play the recording again, and give pupils time to write the words.

16 🔊 **3:38 Listen and write the words.**

- Play the recording, pausing if necessary to give pupils time to write the words. Play it again for them to check what they have written. Check answers.

17 🔊 **3:39 Read aloud. Then listen and check.**

- Ask different pupils to read the text aloud, one sentence each. Then play the recording: pupils listen and check.

Ending the lesson

- Divide the class into four groups. Allocate one of the pictures in PB Activity 15 to each group. Call out a number from 1 to 4: that group must stand up and chorus their sentence as quickly as they can, then sit down again. Continue, calling out the numbers in random order, speeding up the game as you go along. Swap groups around if your class can cope.
- (For AB Answer Key, see p. 252. For Audioscript, see p. 254.)

PHONICS

12 (3:34) **Listen and repeat.**

1 **ph**   2 **wh**

13 (3:35) **Listen, point and say.**

14 (3:36) **Listen and blend the sounds.**

1 ph – o – ne   phone   2 d - o - l - ph - i - n   dolphin

3 e - l - e - ph - a - n - t   elephant   4 a - l - ph - a - b - e - t   alphabet

5 wh – ee – l   wheel   6 wh – i – te   white

7 wh – a – le   whale   8 wh - i - s - p - er   whisper

15 **Read the sentences aloud. Then find *ph* and *wh*.**

1 Can a sheep whisper?   2 Can a whale sing the alphabet song?

baaa

A C D B E

3 Can a dolphin talk on the phone? 4 Can a white elephant juggle a wheel?

Lesson 6 phonics (ph / wh)   AB p.83   **87**

OPTIONAL ACTIVITIES
OPTIONAL ACTIVITIES

Phonics game
Play *Sound snake* see p. 302.

Phonics game
Play *Sound hunt* see p. 302.
Photocopiable 8.5 see Teacher's notes p. 293.

Lesson 7

Lesson aims
To connect other areas of the curriculum with English learning; to develop the cross-curricular topic through a short project

Cross-curricular focus
Science (Saving coral reefs)

Target language
save, coral reef, skeleton, seahorse, starfish, global warming, dead

Materials
Audio CD

Optional materials
World map or globe; pictures of sea animals, plastic bottle; Active Teach; Digital Activity Book; CLIL poster; Photocopiable 8.6

Starting the lesson

- Whisper an action to a pupil, e.g. *I'm horse-riding/ sailing/windsurfing.* He/She mimes it for the class to guess.

Pupil's Book page 88

Presentation

- Point to the photo on the right. Say *This is a coral reef. Where can you find coral reefs?* Locate some on a map, e.g. the Great Barrier Reef in Australia, Belize Barrier Reef in the Caribbean, the Red Sea Coral Reef.

16 **Listen and read. Then say *True* or *False*.**

- Ask *Which animals live on coral reefs?* Tell pupils to listen, read and find out. Play the recording. When they have answered, discuss the questions at the end of each paragraph.
- Pupils reread the article. Explain the meaning of *dead.* Read out the sentences and check that they understand. Give pupils time to read and work out if the sentences are true or false. Check answers with the class. Ask them to change false sentences into true ones.

> **KEY** **1** False (They are in hot and sunny places.), **2** True, **3** False (There are butterfly fish and parrotfish.), **4** True, **5** True

Practice
Mini-project

- In small groups, pupils find out about animals that live on coral reefs, either in reference books or on the internet. They choose three animals. On poster paper, they stick or draw pictures of the animals and write some information about them. When they have finished, display their posters around the classroom. Give pupils time to look at and comment on the other groups' work.

Think!

- Ask pupils to read the text in the Think! box. They could look on the internet for information about the places where coral reefs can't survive.

Activity Book page 84

18 **Write.**

- Focus the pupils' attention on the word bank. Check that they understand the vocabulary. They must complete the sentences with the words. Check the answers with the class.

19 **Write.**

- Check the meaning of *land* and elicit with pupils animals that live in the sea and on land. Then ask them to read the words in the word bank. They complete the word maps. Check with the class by asking pupils to help you write the word maps on the board.

20 **Write.**

- Pupils read the text (PB p. 88 Activity 16) again and answer the question. Check as a class.

Ending the lesson

- Say *In the coral reef, I can see a seahorse.* Nominate a pupil to add to the sentence, e.g. *In the coral reef, I can see a seahorse and red coral.* Continue round the class, with each pupil adding something new to the list, until someone makes a mistake. Then start again.
- (For AB Answer Key, see p. 252. For Audioscript, see p. 254.)

16 **Listen and read. Then say *True* or *False*.**

save   coral reef   skeleton   seahorse   starfish   global warming   dead

Save the Reefs!

Coral reefs are made of small sea animals and their skeletons. You can find coral reefs in the sea where it's hot and sunny. They are called the rainforests of the sea because a lot of fish and sea animals live on them. There are seahorses, sea snakes, starfish, butterfly fish, parrotfish and many more. There are a lot of pretty colours in the reef. How does this coral reef make you feel?

Now look at this coral reef. It's white and there are no fish or sea animals on it. The sea is too hot because of global warming and the coral is dead. Fish don't like dead coral. How does this coral reef make you feel?

Please help us save the coral reefs.

1 There are coral reefs in cold seas.

2 A lot of fish and sea animals live on coral reefs.

3 There are parrots and butterflies on the reef.

4 Dead coral is white.

5 Fish don't like dead coral.

MINI-
PROJECT
Make a poster about five of the sea animals in the passage and write about them.

THINK!
Coral reefs need sunlight and warm temperatures. Name two places where coral reefs can't survive.

Lesson 8

Lesson aims
To learn about other cultures and respect cultural differences

Cross-cultural focus
To learn about summer camps in the world

Target language
beach summer camp, rafting, beach volleyball

Materials
Audio CD

Optional materials
World map or globe; Active Teach; Digital Activity Book; CLIL poster; Photocopiable 8.7

Starting the lesson

- Write the words *beach summer camp, rafting, beach volleyball* on the board. Explain the meaning or point to the pictures to show the meaning. Brainstorm other words for summer camps and write them on the board.

Pupil's Book page 89

Presentation

- Focus on the photos. Pupils describe what they can see.
- Pupils look at the texts, find the names of the places where the children live and locate them on the map or globe.

17 **Listen and read.**

- Play the recording. Pupils listen and follow the text in their books. Ask pupils to find the names of the children. Write them on the board.
- Ask a few comprehension questions: *Where is Elliot going? What is he going to do there? Where is Carolina going? What is she going to do there?*

Practice

18 **Ask and answer.**

- Direct pupils' attention to the sentences. Check that they understand. Allow pupils time to reread the text and decide if the sentences are true or false. When they have finished, check answers with the class.
- Divide the class into pairs. Pupils ask and answer about the texts.

> **KEY** **1** False, **2** False, **3** True, **4** True, **5** False, **6** True

Portfolio project

- Ask pupils to imagine they are going to go to a summer camp. Ask them to write about what they are going to do there.
- Pupils can write in their notebooks, using the texts in PB p. 89 as a model.

Activity Book page 85

21 **Look and write.**

- Ask the pupils to look at the pictures and read the words in the word bank. Check that they understand. Pupils label the pictures and complete the sentence. Check answers with the class.

22 **Plan a summer camp. Then write.**

- Ask the pupils to look at the diary day grids for Monday, Tuesday, Wednesday. They must plan summer camp activities for three days. First they have to write what activities they are going to do on the three days. Then they must write sentences saying what they are going to do. When they have finished, they tell their partners. Check with the class.

Ending the class

- Play *Picture charades* see p. 298 with vocabulary for summer camps.
- (For AB Answer Key, see p. 252. For Audioscript, see p. 255.)

Wider World
Summer camps

17 🔊 3:41 **Listen and read.**

1
Hi, I'm Elliot. I live in Scotland. In August I'm going to go to a summer camp for two weeks. It's near a national park and it's fantastic! I'm going to do adventure activities like kayaking and rafting. I like sports too. I'm also going to play football and volleyball. I love sports and adventure.

Elliot, 10, Scotland

beach volleyball

My name's Carolina and I live in Los Angeles. This summer I'm going to go to a beach summer camp for three weeks. It's a wonderful place at the seaside. I can practise lots of fun activities for kids. I'm going to go surfing and snorkelling. I'm also going to play beach volleyball, and I'm going to go on sea life safaris. I love the beach!

Carolina, 10, United States

2

18 **Read and say *True* or *False*.**

1 Elliot is from Los Angeles.
2 He's going to go to beach camp.
3 He's going to do adventure activities at camp.
4 Carolina is from the United States.
5 She doesn't like the beach.
6 She's going to go surfing and snorkelling this summer.

PORTFOLIO

Think and write.

Imagine you are going to go to a summer camp. Write about what you are going to do.

OPTIONAL ACTIVITIES

Team game
Play *Unscramble* see p. 300 revising weather, sports and seaside activities.

Research
Divide the class into pairs. Tell pupils to look for information about summer camps in their country.

They could use brochures or internet links that you recommend. They write sentences about them and draw pictures.
Photocopiable 8.7 see Teacher's notes p. 293.

Lesson 9

Lesson aims
To review the unit language with a game and the Picture Dictionary

Materials
Audio CD

Optional materials
Active Teach; Digital Activity Book; CLIL poster; Reading and Writing Booklet

Starting the lesson

- Play *Hit the card* see p. 299 using a variety of language from the unit.

Pupil's Book page 90

19 Write in your notebook. Then play.

- Focus pupils' attention on the example question and answer, and the pictures. Revise the vocabulary using the flashcards (nature activities, extreme sports, emotions, activities). Practise with the pupils the language to be used: *Are you crazy about surfing? No, I'm not. My turn.*
- Pupils copy the table into their notebooks and complete the information about themselves, in the left-hand column. Then they work in pairs, taking turns to ask and answer and complete the information about their partners.
- Pupils can use the Picture Dictionary (AB p. 111.)

Activity Book page 86

23 Look and write.

- Direct pupils' attention to the pictures and the beginning of the sentences. Explain (L1) that they are going to revise words and structures for giving suggestions and feelings. Pupils complete the sentences. Check as a class.

Ending the lesson

- Divide the class into pairs. Write these categories on the board: *sports, food, clothes, actions.* Ask the pupils to write as many words as they can think for each category within a time limit. The pair that comes up with the most words wins.
- (For AB Answer Key, see p. 252.)

19 Write in your notebook. Then play.

Me		My friend	
Round 1			
Fond of		Crazy about	
1 …	2 …	1 …	2 …
3 …	4 …	3 …	4 …
Round 2			
Bored with		Scared of	
1 …	2 …	1 …	2 …
3 …	4 …	3 …	4 …

Are you are crazy about surfing?

No, I'm not. My turn.

Guess!

Picture Dictionary

AB p.111

90 Lesson 9 review and consolidation

AB p.86

OPTIONAL ACTIVITIES

Guessing game

Divide the class into two or more groups. Ask a pupil from one group to come up to the front and show him/her a flashcard from the unit. His/Her group asks questions to guess what it is. The answer can only be *Yes* or *No*, e.g. *Can I wear it?* The first pupil to guess correctly gets a point for the team. If he/she can say a sentence correctly using the word, she/he gets an extra point for the team.

Poster activity

See the notes on CLIL poster on p. 27.

Reading and Writing Booklet p. 24 see Answer Key p. 283.

Lesson 10

Lesson aims
To personalise and assess efforts

Materials
Audio CD

Optional materials
Digital Activity Book; CLIL poster; Online material –
Film Studio Island, Active Teach; Grammar reference
and Review for Unit 8 (PB p. 116 and AB p. 103); Test
Booklet; Grammar Booklet

Starting the lesson

- This is a self assessment activity. Tell the pupils that
the activities on this page will show what they have
learnt in this unit.
- Play *Ball throw* see p. 300 to revise groups of words
from the course: weather, landscape, feelings, animals,
hobbies, etc.

Pupil's Book page 91

20 Listen and point.

- Tell the pupils that they must choose the correct
picture for each question. Play the recording more
than once if necessary.
- Pupils listen, look at the pictures and choose the
correct ones.

> **KEY** **1** a, **2** b, **3** b, **4** b, **5** b, **6** a

21 Read and say.

- In questions 1 and 2, pupils complete the gapped
questions. In questions 3 and 4, they give their own
answers.

> **KEY** **1** kayaking, **2** fishing rod

Activity Book page 87

- Focus on the *I can* sentences at the bottom of the
page. Tell the pupils that they have to tick the boxes,
depending on whether they think they can do the *I
can* points.

24 Look and write.

- Direct pupils' attention to the postcard. Explain that
they are going to complete the text. Ask them to look
at the pictures before they write. When they have
finished, they exchange texts with their partners and
check them. Check by asking a few pupils to tell the
whole class.

25 Pretend you are on holiday. Write an email to a friend.

- Elicit a description about holidays by asking questions:
Do you go to the seaside? What do you like doing? Elicit
vocabulary and expressions to be used. Then ask
pupils to write an email to a friend describing what
they do on holiday. Ask volunteers to read their
emails to the class.

Ending the lesson

- Pupils use their emails (AB Activity 25) as the basis of
an illustrated blog post holiday poster, adding photos
or drawings which they label, e.g. *I'm going kayaking*.
Display the finished work.
- (For AB Answer Key, see p. 252. For Audioscript,
see p. 255.)

> **OPTIONAL ACTIVITIES**
> **Flashcard relay**
> Put all the Unit 7 and 8 wordcards face up at
> one end of the classroom and the Unit 7 and 8
> flashcards at the other, all in jumbled order. Divide
> the class into two or four teams, depending on the
> size of your class (there should be no more than
> seven pupils in a team). Two teams stand in a line.
> When you say *Go*, the first member of each team
> runs to the wordcards, takes one, then runs to the
> other end of the room to find the corresponding
> flashcard. Then he/she runs back to the second
> member of the team, who does the same. The first
> team to collect seven pairs of cards is the winner.
> If you have two more teams, they then play the
> game. You could also have a final between the two
> winning teams to find a class champion.

20 (3:42) **Listen and point.**

1 a

b

2 a

b

3 a

b

4 a

b

5 a

b

6 a

b

21 **Read and say.**

1 Let's go … Have you got a paddle?

2 Let's go fishing. Have you got a …?

3 What are you going to do this summer?

4 What's your family going to do this winter?

Team game
Play *Stop!* see p. 301.
Activity Book Review see p. 103.
Grammar Booklet p. 24 see Answer Key p. 285.

Test Booklet Unit 8 see Answer Key p. 296.
Online World
Pupils can now go online to *Film Studio Island* and enjoy the fun and games.

Activity Book Answer Key

p. 78, Activity 1
1 kayaking, 2 snorkelling, 3 horse-riding, 4 fishing, 5 surfing, 6 sailing

p. 78, Activity 2
1 fishing, fishing rod, 2 riding boots, riding, 3 sailing, life jacket, 4 kayaking, paddle, 5 surfboard, surfing, 6 snorkel, snorkelling

p. 79, Activity 3
Number: 1 fishing, 2 surfing, 3 snorkelling, 4 sailing
Tick: 1 a, 2 a, 3 b, 4 b

p. 79, Activity 4
1 horse-riding
2 Let's go kayaking! kayaking
3 Let's go fishing! Sorry, I don't like fishing.
4 Let's go surfing! Great idea! I love surfing.
   a surfboard

p. 80, Activity 5
1 hang gliding, 2 rafting, 3 scuba diving, 4 bungee jumping, 5 rock climbing

p. 80, Activity 6
1 crazy about scuba diving, 2 terrified of bungee jumping, 3 scared of hang gliding , 4 fond of rock climbing, 5 bored with rafting

p. 81, Activity 7
1 crazy about, crazy about scuba diving
2 is she terrified of, She's terrified of bungee jumping
3 What's she scared of? She's scared of hang gliding
4 What's she fond of? She's fond of rock climbing
5 What's she bored with? She's bored with rafting

p. 81, Activity 8
1 I'm going to go sailing.
2 What are, going to do, They're going to go fishing.
3 What is, going to do, She's going to go rafting.

p. 82, Activity 10
She opens his diving helmet.

p. 82, Activity 11
a 3, b 5, c 2, d 1, e 4

p. 82, Activity 12
1 film star, 2 making, 3 sharks, 4 scared of, 5 good, 6 acting

p. 82, Activity 13
1 He's crazy about making adventure films.
2 He's scared of sharks.

p. 83, Activity 15
paint, bump, tickle, funny

p. 83, Activity 16
1 elephant, 2 alphabet, 3 wheel, 4 white

p. 84, Activity 18
1 rainforests
2 fish, sea animals
3 colourful
4 sea, hot
5 white

p. 84, Activity 19
Sea: butterfly fish, seahorse, parrot fish, sea snake, starfish
Land: butterfly, lion, parrot, horse, snake

p. 84, Activity 20
Because they are in the sea in places where it's hot and sunny.

p. 85, Activity 21
1 horse-riding, 2 beach volleyball, 3 kayaking, 4 rafting, 5 snorkelling, 6 surfing

p. 86, Activity 23
1 A: sailing, life jacket, B: I haven't.
2 A: Let's go kayaking! you got a paddle B: I have
3 A: Let's go scuba diving! B: scuba diving
4 A: Let's go surfing! B: I don't like surfing
5 B: going to go rafting
6 A: you going to do
   B: going to go snorkelling

p. 87, Activity 24
1 horse-riding, 2 fishing, 3 bored with, 4 snorkelling, 5 excited/happy about, 6 rock climbing

Audioscript

Lesson 1 Activity 1 CD3:23
D = DIRECTOR   C = CREW

D OK. Are we ready? Is everyone on the beach?
C Yes, sir. On the beach or in the sea, sir.
D This is Madley Kool's big scene. Is he ready?
C Errr ...
D Good! Let's start. What's everyone doing? Where's Joe?
C He's sailing.
D OK. Where's Julian?
C He's fishing.
D Right. Where's Jane?
C She's snorkelling.
D Right. Where's James?
C He's ... er, he's horse-riding.
D He's WHAT??? And why is James horse-riding?
C Because he's scared of sharks.

Lesson 1 Activity 2 CD3:24
a snorkelling
  snorkel
b surfing
  surfboard
c sailing
  life jacket
d kayaking
  paddle
e fishing
  fishing rod
f horse-riding
  riding boots

Lesson 1 Activity 3 CD3:25
1 I like kayaking.
2 I like surfing.
3 I like horse-riding.
4 I like sailing.
5 I like fishing.
6 I like snorkelling.

Lesson 2 Activity 4 CD3:26
What are you scared of?
I'm scared of sharks.
What are you scared of?
I'm scared of sharks.
I like the beach and I like the sea.
But I'm scared of sharks.
And they're scared of me!

Lesson 2 Activity 5 CD3:27
S = SAM   R = RUBY   JO = JOHN   JE = JENNY

S Let's go snorkelling!
R Sorry, I don't like snorkelling.
JO Let's go sailing!
S Great idea! I love sailing.
S Let's go fishing!
JO Sorry, I don't like fishing.
R Let's go horse-riding!
JE Great idea! I love horse-riding.
JE Let's go kayaking!
JO Sorry, I don't like kayaking.

Lesson 2 Activity 3 (AB) CD3:28
1 Let's go fishing.
  Great idea! I love fishing.
2 Let's go surfing.
  Sorry, I don't like surfing.
3 Let's go snorkelling.
  Sorry, I don't like snorkelling.
4 Let's go sailing.
  Great idea! I love sailing.

Lesson 3 Activity 6 CD3:29
a fond of
b crazy about
c bored with
d scared of
e terrified of
f rafting
g bungee jumping
h rock climbing
i scuba diving
j hang gliding

Lesson 3 Activity 7 CD3:30
What are you fond of?
I'm fond of these:
Scuba diving and climbing
Big rocks, and the sea.

Whar are you bored with?
I'm bored with these:
Fishing and sailing.
Not exciting, you see?

What are you scared of?
Being up in the air.
Bungee jumping, hang gliding
Not safe, you see?

Anything else, you ask?
I'm terrified of sharks!

Lesson 3 Activity 6 (AB)   CD3:31

1 What is she crazy about?
   She's crazy about scuba diving.
2 What is she terrified of?
   She's terrified of bungee jumping.
3 What is she scared of?
   She's scared of hang gliding.
4 What is she fond of?
   She's fond of rock climbing.
5 What is she bored with?
   She's bored with rafting.

Lesson 4 Activity 9   CD3:32

Dear Grandma and Grandpa,
I'm having a great holiday at the beach. It's warm and sunny and there are a lot of exciting things to do. Every morning I go swimming with the dolphins in the sea. It makes me feel happy because dolphins are so intelligent! In the afternoon I go snorkelling. I love to see all the amazing animals in the sea.
Mum is bored with the beach. Today she's hang gliding!
I'm crazy about water sports, and next Monday I'm going to go scuba diving. I'm so excited!
Then next Wednesday Sue and I are going to go rafting on the river. It's going to be so much fun! Finally, on Friday, we're all going to hike along the coast to the next town. My friend is going to be there and we're going to visit him.
I miss you.
Lots of love.
Tara

Lesson 6 Activity 12   CD3:34

p   h
/f/ /f/ /f/
w   h
/w/ /w/ /w/

Lesson 6 Activity 13   CD3:35

/f/ /f/
/w/ /w/
/f/ /f/
/w/ /w/
/w/ /w/
/f/ /f/

Lesson 6 Activity 14   CD3:36

1 /f/ /oh/ /n/
   phone
2 /d/ /o/ /l/ /f/ /i/ /n/
   dolphin
3 /e/ /l/ /e/ /f/ /a/ /n/ /t/
   elephant
4 /a/ /l/ /f/ /a/ /b/ /e/ /t/
   alphabet
5 /w/ /ee/ /l/
   wheel
6 /w/ /eye/ /t/
   white
7 /w/ /ay/ /l/
   whale
8 /w/ /i/ /s/ /p/ /er/
   whisper

Lesson 6 Activity 15 (AB)   CD3:37

1 /p/   /ai/   /n/   /t/
2 /b/   /u/   /m/   /p/
3 /t/   /i/   /k/   /l/
4 /f/   /u/   /n/   /y/

Lesson 6 Activity 16 (AB)   CD3:38

1 elephant
2 alphabet
3 wheel
4 white

Lesson 6 Activity 17 (AB)   CD3:39

Look, the whale and the dolphin are on the phone!
Here comes the shark. The fish are whispering.
What's that on his head? Oh, it's a funny hat!

Lesson 7 Activity 16   CD3:40

Save the Reefs!
Coral reefs are made of small sea animals and their skeletons. You can find coral reefs in the sea where it's hot and sunny. They are called the rainforests of the sea because a lot of fish and sea animals live on them. There are seahorses, sea snakes, starfish, butterfly fish, parrotfish and many more. There are a lot of pretty colours in the reef. How does this coral reef make you feel?
Now look at this coral reef. It's white and there are no fish or sea animals on it. The sea is too hot because of global warming and the coral is dead. Fish don't like dead coral. How does this coral reef make you feel?
Please help us save the coral reefs.

Lesson 8 Activity 17 CD3:41

Hi, I'm Elliot. I live in Scotland. In August. I'm going to go to a summer camp for two weeks. It's near a national park and it's fantastic! I'm going to do adventure activities like kayaking and rafting. I like sports too. I'm also going to play football and volleyball. I love sports and adventure. Elliot, 10, Scotland

My name's Carolina and I live in Los Angeles. This summer I'm going to go to a beach summer camp for three weeks. It's a wonderful place at the seaside. I can practise lots of fun activities for kids. I'm going to go surfing and snorkelling. I'm also going to play beach volleyball, and I'm going to go on sea life safaris.
I love the beach! Carolina, 10, United States

Lesson 10 Activity 20 CD3:42

1 I'm crazy about snorkelling.
2 I'm bored with sailing.
3 What are you fond of?
  I'm fond of horse-riding.
4 What are you scared of?
  I'm scared of hang gliding.
5 Let's go scuba diving!
  Great idea! I love scuba diving.
6 Have you got a life jacket?
  Yes, I have.

Goodbye

Lesson 1

> **Lesson aims**
> To finish the story
>
> **Materials**
> Audio CD; Story cards; Photocopiable G.1
> Active Teach; Digital Activity Book

Starting the lesson

- Ask pupils (L1) what they can remember about the story from the previous episode. Use the story cards as prompts.

Pupil's Book page 92

Pupil's Book page 92

Presentation

- Ask pupils to revise the story to give a brief summary. They can look at the story pages in the book to get ideas. Ask the class to describe the ending of the story.

1 **Listen and find.**

- Tell pupils they are going to hear a recording and they have to point to the characters. Play the recording. Pause if necessary to give pupils time to find the characters and point to them.

2 Read and match.

- Pupils read the names of the characters and the sentences. Pupils match the halves to make sentences about the characters. Check with the class. Then ask individual pupils to say the sentences for the class.

> **KEY**
> 1 Cleo wants to be a detective.
> 2 Sam wants to be a basketball player.
> 3 Jenny likes Madley Kool.
> 4 John likes playing football.
> 5 Ruby likes keeping things clean.

Practice

- Divide the class into six groups and assign a character to each one (Madley Kool, John, Jenny, Ruby, Sam, Cleo). Select chapters from the story and ask the groups to read their parts as a class from their seats.
- Make sentences about the story, some true and some false, e.g. *John wants to be a film star.* When pupils hear a false sentence, they stand up and correct it.

Activity Book page 88

Activity Book page 88

1 Look and write.

- Pupils look at the picture and complete the questions and answers. Check answers as a class. Invite volunteers to make up new questions for the class to answer, e.g. *What is he wearing?*

2 **Listen and circle.**

- Tell pupils they are going to hear a recording and they have to circle the correct picture. Explain that there are questions from all the episodes. Play the recording. Give pupils time to find the picture and circle it.
- Play the recording again. Pause after each piece of information. Pupils check again. Check with the class.

Ending the lesson

- Divide the class into the same six groups as in the Practice section, with each group being assigned their character. Discuss with pupils what each of the characters likes doing and wants to be or do. Tell them to make a list, as a group, of information about their character. Then they report to the class.
- For AB Answer Key, see p. 264. For Audioscript, see p. 264.

> **NOTES**

Goodbye

1 🔊 3:43 **Listen and find.**

GREAT WHITE SHARKS
starring
MADLEY KOOL

THE GREAT CAT DETECTIVE
STARRING
CLEO

PIZZA

2 **Read and match.**

(John) (Jenny) (Ruby) (Sam) (Cleo)

1 wants to be a detective

2 wants to be a basketball player

3 likes Madley Kool

4 likes playing football

5 likes keeping things clean

OPTIONAL ACTIVITIES

Memory
Ask the pupils to try to repeat the names of the characters in the same order as they appear in the last episode.

Drawing activity
Pupils draw a picture of their assigned, or their favourite, story character and describe him/her. Photocopiable G.1 see Teacher's notes p. 293

Lesson 2

Lesson aims
To practise talking about favourite film stars

Materials
Photos of film stars; Active Teach; Digital Activity Book

Starting the lesson

- Bring magazine cut outs of famous film stars. Check with the pupils their names and what they are famous for.

Pupil's Book page 93

Presentation

- Revise the characteristics of Madley Kool. Go through the different episodes and revise what he does and what happens to him.
- Elicit the name of a film star who is popular with the class. Ask questions about him/her: *Where's he/she from? Has he/she got long hair?*

3 Look, read and say *True* or *False*.

- Focus on the sentences. Check that pupils understand them. You may want to play the Activity 1 recording CD3:43 from Lesson 1 before the class reads the sentences and decides if they are true or false.
- Allow pupils time to think about the answers. Then ask individual pupils to read out a sentence and the class says *True* or *False*. Correct the false sentences.

> **KEY**
> 1 False (He likes meeting his fans.)
> 2 False (It's about the sea.)
> 3 True
> 4 False (He plays football.)
> 5 False (His house is messy.)

4 Think of your favourite film star. Answer the questions in your notebook.

- Read out the questions and check that pupils understand. Check the class's favourites. They then write their answers to the questions in their notebooks.

5 Ask and answer questions about your favourite film stars.

- Organise the class in pairs. Point out the model dialogue. Pupils choose their favourite film stars. They prepare a set of questions each. Then they take it in turns to ask and answer questions about their favourite stars.

Practice

- Divide the class into pairs. Each pupil writes a short description of his/her favourite film star (this could be based on what they wrote for AB Activity 4). Then they ask each other questions, without referring to their text to check if their partner has memorised the information.

Activity Book page 89

3 Write.

- Read out the questions in the bubbles and check that pupils understand. Explain that they must give personal answers. Check answers as a class. Ask all the questions to the class to answer.

4 Think of your favourite film star. Stick a picture of him/her in a scene from a film. Then write.

- Allow pupils time to draw or stick a picture of a film scene with their favourite film star and complete the text describing the scene. Demonstrate with your own favourite if they need support. When they have finished, organise an exhibition with all the pictures. Vote for their favourite film star.

Ending the lesson

- Sing tunes from famous films as a whole-class activity: if possible, play recordings and sing along.
- For AB Answer Key, see p. 264.

3 Look, read and say *True* or *False*.

1 Madley Kool doesn't like meeting his fans.

2 Madley Kool's new film is about the rainforest.

3 Ruby thinks Madley's house is messy.

4 John plays basketball and skateboards.

5 Madley Kool cleans his house every day.

4 Think of your favourite film star. Answer the questions in your notebook.

1 Who's your favourite film star?

2 What country is he/she from?

3 What's his/her best film?

4 Why do you like him/her?

5 What's your favourite film?

6 Why do you like this film?

5 Ask and answer questions about your favourite film stars.

Who's your favourite film star?

My favourite film star is ...

OPTIONAL ACTIVITIES

Flashcard game
Play *Picture charades* see p. 298.

Team game
Play *Unscramble* see p. 300, using names of famous film stars.

Lesson 3

Lesson aims
To revise vocabulary and structures

Materials
Audio CD; Flashcards (All units); ball or beanbag; game counters, dice or spinners; Active Teach; Digital Activity Book

Starting the lesson

- Play a game. With a small class, sit in a circle on the floor and have pupils throw a ball or beanbag to each other. With a larger class, keep the usual seating arrangement and ask pupils to stand up and give the ball to each other. Explain that pupils should take a flashcard from a pile and make a sentence with that word, e.g. *I'm fond of surfing,* when they throw or give the ball to another pupil. When a pupil catches or receives the ball they should repeat the sentence before taking another flashcard.

Pupil's Book page 94

Presentation

- Tell pupils (L1) they are going to do activities to revise vocabulary and structures they have learnt throughout the course year. Give them time to go through the book and look at main vocabulary and language patterns in pairs.

6 Play.

- Divide the class into groups of four and distribute game counters (one for each pupil). Revise the vocabulary using the flashcards. Practise with the pupils the language to be used: *Cleo likes ... .* Check that pupils understand that they take turns to throw/ spin and move the number of spaces: they must answer the questions or complete the sentences. An incorrect answer means the player must move back two spaces and try that question. The winner is the first pupil to reach question 20 (the throw/spin must be exact) and answer it correctly.

Activity Book page 90

5 Listen and read about Willie. Then write about yourself.

- Tell the class that they are going to read a text about Willie and they must take it as a model to write about themselves. Ask questions to check that they understand the text: *What's his name? What does he like doing?* Tell them they can write a draft in their notebooks before they write the final version in the Activity Book. Ask a few pupils to read out their text to the class.

6 Look and write.

- The pupils look at the pictures and answer the questions about the weather. When they have finished, they read out the answers in pairs. Then ask volunteers to read out their answers to the class.

Ending the lesson

- Play *Spelling bee* to practise spelling words from all units. Pupils listen to the words you say and, in turn, they try to spell them correctly.
- For AB Answer key, see p. 264. For Audioscript, see p.264.

6 Play.

 Try to remember as much as you can from the story. Count your correct answers.

1 The children are looking for …	**2** Cleo likes … and …	**3** Two … are under John's feet.	**4** Crocodiles eat …!
5 Jenny likes the beach because it's …	**6** Cleo wants to … on the beach.	**7** On the boat Sam is ill because of the … weather.	**8** Madley Kool does … on Mondays.
9 Madley Kool goes … on Saturdays.	**10** Can Madley Kool swim?	**11** What does Sam want to be?	**12** What does Ruby want to be?
13 What does John want to be?	**14** True or false: The spider near Ruby is real.	**15** Cleo's full name is …	**16** Madley Kool's new film is about …
17 What's Ruby scared of?	**18** The man in the water writes the word ' … ' on the glass wall.	**19** Who finds Madley Kool in the end?	**20** Is Madley Kool scared of sharks?

OPTIONAL ACTIVITIES

Team game
Play *Can I cross the river?* see p. 300 to revise questions and answers learnt: *What are you scared of? Can you swim?* etc.

Flashcard game
Play *Countdown* see p. 298, using words from different units and categories.

Lesson 4

Lesson aims
To revise vocabulary and structures

Materials
Audio CD; Flashcards (Prepositions); Active Teach;
Digital Activity Book

Starting the lesson

- Hold up the flashcards for prepositions and say the words. Pupils say all the words.

Pupil's Book page 95

Presentation

- Tell pupils (L1) they are going to do activities to revise vocabulary and structures they have learnt throughout the course year.
- Play a chain game saying sentences from the book, e.g. to describe animals: *Giraffes eat ....* One pupil starts a sentence, and the other pupils continue the chain.

7 Look and answer.

- Focus on the picture. Read out the questions and check that pupils understand. Revise the prepositions. Give pupils time to ask and answer in pairs or to write the answers. Check answers with the class.

> **KEY**
> 1 They are near the river, under the bridge.
> 2 They are in the river, near the waterfall.
> 3 The monkey is in the tree, between the waterfall and the bridge.
> 4 The parrot is flying over the hut.
> 5 The snake is between the bridge and the hut
> 6 The hut is next to the tree.

8 Talk about your favourite animal.

- Focus first on the two model questions. Give pupils time to complete the questions and check that they understand the meaning. Then point out the answer speech bubbles. Give them time to think about their answers. They work in pairs and exchange information about their favourite animals.

9 Ask and answer.

- Focus on the questions the pupils have to use to talk about themselves. Check that they understand them.
- Pupils work in pairs. They take it in turns to ask and answer questions about themselves. Model a dialogue with a confident pupil as an example. Practise with the whole class before they work in pairs.

Activity Book page 91

7 Listen and read about Judy. Then write about yourself.

- Tell the class that they are going to read a text about Judy and use it as a model to write about themselves. Ask questions to check that they understand the text: *What does she do on Wednesdays? What does she want to be?* Tell them to write a draft in their notebooks before writing the final version in the Activity Book. Then they write the texts. Ask volunteers to read out their text to the class.

8 Listen and write.

- Explain that pupils are going to listen to a recording and they must write the correct information. Play the recording. The pupils write. Play the recording again. Once they have finished, check answers with the whole class.

9 Write.

- The pupils try to answer all the questions. Explain that if they can't remember the answers, they can ask their partner or look them up in the book. Give them a time limit to answer as many questions as possible. Check answers with the class.

Ending the lesson

- Ask the pupils to give a summary of the story.
- (For AB Answer key, see p. 264. For Audioscript, see p. 264.)

7 Look and answer.

1   Where are the crocodiles?

2   Where are the hippos?

3   Where's the monkey?

4   Where's the parrot?

5   Where's the snake?

6   Where's the hut?

8 Talk about your favourite animal.

What do … eat?

They eat …

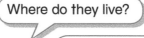

Where do they live?

They live in …

9 Ask and answer.

1	What makes you feel happy?
2	What makes you feel angry?
3	What are you scared of?
4	What are you bored with?
5	What do you want to be?

OPTIONAL ACTIVITIES
Flashcard game
Play *Who's the fastest?* see p. 298.

Team game
Play *Anagrams* see p. 301.

Activity Book Answer Key

p. 88, Activity 1
1 Madley Kool
2 does he like
3 is he smiling

p. 88, Activity 2
1 c, **2** a, **3** b, **4** b **5** a, **6** c **7** b, **8** b

p. 90, Activity 6
1 wet
2 24 degrees
3 Yes, is
4 thunder and lightning
5 No, it isn't. (It's sunny.)
6 Yes, it is.

p. 91, Activity 8
1 a playing the piano, **b** playing the guitar
2 a sports, **b** hiking

p. 91, Activity 9
1 chatting online, **2** a crocodile, **3** stormy
weather, **4** midday, **5** a photographer, **6** a nest,
7 proud (happy), **8** a paddle (a kayak, a life jacket)

Audioscript

Lesson 1 Activity 1   CD3:43

R = RUBY   M = MADLEY   JE = JENNY   S = SAM
JO = JOHN   C = CLEO

R   Whew! It's messy here. Mr Kool, do you like cleaning?

M   No! But I like meeting my fans.

JE   Mr Kool, I'm crazy about film stars. What are you crazy about?

M   I'm crazy about my fans and I want to make you the president of my fan club.

S   I play basketball and I want to be famous like you, Mr Kool. What should I do?

M   That's great! Just work hard and keep practising.

JO   I play football on Saturday. How about you, Mr Kool? When do you play football?

M   I play football on the weekend, when I'm not working. But let's watch the trailer of my new film now.

C   Hmm! Cleo the great cat detective. Starring Cleo, of course!

Lesson 1 Activity 2 (AB)   CD3:44

Unit 1 story
What are John, Jenny, Ruby, and Sam doing?
Unit 2 story
What do the crocodiles like eating?
Unit 3 story
What does Cleo like to do on the beach?
Unit 4 story
What lessons does Madley have on Friday?
Unit 5 story
What does Jenny want to be?
Unit 6 story
Who is the film star?
Unit 7 story
How does the man in the water feel?
Unit 8 story
How many new friends does Madley Kool have?

Lesson 3 Activity 5 (AB)   CD3:45

My name is Willie. I'm 10 years old. I like playing the guitar and surfing the internet in my free time. I don't like painting or drawing. My favourite wild animal is the gorilla. Gorillas live in the rainforest and they eat leaves and fruit.

Lesson 4 Activity 7 (AB)   CD3:46

My name is Judy. I'm 11 years old. I study hard every day. I play basketball with my friends on Wednesdays. I learn to cook with my grandmother on Saturdays. When I grow up I want to be a lawyer or a journalist.

Lesson 4 Activity 8 (AB)   CD3:47

I'm Amy. I'm crazy about music. I love playing the piano, and I feel proud when I play the piano for my family and friends. I feel nervous when I play the guitar, well ... because I'm not very good at it. I'm fond of sports. I love playing tennis and basketball. I also go hiking in the mountains with my family, but I'm bored with hiking.

Halloween

Lesson aims
To learn about Halloween celebrations

Target language
moon, owl, skeleton, monster, bone

Materials
Audio CD

Optional materials
Coloured card; glue; ribbon; glitter; large sheet of poster paper

Cultural note: Halloween in the UK

- Halloween is on 31st October. It includes activities such as trick-or-treating, costume parties, carving lanterns and telling scary stories.

Starting the lesson

- Put a calendar up on the board and ask the class (L1) if and when they celebrate Halloween.
- Ask pupils how they celebrate Halloween. Talk about presents, costumes, etc. Tell them (L1) about British Halloween customs.
- Sing with the pupils any Halloween song they may remember from previous years.

Pupil's Book pages 96–97

Presentation

1 **Listen, find and say.**

- Ask pupils to look at the picture. Play the recording, pausing after each word for pupils to point to the items and say the words.

Practice

- Hold up the Pupil's Book, point to one of the labelled items and ask *What's this?* Pupils answer using the target vocabulary. Then pupils take turns to choose and say a word, e.g. *moon*.

2 **Listen and sing.**

- Tell pupils that you are going to play the Halloween song. Play the recording once for pupils to listen and follow in their books. Play the song again and pupils point to the labelled objects in the picture. Play it a third time for pupils to join in. Repeat until the class remembers the song without help from the book.

3 **Look and say *True* or *False*.**

- Focus on the main illustration and ask *What's this?* Pupils answer *It's an owl. It's a witch,* etc. Explain to the class that they must look at the picture, read the sentences and decide if they are true or false. Allow pupils time to think about the answers. Then ask individual pupils to read out a sentence and the class says *True* or *False.* Correct the false sentences.

> **KEY** **1** True, **2** False (It hasn't got a broom.), **3** False (They aren't scared.), **4** False (They have got sweets.), **5** True

4 **Read and answer.**

- Tell the pupils that they have to answer the questions giving personal information. Read out the questions and check that pupils understand. Allow them time to answer the questions individually in their notebooks. Then check answers with the class.

AB p.92 97

Activity Book page 92

① Find, circle and write the Halloween words.

- Ask the pupils to circle the words in the wordsearch and then write each word next to the corresponding picture. Check answers with the class when they have finished.

② Look and write.

- Pupils look at the picture and describe what they can see. They write the answers individually. Then check answers with the class.

Ending the lesson

- Pupils work in groups to draw and decorate a Halloween poster using the materials you and they can supply.
- For AB Answer Key, see p. 274. For Audioscript, see p. 267.

OPTIONAL ACTIVITIES

Sing Halloween songs
Sing with the class Halloween songs.
Drawing activity
Ask the pupils to draw Halloween items. Organise an exhibition in class.

Audioscript

Halloween Activity 1   CD 3:48
moon
owl
skeleton
monster
bone

Halloween Activity 2   CD 3:49
It's Halloween!
It's Halloween!
Don't be scared!
It' so much fun!

The moon is full and bright,
Monsters play tonight.
Witches on their brooms
fly across the moon.

It's Halloween!
It's Halloween!
Don't be scared!
It' so much fun!

Skeletons move their bones.
Ghosts leave their homes.
Owls go 'twit-twoo'.
Bats fly to you!

It's Halloween!
It's Halloween!
Don't be scared!
It' so much fun!

A bag full of sweets
Such a great treat!
It's getting late!
Halloween is great!

LESSON AIMS
To learn about Christmas celebrations

Target language
Christmas crackers, play with presents, Christmas lunch, open presents, snowball, snowman, Christmas pudding

Materials
Audio CD

Optional materials
Calendar, card of different colours, glue, ribbon, cotton, glitter, poster paper; Photocopiable F.1

Cultural note: Christmas in the UK

- Christmas is an important celebration in the UK. For weeks before, people buy presents and put up decorations.
- On Christmas Day (25th December), children get up early to find stockings filled by Father Christmas/ Santa Claus. Families usually have a big lunch as part of the celebrations.

Starting the lesson

- Put a calendar up on the board and ask the class (L1) if they celebrate Christmas. If they do, ask when and how they celebrate. Talk about food and presents.

Pupil's Book pages 98–99

Presentation

- Tell the class (L1) about British Christmas customs. Direct pupils' attention to the pictures and use them to present the words.
- Explain (L1) that Christmas crackers are an important part of Christmas celebrations in the UK. A cracker is a cardboard tube wrapped in a decorated twist of paper. It is pulled from each end by two people. When it breaks there is a small bang. Inside the cracker there is usually a paper hat, a joke and a gift.

1 🔵 Listen, find and say.

- Ask pupils to look at the picture. Play the recording, pausing after each word for pupils to point to the items and say the words.

Practice

- Hold up the Pupil's Book, point to one of the labelled items and ask *What's this? Who's this?* Pupils answer using the target vocabulary.

2 🔵 Listen and find the order.

- Tell the class that they are going to listen to a girl (Grace) speaking about Christmas traditions. Play the recording and pupils listen and follow in their books. Then ask pupils to listen again and find the order of the pictures. Check answers.

> **KEY** **d** open presents, **c** Christmas lunch, **f** Christmas pudding, **a** Christmas crackers, **b** play with presents, **e** snowball and snowman

3 🔵 Listen and sing.

- Play the recording. Pupils listen and follow the words. Elicit/Explain (L1) that the song has four verses, each like the verse for Dad that is written out in full. Verse 2 has *My mum is cooking Christmas lunch* and so on.
- Play the song again and pupils join in, until they can remember the song without help from the book.

4 🔵 Listen to the song again and answer.

- Focus on the questions and check that pupils understand them. Play the song again. Then give pupils time to answer the questions.

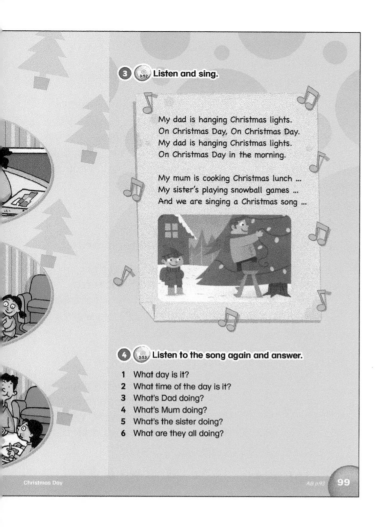

Christmas Day

99

AB p.93

Make Christmas crackers

For instructions, see http://www.oldenglishcrackers.com/make-your-own-crackers.htm.
Photocopiable F.1 see Teacher's notes p.293

Audioscript

Christmas Day Activity 1 CD3:50

Christmas crackers
Christmas pudding
snowball
play with presents
snowman
Christmas lunch
open presents

Christmas Day Activity 2 CD3:51

Hi! I'm Grace. This is me and my family on Christmas Day. We open our presents in the morning, then my mum cooks a special lunch. We eat turkey, potatoes, carrots and sprouts. Then we have Christmas pudding. Yum! We pull Christmas crackers. They go 'bang' and inside there are little presents, jokes and paper hats. What colour is my hat in the photo? In the afternoon I play with my presents. If it's snowy I play snowball games with my brother or make a snowman in the garden.

Christmas Day Activity 3 CD3:52 and CD3:53

My dad is hanging Christmas lights.
On Christmas Day, On Christmas Day.
My dad is hanging Christmas lights.
On Christmas Day in the morning.

My mum is cooking Christmas lunch.
On Christmas Day, On Christmas Day.
My mum is cooking Christmas lunch.
On Christmas Day in the morning.

My sister's playing snowball games.
On Christmas Day, On Christmas Day.
My sister's playing snowball games.
On Christmas Day in the morning.

And we are singing a Christmas song.
On Christmas Day, On Christmas Day.
And we are singing a Christmas song.
On Christmas Day in the morning.

KEY 1 It's Christmas Day (25th December). **2** Morning. **3** Dad is hanging Christmas lights. **4** Mum is cooking Christmas lunch. **5** She's playing snowball games. **6** They're all singing a Christmas song.

Activity Book page 93

1 **Find, circle and write the Christmas words.**

● The pupils must circle the Christmas words in the wordsearch and write them next to the pictures. Check answers with the class when they have finished.

2 **Write.**

● Direct pupils' attention to the picture in the PB pp. 98–99 and the words of the song. Explain that they have to use the words in the word bank. Check answers.

Ending the lesson

● Write some new verses for the song, e.g. *And we are eating Christmas lunch. My granny's wearing a paper hat,* etc. Write them on the board and then sing them to the karaoke version of the song CD3:52 as a class.

● For AB Answers Key, see p. 274. For Audioscript, see p. 274.

Lesson aims
To learn about Easter celebrations

Target language
Easter eggs, chocolate bunny, jelly beans, trail

Materials
Audio CD

Optional materials
Calendar, basket, jelly beans, coloured eggs, flowers, small chocolate bunnies/eggs, hard-boiled eggs, felt pens

Cultural note: Easter in the UK

- On Easter Sunday, exchanging and eating Easter eggs is a popular custom in the UK. Traditionally, these were hard-boiled eggs painted in bright colours. Nowadays, Easter eggs are made of chocolate and sometimes filled with sweets. Children hunt for Easter eggs hidden in the home or garden by the Easter bunny.

Starting the lesson

- Put a calendar up on the board and ask pupils (L1) if or when they celebrate Easter.
- Ask pupils (L1) how they celebrate Easter. Tell them (L1) about British Easter customs.

Pupil's Book page 100

Presentation

- Ask pupils to look at the picture and explain (L1) that *bunny* is a (children's) word for *rabbit*.

1 **Listen, find and say.**

- Play the recording, pausing after each word. Pupils listen, point to the items and say the words.

Practice

- Hold up the Pupil's Book, point to one of the labelled items and ask *What's this? Who's this?* Pupils answer using the target vocabulary. Then pupils take turns to choose a word and say a sentence, e.g. *Peter Cottontail is hiding Easter eggs.*

2 **Listen and sing.**

- Tell pupils you are going to play the Easter song. Play the recording once for pupils to listen and follow. Explain (L1) the meaning of some words if necessary. Play the song again and pupils point to the labelled objects in the picture. Play the song again and pupils join in, until they can remember the song without help from the book.

3 **Ask and answer.**

- Ask individual pupils to read the questions aloud to the class. Help them understand if necessary. Tell the class that they must give personal answers to the questions. Then organise the class in pairs. They take turns to ask and answer the questions. Ask a pair to model the dialogue in front of the class.

Activity Book page 94

1 **Find, circle and write the Easter words.**

- The pupils must circle the Easter words in the wordsearch and write them next to the pictures. Check answers with the class when they have finished. Ask volunteers to make sentences using the words.

2 **Look, match and write.**

- The pupils look at the pictures and the word bank. Ask pupils a few questions to focus their attention on the pictures, e.g. *Who is eating a chocolate bunny? Who has got two Easter eggs?* Allow pupils time to complete the sentences with the words from the word bank.

Ending the lesson

- Play CD3:55 and sing the Easter song as a class.
- For AB Answers Key, see p. 274. For Audioscript, see p. 274.

OPTIONAL ACTIVITIES

TPR game
Give pupils commands taken from the song and organise a TPR game: *Hop. Take a basket. Put jelly beans in the basket. Put eggs in the basket,* etc.

Decorate eggs
Ask pupils to decorate eggs using felt pens. Organise an exhibition in class.

Mother's Day

Lesson aims
To learn about Mother's Day celebrations

Target language
Mother's Day, breakfast in bed, tea, toast, rose, box of chocolates

Materials
Audio CD

Optional materials
World map or globe, British calendar, poster paper, markers, assorted items to decorate a poster; Photocopiable F.2

Cultural note: Mother's Day in the UK

- On Mother's Day children give their mothers cards and presents, and give them extra help like doing the cooking or cleaning. Some families like to go out for lunch on Mother's Day. It is always in spring and on a Sunday, three weeks before Easter. It is traditional in some areas to eat a special cake on Mother's Day.

Starting the lesson

- Put the calendar up on the board and ask pupils (L1) if they celebrate Mother's Day. If they do, ask (L1) when and how they celebrate it. Talk about special gifts, meals or decorations.

Pupil's Book page 101

Presentation

- Ask the pupils what type of presents they would give to their mothers for Mother's Day. Sensitivity may be required depending on your pupils' family circumstances.

● Read.

- Ask pupils to look at the text about Mother's Day. Explain that in different countries the day is on different dates. Write on the board the date when it's celebrated in the country where the pupils live.

Practice

- Play a memory game. Say *It's Mother's Day and Mum has got a rose.* Nominate a pupil to add a present or food item to the sentence, e.g. *It's Mother's Day and Mum has got a rose and a book.* Continue round the class, with each pupil repeating what went before and adding something new to the list, until someone makes a mistake. Then start again.

② Listen, find and say.

- Introduce any new words, pointing to the pictures. Say the words for pupils to repeat. Ask individual pupils to say the words. Play the recording for pupils to listen, point and repeat.

③ Listen and read.

- Tell the class that they are going to listen to a boy speaking about Mother's Day. Play the recording. Pupils listen and follow in their books. Ask pupils to reread the text. Ask some comprehension questions: *What day is it? (Sunday). Where is his mum? (In bed).*

④ Read again and answer.

- The pupils read the text again. Read out the questions and check that pupils understand. They answer individually. Check answers with the class.

> **KEY 1** It's Sunday. **2** She's having toast and tea. **3** Yes, she has. **4** The boy/Her son. **5** A box of chocolates.

Activity Book page 95

① Match.

- Ask pupils to read the labels and draw lines connecting the labels to the items in the picture. Check answers with the class.

② Read. Then write your own note.

- Direct pupils' attention to the layout of the card. Ask *Do you give cards to your mother on Mother's Day?* Explain that they are going to write a card in English. Show them the example and tell pupils that they can use some of this text but should write some text of their own. Ask a few pupils to read their sentences.

Ending the lesson

- You can use this card as a model to make a real card. Then they draw and colour the card and write the text. Display the cards in the classroom.
- (For Audioscript, see p. 274.)

OPTIONAL ACTIVITIES

Make a 'Dear Mum, I promise ...' poster
Discuss (L1) with the class what makes their mothers happy, e.g. that they tidy their bedrooms. Pupils write 'Dear Mum, I promise ...' on a piece of paper. Pupils each write a promise on the poster. Then they decorate it.
Photocopiable F.2 see Teacher's notes p.293

Lesson aims
To learn about Pancake Day celebrations

Target language
Pancake Day, toss, frying pan

Materials
Audio CD

Optional materials
Coloured card, white card, glue, colouring pens

Cultural note: Pancake Day in the UK

- Pancake Day is celebrated on Shrove Tuesday which is the day before Lent. Lent is a Christian holiday when people traditionally used to eat no meat – nowadays they sometimes give up something they like (e.g. chocolate). People used to eat a lot and have fun the day before Lent begins. Shrove Tuesday is often referred to as Pancake Day because fats, which were not allowed during Lent, had to be used up. People would take all the eggs and dairy products that they had left in their kitchens and use them to make delicious pancakes. Nowadays people still make pancakes on Shrove Tuesday even if they do not observe Lent.

Starting the lesson

- Explain when Pancake Day is celebrated and how. Ask pupils (L1) if they have a similar celebration in their country.

> Pupil's Book page 102

Presentation

- Ask pupils to look at the picture and discuss what happens in a pancake race.

1 Listen, look and read.

- Play the recording, pausing after each phrase. Pupils listen, point to the relevant part of the picture, and say the phrases.
- Play the rest of the recording and ask the pupils to listen.
- Explain (L1) any unknown words.

Practice

- Hold up the Pupil's Book, point to the picture showing a pancake race and make a simple description of it.

2 Read and answer.

- Tell pupils they are going to read the text while they listen to it. Play CD3:58 once for pupils to listen and follow. Explain (L1) the meaning of some words if necessary. Play the recording again and ask a few comprehension questions: *Are the people tossing the pancakes? (Yes). Are they running? (Yes).*
- Explain to the class that they are going to read questions about the text and they have to answer them. Read out the questions and check that they understand. They find the answers individually. Then check answers with the class. Make sure pupils realise that they must find the answers in the text.

> **KEY**
> 1 In the United Kingdom
> 2 Sugar and lemon
> 3 They have pancake races.
> 4 Yes, they do.
> 5 Yes, they do.

Ending the lesson

- Write the words *pancake*, *celebrate* and *race* on the board. Ask pupils to write or say as many sentences as they can, using these words. They could do this in competing groups, in pairs or individually.
- For Audioscript, see p. 274.

> **OPTIONAL ACTIVITIES**
> **Pancake recipes**
> Ask pupils to find a pancake recipe and write it in their notebooks. Groups could compare their recipes and report how similar or different they are. Which one sounds nicest?
> **Make a Pancake Race poster**
> Organise the class in small groups. Give each pupil a sheet of card. Pupils draw and make a poster about a pancake race.

Earth Day

Lesson aims
To learn about Earth Day celebrations

Target language
Recycle plastic, Reuse paper, Don't use plastic bags, Recycle cans, Reuse glass bottles, Give old clothes to other people

Materials
Audio CD

Optional materials
Calendar, coloured card, white card, glue, colouring pens; Photocopiable F.3

Cultural note: Earth Day

- Earth Day is the 22nd April every year. It's a day to think about our planet and how we can protect the environment.

Starting the lesson

- Explain when Earth Day is celebrated and show the date on a calendar. Ask pupils (L1) if they have a similar celebration in their country.

Pupil's Book page 103

Presentation

- Ask pupils to look at the pictures and discuss the actions that they show. Ask if they do any of them.

Practice

- Hold up the Pupil's Book, point to the pictures and make or elicit a simple description of each one.

1 **Listen and point.**

- Ask questions as a whole-class activity, e.g. *When is Earth Day? How do people celebrate it? Do you celebrate it?* Play the recording; pupils listen and find the corresponding pictures.

2 **Ask and answer.**

- Organise the class in pairs. Explain to the class that they are going to take turns to ask and answer about actions to look after the Earth. Tell the pupils to look at the model dialogue as an example. Allow pupils time to ask and answer. Ask volunteers to demonstrate some of their questions and answers.

Ending the lesson

- Ask pupils to give information about the things they recycle and reuse. Draw two circles on the board, one with the word *reuse*, and the other with the word *recycle*. Write in the corresponding circle what pupils say. Pupils copy that into their notebooks.
- (For Audioscript, see p. 274.)

OPTIONAL ACTIVITIES

Make a survey
Organise the class in small groups. They collect information about actions that each pupil takes. Then collect actions from the whole class. Draw a diagram with the results on the board. The pupils draw it into their notebooks.

Make a recycle poster
Organise the class in small groups. Give each pupil a sheet of card. Pupils draw and make a poster about things they recycle.

Photocopiable F.3 see Teacher's notes p. 293

Activity Book Answer Key

Halloween

p. 92, Activity 1
1 moon, 2 owl, 3 skeleton, 4 monster, 5 bone

p. 92, Activity 2
1 sweets, 2 two, 3 skeleton, 4 broomstick, 5 monsters

Christmas Day

p. 93, Activity 1
1 lunch, 2 lights, 3 pudding, 4 cracker, 5 present,
6 snowball, 7 snowman

p. 93, Activity 2
1 lights, 2 presents, 3 turkey, 4 pudding, 5 snowballs,
6 snowman, 7 songs

Easter

p. 94, Activity 1
1 jelly beans, 2 bunny, 3 eggs, 4 chocolate, 5 trail,
6 basket

p. 94, Activity 2
1 d trail, 2 a chocolate, 3 c eating, 4 b flowers

Audioscript

Easter Activity 1 — CD3:54
1 chocolate bunny
2 jelly beans
3 trail
4 Easter eggs

Easter Activity 2 — CD3:55
Here comes Peter Cottontail
Hopping down the bunny trail,
Hip hop, hip hop,
Easter's on its way.

He's bringing every girl and boy
A basket full of Easter joy!
Things to make your Easter
Such a wonderful day!

He's got jelly beans for Tim,
Coloured eggs for Kim.
There's a flower for Mummy,
Chocolate bunnies for your tummy.

Here comes Peter Cottontail
Hopping down the bunny trail,
Hip hop, hip hop,
it's Easter Day!

Mother's Day Activity 2 — CD3:56
breakfast in bed
toast
box of chocolates
tea
rose

Mother's Day Activity 3 — CD3:57
Today is Sunday and it's Mother's Day. This is breakfast in bed for my mum. It's a treat because she makes breakfast for me and my dad every day. My mum likes toast and tea for breakfast. Today she's got a rose and some presents too. My present for my mum is a box of chocolates!

Pancake Day Activity 1 — CD3:58
Pancake Day
toss
frying pan

In the United Kingdom, many people celebrate Pancake Day. They eat pancakes with sugar and lemon. Some people also have pancake races! They race with pancakes in frying pans. Racers toss the pancakes and try to catch them as they run. It's a very funny race!

Earth Day Activity 1 — CD3:59
a Recycle plastic.
b Reuse paper.
c Don't use plastic bags.
d Recycle cans.
e Reuse glass bottles.
f Give old clothes to other people.

Extensive reading

Unit 1 Pupil's Book page 104

1 Look and say *True* or *False*.

- Focus pupils' attention on the illustration that goes with the text. Ask a few general questions (L1): *What can you see in the illustration? (A summer camp, A boy and a girl)*. Then ask the class *What type of text is it? (A dialogue). What do you think the dialogue is about? (Activities they like doing in the summer camp)*. Listen to their answers.
- The pupils look at the text and the picture again. Read out sentences (1–5) and check that they understand. Read the sentences one by one and elicit answers from the class: pupils say *True* or *False*. Alternatively, they could write the answers in their notebooks (check as a class). Ask pupils to correct the false sentences.

> **KEY** 1 True, 2 False (There are no skiing lessons.), 3 True, 4 True, 5 False (There is swimming, not lessons.)

2 Look and read.

- Direct the pupils' attention to the dialogue and ask, e.g. *What are their names? (Tom and Elisa). Where's Elisa from? (Spain).* Ask the pupils to read the text. Tell them to ask you about any words they might not understand and help them. Ask them to pay special attention to the words for free time activities and the meanings.

3 Read again and answer.

- Tell pupils to read the dialogue (Activity 2) again and find the information to answer the questions. Allow pupils time to think about the answers. When they have finished, they check answers in pairs. Then ask individual pupils to read out a question and the class answers. Correct if necessary.

> **KEY** 1 Yes, he does. 2 No, he doesn't. 3 Yes, she does. 4 No, she doesn't. 5 Yes, they do.

4 Tell your partner about activities you like.

- Use the flashcards for leisure activities to revise the vocabulary. If possible, bring to the class magazine cut outs showing more activities. Organise the class in pairs. Give them time to write notes about the activities they like. Then they take turns to tell their partners. Ask them to bring pictures of their favourite activities to the class if possible and organise an exhibition in the classroom.

5 Describe these activities to a partner.

- Show cut outs to the class with these activities: *swimming* and *cooking*. Organise the class in pairs. Tell them to take turns to mime the activity and then to use their own words to explain the meaning. If necessary, let them do that in L1. They can check the answers looking up in a dictionary. Check answers with the class.

Unit 2 Pupil's Book page 105

1 Look and say *True* or *False*.

- Focus pupils' attention on the illustration that goes with the text. Ask a few general questions (L1) *What can you see in the illustration? (Alligators)*, etc. After that, ask the class *What type of text is it? (A description). What do you think the text is about?* Listen to their answers.
- The pupils look at the text and the picture again. Read out sentences (1–5) and check that they understand. Read the sentences one by one and elicit answers from the class: pupils say *True* or *False*. Alternatively, they could write the answers in their notebooks (check as a class). Ask pupils to correct the false sentences.

> **KEY** 1 False (They can swim), 2 True, 3 True, 4 True, 5 False (They live in rivers/near rivers/on land and in water.)

2 Look and read.

- Ask the pupils to read the text silently. Tell them to ask you about any words they might not understand and help them. Ask them to pay special attention to the words for wild animals and the meanings. Show where North America, South/Central America, Africa and Australia are on a world map or globe.

3 Read again and answer.

- Tell pupils to read the text (Activity 2) again and find the information to answer the questions. Allow pupils time to think about the answers. When they have finished, they check answers in pairs. Then ask individual pupils to read out a question and the class answers. Ask them to explain any *No* answers. Correct if necessary.

> **KEY** 1 No, they are reptiles. 2 They live on land and in water. 3 Yes, they can. 4 They eat frogs, turtles, birds, fish and other animals. 5 There are two kinds of alligators (Chinese and American).

4 Tell your partner about alligators.

- Organise the class in pairs and focus their attention on the characteristics of the animals. The pupils write a list with the characteristics. They can read the text again if necessary. Then they take turns to describe the animals to each other.

5 Find these words in the text. Explain their meaning.

- Say the two words: *skin* and *sharp*. Ask the pupils to read the text again and find these words. They have to find out their meaning. Tell them to use their own words and write the definition. If necessary, let them do that in L1. They can check the answers looking up in a dictionary. Check answers with the class.

> **KEY Suggested answers: 1** skin: external part of the animal, **2** sharp: can cut

Unit 3 Pupil's Book page 106

1 Look and say *True* or *False*.

- Focus pupils' attention on the pictures that go with the descriptions. Ask a few general questions (L1): *What can you see in the illustration? (A pond)*, etc. Then ask *What type of text is it? (A description). What's the title of the text? (The pond). What do you think the text is about? (The pond in summer and winter).*
- The pupils look at the text and the picture again. Read out sentences (1–5) and check that they understand. Read the sentences one by one and elicit answers from the class: pupils say *True* or *False*. Alternatively, they could write the answers in their notebooks (check as a class). Ask pupils to correct the false sentences.

> **KEY 1** True, **2** True, **3** False (The pond is frozen.), **4** False (It's sunny and warm.), **5** True

2 Look and read.

- Ask the pupils to read the text silently. Tell them to ask you about any words they might not understand and help them. Ask them to pay special attention to the words for the seasons and the meanings. Tell them to compare the pictures of the pond in summer and winter and read the descriptions finding the differences.

3 Read again and answer.

- Tell pupils to read the description again and find the information to answer the questions. Allow pupils time to think about the answers. Check answers in pairs. Ask individual pupils to read out a question and the class answers. Correct if necessary.

> **KEY 1** Yes, you can. **2** It's −5 degrees. **3** Yes, you can. **4** It's 27 degrees. **5** It's sunny and warm.

4 Describe the pond in both seasons to your partner.

- Organise the class in pairs and focus their attention on the descriptions of the same pond in summer and winter. Pupils write the draft of the description in their notebooks. Revise drafts when pupils ask for help. They take turns to read their descriptions to each other.

5 Find these words in the text. Explain their meaning.

- Say the two words *pond* and *skates*. Direct the pupils' attention to the pictures that go with the text. Ask them to read the text again and find these words. They have to find out their meaning. Tell them to use their own words and write the definition. If necessary, let them do that in L1. They can check the answers looking up in a dictionary. Check answers.

> **KEY Suggested answers: 1** pond: It's water but smaller than a lake. **2** skates: You wear them on your feet to skate on ice.

Unit 4 Pupil's Book page 107

1 Look and say *True* or *False*.

- Focus pupils' attention first on Mary's week plan. Ask a few general questions (L1): *What type of text is it? (A week plan)*, etc. Then focus on the title: *Mary's week*. After that, ask about the blog: *What type of text is it? (A blog). What do you think the text is about?*
- The pupils look at the text and the picture again. Read out sentences (1–5) and check that they understand. Read the sentences one by one and elicit answers from the class: pupils say *True* or *False*. Alternatively, they could write the answers in their notebooks (check as a class). Ask pupils to correct the false sentences.

> **KEY 1** True, **2** True, **3** False (She practises the piano.), **4** False (She doesn't do gymnastics.), **5** True

2 Look and read.

- Ask pupils about their week plan: *Do you have ballet lessons? Do you do karate? Do you practise the piano?* Tell the pupils to read the blog and look at the week plan. Tell them to ask you about any words they might not understand and help them. Ask them to pay special attention to the words for activities and the meanings.

3 Read again and answer.

- Tell pupils to read the blog, look at the week plan again and find the information to answer the questions. Allow pupils time to think about the answers. When they have finished, they check answers in pairs. Then ask individual pupils to read out a question and the class answers. Correct if necessary.

KEY **1** She has ballet lessons at 3 o'clock. **2** She has piano lessons at 2 o'clock. **3** She does karate at half past 4. **4** She has cooking lessons on Tuesdays at half past 3. **5** Yes, she does.

4 Describe your week to your partner.

- Organise the class in pairs and focus their attention on the week plan. The pupils write a similar table with their week's activities in their notebooks. Then they write the draft of a blog like the one in Activity 2 in their notebooks. Revise drafts when pupils ask for help. Then they take turns to read their blogs to each other.

5 Find these words in the text. Explain their meaning.

- Say the two words: *busy* and *practise*. Direct the pupils' attention to the text. Ask the pupils to read the text again and find these words. They have to find out their meaning. Tell them to use their own words and write the definition. If necessary, let them do that in L1. They can check the answers looking up in a dictionary. Check answers with the class.

KEY **Suggested answers: 1** busy: doing lots of activities, having lots to do, **2** practise: do something often, because you want to be good at it

Unit 5 Pupil's Book page 108

1 Look and say *True* or *False*.

- Focus pupils' attention on the illustration. Ask a few general questions (L1): *What can you see in the picture? (A boy – Rob and a girl – interviewer/Sarah). What's Rob thinking about? (He wants to be an astronaut).* Then ask *What type of text is it? (An interview). What do you think the text is about? (Jobs for the future).*

- The pupils look at the text and the picture again. Read out the sentences and check that they understand. Read the sentences one by one and elicit answers from the class: pupils say *True* or *False*. Alternatively, they could write the answers in their notebooks (check as a class). Ask pupils to correct the false sentences.

KEY **1** True, **2** True, **3** False (He likes space.), **4** False (He wants to be an astronaut.), **5** True

2 Look and read.

- Direct the pupils' attention to the layout of the interview. Ask *Who's the interviewer? (Sarah). Who answers the questions? (Rob). How do you write an interview? (With questions and answers).* Then ask the pupils to read the text silently. Tell them to ask you about any words they might not understand. Ask them to pay special attention to the words for jobs.

3 Read again and answer.

- Tell pupils to read the interview and find the information to answer the questions. Allow pupils time to think about the answers. When they have finished, they check answers in pairs. Then ask individual pupils to read out a question and the class answers. Correct if necessary.

KEY **1** She is interviewing Rob. **2** He wants to be an astronaut. **3** He likes space, rockets and flying. **4** Yes, he does. **5** No, it isn't.

4 Tell your partner about a job you want to do.

- Use the flashcards for jobs and revise them with the class. Organise the class in pairs. Ask the pupils to choose their favourite jobs. The pupils write a draft describing the job in their notebooks. Revise drafts when pupils ask for help. Then they take turns to describe their favourite jobs. Make a survey with the class to identify the job that most pupils like. Draw a diagram with the class results. Pupils could copy it into their notebooks.

5 Find these words in the text. Explain their meaning.

- Direct the pupils' attention to the text. Say the two words: *interview* (v) and *space*. Ask the pupils to read the interview again and find these words. They have to find out their meaning. Tell them to use their own words and write the definition. If necessary, let them do that in L1. They can check the answers looking up in a dictionary. Check answers with the class.

KEY **Suggested answers: 1** interview: ask someone questions (one person asks, the other person answers), **2** space: outside the Earth

Unit 6 [Pupil's Book page 109]

1 Look and say *True* or *False*.

- Focus pupils' attention on the illustration. Ask a few general questions (L1): *What can you see in the picture? (A rainforest landscape). Is Tony outside a hut? (Yes, he is),* etc. After that, ask the class *What type of text is it? (A letter). What do you think the letter is about?* Listen to their answers.
- The pupils look at the text and the picture again. Read out sentences (1–5) and check that they understand. Read the sentences one by one and elicit answers from the class: pupils say *True* or *False*. Alternatively, they could write the answers in their notebooks (check as a class). Ask pupils to correct the false sentences.

> **KEY 1** False (There isn't a desert.), **2** True, **3** False (The hut is near the lake.), **4** True, **5** True

2 Look and read.

- Direct the pupils' attention to the greeting and farewell in the letter. Ask them to complete this sentence: *This letter is to ... (Bill).* Read out the letter to the class. Then ask the pupils to read it silently. Tell them to ask you about any words they might not understand and help them. Ask them to pay special attention to the words for the rainforest and the meanings.

3 Read again and answer.

- Tell pupils to read the letter again, look at the picture, and find the information to answer the questions. Allow pupils time to think about the answers. When they have finished, they check answers in pairs. Then ask individual pupils to read out a question and the class answers. Correct if necessary.

> **KEY 1** He's outside a hut. **2** It's between a mountain and a lake. **3** Yes, it is. **4** There were monkeys and gorillas. **5** Yes, it is.

4 Describe the rainforest to your partner.

- Bring some magazine cut outs if possible or science books about the rainforest. Pupils can also find information via internet links that you recommend. Pupils write a list of characteristics of rainforests in their notebooks. Revise drafts when pupils ask for help. Organise the class in pairs and tell the pupils to tell each other the information they have prepared about the rainforest. They can illustrate their lists with pictures or photos. Display the pupils' work in the class.

5 Find these words in the text. Explain their meaning.

- Say the two words *near* and *fantastic*. Direct the pupils' attention to the letter. Ask them to read it and find the words. They have to find out their meaning. Tell them to use their own words and write the definition. If necessary, let them do that in L1. They can check the answers looking up in a dictionary. Check answers with the class.

> **KEY Suggested answers: 1** near: preposition of place, close to something, **2** fantastic: really good, amazing, exciting

Unit 7 [Pupil's Book page 110]

1 Look and say *True* or *False*.

- Focus pupils' attention on the illustration and the conversation. Ask a few general questions (L1): *Is the girl worried? (No, she isn't). Is the boy nervous? (Yes, he is). Is he wearing glasses? (No, he isn't),* etc. Then ask *What type of text is it? (A conversation). What do you think the conversation is about? (Feelings).*
- The pupils look at the text and the picture again. Read out sentences (1–5) and check that they understand. Read the sentences one by one and elicit answers from the class: pupils say *True* or *False*. Alternatively, they could write the answers in their notebooks (check as a class). Ask pupils to correct the false sentences.

> **KEY 1** False (They're in the playground.), **2** True, **3** False (She's excited.), **4** False (The girl is going to a party.), **5** False (The boy is worried about his Maths test.)

2 Look and read.

- Direct the pupils' attention to the text and ask them to explain how to write a dialogue. Read out the text to the class. Then ask the pupils to read the text silently. Tell them to ask you about any words they might not understand and help them. Ask them to pay special attention to the words for feelings and the meanings.

3 Read again and answer.

- Tell pupils to read the text again and find the information to answer the questions. Allow pupils time to think about the answers. When they have finished, they check answers in pairs. Then ask individual pupils to read out a question and the class answers. Correct if necessary.

4 Tell your partner how you feel.

- Revise the words to express feelings, and the structure *makes me feel*, using the flashcards. Pupils write in their notebooks a description of how things make them feel. Tell them to explain what makes them feel sad, worried, happy, etc. Revise drafts when pupils ask for help. Organise the class in pairs and tell the pupils to tell each other the information they have prepared about how things make them feel. They can illustrate their descriptions with pictures. Display the pupils' work in the class.

5 Find these words in the text. Explain their meaning.

- Say the two words *nervous* and *excited*. Ask the pupils to read the text again and find these words. They have to find out their meaning. Tell them to use their own words and write the definition. If necessary, let them do that in L1. They can check the answers looking up in a dictionary. Check answers with the class.

Unit 8   Pupil's Book page III

1 Look and say *True* or *False*.

- Focus pupils' attention on the illustration. Ask a few general questions (L1): *What can you see in the picture? (Two girls and a boy, A horse)*, etc. Then ask *What type of text is it? (A conversation). What do you think the conversation is about? (Activities).* Ask the pupils to look at the thought bubble for each character and describe them.
- The pupils look at the text and the picture again. Read out sentences (1–5) and check that they understand. Read the sentences one by one and elicit answers from the class: pupils say *True* or *False*. Alternatively, they could write the answers in their notebooks (check as a class). Ask pupils to correct the false sentences.

2 Look and read.

- Revise with the class the characteristics of conversations. Ask the pupils to read the conversation silently. Then divide the class in groups of three, assign a role to each pupil and tell them to read the conversation. Tell them to ask you about any words they might not understand and help them. Ask them to pay special attention to the words for activities and the meanings.

3 Read again and answer.

- Tell pupils to read the conversation again and find the information to answer the questions. Allow pupils time to think about the answers. When they have finished, they check answers in pairs. Then ask individual pupils to read out a question and the class answers. Correct if necessary.

4 Tell your partner about your plans.

- Revise the words to express plans and say the activities they are going to do, using the flashcards. Pupils write notes about their plans in their notebooks. Tell them to explain why they are going to do things. Revise drafts when pupils ask for help. Organise the class in pairs and tell the pupils to tell each other about their plans. They can illustrate their plans with pictures. Display the pupils' work in the class.

5 Find these words in the text. Explain their meaning.

- Say the words *snorkelling* and *fond of*. Direct the pupils' attention to the text. Ask them to read the text again and find these words. They have to find out their meaning. Tell them to use their own words and write the definition. If necessary, let them do that in L1. They can check the answers looking up in a dictionary. Check answers with the class.

Activity Book unit review Answer Key

Welcome and Unit 1

Activity Book Page 96

1 Answer the questions.
Students' personal answers

2 Complete the sentences.
1 taller than, 2 smaller than, 3 bigger than,
4 younger than, 5 older than

3 Write sentences about yourself.
Students' personal answers

4 Ask a partner the questions. Then write the answers
Students' personal answers

Unit 2 Activity Book Page 97

1 Find 8 animals and write.
2 gorilla, 2 zebra, 3 panda, 4 camel, 5 elephant,
6 lion, 7 crocodile, 8 hippo,

2 Write about the animals.
1 grass, 2 rivers, 3 leaves, 4 deserts, 5 meat,
6 forests

3 Answer the questions.
1 No, they don't.
2 Yes, they do.
3 They live in rainforests.
4 They live in grasslands.
5 They eat fruit.

4 Match.
1 e, 2 a, 3 b, 4 d, 5 c

Unit 3 Activity Book Page 98

1 Answer the questions.
Students' personal answers

2 Write about what you and your partner do in each season.
Students' personal answers

3 Draw and write about the weather.
Students' personal answers

4 Write about your favourite season.
Students' personal answers

Unit 4 Activity Book Page 99

1 Write do or have.
1 have 2 do, 3 do, 4 have

2 Write practise or learn to.
1 practise 2 learn, 3 learn, 4 practise

3 Write about your week.
Students' personal answers

4 Ask your partner about his/her week. Then write the answers.
Students' personal answers

5 Write about yourself.
Students' personal answers

Unit 5 Activity Book Page 100

1 Write the words in alphabetical order.
1 astronaut, 2 builder, 3 carpenter, 4 firefighter,
5 journalist, 6 lawyer, 7 mechanic, 8 photographer,
9 singer

2 Write about what you and your partner want to be and don't want to be.
Students' personal answers

3 Write.
Students' personal answers

4 Draw and write about your dream job.
Students' personal answers

Unit 6 Activity Book Page 101

1 Find 8 nature words and write.
1 river, 2 hut, 3 bridge, 4 mountain, 5 sea, 6 lake,
7 coast, 8 hill

2 Read and draw.
Students' personal answers

3 Describe what you could and couldn't do.
Students' personal answers

4 Write.
1 hiked, 2 climbed, 3 watched, 4 walked

Unit 7 Activity Book Page 102

1 Write the words in alphabetical order.
1 blushing, 2 crying, 3 drinking, 4 frowning,
5 laughing, 6 shaking, 7 shouting, 8 smiling,
9 yawning

2 Write.
1 smiling, 2 nervous, 3 crying, 4 blushing, 5 angry,
6 feel

3 Write the questions.
1 Why are you crying? 2 Why is she nervous?
3 Why is he shouting? 4 Why are you blushing?
5 Why are you smiling?

4 Answer about yourself.
Students' personal answers

Unit 8 Activity Book Page 103

1 Write the words in alphabetical order.
1 bungee jumping, 2 fishing, 3 hang gliding, 4 horse-
riding, 5 kayaking, 6 rafting, 7 rock climbing, 8 scuba
diving, 9 snorkelling

2 Write.
1B: love snorkelling, 2A: Let's go hang gliding.,
3B: I haven't., 4A: Have you got a fishing rod?

3 Answer about yourself.
1B: love s

4 Answer about yourself.
Students' personal answers

Reading and Writing Booklet

Answer Key

Unit 1

Free time

1 Santiago
2 2 Ta
  3 F
  4 T
  5 T
  6 F
  7 F
  8 T
3 2 e
  3 a
  4 b
  5 f
  6 d
4 skiing
  skateboarding
  skipping
  cooking
5 2 painting, a
  3 skipping, f
  4 watching films, b
  5 cooking, e
  6 reading magazines, d
6 (open question)
7 (open question)

Unit 2

Wild animals

1 2 can
  3 like
  4 herbivores
  5 sleep
2 2 Yes, they do.
  3 They live in grasslands (in Africa).
  4 They eat grass, leaves and fruit.
  5 Yes, they do.
3 2 gorilla
  3 lion
  4 elephant
  5 crab
  6 monkey
4 2 giraffe
  3 crocodile
  4 camel
  5 hippo
  6 panda
5 river
  grassland
  rainforest
  desert
6 (open question)
7 (open question)

Unit 3

The seasons

1 (open question)
2 2 thirty-five
  3 twenty-four
  4 twenty
3 2 F
  3 F
  4 T
  5 T
4 2 autumn
  3 spring
  4 summer
5 humid
  thunder
  warm
  wet
  lightning
6 2 go camping
  3 go snowboarding
  4 go hiking
7 (open question)
8 (open question)

Unit 4

My week

1 2 four o'clock
  3 a quarter to two
  4 Maths
  5 three o'clock
  6 afternoon
2 2 On Tuesdays she has a ballet lesson at three o'clock.
  3 On Wednesdays she practises the piano at half past two.
  4 On Thursdays she studies English in the morning.
  5 On Fridays she does gymnastics at four o'clock.
  6 On Saturdays she does karate in the morning.
3 have: music lessons
  do: gymnastics, karate
  practise: the violin, the saxophone
  study: English, Maths
4 2 practise the violin
  3 do gymnastics
  4 study Maths
  5 have music lessons
  6 do karate
5 (pictures)
6 (open question)
7 (open question)

Unit 5

Jobs

1 (open question)
2 2 He's writing to see if his uncle (Rob) can help him.
   3 The project is about different jobs.
   4 He wants to be a chef.
   5 He wants to go to the restaurant (one morning) next week.
3 2 journalist
   3 doctor
   4 police officer
   5 lawyer
   6 astronaut
4 2 farmer
   3 firefighter
   4 film star
5 2 photographer
   3 builder
   4 carpenter
   5 athlete
   Secret word: model
6 2 d
   3 b
   4 a
7 (open question)

Unit 6

In the rainforest

1 2 T
   3 F
   4 F
   5 F
   6 T
   7 T
2 2 bridge
   3 waterfall
   4 vines
   5 nest
   6 lake
3 1 b
   2 d
   3 c
   4 a
4 2 giant tarantula
   3 tapir
   4 hummingbird
5 (open question)
6 (open question)

Unit 7

Feelings

1 Yes, (he/she does,) because it can make you feel lots of different things.
2 2 a group of children
   3 plane
   4 plane
   5 aren't
   6 sad
3 2 shaking
   3 yawning
   4 crying
   5 shouting
4 2 proud, c
   3 nervous, a
   4 relaxed, e
   5 relieved, d
5 (open question)

Unit 8

Action!

1 Alberto is going to go to Wales.
  Carla is going to go to Scotland.
2 2 A
   3 C
   4 C
   5 C
   6 A
   7 C
   8 A
3 Across:
   4 scuba
   6 rafting
   8 paddle
   Down:
   1 rod
   3 surfboard
   5 bungee
   7 jacket
4 2 kayaking
   3 beach volleyball
   4 rafting
   5 horse-riding
   6 surfing
5 (open question)

Grammar Booklet

Answer Key

Unit 1

1
2 a, She likes
3 g, They don't like
4 f, She likes
5 b, He likes
6 d, He doesn't like
7 e, He likes

2
1 A: He likes playing computer games.
2 Q: What do Mum and Dad like doing?
A: They like reading the newspaper.
3 Q: What does Mary like doing?
A: She likes cooking.

3
2 doesn't
3 like
4 Do
5 like
6 do

4
3 Sara likes chatting online.
4 They like playing computer games?
5 We don't like watching films.

5
1 What do you like doing? I like chatting online.
2 Do your friends like playing hockey? No, they don't.

Unit 2

1
2 They eat fruit.
3 Do elephants live in forests?
4 Yes, they do.
5 Do hippos eat fruit?
6 Giraffes eat leaves.

2
2 are
3 eat
4 got
5 like

3 (open question)

4
1 live
2 Where, lives
3 does, eats
4 What, eat

5
2 Where do crocodiles live?
3 What do they eat?

6
2 a
3 d
4 c

7
1 a lot
2 How much, a lot
3 How many, There are

8
2 walk
3 swim
4 fast
5 climb
6 slowly

Unit 3

1
2 c
3 b

2
2 There's thunder and lightning.
3 It very snowy in winter.
4 It's 17 degrees today. / Today it's 17 degrees.

3
2 Kim and Mark go hiking in autumn.
3 Tom goes surfing in spring and summer.
4 Jo and Sue go camping in summer.
5 Ben goes cycling in autumn.
6 Tom goes camping in autumn.

4 (open question)

5
2 was
3 is
4 was
5 was
6 is

6
3 What was the weather like in January?
4 What was the temperature in December?
5 What was the temperature in January?
6 What was the weather like in December?

Unit 4

1
2 f, they
3 e, he
4 b, have
5 c, practise
6 a, does

2 (open question)

3
2 past
3 do
4 practises
5 learns
6 do

4
2 He does his homework every day at four o'clock.
3 What does Liam's sister do on Thursdays?
4 When does Liam play basketball?/What does Liam do on Fridays?

5
2 Jo never has music lessons.
3 Jo often learns to cook.
4 Jo often studies English.

6 (open question)

Unit 5

1
2 d, I don't want to be a police officer.
3 a, I don't want to be an astronaut.
4 b, I want to be a film star.

2
2 What do you want to be?
3 What does he want to be?

3
2 g
3 a
4 f
5 d
6 c
7 e

4 **2** Does, want to be, Yes, he does.

3 Does, want to be, Yes, she does.

4 Does, want to be, No, he doesn't. He wants to be a mechanic.

5 Do, want to be, Yes, they do.

6 Do, want to be, No, they don't. They want to be film stars.

7 Does, want to be, Yes, he does.

5 **2** because

3 like

4 good

5 be

6 because

7 like

8 at

6 **1** helping

2 does, good

3 you, do

4 What, want

7 (open question)

Unit 6

1 **2** There's a waterfall between the mountains.

3 There's a river near the rainforest.

4 There's a bridge across the river.

5 There are huts near the bridge.

2 (picture)

3 **2** Could Sara speak English when she was little? Yes, she could.

Can she speak English now? Yes, she can.

3 Could Jo and Sam skateboard when they were little? No they couldn't.

Can they skateboard now? No, they can't.

4 Could Kim and Mike run when they were little? Yes, they could.

Can they run now? Yes, they can.

4 (open question)

5 **2** climb

3 plays

4 hiked

5 watched

6 practises

6 **2** camped

3 was

4 walked

5 could go

6 could not give

7 were

8 could walk

9 was

10 was

7 (open question)

Unit 7

1 **2** e

3 a

4 b

5 c

6 f

2 **2** Q: Why is your brother crying? A: He's crying because he's hurt.

3 Q: Why are you shaking? A: I'm shaking because I'm angry.

3 **2** Walking to school makes me feel tired.

3 Passing a test makes me feel relieved.

4 Playing football well makes me feel proud.

4 **2** What's the matter?

3 How do you feel?

5 (open question)

6 **1** I

2 me

3 He

4 us

5 he

6 we

7 them

7 **2** c, it

3 a, him

4 b, them

8 **2** My Mum always gives me a book for my birthday.

3 My grandma often tells us interesting stories.

Unit 8

1 **2** water skiing

3 rafting

4 scuba diving

5 hang gliding

6 surfing

2 **2** with

3 of

4 of

5 about

6 of

3 (open question)

4 7, 6, 2, 4, 1, 5, 3, 8

5 **2** I'm not good at kayaking.

3 Have you got a fishing rod?

4 Are you fond of fishing?

5 I'm crazy about fishing.

6 **2** She's going to play the guitar.

3 He's going to go horse-riding.

5 What's Tom going to do next year?

6 What's Sara going to do next year?

7 (open question)

Photocopiables notes

Look and match. (Lesson 1)

- Revise with the class the Welcome episode and focus their attention on the characters. Point to each of the characters and ask the pupils to say their names one by one. Explain that they must cut out the names and glue them in the corresponding boxes. Give them time to do that. Check answers with the class.
- Ask the class questions about the characters and what they like: *Who's this? It's (Jenny). What does she like? She likes (films),* etc.

KEY Ruby, Sam, John, Jenny, Madley Kool, Cleo

Unit 1 Free time

1.1 Look and match. (Lesson 1)

- Organise the class in pairs. Direct the pupils' attention to the cue cards and revise all the actions. Tell them that they have to cut out the cue cards to play a guessing game. Once they have cut out the cards, tell the pupils to shuffle them and put them facing the table. Pupils take turns to mime an action to be guessed by their partners. The winner in each pair is the pupil with the most guesses. Finally, the pupils match the pictures with the actions.

1.2 Mime and guess. Then match. (Lesson 3)

- Organise the class in pairs again. Explain that this time they have to read the reading cards and act out the actions for their partners to guess. Revise all the actions with the class. Start a 'Simon says' game to practise them. Pupils take turns to read a reading card and act out an action. When the partner guesses, it's his/her turn. Finally, the pupils match the pictures with the actions.

1.3 Listen. Then cut and play. (Lesson 3)

- Play CD 1.18 and mime the actions with the class to make meaning clear. The pupils look at the pictures and describe them.
- Play the song again. The pupils listen and point to the corresponding pictures.

KEY Boy riding his bike, Boy playing the guitar, Girl riding her scooter, Girl skateboarding

Write four true answers.

- Focus on the pictures and ask the class to say true answers from the song. Then the pupils write four true answers. Check answers with the class.

KEY 1 I like riding my bike, 2 I like playing the guitar, 3 I like riding my scooter, 4 I like skateboarding.

1.4 Cut and order. (Lesson 5)

- Tell pupils to cut out the story cards and try to put them in order without looking at the book. When they have finished, they can check their results with their partners and look at the book. After that, they shuffle the story cards. Play CD 1.22 for the pupils to listen to the story and order the pictures. Repeat the stage if necessary until they do it correctly.

1.5 Cut and stick. (Lesson 6)

- Read out the words and ask the pupils to repeat them. Explain that they have to cut out the words and place them in the correct column. Provide an example for each sound if necessary. The pupils work individually. When they have finished play CD 1.23 for pupils to listen and check the answers.

KEY	
/ou/	/ow/
out	low
loud	snow
shout	blow
cloud	yellow

1.6 Cut and order. (Lesson 7)

- Show the page with the cut outs of the two texts to the class. Explain the meaning of the word *jigsaw.* Tell the pupils that they are going to cut out the pieces of the texts and then they must reconstruct the two texts. They work individually and try to put the pieces together. Walk around the class and help them when necessary. Check that they have been able to reconstruct the texts. Then they glue the pieces together. After that, ask the pupils about the clues they followed to put the pieces together.

KEY
Text 1
This is Rosa. Look at her house. It's a boat. Rosa likes her boat. She doesn't like watching TV. She likes reading and playing the guitar. She also likes riding her bike but not on the boat! She's got a cat. He likes sleeping on the boat.

Text 2
This is Will. This is his house. It's a lighthouse! There are a lot of stairs. Will likes living in the lighthouse but he doesn't like climbing the stairs. He likes playing computer games and watching TV. He likes cooking too. His favourite food is fish.

1.7 Read, write and draw. (Lesson 8)

- Pupils must draw a picture of themselves or stick a photo describing what they do at the weekend (play football, swim, etc.). Tell them to complete the sentences in each caption providing personal information. Tell them to reread the texts in *Wider World* if necessary.
- Allow pupils time to think about the information they are going to provide. Let them complete the sentences. Then ask individual pupils to read out their sentences. You can collect their work and display them in the classroom.

1.8 Cut and stick. (Lesson 9)

- Pupils read the sentences. Then they cut out the sentence strips and stick them next to the corresponding picture boxes.

Unit 2 Wild animals

2.1 Match. Then draw and write. (Lesson 1)

- Give each pupil a worksheet and ask them to match the pictures of the animals with the pictures of where the animals live. Check answers.
- Ask pupils to think about their favourite animal and then draw a picture of it. Ask them to complete the sentences. Check answers.

> **KEY**
> gorilla/rainforest; camel/desert; crab/river; zebra/grassland; panda/forest

2.2 Read and match. Then stick. (Lesson 3)

- Talk about animals and what they eat. Say a few mistakes and ask the pupils to correct you. Then tell the pupils to match to the corresponding pictures of food. Check answers with the class.
- Ask the pupils to stick the animal pictures in the correct spaces opposite the pictures of food.

> **KEY**
> Giraffes eat leaves. Hippos and elephants eat grass. Monkeys eat fruit. Lions and crocodiles eat meat.

2.3 Listen. Then write. (Lesson 3)

- Play CD 1.41. Pupils listen and follow the words, identifying the information about animals in the song. Then they read the text and write the correct word from the word bank. Check answers.

Draw and describe an animal.

- Ask pupils to draw an animal and describe it. Ask a few pupils to show their pictures and read out their descriptions. Display the pictures in the classroom.

2.4 Cut and order. (Lesson 5)

- Tell pupils to cut out the story cards and try to put them in order without looking at the book. When they have finished, they can check their results with their partners and look at the book. After that, they shuffle the story cards. Play CD 1.45 for the pupils to listen to the story and order the pictures. Repeat the stage if necessary until they do it correctly.

2.5 Cut and stick the words that sound the same. (Lesson 6)

- Read out the words and ask the children to repeat them. Explain that they have to cut out and sort the words. Organise the class in pairs and let them find the words that sound the same. Then, the pupils work individually and glue the words in the boxes. When they have finished, play CD 1.46 for pupils to listen and check the answers.

> **KEY** yawn

2.6 Cut and stick. Then reorder to make a food chain. (Lesson 7)

- Ask pupils to look at the pictures that describe a food chain. Then read out the sentences and check that pupils understand. Tell them to cut out the sentences and place each one below the corresponding picture. Check answers. Let them glue the sentences in the corresponding box. Then ask them questions, e.g. *What do eagles eat? Snakes*, etc. Pupils order the pictures to make a food chain.

2.7 Draw. Then write. (Lesson 8)

- Pupils must draw a picture of themselves, a wildlife park they know and an animal in the three boxes. Tell them to complete the sentences in each caption providing personal information. Tell them to reread the texts in *Wider World* and find information on the Internet.
- Ask individual pupils to read out their sentences. You can collect their work and display them in the classroom.

2.8 Ask and answer. Then complete. (Lesson 9)

- Put the pupils into pairs. Pupils should take it in turns to ask and answer questions about the animals in the table, using the prompts.

Unit 3 The seasons

3.1 Find eight words about the weather. Write sentences. (Lesson 1)

- Pupils look at the word puzzle and try to identify the words about weather. Then they have to write sentences in the spaces below. Check answers.

3.2 Cut and play. (Lesson 3)

- Pupils cut out the pictures. Organise the class in pairs. Ask them to make sentences. Pupil 1 holds up a picture of a tree, e.g. summer. Pupil 2 has to make a sentence using, e.g. the girl on the bike and say *I ride my bike in summer.* Then they swap.

3.3 Listen and draw the activities you hear. (Lesson 3)

- Play CD 1.62. Pupils listen and follow the words, identifying the information about the seasons in the song. Then they read the text and draw a picture for each season in each frame. When they have finished, ask a few pupils to show their pictures to the class.

Write about your favourite season.

- Pupils write about their favourite season, using the prompts from the song.

3.4 Cut and order. (Lesson 5)

- Tell pupils to cut out the story cards and try to put them in order without looking at the book. When they have finished, they can check their results with their partners and look at the book. After that, they shuffle the story cards. Play CD 1.65 for the pupils to listen to the story and sequence the pictures. Repeat the stage if necessary until they do it correctly.

3.5 Cut and stick the words that sound the same. (Lesson 6)

- Read out the words and ask the pupils to repeat them. Explain that they have to cut out the words and find the words that sound the same. Organise the class in pairs and let them find the words. Then the pupils work individually and glue the words in the boxes. When they have finished, play CD 1.66 for pupils to listen and check the answers.

3.6 Cut and stick. (Lesson 7)

- Focus pupils' attention on the layout of the text and ask: *What is it about?* Let the pupils answer: *Hurricanes.* Ask: *What's missing?* Elicit answers from the class: *pictures and headings* (L1).
- The pupils read the text. Then they cut out the photos and the headings and try to place them in the correct place. They check results looking at the text in the Pupil's Book. Check as a class. Then they glue them.

Draw. Then write.

- Pupils draw a picture describing a natural disaster. Tell them to complete the sentences in each caption providing information. Tell them to read again the

texts in *Wider World* and find information on the internet if necessary.
- Ask individual pupils to read out their sentences. You can collect their work and display them in the classroom

3.7 Play a game using a dice. (Lesson 9)

- Ask pupils to work in small groups. Give each group a game sheet and a dice. Give each pupil a counter (or ask them to use a small object from their pencil case).
- Read the sentence prompts and check that pupils understand.
- Begin the game. Pupils take turns to throw their dice and move forward. They make questions and answers about the picture on the square they land on. If the sentence is correct, they move forward one space. If it is wrong, they move back one space.
- Go round the class, helping and checking.

Unit 4 My week

4.1 Cut and play. Then mime and guess. (Lesson 1)

- Organise the class in pairs. Direct the pupils' attention to the cue cards and revise all the activities. Tell them that they have to cut out the cue cards to play a guessing game. Once they have cut out the cards, tell the pupils to shuffle them and put them facing the table. Pupils take turns to mime an activity to be guessed by their partners. The winner in each pair is the pupil with the most guesses.

4.2 Ask and answer. (Lesson 3)

Make sentences. Play a memory game.

- Pupils look at the pictures for the parts of the day and the clocks. Check the times with the class: *It's half past two. It's quarter to three,* etc. Then focus their attention on the activities.
- Tell pupils to get into pairs. Pupils should take it in turns to ask and answer questions relating to the activities and the times that they occur.

4.3 Listen and choose the correct answer. Then stick. (Lesson 3)

- Play CD 2.07. Pupils listen and identify the times in the song. Then play the song again. Pupils read the text and place the correct cut out times in the corresponding place. When they have finished, ask a few pupils to say the results. Check as a class.

4.4 Cut and order. (Lesson 5)

- Tell pupils to cut out the story cards and try to put them in order without looking at the book. When they have finished, they can check their results with their partners and look at the book. After that, they shuffle the story cards. Play CD 2.11 for the pupils to listen to the story and sequence the pictures. Repeat this stage if necessary until they do it correctly.

4.5 Cut out and stick the words that sound the same. (Lesson 6)

- Read out the words and ask the pupils to repeat them. Explain that they have to cut out the words and find the words that sound the same. Organise the class in pairs and let them find the rhyming words. Then the pupils work individually and glue the rhyming words in the boxes. When they have finished, play CD 2.12 for pupils to listen and check the answers.

> **KEY** Fried

4.6 Write. (Lesson 7)

- Focus pupils' attention on the layout and the title of the text and ask *What is it about?* Let the pupils answer *How children go to school.* Ask *What's missing?* Elicit answers from the class: *headings* (L1).
- The pupils read the text. Then they fill in the gaps, using the word bank.

Draw. Then write about how you go to school.

- Pupils draw a picture of how they get to school. Then they write sentences using the prompts.
- Ask individual pupils to read out their sentences. You can collect their work and display them in the classroom.

4.7 Cut out and stick. Then ask and answer. (Lesson 8)

- Pupils cut and stick the pictures on the page into the table to make sentences about themselves and their friends.
- Split the class into pairs. Pupils should take it in turns to ask and answer questions relating to the pictures in the tables. For example: *Do you study Maths on Wednesday afternoons? Yes, I do./No, I don't.* Pupils add a tick or a cross, based on their answers.

Unit 5 Jobs

5.1 Cut and play. Then mime and guess. (Lesson 1)

- Organise the class in pairs. Direct the pupils' attention to the cue cards and revise all the jobs. Tell them that they have to cut out the cue cards to play a guessing game. Once they have cut out the cards, tell the pupils to shuffle them and put them facing the table. Pupils take turns to take a cue card and mime a job to be guessed by their partners. The winner in each pair is the pupil with the most guesses.

5.2 Play a game. (Lesson 3)
Anagrams.

- Tell the class that now they have to put the letters in order to make words for jobs described in the pictures. Ask them to cover the pictures and try to find the words. Do an example with the class so that they know what they have to do. Pupils find the words and check answers looking at the pictures. Organise the class in pairs. Pupils take turns to point to the words and suggest the correct form of each word. Finally, check answers with the class. Pupils can write more anagrams and continue the game with their partners.

5.3 Listen. Then look and match. (Lesson 3)

- Play CD 2.31. Pupils listen and follow the words, identifying the jobs in the song. Then play the recording again and ask the pupils to cut and stick the pictures in the correct order that they appear in the song.

> **KEY** farmer, builder, teacher, doctor

5.4 Cut and order. (Lesson 5)

- Tell pupils to cut out the story cards and try to put them in order without looking at the book. When they have finished, they can check their results with their partners and look at the book. After that, they shuffle the story cards. Play CD 2.35 for the pupils to listen to the story and order the pictures. Repeat this stage if necessary until they do it correctly.

5.5 Cut and stick the words that sound the same. (Lesson 6)

- Read out the words and ask the pupils to repeat them. Explain that they have to cut out the words and find the words that sound the same. Organise the class in pairs and let them find the rhyming words. Then the pupils work individually and glue the rhyming words in the boxes. When they have finished, play CD 2.36 for pupils to listen and check the answers.

5.6 Cut and order. (Lesson 7)

- Show the page with the cut outs of the three texts to the class. Revise the meaning of the word *jigsaw*. Tell pupils that they are going to cut out the pieces of the three texts and then they must reconstruct them. They work individually. Walk around the class and help them when necessary. Check answers.
  Then they stick the pieces together. Ask pupils about the clues they followed to put the pieces together.

Draw. Then write.

- Pupils must draw a picture describing their heroes. Tell them to complete the sentences in each caption providing personal information. Tell them to read again the texts in *Wider World* if necessary.
- Ask individual pupils to read out their sentences. You can collect their work and display them in the classroom.

5.8 Ask. Then cut and stick.

- Pupils ask and answer questions about what they want to be, using the model question and answer in the speech bubbles. Pupils write the names of their classmates and cut and stick the jobs in the table.

Unit 6 In the rainforest

6.1 Play Battleships. (Lesson 1)

- Explain to the class that they are going to play a game called *Battleships*. Check if they have played this game before. Organise the class in pairs. Tell them to cut out the labelled pictures. They have to take turns to place the pictures in the squares they want without showing their partners. Then they give instructions to their partner to put the words in the same squares. For example: 'Nest' is in A1.
- Direct the pupils' attention to the model dialogue. Tell them to take turns to ask and answer questions about the pictures using the prepositions.

6.2 Do the crossword. (Lesson 3)

- Pupils look at the crossword and try to identify the words for the pictures. Then they have to write the words. Draw the crossword on the board and ask a few pupils to come to the board and write the words for the class.

6.3 Listen and reorder. Then circle. (Lesson 3)

- Play CD 2.55. Pupils listen and follow the words, identifying the animals and their habitats in the song. Then play the recording again and ask the pupils to put the strips of paper in the correct order, to match the song. Finally, pupils circle the correct words.

6.4 Cut and order. (Lesson 5)

- Tell pupils to cut out the story cards and try to put them in order without looking at the book. When they have finished, they can check their results with their partners and look at the book. After that, they shuffle the story cards. Play CD 2.59 for the pupils to listen to the story and order the pictures. Repeat this stage if necessary until they do it correctly.

6.5 Read the sentences. Circle the *ce, ci, cir*. (Lesson 6)

- The pupils read the sentences and circle /ce/, /ci/, /cir/. Play CD 2.60 for the pupils to listen and check.

Match the words to the sounds.

- Pupils read the words and match them to the corresponding sounds. Play CD 2.62 for the pupils to listen and check.

6.6 Read, cut and stick. (Lesson 7)

- Focus pupils' attention on the layout and the title of the text. Ask *What is it about?* Let the pupils answer *The Amazon rainforest.* Ask *What's missing?* Elicit answers *title, photos and labels* (L1).
- The pupils read the text. Ask pupils to place strips and photos in the corresponding place. Check as a class. Then they stick them.

6.7 Draw. Then write about your country. (Lesson 8)

- Pupils must draw a picture describing a forest in the country where they live. Tell them to complete the sentences in each caption providing information. Tell them to reread the texts in *Wider World* and find information on the Internet.
- Ask individual pupils to read them out. You can collect their work and display them in the classroom.

6.8 Look at the map. Then ask and answer.

- Pupils are put into pairs. Using the model sentence, pupils ask and answer questions relating to the items that appear on the map. For example: *Where's the river? It's between the elephant and the lion.* Check as a class.

Unit 7 Feelings

7.1 Play Dominoes. (Lesson 1)

- Explain to the class that they are going to play a game called *Dominoes*. Check if they have played this game before. Organise the class in pairs. Tell them to cut out the counters. They have to take turns to place counters next to the matching pictures and the corresponding words. The winner is the pupil who gets rid of the counters first.

7.2 Find and write. (Lesson 3)

- Pupils look at the wordsearch and try to identify the words for feelings. They have to write the words on the empty lines. Ask a few pupils to come to the board and write the words for the class.

> **KEY** nervous, proud, relieved, surprised, relaxed, embarrassed, worried

7.3 Listen and answer. (Lesson 3)

- Play CD 3.08. Pupils listen and follow the words, identifying the feelings. Play the recording again and ask the pupils to answer the questions and stick the matching pictures into the spaces.

7.4 Cut and order. (Lesson 5)

- Tell pupils to cut out the story cards and try to put them in order without looking at the book. When they have finished, they can check their results with their partners and look at the book. After that, they shuffle the story cards. Play CD 3.11 for the pupils to listen to the story and order the pictures. Repeat this stage if necessary until they do it correctly.

7.5 Read the sentences. Circle the *ge, dge* sounds. (Lesson 6)

- The pupils read the sentences and circle /ge/, /dge/. Play CD 3.12 for the pupils to listen and check.

Match the words to the sounds.

- Pupils read the words and match them to the corresponding sounds. Play CD 3.14 for the pupils to listen and check.

> **KEY** ge: gem, gentleman, page, large
> dge: edge, badge, hedge, bridge

7.6 Read. Then cut and stick. (Lesson 7)

- The pupils look at the pictures and read the texts. Then they put each text in the corresponding place. Check with the class. Then they stick the texts.

7.7 Read. Then draw yourself and write. (Lesson 8)

- Pupils must draw a picture of themselves and then describe what makes them feel happy. Tell them to complete the sentences in each caption providing personal information. Tell them to reread the texts in *Wider World*.
- Ask individual pupils to read them out. You can collect their work and display them in the classroom.

7.8 Cut and stick. Then write about what makes you feel ...

- Pupils read the text and cut and stick the corresponding picture to the correct word, in each instance.
- Pupils write sentences about how they feel in certain situations. For example: *Crocodiles make me feel nervous.*

Unit 8 Action!

8.1 Cut and play. Then mime and guess (Lesson 1)

- Organise the class in pairs. Direct the pupils' attention to the cue cards and revise all the nature activities. Tell them that they have to cut out the cue cards to play a guessing game. Once they have cut out the cards, tell the pupils to shuffle them and put them facing the table. Pupils take turns to take a cue card and mime a nature activity to be guessed by their partners. The winner in each pair is the pupil with the most guesses.

8.2 Mime and guess. Then match. (Lesson 3)

- Organise the class in pairs again. Explain that they have to look at the picture cards, match the pictures to the text, then act out the sports for their partner to guess. Revise all the extreme sports with the class. Pupils take turns to read a reading card and act out an action. When the partner guesses, it's his/her turn.

8.3 Listen. Then cut and stick. (Lesson 3)

- Play CD 3.30. Pupils listen and follow the words. Play the recording again and ask the pupils to cut and stick the pictures in the correct column. Play the recording again and check as a class.

> **KEY**
> bored with: fishing, sailing
> fond of: scuba diving, climbing
> scared of: bungee jumping, hang gliding

8.4 Cut and order. (Lesson 5)

- Tell pupils to cut out the story cards and try to put them in order without looking at the book. When they have finished, they can check their results with their partners and look at the book. After that, they shuffle the story cards. Play CD 3.33 for the pupils to listen to the story and order the pictures. Repeat this stage if necessary until they do it correctly.

8.5 Read the sentences. Circle ph and *wh*. (Lesson 6)

- The pupils read the sentences and circle /ph/, /wh/. Play CD 3.34 for the pupils to listen and check.

Match the words to the sounds.

- Pupils read the words and match them to the corresponding sounds. Play CD 3.36 for the pupils to listen and check.

> **KEY**
> ph: phone, dolphin, elephant, alphabet
> wh: wheel, white, whale, whisper

8.6 Read. Then cut and stick. (Lesson 7)

- Focus pupils' attention on the layout of the text and ask *What is it about?* Let the pupils answer *Save the Reefs!* Ask *What's missing?* Elicit answers from the class *title and photos* (L1).
- The pupils read the text. Ask pupils to place the text and photos in the corresponding places. Check as a class. Then they stick them.

8.7 Draw. Then write. (Lesson 8)

- Pupils draw a picture of a summer camp and another to show what activities can be done there. Tell them to complete the sentences in each caption providing information. Tell them to reread the texts in *Wider World* and find information on the Internet.
- Ask individual pupils to read them out. You can collect their work and display them in the classroom.

8.8 Read. Then cut and stick. (Lesson 9)

- Pupils cut and stick the activity pictures with the corresponding text. Check as a class.

Goodbye

G.1 Cut and play. (Lesson 1)

- Tell the pupils to cut the cards and make sentences about the characters on them. Check as a class.

> **KEY**
> 1 John likes playing football.
> 2 Jenny wants to be a film star.
> 3 Ruby likes to keep things clean.
> 4 Sam wants to be a basketball player.
> 5 Cleo likes Madley Kool.

Festivals

F.1 Christmas

1 Make a Christmas cracker.

- Pupils make a Christmas cracker using the information provided.

F.2 Mother's Day

1 Make a Mother's Day card. Then cut and fold.

- Pupils cut, fold and decorate their own Mother's Day card using the instructions provided.

Game.

- Play a memory game. Say *It's Mother's Day* and *Mum has got a rose*. Nominate a pupil to add a present or food item to the sentence, e.g. *It's Mother's Day and Mum has got a rose and a book*. Continue round the class, with each pupil repeating what went before and adding something new to the list, until someone makes a mistake. Then start again.

F.3 Earth Day

1 Write. Then make a collage for Earth Day.

- Pupils fill in the gaps, using the word bank provided. Then they cut out the pictures and text and glue them down to make a collage.

Certificate

Pupils write their name on the certificate.

Portfolio

Pupils stick a photo of themselves on the page and add their personal details.

Test Booklet Answer Key

Placement

Reading
1 a 3 b 5 c 2 d 1 e 4 f 6
2 1 do, b 2 Does, a 3 run, d 4 Has, f 5 wearing, c
   6 it, e
3 1 True 2 False 3 False 4 True 5 True 6 False

Writing
1 1 name 2 nine 3 brother 4 is 5 younger 6 like
   7 reading
2 (open answers)
3 (open answers)

Listening and speaking
1 **Alice:** 24, brown
   Amy: 9, watching TV
   Bill: 19, black, playing the guitar
   Tom: 11, 55, skateboarding
2 19, 15, 20, 80, 14, 70, 30, 16
3 **Alice:** chatting online – at the weekend
   Darren: skiing – in the winter
   Jo: walking the dog – every morning
   Alex: cooking – after school
4 (open answers)

Unit 1

Reading and writing A
1 1 ✓ 2 ✗ What does Anna like doing? 3 ✗ They like
   chatting online. 4 ✓ 5 ✗ We don't like reading the
   newspaper. 6 ✗, Tom likes watching TV.
2 1 b 2 d 3 e 4 a 5 c
3 1 doing 2 dog 3 playing 4 What 5 guitar
   6 magazines 7 swimming 8 love 9 in
4 (open answers)

Reading and writing B
1 1 ✗ What do you like doing? 2 ✓ 3 ✗ We don't like
   reading the newspaper. 4 ✓ 5 ✗ I don't like skiing.
   6 ✗ Richard doesn't like skateboarding.
2 1 Do you like walking the dog? No, I don't.
   2 Does your dad like surfing the Internet?
     Yes, he does.
   3 Does she like riding a scooter? No, she doesn't.
   4 Do they like painting? No, they don't.
   5 Do you like playing hockey? Yes, I do.
3 1 like 2 scooters 3 chatting 4 playing 5 don't
   6 TV 7 loves 8 breakfast 9 cooking 10 doesn't
4 (open answers)

Listening and speaking A
1 1 b 2 c 3 c 4 a
2 1 ✓ 2 ✗ 3 ✓ 4 ✗ 5 ✗
3 (open answers)

Listening and speaking B
1 1 b 2 a 3 c 4 b
2 1 ✓,✗ 2 ✓,✓ 3 ✗,✓ 4 ✗,✗ 5 ✗,✓
3 (open answers)

Unit 2

Reading and writing A
1 1 grasslands – e 2 forests – a 3 deserts – c
   4 rivers – b 5 rainforests – d
2 1 b 2 d 3 a 4 c
3 1 many 2 much 3 have 4 eat 5 run quickly
4 (open answers)

Reading and writing B
1 1 crocodile – d 2 hippo – a 3 leaves – e 4 giraffe – f
   5 lion – c 6 grass – b
2 1 Where do zebras live? – c
   2 What do pandas eat? – d
   3 Where do crocodiles live? – b
   4 What do birds eat? – a
   5 Where do gorillas live? – e
3 1 much 2 swim well 3 many 4 live 5 a lot 6 climb
4 (open answers)

Listening and speaking A
1 1 lion 2 crocodile 3 elephant 4 monkey
2 grasslands, rainforest, river, crocodile, monkey,
   zebra
3 (open answers)

Listening and speaking B
1 1 b 2 c 3 c 4 a
2 desert, rainforest, river, camel, crocodile, zebra
3 (open answers)

Unit 3

Reading and writing A
1 1 humid 2 wet 3 lightning 4 warm 5 stormy
   6 thunder
2 1 like – c 2 temperature – d 3 was – a
   4 hurricane – b
3 1 F 2 T 3 T 4 T 5 F 6 T
4 (open answers)

Reading and writing B
1 1 c 2 d 3 b 4 a
2 1 What's the weather like today? / b 2 What's
   the temperature today? / d 3 What was the
   temperature yesterday? / c 4 What was the
   weather like last week? / a
3 1 It's warm and sunny.
   2 It's 30 degrees.
   3 It was humid and hot.
   4 They go skiing in winter.
4 (open answers)

Listening and speaking A

1 1 b 2 b 3 b 4 a
2 1 d 2 b 3 a 4 c
3 (open answers)

Listening and speaking B

1 1 a 2 b 3 c 4 b
2 1 **Jim/Claire** – camping – spring 2 **Carol** –
   snowboarding – winter 3 **Pete/Nick** – water skiing
   – summer 4 **Pat/Helen** – hiking – autumn
3 (open answers)

Unit 4

Reading and writing A

1 1 b 2 d 3 e 4 c 5 a
2 1 have music lessons 2 morning 3 quarter to three
   4 karate 5 half past three
3 1 Jane always has piano lessons in the morning.
   2 When does Henry do gymnastics?
   3 They often learn to cook at midday.
   4 What does she do on Saturdays?
   5 I practise the violin at a quarter past five.
4 (open answers)

Reading and writing B

1 1 study 2 practise 3 have 4 learn 5 do
2 1 Roger always has violin lessons in the afternoon.
   2 When does Karen do karate?
   3 They often learn to draw at midday.
   4 What does she do on Fridays?
   5 I practise the piano at a quarter past four.
3 1 Kim studies maths on Mondays at a quarter
     to five.
   2 Kim has ballet lessons on Tuesdays.
   3 John learns to cook on Saturdays/on Saturday
     evenings.
   4 John does gymnastics on Fridays
4 (open answers)

Listening and speaking A

1 1 piano 2 Sunday 3 afternoons 4 violin 5 Saturdays
2 1 b 2 e 3 d 4 f 5 a 6 c
3 (open answers)

Listening and speaking B

1 1 today / Thursday 2 karate / Saturday
   3 gymnastics / Thursday 4 Maths / lesson
   5 draw / cook 6 Sunday / piano
2 1 have ballet lessons – Monday – 12.00
   2 study Maths – every day – 11.30
   3 learn to cook – Wednesday afternoon – 3.15
   4 do karate – Saturday afternoon – 4.00
   5 practise the violin – every morning – 6.30
   6 learn to draw – evening – 6.45
3 (open answers)

Unit 5

Reading and writing A

1 1 firefighter 2 police officer 3 basketball player
   4 film star
2 1 do – b 2 does – c 3 want – a 4 you – d
3 1 want 2 basketball player 3 jump 4 always
   5 helps
4 (open answers)

Reading and writing B

1 1 firefighter 2 astronaut 3 basketball player
   4 film star 5 builder 6 police officer.
2 1 do – b 2 does – c 3 want – d 4 be – a
3 1 Does he want to be a journalist? Yes, he does.
   2 Does she want to be a lawyer? No she doesn't.
   3 Does he want to be a model? No, he doesn't.
   4 Does she want to be a ballet dancer?
      Yes, she does.
4 (open answers)

Listening and speaking A

1 1 ballet dancer 2 wants to be 3 police officer
   4 doesn't want to be
2 1 False 2 True 3 True 4 True 5 False 6 True
3 (open answers)

Listening and speaking B

1 1 Fran – a ballet dancer 2 Tim – a builder
   3 Rob – a basketball player 4 Jamie –firefighter
   5 Ann – a film star 6 Claire – a police officer
2 1 False – Jim wants to be a carpenter. 2 True –
   Paul wants to be a mechanic. 3 False – Karen
   wants to be a model. 4 False – Simon wants to be
   a singer. 5 True 6 False – Pam wants to be
   an athlete.
3 (open answers)

Unit 6

Reading and writing A

1 1 vines – c 2 nest – d 3 valley – b 4 bridge – a
2 1 walked 2 looked 3 could see 4 climbed 5 was
   6 couldn't play
3 1 Yes, he could. 2 No, they couldn't.
   3 Yes, he could. 4 No, she couldn't.
4 (open answers)

Reading and writing B

1 1 vines – d 2 waterfall – c 3 nest – e
   4 mountain – f 5 valley – b 6 bridge – a
2 1 walked 2 looked 3 could see 4 climbed
   5 jumped 6 was 7 couldn't play 8 stayed
3 1 Could he swim through the river? / No, he
   couldn't. 2 Could they go towards the hills? / Yes,
   they could. 3 Could he walk around the mountain?
   / No, he couldn't. 4 Could she walk around the
   lake? / Yes, she could.
4 (open answers)

Listening and speaking A

1 1 across 2 around 3 through 4 towards 5 past
6 over
2 1 could 2 near 3 through 4 vines
3 (open answers)

Listening and speaking B

1 1 past – waterfall 2 over – hills 3 couldn't –
could 4 lake – hills 5 mountains – coast
6 nests – hut
2 1 could – over 2 tarantula – behind 3 nests – birds
4 couldn't – could
3 (open answers)

Unit 7

Reading and writing A

1 1 frowning 2 smiling 3 blushing 4 shaking 5
crying 6 shouting
2 1 b 2 d 3 a 4 f 5 c 6 e
3 1 T 2 F 3 F 4 T 5 F 6 F
4 (open answers)

Reading and writing B

1 1 Why – e 2 matter – f 3 is – a 4 are – d
5 makes – c 5 feel – b
2 1 T 2 F 3 T 4 T 5 F 6 F
3 1 him 2 them 3 me 4 her 5 it 6 you
4 (open answers)

Listening and speaking A

1 1 e 2 b 3 a 4 f 5 c 6 d
2 Al: worried, tired, surprised, relaxed
   Brenda: angry, can't, surprised, relaxed
3 (open answers)

Listening and speaking B

1 1 Barry – is worried – because the test results
come out today. 2 Helen – is tired – because she
went to bed late. 3 James – feels embarrassed –
when the teacher makes him sing.
4 Sonia – isn't happy – because her brother has
got her bike. 5 Gary – feels relieved – because he's
not going to the dentist. 6 Cindy – feels nervous –
when she's got a Maths test.
2 1 crying – relieved 2 worried – picture 3 great
and proud – celebration 4 on holiday – reading 5
nervous – spider
3 (open answers)

Unit 8

Reading and writing A

1 1 snorkelling 2 kayaking 3 fishing 4 sailing
5 horse-riding
2 1 b 2 c 3 c 4 a
3 1 Let's go snorkelling! 2 Have you got a life
jacket? 3 What are you going to do this
summer? 4 He's going to go surfing next summer.
4 (open answers)

Reading and writing B

1 1 fishing 2 snorkelling 3 horse-riding 4 kayaking
5 surfing
2 1 c 2 b 3 a 4 c 5 a 6 c
3 1 Let's go snorkelling! / Sorry, I don't like
snorkelling. 2 Have you got riding boots? / No,
I haven't. 3 Let's go horse-riding! / Great idea! I
love horse–riding. 4 Have you got a life jacket? /
Yes, I have.
4 (open answers)

Listening and speaking A

1 1 b 2 a 3 b 4 a
2 bored – fishing; scared of – diving; terrified of –
bungee jumping; crazy about – sailing
3 (open answers)

Listening and speaking B

1 1 b 2 b 3 a 4 c
2 1 bored-beach volleyball 2 terrified-rock climbing
3 scared-snorkelling 4 crazy about-fishing
3 (open answers)

End of term 1

1 1 g 2 c 3 d 4 a 5 h 6 e 7 f 8 b
2 (check pictures against text)
3 (own answers)
4 1 ✗ skiing 2 ✗ skateboarding 3 ✓ 4 ✗ crocodile
5 ✓ 6 ✗ humid
5 Weather: thunder, warm, humid, degrees
   Habitats: desert, grasslands, rainforest, forest
   Seasons: autumn, summer, spring, winter
6 (open answers)

End of term 2

1 1 f 2 d 3 h 4 a 5 g 6 c 7 e 8 b
2 (compare pictures with text)
3 (own answers)
4 1 ✗ gymnastics 2 ✓ 3 ✗ journalist 4 ✗ mechanic
5 ✗ through 6 ✓
5 Rainforest: nest, waterfall, vines, hut
   Propositions: over, across, towards, around
   Jobs: lawyer, model, photographer, singer
6 (open answers)

End of term 3

1 1 e 2 h 3 g 4 b 5 f 6 c 7 a 8 d
2 (compare pictures with text)
3 (own answers)
4 1 ✗ shaking 2 ✗ nervous 3 ✓ 4 ✗ kayaking 5 ✓
6 ✗ terrified
5 Extreme sports: rafting, sailing, snorkelling, surfing
   Feelings: embarrassed, nervous, worried, excited
   Things: snorkel, life jacket, surfboard, riding boots
6 (open answers)

Final

Reading A
1 1 b 2 b 3 c 4 c
2 1 F 2 T 3 T 4 F 5 F 6 T
3 1 It's sunny and windy 2 They often go sailing in the summer. 3 No, they couldn't 4 Bill/He wants to be a famous basketball player.

Reading B
1 1 c 2 a 3 b 4 a 5 b 6 c
2 1 F 2 T 3 T 4 T 5 F 6 T 7 T 8 F
3 1 To be sick on a boat/at sea.
   2 To be safe.
   3 Kim likes looking for crabs more.
   4 In the desert.

Writing A
1 (open answers)
2 1 Why is she laughing? 2 What was the weather like? 3 What makes you nervous? 4 What does he want to be? 5 What do monkeys eat?
3 (open answers)

Writing B
1 (open answers)
2 1 How do you feel? 2 What's the temperature today? 3 What makes you feel scared? 4 Do you want to be a journalist? 5 What does he want to be? 6 Why is she crying?
3 (open answers)

Listening A
1 **Julie:** is going to go hiking; likes autumn; wants to be a ballet dancer; is laughing at the dog
   Ben: is going to walk the dog; likes spring; wants to be a builder; is shouting at the dog
2 1 playing computer games / riding a scooter 2 black and white / Monkeys 3 autumn / cloudy and wet 4 quarter past / reads and does homework.
3 1 False 2 True 3 True 4 False
4 **John:** ✓ sailing; ✗ horse-riding, hiking
   Ron: ✓ horse-riding, hiking; ✗ fishing
   Judith: ✓ horse-riding, hiking; ✗ fishing
   Sue: ✓ horse-riding, hiking; ✗ sailing

Listening B
1 **Janet:** is going to play hockey; is going to go hang gliding; plays tennis in spring and summer; does karate; practises Tuesday, Thursday and Saturday; loves the sea and coast
   Billie: is going to play beach volleyball; is going to chat online; usually plays volleyball in summer; plays piano; practises before school; loves lakes and waterfalls
2 1 walking in the park, likes, doesn't like 2 crocodiles, lakes, hippos 3 winter, cloudy and humid, afternoon 4 doesn't like, watch TV, always
3 1 F, First you go around the lake. 2 F, Next you go around the forest. 3 T 4 T

4 **Silvia:** ✓ ski, play football, watch films; ✗ skateboard
   Joanne: ✓ watch films; ✗ skateboard, ski, play football
   Pete: ✓ skateboard, play football, watch films; ✗ ski
   Lenny: ✓ skateboard, ski, play football; ✗ watch films
5 1 skateboarding 2 watching films 3 skiing 4 watching films

Speaking A
1 (open answers)

Speaking B
1 (open answers)

Exam preparation

Reading and writing A
1 1 paddle 2 firefighter 3 bridge 4 elephant 5 watching TV 6 thunder
2 1 yes 2 no 3 yes 4 yes 5 no 6 yes
3 1 b 2 a 3 c 4 a
4 1 mountains 2 lake 3 fishing 4 always 5 dog 6 scared

Listening A
1 (Compare against audio script)
2 1 Blue Forest 2 three children on a hiking holiday 3 William 4 When the children see the thunder and lightning 5 60 to 100 pages.
3 Monday – c; Tuesday – b; Wednesday – a; Friday – d
4 1 c 2 a
5 (compare against audio script)

Reading and writing B
1 1 police officer 2 lightning 3 snorkel 4 crocodile 5 mountain 6 skateboarding
2 1 no 2 no 3 yes 4 yes 5 no 6 yes
3 1 b 2 a 3 c 4 b
4 1 coast 2 swimming / snorkelling 3 paddles 4 Tuesday / Thursday 5 journey 6 faster

Listening B
1 (Compare against audio script)
2 1 Hugh 2 Near a big forest and lake. 3 lions, giraffes and monkeys 4 One o'clock 5 Mr Thomas
3 Monday – a; Tuesday – d; Thursday – c; Friday b
4 1 B 2 a
5 (compare against audio script)

Speaking A and B
1 (open answers)
2 (open answers)
3 (open answers)
4 (open answers)

Games bank

Flashcard and wordcard games

Pass the actions Use action wordcards. Distribute these to eight pupils in the class. Play some music and ask pupils to pass the action cards round the class between themselves while they are listening. Stop the music. Pupils with an action card take turns to read their action silently and act it out for the rest of the class to guess. Repeat until all members of the class have had a turn.

Mix-matched flashcards Stick four flashcards on the board face down so pupils can't see the pictures. Divide the class into teams of four. Invite Team 1 to the board and give each person a wordcard. Pupils stick the wordcards face up below the flashcards so they can be read. Now point to the first wordcard and pupils read out the word. Turn over the flashcard above it. The team receives one point if the flashcard corresponds with the wordcard below it. Continue with the remaining cards. Write the total number of points earned by each team on the board. Mix the cards and continue with the other teams.

Pass the wordcards This is a reading game. Write the words for any target vocabulary set (e.g. numbers, colours, animals, etc.) on pieces of paper or card and fold them up. Pupils sit in a circle. Distribute the cards to different pupils around the circle. Play some music and ask pupils to pass the cards around the circle. Stop the music. The pupils holding cards open them, show them to the class, and read the words on them. Pupils then fold up their cards. Start the music again and ask pupils to pass the cards again.

What's missing? Lay several flashcards facing upwards on the floor or a large table. Allow pupils a few minutes to study them. Tell pupils to close their eyes and remove a flashcard. Pupils have to correctly identify the missing card.

Pass the flashcards Choose a number of flashcards and pass them face down round the classroom at intervals so pupils can't see the cards. When you say stop, ask *Who's got (purple)?* Pupils guess who's got the flashcard of the colour purple and get a point if their guess is correct. Alternatively, you can just ask pupils who have got flashcards to stand up and name their card when the music stops.

Picture charades Choose a selection of words you want to revise. Use flashcards or draw simple pictures of them on pieces of paper. Put these into a bag. Ask a pupil to choose a picture. They have to act out the meaning of the word for the rest of the class to guess.

Snap Write a word on the board or say an item from a specific group of flashcards. Show several flashcards one by one. Pupils shout *Snap!* when they see the corresponding flashcard.

Bluff Invite several pupils to the board and ask them to stand in a row. Give them each a flashcard and ask them to keep it secret from the class. The first pupil in the row says a word that might or might not correspond with the flashcard they are holding. Pupils guess whether or not they're bluffing. Pupils say *Bluff* if they think they're bluffing. Divide the class into teams and award points when pupils guess correctly.

Basketball Divide the class into teams. Show a pupil from Team 1 a flashcard. If he/she correctly states the content of the flashcard, he/she is allowed to 'shoot' at a specific target (e.g. the bin or a small box) with a ball of paper. If the 'ball' enters the target, he/she is awarded two points. If the 'ball' hits the target without going in, he/she is awarded one point.

Countdown Divide the class into small groups. Mix flashcards from different units together and divide into piles according to the number of groups. Pupils arrange them back into categories, e.g. Colours, Classroom objects, Family, etc. The first group to finish is the winner.

Collect the cards Hold up any flashcard. If a pupil can correctly identify it, he/she is allowed to keep it. The pupil with the most flashcards at the end of the game is the winner.

Who's the fastest? Divide the class into two teams. Stick a number of flashcards on the board. Invite two pupils to stand facing the flashcards on different sides of the board. Call out one of the words and the pupil who is the fastest to touch the card wins a point for his/her team.

Noughts and crosses Divide the class into two teams. One is noughts and one crosses. Draw a large grid on the board with nine spaces. Stick one flashcard in each space facing towards the board. Pupils select a card, turn it over and say the word on the flashcard. If it's correct, remove the flashcard and write a nought or a cross accordingly. The first team to have three noughts or crosses in a row wins.

Correct order Call four to eight pupils to the front of the class (depending on the number of flashcards) and give them each a flashcard. Then call out four flashcards in random order. Pupils have to arrange themselves in the correct order.

Who's got it? Invite several pupils to the board and give a different flashcard to each. Pupils hold their flashcards up to show the class. Ask *Who's got the (cat)?* Pupils answer *He's/She's got the cat.* Pupils have to say the name of the pupil who has that flashcard.

Name it Divide the class into two teams. Invite a pupil from each team to come to the front of the class and turn their back to you. Hold up a flashcard and count to three and say *Turn around*. The first pupil to turn around and correctly identify the card is awarded a point for his/her team.

Animal farm Call a pupil to the front of the class and secretly show him/her an animal flashcard, e.g. a cat. Blindfold the pupil. Give out several animal flashcards around the classroom including the one you've shown to the blindfolded pupil. Pupils make the appropriate sound for their given animal. The blindfolded pupil has to walk round the classroom listening to the different animal sounds until he or she finds the pupil making the correct animal noise, e.g. a cat sound. Be prepared for a lot of noise!

Hide from the monster Put the wordcards for the four rooms in a bag, and stick the four room flashcards on the wall in different parts of the classroom. Choose one pupil to be the monster. Everyone else has to hide from the monster in one of the 'rooms', while you and the monster count to 10. The monster then takes a wordcard from the bag and visits that room. Everyone in that room loses a life. Play several times with different pupils as the monster.

Guess the card Cut out a small square in the centre of a piece of A4 paper. Hold the paper in front of a flashcard allowing pupils to see only a small bit of the card through the hole. Pupils guess the item.

Sponge throw Place the flashcards on the floor facing the floor. Pupils throw a sponge or other soft object and identify the flashcard it lands on.

Hit the card Stick all the flashcards of one vocabulary category on the board in mixed order. Call two pupils to the front of the room to stand a metre or two from the board. Call out a word. The first pupil to run to the board and 'hit' the correct flashcard wins. Play the game in teams and award points for each correct 'hit'.

Tick or cross Explain the meaning of a tick and a cross. Hand out two large squares of paper to each pupil. Ask them to draw a tick on one card and a cross on the other. Tell pupils you will show them one flashcard and one wordcard at the same time. If the flashcard corresponds with the wordcard, they hold up the 'tick' card. If it doesn't, they hold up the 'cross' card. Make lots of intentional mistakes. Stick the cards on the board when you make a match.

Echo Explain (L1) the meaning of the word *echo*. Ask pupils to be your echo. Show them an emotion card and say the item on it, using an appropriate tone of voice to match the emotion. Ask pupils to echo it by repeating several times, becoming quieter and quieter.

Memory Stick four or five flashcards on the board. After pupils memorise the cards, remove them from the board and pupils say the items. To make this more challenging, ask pupils to say the cards in the order they appeared on the board.

Drawing games

Alternative bingo Pupils each draw a simple picture of one of the items from a unit (e.g. Pets). Write the words on the board to remind them. Also include others from previous units of the same category (e.g. bird, butterfly, frog). As they draw, write the words on small pieces of paper and put them in a small box or bag. Ask pupils to stand up. Pull out the pieces of paper in turn and read the animal names. Pupils who have drawn that particular animal sit down. Continue until there's only one piece of paper remaining in the bag.

Dice game Divide the class into two teams. Tell pupils to draw an item from the target vocabulary. If he/she draws correctly, he/she rolls the dice and wins that number of points for his/her team.

Feed the monster Draw a simple picture of a monster on the board and ask *What's this?* (It's a monster.) Then tell pupils to imagine that they are a very hungry monster. Ask *What do you want for lunch?* Pupils have to 'feed the monster' by playing a food game chain around the class. Start by saying *I'm a hungry monster and I want chicken for lunch.* The nearest pupil to you repeats and adds to this: *I'm a hungry monster and I want chicken and peas for lunch.* Continue with different pupils adding one food to the chain until one of them forgets or makes a mistake and is out of the game. Repeat the game a couple of times.

TPR games

Teacher says Give the pupils instructions, but tell them to follow the instructions only if they are preceded by *Teacher says*. For example, if you say, *Stand up*, pupils should do nothing, but if you say *Teacher says 'Stand up!'* pupils must stand up. Vary the speed of the instructions to make the game more interesting. You could also ask pupils in stronger classes to give the instructions.

Grab it Pupils sit in a circle. Place some classroom objects (no sharp pencils or scissors) or flashcards in the middle of the circle. Pupils put their hands behind their backs. Call out an object and pupils race to find and touch it. Play this in teams and award points to the winner.

Pass the ball Pupils sit in a circle. Make a paper ball. Choose a category and pupils pass the ball around the circle. Each pupil must say a word from the given category when he/she's got the ball. A pupil leaves the circle when he/she can't say a word from the given category. Alternatively, play music while pupils pass the ball and say words. Stop the music. The pupil holding the ball when the music stops leaves the game.

Memory Play a memory game in teams. Put eight classroom objects of different colours on a tray or desk and let all the pupils have a good look for one minute. Then take all the objects away so that pupils can't see them. Say classroom objects, e.g. a blue rubber. In teams, pupils have to decide if that object was on the tray and say *Yes* or *No*. Continue until you have mentioned everything on the tray and several other objects. Teams get a point for each correct answer.

Ball throw Pupils stand in a large circle. Make a paper ball, call out a category (e.g. Family) and throw the ball to a pupil. He/She must say a word in the category you mentioned. He/She then throws the ball to another pupil who says another word in the same category. If a pupil drops the ball or can't say a word in the category, he/she must sit down. Continue until one pupil remains.

Guess the object Put an object in a bag for a pupil to feel (e.g. toy food or plastic animals). He/She must guess what the object is without looking.

Number groups Play some lively music and ask pupils to perform a specific action (e.g. jump, walk and hop) around the classroom. Stop the music and call out a number from 2–5. Pupils must quickly get together in groups of that number. The odd pupil must sit out until the next round. Start with the numbers 2–5 then move on to numbers 6–10 when pupils feel confident.

Pairwork games

Snap Pupils can use cards they make with the cut outs or photocopiables. Pupils shuffle their cards and hold them in front of them face down. Pupils take turns to place one card from their pile face up on the table. If their card matches with the one their partner has laid down, they say *Snap!* And place their hand on the cards. The first pupil to say *Snap!* adds the cards to their pile. The game continues until one player has all the cards. This player is the winner.

Matching pairs Pupils can use cards they make with the cut outs or photocopiables. Pupils shuffle their cards together and place them on the table face down in front of them. Pupils take turns to turn two cards face up, naming the words as they do so. If the cards match, the pupil who has found the matching pair keeps it and has another turn. If they don't match, the pupil puts the cards back in the same location they found them in.

Team games

Colour race Divide the class into two teams. Say a colour, e.g. Red. One member from each team finds something red in the classroom. Alternatively, stick the colour flashcards on the board. Say a colour. Pupils point to the correct flashcard to win a point for their team.

Missing numbers Divide the class into groups or teams. Write a sequence of numbers on the board, leaving some out. Pupils work in their groups or teams to find the missing numbers. The sequences you use can vary in difficulty. Start with numbers in the correct numerical sequence, then include some different mathematical sequences, e.g using even numbers, 2, 4, 6, 8 or odd numbers, 1, 3, 5, 7, 9.

Drawing race Divide the class into two teams and invite a pupil from each team to the front of the class. Show a wordcard to each or whisper a word. Each pupil draws the word on the board. The first team to identify the picture correctly wins a point.

Twenty seconds Set a time limit of twenty seconds for pupils, groups of pupils or teams to complete a task. E.g. Find fifteen pencils. The rest of the class counts to twenty while that pupil, group or team tries to complete the task. They can score a point for each task completed correctly before the twenty seconds runs out.

Unscramble Divide the class into groups. Write a word on the board in jumbled order. The first group to guess the word wins a point.

Clothes line Cut out several clothes items from different colours of sturdy card. Draw a clothes line on the board and stick the clothes on the line (e.g. a pink skirt, a black T-shirt, a green shoe and an orange dress). Alternatively, pin them to a real length of string hung to look like a clothes line. Give pupils a few minutes to study the order of the clothes. Remove the clothes cards. Now pupils draw and colour the clothes in the same order. Pupils could also label the clothes to make this more challenging. If you haven't got much time, pupils could simply recite the order. Do this game in teams and award points for correct answers.

Can I cross the river? Divide the class into two teams. Each team stands on one side of the classroom facing the other. Tell them to pretend that there is a river running between them with crocodiles swimming in it. Pupils take turns to try and cross the 'river' (i.e. from one team to the other) by asking *Please Mr Crocodile, can I cross the river?* The team replies *Only if you've got (green socks)*. If they do, they can cross the river. If they don't, they fall in the river and are out of the game. Set a time limit for the game. The winning team is the one with most people left at the end of this time limit.

Board game Draw a large race track on the board. Divide the class into two teams. Use small coloured circles as markers for each team. Ask questions, e.g. show flashcards/story cards and ask *What's this?* or show classroom objects in different numbers and ask *How many?* Pupils move ahead one space if they guess correctly. The winning team are the ones to reach the finish first.

Stop! Divide the class into two teams. Write the target vocabulary on small pieces of paper and put them in a bag or a small box. Write the word *STOP* on a few pieces of paper and add them to the others. Pupils reach into the bag/box without looking, choose a piece of paper and say the word. If he/she says the word correctly, his/her team wins a point. If a pupil chooses the word STOP, the team loses all of its points.

Last man standing Ask pupils to write the names of three foods they like and three foods they don't like on a piece of paper. (They can write full sentences, or just the food words with a tick or cross next to them as you prefer.) Then ask pupils to stand up. Ask a food question, e.g. *Do you like cake?* All pupils who have written they like cake answer *Yes, I do* and remain standing. Pupils who haven't written cake, reply *No, I don't* and sit down. Continue with more food questions until there is only one pupil left standing up. That pupil is the winner.

Yes or no? Bring in several toys, classroom objects or toy animals of different colours and sizes. You may also use flashcards. Put them on a table at the front of the class. Explain that you will choose one of the items and pupils will guess the item, but you can only say *Yes* or *No*. Pupils ask *Is it big? Is it red? Is it a duck?*

Whoops! Write as many words as possible (from any unit or combination of units) on small pieces of paper. Fold them and put them in a box or a bag. Also write the word *Whoops!* on several pieces of paper and add them to your bag or box. Pupils come to the front of the class, choose a piece of paper and read the word. If they read it correctly, they keep the paper and receive one point for their team. If the word is read incorrectly, you keep the paper. If pupils choose the word Whoops! they sit down and don't receive any points. Alternatively, you could add some suspense by taking away all points when the Whoops! card is chosen.

Reading race Write sentences on long strips of paper describing a set of flashcards (e.g. Food, Toys, Family or Animals). *It's big. It's black and white. It's got four legs,* etc. Divide the class into two or more teams and ask each team to stand in a queue. Put a set of sentences face down at the front of the queue.

Stick the flashcards on the board. When you say go, one pupil from each team picks up a sentence, sticks it below the appropriate flashcard on the board, and runs back to touch the hand of the next person in his team. Check that pupils are sticking the sentences in the correct place, and call them back to the board if they make a mistake. The first team to stick up all its sentences is the winner.

Anagrams Tell the class to make anagrams with all the new words from this unit. Organise the class in pairs. They must work out their partner's anagrams and write the words in their notebooks.

Hide and seek Collect pictures of relevant vocabulary and cut them in halves. Put one set of halves on your table and hide the other set around the classroom. Explain to pupils (L1) that they have to find the missing halves, match them to the ones on your table and say what they are, e.g. *It's a belt.* You may like to turn the activity into a competition: hand out the same number of picture halves to two groups and ask them to find the matching pictures; the team who finds their set of pictures first and describes them correctly wins.

Miming competition Mime putting on an item of clothing or doing an action. The class guesses what it is. Then divide the class into two teams and have a competition. Whisper an item of clothing or action to a pupil to mime. His/Her own team has to guess the item within a twenty second time limit. Then do the same for the other team. Teams win a point for every correct guess.

Spin the bottle Draw pictures or write words around a circle. Take a pen or a plastic bottle and spin it to point to one of the pictures or words. A speaker from each group must say the word or describe the picture.

Phonics games

Build the word Use letter cards for the target phonic sounds, e.g. /a/, /p/, /s/, /t/ and attach these to the board or face up on a table. Say one of the sample words, e.g. *tap.* Ask a pupil to come and arrange the letter cards in the correct sequence. Read the word out to check it as a class. Repeat with the other sample cards.

Sound trail Put the letter cards face up on the floor at the front of the class. Ask a pupil to the front of the class. Call out the phonics sounds for the letters on the floor in a random order. Pupils step from letter card to letter card, according to the sounds you call out.

Scrambled words Use a selection of letter cards, e.g. /a/, /p/, /s/, /t/, /i/, /d/, /m/, /n/. Choose a word made from these letters, e.g. *man.* Put these letters on the board in a jumbled order. Pupils unscramble the letters to make a word. Check by asking a pupil to sound out the letters in the correct order for another pupil to come and unscramble on the board. Check the word with the rest of the class and repeat with another scrambled word.

Pass the parcel Use a wrapped parcel for this game. Pupils sit in a circle. Play some music and ask them to pass the parcel. They pass it round the circle. Then stop the music and ask the pupil holding the parcel a question, e.g. *How old are you?* If the pupil answers correctly, he/she can unwrap one layer of the parcel. Continue until one pupil ends up opening the small gift. NOTE, to add a reading element to this game, you can include a written instruction inside each layer, e.g. *Stand up. Open your book.* Instead of answering a question, the pupil who unwraps the layer, reads and follows the instruction.

Hunting for letter sounds Prepare a word puzzle with the words from the lesson that contain the studied sounds. Make photocopies for the class. The children must identify and circle them. Ask them to report to the class.

Odd one out Write on the board a list of words with the same sound and add one with a different sound. Pupils must find the odd one out, e.g.; eat, tea, coin, leaf, peach.

Slow motion game Begin by saying a word from the lesson in slow motion, stretching out each sound as you say it. Repeat it so that pupils hear each sound clearly. Try with more words stretching out sounds as you say them. Ask your pupils to guess what word you said, saying the word as it is normally pronounced.

Snap Prepare pairs of cards: one with the sound, the other with the word. For example: /ge/ *bridge*. Organise the class in pairs. Pupils play *Snap!*

Sound hunt Ask pupils to bring a small container (a shoebox, plastic tub, etc.) to class. Ask them to go on a 'sound hunt'. They have to fill the container with items that rhyme with the lesson vocabulary. For example, if the word 'glue' has appeared in the lesson, they could find something blue, a shoe, etc.

Sound snake The pupils write all the words that they have seen in a lesson that contain the studied sounds and write them making a sound snake. Tell them to write the sounds in a different colour, e.g. /ce/ (red), /ci/ (green), /cir/ (blue).

Sound spy Write on the board the sounds of the unit. The pupils write them in their notebooks. Now think of two words that end with the same sounds. The pupils say them with you. Then say a word and ask *Can you sound spy?* The pupils write a rhyming word. Check with the class. The pupils with correct rhyming words score a point.

Words in the air Write some of the words from the lesson with your finger in the air. Pupils guess the words and say another word with the same sound. Each pupil writes a word on his/her partner's back. The partner guesses the word and says another word with the same sound.

Classroom language

Using classroom language is a good way to get pupils to react in English rather than in L1. The more they use these new phrases and expressions, the more confident they become and the less they will need to rely on L1 to communicate with the teacher. If classroom language is used consistently, it becomes a natural part of pupils' vocabulary. It is important to teach both the classroom language the pupils have to understand as well as language they need to produce. The following is a list of common English expressions that could easily be introduced in the classroom and used on a daily basis. It's best to begin with a few expressions and increase the number gradually.

Greeting the class
Good morning/afternoon. Come in. Sit down/stand up, please. What day is it today? How are you today? Is everyone here? Is anyone away today? Where is (John)?

Starting the lesson
Are you ready? Let's begin. Listen (to me). Look (at me/at the board). Take out your books/notebooks/coloured pencils. Give this/these out, please. Have you got a (pencil)? Open your books at page (4). Turn to page (6). Open the window/door. Close the window/door.

Managing the class
Be quiet, please. Come to the front of the class. Come to the board. Come here, please. Put your hands up/down. Who's next? Queue/Line up! Repeat after me. Wait a minute, please. Hurry up.

During the lesson – instructions
Hold up your picture.
Show me/the class your picture.
Draw/Colour/Stick/Cut out ...
Write the answer on the board/in your book.
Let's sing.
All together now.
It's break time/lunch time.
Wait a minute, please.
Be careful.
Sorry, guess/try again.
Next, please.
Again, please.

During the lesson – questions
Do you understand? What do you think? Anything else? May/Can I help you? Are you finished? Who's finished? Who would like to read? What can you see? Any questions?

Words of praise
Well done! Excellent! Fantastic! That's nice. Much better. Good job. Congratulations. That's correct! Great work! Good luck! Thank you.

Pairwork/Group work
Find a partner.
Get into twos/threes.
Who's your partner?
Work in pairs/groups.
Make a circle.
Work with your partner/friend/group.
Show your partner/friend/group.
Tell your partner/friend/group.
Now ask your partner/friend/group.

Language used for playing games
It's my/your/his/her turn. Whose turn is it? You're out. Don't look. No cheating. Turn around. Shut your eyes. Pass the (ball, cup, etc.) Wait outside. Spin the spinner. Move your/my counter (3) spaces. Miss a turn. Go back (2) spaces. Spin again. I've won! You're the winner!

Ending the lesson
Put your books/notebooks/coloured pencils away.
Tidy up.
Put that in the bin/rubbish bin, please.
That's all for today.
Collect the stickers/cards/spinners/scissors, please.
The lesson is finished.
Goodbye!
See you tomorrow.
Have a nice weekend/holiday.

Useful phrases for the pupils
May/Can I go to the toilet?
I understand/I don't understand.
Excuse me/Pardon me?
I'm sorry.
Can you help me?
I'm finished.

Pearson Education Limited
Edinburgh Gate
Harlow
Essex CM20 2JE
England
and Associated Companies throughout the world.

www.islands.pearson.com

First published 2012
Fourth Impression 2017
ISBN: 978-1-4082-9055-2

Set in Fiendstar 10.5/12pt
Printed in Great Britain by Ashford Colour Press Ltd

Islands

4

TEST BOOKLET

PEARSON

Contents

1 **Read. Then number.**

1 She's doing homework.	**2** He's walking.
3 He's sleeping.	**4** He's listening to music.
5 She's eating.	**6** She's dancing.

a ☐   b ☐

c ☐   d ☐

e ☐   f ☐

2 **Read and circle. Then match.**

1 What (*do* / *does*) you like doing?	**a** No, she doesn't.
2 (*Do* / *Does*) Anna like peas?	**b** I like playing the guitar.
3 Can he (*run* / *running*)?	**c** I'm wearing a blue a shirt.
4 (*Has* / *Have*) she got a round chin?	**d** Yes, he can.
5 What are you (*wear* / *wearing*)?	**e** It's got a tail and big ears.
6 What does (*it* / *they*) look like?	**f** No, she hasn't.

3 **Read. Then write *True* or *False*.**

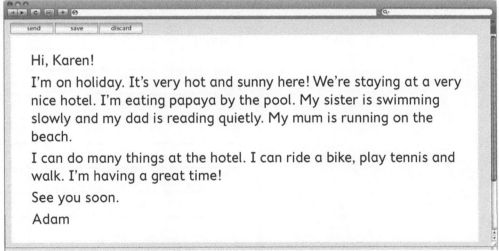

| send | save | discard |

Hi, Karen!

I'm on holiday. It's very hot and sunny here! We're staying at a very nice hotel. I'm eating papaya by the pool. My sister is swimming slowly and my dad is reading quietly. My mum is running on the beach.

I can do many things at the hotel. I can ride a bike, play tennis and walk. I'm having a great time!

See you soon.

Adam

1 Adam is on holiday.	_____
2 It's cold and rainy.	_____
3 His sister is reading slowly.	_____
4 His mum is running on the beach.	_____
5 He can play tennis at the hotel.	_____
6 He can't ride a bike at the hotel.	_____

1 **Read. Then complete.**

like   younger   name   brother   nine   is   reading

My ¹ _____ is Mary. I'm ² _____ years old.
This is my ³ _____ Rob. He ⁴ _____ six. He's
⁵ _____ than me. I ⁶ _____ writing but I don't like
⁷ _____ .

2 **Read. Then answer.**

1   When were you born?   _____
2   Have you got brown hair?   _____
3   Can you swim?   _____
4   Are you writing?   _____
5   What do you do after school? _____
6   Where were you yesterday?   _____
7   Has your teacher got glasses? _____
8   Are you wearing a tracksuit? _____

3 **Draw. Then write about your family.**

My family

There are _____ people in my family.

I've got _____

_____ .

My _____ likes _____

_____ .

_____

_____

_____

_____

_____

_____

_____

_____

_____

_____

1 (4:01) **Listen. Then write.**

		Age	Favourite number	Hair colour	Favourite hobby
1	Alice	9			painting
2	Amy		62	blond	
3	Bill	10			
4	Tom			brown	

2 (4:02) **Listen. Then circle.**

1 19 / 90	**2** 15 / 50	**3** 20 / 30	**4** 18 / 80
5 14 / 40	**6** 17 / 70	**7** 13 / 30	**8** 16 / 60

3 (4:03) **Listen. Then match.**

1 Alice	skiing	every morning
2 Darren	walking the dog	after school
3 Jo	cooking	at the weekend
4 Alex	chatting online	in the winter

4 **Look at the picture. Then talk.**

on   in   next to   opposite   behind   in front of   above   under

There is / are …

It's …

1 **Read and tick (✓) or cross (✗). Then correct the sentences.**

1 What do you like doing? ☐ _____

2 What do Anna like doing? ☐ _____

3 They likes chatting online. ☐ _____

4 I like playing the guitar. ☐ _____

5 We do'nt like reading the newspaper. ☐ _____

6 Tom likes watch TV. ☐ _____

2 **Read. Then match.**

1 Do you like walking the dog?   **a** No, she doesn't.

2 Does your brother like riding a scooter?   **b** Yes, I do.

3 Do you like watching films?   **c** No, they don't.

4 Does your sister like painting?   **d** Yes, he does.

5 Do your friends like skipping?   **e** Yes, we do. We love films.

3 **Read. Then write.**

> playing   love   What   in   magazines   dog   swimming   guitar   doing

Donna: What do you like [1] _____ , Emily?

Emily: I like walking my [2] _____ and I like [3] _____ with my friends.

Donna: [4] _____ else do you like doing?

Emma: I also like singing and playing the [5] _____ with my family. What about you, Donna?

Donna: I like reading [6] _____ . My dad likes [7] _____ at the water park but I don't. Do you like swimming, Emily?

Emily: Yes, I do. I [8] _____ swimming. I really like swimming [9] _____ the sea.

4 **Write about what you like and don't like doing.**

I like _____ .

_____

_____

_____

I don't like _____ .

_____

_____

_____

1 Read and tick (✓) or cross (✗). Then correct the sentences.

1 What like you doing? ☐ _____

2 What does Zoe like doing? ☐ _____

3 We doesn't like reading the newspaper. ☐ _____

4 I like playing computer games. ☐ _____

5 I don't like ski. ☐ _____

6 Richard don't like skateboarding. ☐ _____

2 Write questions and answers.

1 _____ (you / like / walk the dog / ?)
_____ (✗)

2 _____ (your dad / like / surf the Internet / ?)
_____ (✓)

3 _____ (she / like / ride a scooter / ?)
_____ (✗)

4 _____ (they / like / paint / ?)
_____ (✗)

5 _____ (you / like / play hockey / ?)
_____ (✓)

3 Read. Then write.

| loves   don't   scooters   like   playing   TV   cooking   chatting   breakfast   doesn't |

At the weekend I ¹ _____ skateboarding and riding ² _____ with my friends. I also like ³ _____ online and ⁴ _____ computer games. They're so much fun! I ⁵ _____ like watching ⁶ _____ at the weekend but my brother does. He ⁷ _____ TV! He can watch all day. On Sundays my family has a big ⁸ _____ . My dad likes ⁹ _____ breakfast but my mum ¹⁰ _____ . She likes eating! So do I!

4 Write about what you and a friend like and don't like doing.

I like _____ .

_____

I don't like _____ .

_____

_____ likes _____ .

_____

_____

1 4:04 **Listen. Then circle.**

1 Robert likes
  a skiing.
  b skateboarding.
  c riding his scooter.

3 Jack likes
  a playing the guitar.
  b playing football.
  c watching TV.

2 Daisy likes
  a playing football.
  b reading magazines.
  c reading books.

4 Pat likes
  a cooking.
  b painting.
  c watching TV.

2 4:05 **Listen. Then write a tick (✓) or cross (✗).**

1 Harry and Beth like walking the dog. ☐

2 Peter and Nick don't like painting. ☐

3 Chris likes playing hockey. ☐

4 Vicky doesn't like reading magazines. ☐

5 Charlie doesn't like surfing the Internet. ☐

3 **Draw things you like and don't like doing. Then talk.**

like	don't like

What do you like doing?

I like ... / I don't like ...

Do you like ... ?

1 🔊 4:06 **Listen. Then circle.**

1 Sandy likes
   a chatting online.
   b playing computer games.
   c playing football.

2 Fred doesn't like
   a reading magazines.
   b watching the TV.
   c playing the guitar.

3 Mary likes
   a skiing.
   b chatting online.
   c skateboarding.

4 Matt likes
   a playing computer games.
   b watching films.
   c cooking.

2 🔊 4:07 **Listen. Then write a tick (✓) or cross (✗).**

1 Tom likes running. ☐

He likes skipping. ☐

2 Jo and Sue don't like painting pictures of flowers. ☐

They like painting pictures of animals. ☐

3 Charlie doesn't like playing football. ☐

He doesn't like the rain. ☐

4 Val likes reading newspapers. ☐

Her mum and dad don't like reading newspapers. ☐

5 Tony doesn't like riding bikes. ☐

He doesn't like riding his scooter. ☐

3 **Draw what you and your friends like and don't like doing. Then talk.**

like	don't like

What do you / they like doing?

Do you / they like ... ?

What does he / she like doing?

Does he / she like ... ?

1 **Read and write. Then number.**

1 Zebras live in _____ .   2 Pandas live in _____ .

3 Camels live in _____ .   4 Crabs live in _____ .

5 Gorillas live in _____ .

a  ☐   b  ☐   c  ☐

d  ☐   e  ☐

2 **Read. Then match.**

1 Do monkeys eat fruit?   a They eat worms.
2 Do giraffes eat meat?   b Yes, they do.
3 What do crabs eat?   c They live in rivers.
4 Where do crocodiles live?   d No, they don't.

3 **Read. Then circle.**

1 How (*much / many*) teeth have crocodiles got? They've got 65 teeth.
2 How (*much / many*) meat do lions eat? They eat a lot of meat.
3 Giraffes (*has / have*) got 32 teeth.
4 Monkeys (*eat / eats*) fruit.
5 Zebras (*run quickly / quickly run*).

4 **Look. Then write about an animal that lives in each place.**

1   2

_____ live in _____ .   _____

They eat _____ .   _____

They can _____ .   _____

They can't _____ .   _____

1 Unscramble and write. Then number.

1 dorlcoice _____ 2 pihop _____ 3 veslae _____

4 regfaif _____ 5 oiln _____ 6 srags _____

a  ☐ b  ☐ c  ☐

d  ☐ e  ☐ f  ☐

2 Unscramble and write the questions. Then match.

1 do / live / zebras / where

_____

2 eat / pandas / what / do

_____

3 crocodiles / do / where / live

_____

4 do / what / eat / birds

_____

5 gorillas / live / where / do

_____

a They eat worms.

b They live in rivers.

c They live in grasslands.

d They eat leaves.

e They live in rainforests.

3 Read. Then circle.

1 How (*much* / *many*) meat do lions eat?
2 Fish (*swim well* / *well swim*).
3 How (*much* / *many*) teeth do cats have?
4 Zebras (*live* / *living*) in grasslands.
5 They eat (*a lot* / *quickly*) of leaves.
6 Monkeys (*climb* / *climbs*) well.

4 Write about an animal.

- They've got …
- They live in …
- They eat …
- They can …
- They're omnivores, etc. …

_____

_____

_____

_____

_____

_____

1 **Listen. Then circle.**

1   a   b   2   a   b

3   a   b   4   a   b

2 **Listen and tick the words you hear.**

desert	☐	grasslands	☐	rainforest	☐	river	☐
camel	☐	crab	☐	crocodile	☐	elephant	☐
lion	☐	monkey	☐	panda	☐	zebra	☐

3 **Choose an animal. Then talk.**

1   2   3

Where does it live?

Can it ... fast / well?

What does it eat?

How much / many ... ?

1 (4:10) **Listen. Then circle.**

1   a   b   c

2   a    b   c

3   a    b   c

4   a    b   c

2 (4:11) **Listen and tick the words you hear.**

desert	☐	forest	☐	grasslands	☐	rainforest	☐	river	☐
camel	☐	crab	☐	crocodile	☐	elephant	☐	giraffe	☐
hippo	☐	lion	☐	monkey	☐	panda	☐	zebra	☐

3 **Make notes about an animal. Then talk.**

Animal: _____

Eats: _____

Lives: _____

Can: _____

How much / many: _____

Where does it live?

What does it eat?

Can it ... fast / well?

How much / many ... ?

Is it a herbivore / omnivore / carnivore?

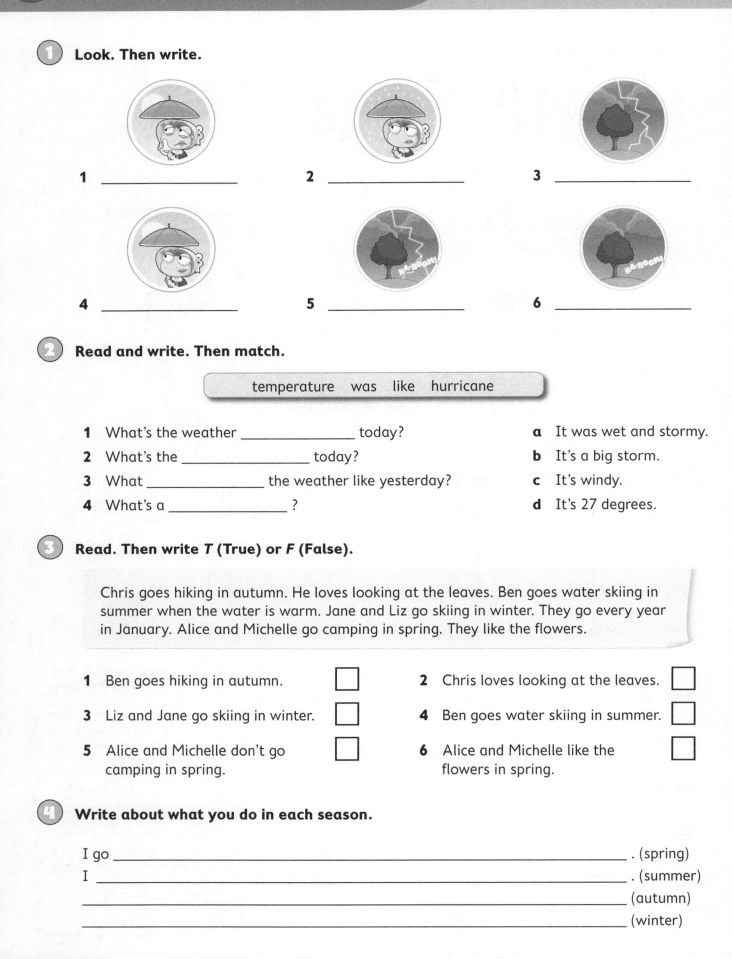

1 **Look. Then write.**

1 _____ 2 _____ 3 _____

4 _____ 5 _____ 6 _____

2 **Read and write. Then match.**

| temperature was like hurricane |

1 What's the weather _____ today?   **a** It was wet and stormy.

2 What's the _____ today?   **b** It's a big storm.

3 What _____ the weather like yesterday?   **c** It's windy.

4 What's a _____ ?   **d** It's 27 degrees.

3 **Read. Then write T (True) or F (False).**

Chris goes hiking in autumn. He loves looking at the leaves. Ben goes water skiing in summer when the water is warm. Jane and Liz go skiing in winter. They go every year in January. Alice and Michelle go camping in spring. They like the flowers.

1 Ben goes hiking in autumn. ☐   **2** Chris loves looking at the leaves. ☐

3 Liz and Jane go skiing in winter. ☐   **4** Ben goes water skiing in summer. ☐

5 Alice and Michelle don't go camping in spring. ☐   **6** Alice and Michelle like the flowers in spring. ☐

4 **Write about what you do in each season.**

I go _____ . (spring)

I _____ . (summer)

_____ (autumn)

_____ (winter)

1 Read. Then number.

1 I go snowboarding in winter. 2 My brother goes water skiing in spring.
3 My family goes hiking in autumn. 4 My aunt goes camping in summer.

a ☐ b ☐

c ☐ d ☐

2 Unscramble and write the questions. Then match.

1 today / weather / what's / like / the

_____

2 temperature / today / what's / the

_____

3 was / temperature / the / what / yesterday

_____

4 weather / last / what / the / was / week / like

_____

a It was wet and stormy.

b There's thunder and lightning.

c It was 14 degrees.

d It's 27 degrees.

3 Read. Then write.

1 What's the weather like today?
_____ (warm / sunny)

2 What's the temperature today?
_____ (30 degrees)

3 What was the weather like on Monday?
_____ (humid / hot)

4 What do they do in winter?
_____ (go skiing)

4 Write about the seasons.

I go _____
_____ . (spring)
I _____
_____ . (summer)
_____
_____ (autumn)
_____
_____ (winter)

Last spring the weather was _____
_____ . (spring)
Last _____
_____ . (summer)
_____
_____ (autumn)
_____
_____ (winter)

1 **Listen. Then circle.**

1 The weather is
a humid.
b sunny.
c stormy.

2 The temperature is about
a 20 degrees.
b 35 degrees.
c 30 degrees.

3 This afternoon
a it's wet.
b it's cloudy.
c it's snowy.

4 The temperature is
a over 30 degrees.
b over 35 degrees.
c cool.

2 **Listen. Then match.**

1 Sally and Susan

2 John and Kim

3 Ian

4 Naomi

a goes snowboarding in winter.

b go hiking in autumn.

c rides a bike in spring.

d go camping in summer.

3 **Look at the pictures. Then talk**

1

What was the weather like / temperature?

2

What does he / she do in ... ?

1 4:14 **Listen. Then circle.**

1 The weather is
   a warm and wet.
   b cold and stormy.
   c humid with thunder and lightning.

2 The temperature is about
   a 23 degrees.
   b 25 degrees.
   c 33 degrees.

3 Today there's
   a a lot of wind.
   b not much rain.
   c thunder, lightning and rain.

4 It's about
   a 11 degrees.
   b 21 degrees.
   c 31 degrees.

2 4:15 **Listen. Then match.**

1	Jim and Claire	water skiing	winter
2	Carol	hiking	spring
3	Pete and Nick	snowboarding	autumn
4	Pat and Helen	camping	summer

3 **Look at the pictures and draw your own. Then talk.**

1

2

3
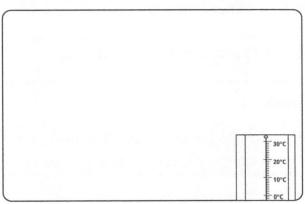

What was the weather like / temperature?

What does he / she do in … ?

What do you do in … ?

1 **Read. Then match.**

1 What do you do on Thursdays?
2 What does Jenny do on Fridays?
3 What does Robert do on Saturdays?
4 When do you learn to cook?
5 When do they have music lessons?

a They have music lessons at midday.
b I practise the violin.
c I learn to cook on Sundays.
d She learns to draw.
e He does gymnastics.

2 **Read. Then circle.**

When do you have music lessons, Bob?

I have music lessons on Mondays at 10.00. When do you have music lessons, Sue?

I have music lessons on Wednesday afternoons at 2:45. When does Frankie do karate?

Frankie does karate at 3.30.

1 Bob and Sue (*have music lessons / do gymnastics*).
2 Bob has music lessons on Monday (*afternoon / morning*).
3 Sue has music lessons at a (*quarter to three / quarter after three*).
4 Frankie does (*gymnastics / karate*).
5 He does it at (*half past four / half past three*).

3 **Unscramble. Write sentences and questions.**

1 the / always / Jane / has / piano / lessons / in / morning

_____

2 Henry / do / gymnastics / does / when

_____

3 midday / to / they / often / learn / at / cook

_____

4 on / does / what / Saturdays / she / do

_____

5 a / five / the / violin / I / practise / at / quarter / past

_____

4 **Write about your week.**

> morning   midday   afternoon   evening   a quarter past
> half past   a quarter to   always   never   often

On Mondays _____ .
On _____ .
_____
_____
_____

1 Read. Then write.

| do   study   have   practise   learn |

1 _____ English   2 _____ the piano
3 _____ ballet lessons 4 _____ to cook
5 _____ karate

2 Unscramble. Write sentences and questions.

1 the / always / Roger / has / violin / lessons / in / afternoon
_____

2 Karen / do / karate / does / when
_____

3 midday / to / they / often / learn / at / draw
_____

4 on / does / what / Fridays / she / do
_____

5 a / four / the / piano / I / practise / at / quarter / past
_____

3 Look. Then answer the questions.

	Activity	Day	When
Kim	MATHS	Monday	(clock)
	(ribbons)	Tuesday	(sun over hills)
John	(stove)	Saturday	(moon over hills)
	(table tennis)	Friday	(clock)

1 When does Kim study Maths?   _____
2 What does Kim do on Tuesdays?   _____
3 When does John learn to cook?   _____
4 What does John do on Fridays?   _____

4 Write about your week.

On Mondays _____ .
On _____ .
_____
_____

1 (4:16) **Listen. Then write.**

1 Jenny has _____ lessons on Wednesday after school.

2 She has ballet on _____ morning.

3 She has art lessons on Friday _____ .

4 She hasn't got _____ lessons.

5 She does gymnastics on _____ .

2 (4:17) **Listen. Then match.**

1 music lessons   **a** Saturday mornings

2 study English   **b** Wednesday and Friday at 10.30

3 practise the violin   **c** Sunday at midday

4 study Maths   **d** in the morning at 7.00

5 have ballet lessons   **e** every day at 11.45

6 learn to cook   **f** every morning at 9.15

3 **Make some notes about the activities you do. Then talk.**

Activity	Day	When

What activities do you do?

What do you do on ... ?

When do you ... ?

1 (4:18) **Listen. Then write.**

1   Ben has his piano lesson _____ and his guitar lesson on _____ .

2   He has _____ on _____ morning.

3   He does _____ on _____ after school.

4   He has a _____ _____ now.

5   On Friday he learns to _____ and _____ .

6   On _____ he does karate and _____ .

2 (4:19) **Listen. Then match.**

1 have ballet lessons	Wednesday afternoon	3.15
2 study Maths	Saturday afternoon	12.00
3 learn to cook	evening	4.00
4 do karate	every morning	11.30
5 practise the violin	Monday	6.45
6 learn to draw	every day	6.30

3 **Make some notes about the activities you and a family member do. Then talk.**

	Activity	Day	When
Me			
Family member:			

What activities do you do?

What activities does he / she do?

When do you ... ?

When does he / she ... ?

What do you do on ... ?

What does he / she do on ... ?

1 **Look. Then write.**

1 _____

2 _____

3 _____

4 _____

2 **Read and circle. Then match.**

1 What (*do / does*) you want to be?
2 What (*do / does*) Tina want to be?
3 Does Helena (*want / wants*) to be a singer?
4 Do (*you / she*) want to be a carpenter?

a Yes, she does. She loves singing.
b I want to be a journalist.
c She wants to be a lawyer.
d No, I don't. I want to be an athlete.

3 **Read. Then write.**

> jump   basketball player   helps   want   always

I ¹_____ to be in the Olympic Games. I want to be a ² _____
someday because I can ³ _____ high and run fast.
I ⁴_____ train at six o'clock in the morning before going to school. My coach is
named Wendy. She ⁵ _____ me a lot.

4 **What do you want to be? Why? Draw and write.**

I want to _____ .

_____

_____

_____

_____

_____

_____

_____

1 Look. Then write.

1 _____

2 _____

3 _____

4 _____

5 _____

6 _____

2 Read and write. Then match.

1 What _____ you want to be?

2 What _____ he want to be?

3 Does Jane _____ to be a photographer?

4 Do you want to _____ a model?

a No, I don't.

b I want to be a journalist.

c He wants to be a mechanic.

d No, she doesn't.

3 Look and write. Then answer.

1 Does he want to be _____
_____ ?
✓ _____

2 COURT
_____
✗ _____
_____

3 _____
✗ _____
_____

4 _____
✓ _____
_____

4 What do you and your friend want to be? Why? Write and draw.

you	your friend

I want to _____ .

_____

_____

_____

My friend _____ .

_____

_____

_____

_____

1 **Listen. Then circle.**

1 Sally wants to be a (*firefighter / ballet dancer*).

2 Dan (*wants to be / doesn't want to be*) a police officer.

3 Pat wants to be a (*journalist / police officer*).

4 Ben (*wants to be / doesn't want to be*) an astronaut.

2 **Listen. Then circle *True* or *False*.**

1 Sasha wants to be a singer.   *True / False*

2 Greg wants to be a photographer.   *True / False*

3 Beth wants to be a lawyer.   *True / False*

4 Graham wants to be an athlete.   *True / False*

5 Vicky wants to be a journalist.   *True / False*

6 Sam wants to be a mechanic.   *True / False*

3 **Draw what you want and don't want to be. Then talk.**

want to be   don't want to be

What do you want to be?

Do you want to be a ... ?

I want to be a / an ... because ...

I don't want to be a / an ... because ...

1 4:22   **Listen. Then circle.**

1 Fran wants to be (*a firefighter* /*a ballet dancer*).

2 Tim wants to be (*a carpenter* / *a builder*).

3 Rob doesn't want to be (*an astronaut* / *a basketball player*).

4 Jamie wants to be (*a police officer* / *a firefighter*).

5 Ann doesn't want to be (*a film star* / *a police officer*).

6 Claire doesn't want to be (*a police officer* / *a basketball player*).

2 4:23   **Listen. Then circle *True* or *False*. Then correct.**

1 Jim wants to be a model.   *True / False* _____

2 Paul doesn't wants to be a carpenter.   *True / False* _____

3 Karen wants to be a lawyer.   *True / False* _____

4 Simon doesn't want to be a singer.   *True / False* _____

5 Lucy wants to be a photographer.   *True / False* _____

6 Pam wants to be an astronaut.   *True / False* _____

3 **Make notes about what you want and don't want to be. Then talk.**

want to be	why

don't want to be	why not

What do you want to be?

I want to be a / an ... because ...

Do you want to be a ... ?

I don't want to be a / an ... because ...

6 In the rainforest

Reading and writing A

1 **Unscramble. Then match.**

1 snive _____

2 tens _____

3 eyallv _____

4 ebrdig _____

a  b 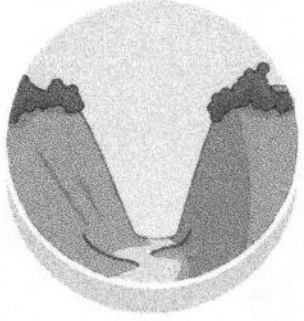 c 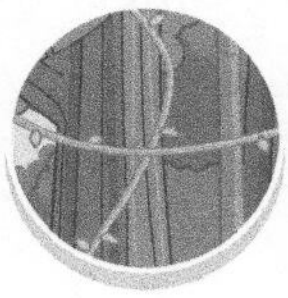 d

2 **Read. Then write in the past.**

I'm on holiday in the rainforest. Yesterday morning I ¹ _____ (walk) through the valley near my hut and I ² _____ (look) at the birds. I ³ _____ (can see) a hummingbird nest in a tree. I ⁴ _____ (climb) the tree but I could not see the hummingbird. In the afternoon it ⁵ _____ (is) very humid. I ⁶ _____ (cannot play) so I stayed in the hut.

3 **Look and read. Then answer the questions.**

1  Could he swim through the river? _____ _____

2  Could they go towards the hills? _____ _____

3  Could he walk around the mountain? _____ _____

4  Could she walk past the lake? _____ _____

4 **Draw your favourite rainforest animal. Then write.**

My favourite rainforest animal

My favourite _____ _____ .

I like them because _____ _____ .

They've got _____ _____ .

They live _____ _____ .

They eat _____ _____ .

© Pearson Education Ltd. 2012

1 Unscramble. Then match.

1 snive _____

2 afwetallr _____

3 tens _____

4 ntainoum _____

5 eyallv _____

6 ebrdig _____

a    b 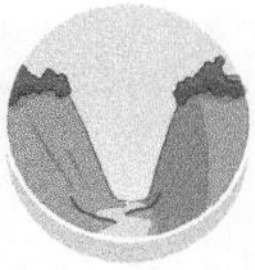   c

d    e 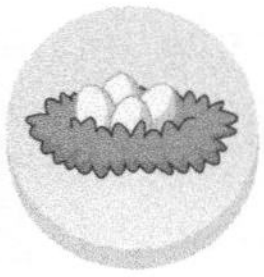   f

2 Read. Then write in the past.

I'm in the rainforest. Yesterday morning I ^{1} _____ (walk) through the valley near my hut. I ^{2} _____ (look) at the birds. I ^{3} _____ (can see) a hummingbird nest in a tree. I ^{4} _____ (climb) the tree but I could not see the hummingbird. Then I ^{5} _____ (jump) down. In the afternoon it ^{6} _____ (is) very hot. I ^{7} _____ (cannot play) so I ^{8} _____ (stay) in the hut.

3 Look and write the question. Then answer.

1  he / swim / through / river

_____   _____

2  they / go / towards / hills

_____   _____

3  he / walk / around / mountain

_____   _____

4  she / walk / around / lake

_____   _____

4 Draw your favourite rainforest animal. Then write.

live   eat   have got

My favourite _____ .

_____

_____

_____

_____

_____

_____

1 (4:24) **Listen. Then write.**

> past   around   over   towards   across   through

1 First she walks on the path and goes _____ the bridge.

2 Then she goes _____ the mountain.

3 After that she walks next to a small river. Then she walks _____ the river.

4 Next she walks _____ the lake.

5 And then she walks _____ the waterfall.

6 After the waterfall she goes _____ the hill. Then she can see her hut.

2 (4:25) **Listen. Then circle.**

1 They (*could / couldn't*) swim in the lake.

2 The hummingbird was (*near / past*) the waterfall.

3 Karen and Tina walked (*through / towards*) the river.

4 The hut was between the bridge and the (*vines / nest*).

3 **Look at the picture and imagine you were on the island. Then talk.**

> bridge   hut   lake   mountain   river   waterfall   climbed   hiked   looked   walked

Where is / are the ... ?

It's / They're ...

I walked / looked at ...

1 **Listen. Then write.**

1 The vines were _____ a big _____ .

2 They walked _____ a bridge to get to some _____ .

3 They _____ swim in the sea. They _____ swim across the river.

4 The _____ was between the forest and the _____ .

5 They weren't near the _____ . Those were near the _____ .

6 There were four hummingbird _____ near their _____ .

2   **Listen. Then circle.**

1 They (*could / couldn't*) run (*over / around*) a mountain.

2 There was a (*tapir / tarantula*). It was (*behind / past*) their hut.

3 There were lots of (*nests / monkeys*). They could hear the (*birds / monkeys*).

4 They (*could / couldn't*) see the coast but they (*could / couldn't*) see a lake.

3 **Look at the picture and imagine you were on the island. Then talk.**

Where is / are the … ?

It's / They're …

Could you … ?

I couldn't / couldn't …

I walked / looked at …

1 **Look. Then write.**

1 He's _____ .

2 She's _____ .

3 He's _____ .

4 She's _____ .

5 He's _____ .

6 She's _____ .

2 **Read. Then match.**

1 What's the matter?	**a** Watching TV.
2 How do you feel?	**b** I'm tired.
3 What makes you feel relaxed?	**c** Let's give him some cake.
4 Why are you crying?	**d** I feel happy.
5 It's John's birthday.	**e** I can make her some lunch.
6 Jane is hungry.	**f** Because I'm sad.

3 **Read. Then write _T_ (True) or _F_ (False).**

Dan: What's the matter, Kate? Why are you crying?

Kate: I'm sad.

Dan: Why are you sad?

Kate: I'm sad because I can't find my hamster.

Dan: Oh, no. I can help you find him. Look! There he is under the sofa.

Kate: Get that box! We can catch him in it.

Dan: I've got him!

Kate: Great! I can put him back in his house.

1 Kate is crying. ☐

2 Kate isn't sad. ☐

3 Dan can't find her hamster. ☐

4 The hamster is under the sofa. ☐

5 They haven't got a box. ☐

6 They didn't catch the hamster. ☐

4 **Write about what makes you feel happy and why.**

_____

_____

_____

_____

1 **Read and write. Then match.**

1 _____ are you crying?

2 What's the _____ ?

3 Why _____ she laughing?

4 Why _____ they shouting?

5 What _____ you feel happy?

6 How does he _____ ?

a Because her book is funny.

b He feels tired.

c Dancing makes me feel happy.

d Because they're angry!

e Because I'm sad.

f I'm ill.

2 **Read. Then write T (True) or F (False).**

Jack: What's the matter, Pete?

Pete: I've got my piano exam later.

Jack: How do you feel?

Pete: Very nervous.

Jack: But you always practise. And you always do well.

Pete: Yes, but I still feel nervous.

Jack: What makes you feel relaxed?

Pete: When I go for a walk.

Jack: We can take a walk by the lake ...

Pete: Yes, a walk is a good idea.

1 Pete has got a piano exam. ☐

2 Pete never practises the piano. ☐

3 Pete feels nervous because of the exam. ☐

4 Pete feels relaxed when he goes for a walk. ☐

5 Jack can't go for a walk. ☐

6 They're going to a waterfall. ☐

3 **Read. Then write.**

1 My little brother is thirsty. Can we give _____ a drink?

2 Your clothes are on the floor. Put _____ in the wardrobe.

3 I think this question is very hard. Can you help _____ ?

4 Today is my sister's birthday. I'm giving _____ a present.

5 The cat is lost. We need to find _____ .

6 You look sad. I can give _____ a hug.

4 **Write about what makes you happy and sad and why.**

happy	sad
_____	_____
_____	_____
_____	_____
_____	_____

1 **Listen. Then match.**

1	Sam		**a**	is laughing because the story was funny.
2	Hilary		**b**	is shouting because her grandad can't hear well.
3	Dan		**c**	feels sick.
4	Kate		**d**	loves parties and celebrations.
5	Bob		**e**	is hungry.
6	Lynn		**f**	is shaking because she's cold.

2 (4:29) **Listen. Then circle.**

1 Al was (*worried / happy*) about his homework.
He was (*tired / excited*) last night.
His mum was (*proud / surprised*).
Al now feels more (*relaxed / nervous*).

2 Brenda is (*angry / excited*).
Brenda's brother (*can / can't*) find her new CD.
She was (*surprised / embarrassed*) by her brother.
Her mum and dad are (*bored / relaxed*).

3 **Draw two pictures of yourself. Then talk about how you feel in each.**

How do you feel?

I feel …

Why are you … ?

I'm … because …

7 Feelings

1 **4:30 Listen. Then match.**

1	Barry	feels embarrassed	because he's not going to the dentist.
2	Helen	is worried	because her brother has got her bike.
3	James	feels relieved	because she went to bed late.
4	Sonia	feels nervous	when she's got a Maths test.
5	Gary	is tired	when the teacher makes him sing.
6	Cindy	isn't happy	because the test results come out today.

2 **4:31 Listen. Then circle.**

1 He's (*laughing / crying*) because he's (*relieved / relaxed*).

2 She's (*worried / sad*) because she broke her mum's (*picture / mirror*).

3 She's feeling (*great and proud / nervous and worried*). There's a big (*celebration / game*) tonight.

4 He feels relaxed (*on holiday / at the park*). He loves (*reading / running*) on the beach.

5 He's (*nervous / happy*) because there was a (*spider / present*) in the kitchen.

3 **Draw pictures of you and your friend. Then talk about how you each feel.**

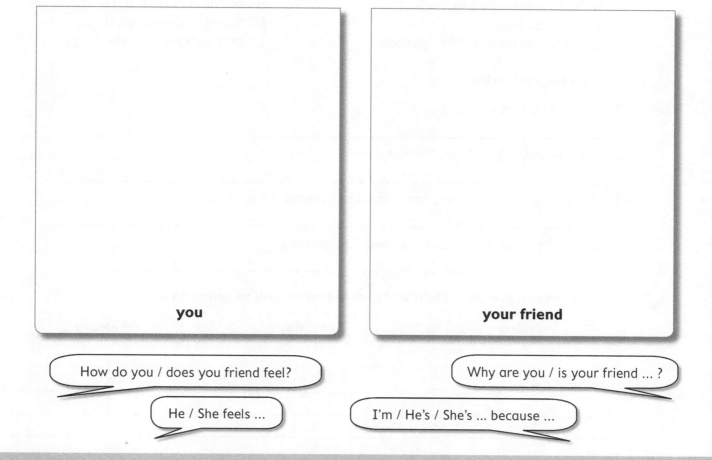

you

your friend

How do you / does you friend feel?

Why are you / is your friend … ?

He / She feels …

I'm / He's / She's … because …

1 **Read. Then write.**

horse-riding   fishing   snorkelling   sailing   kayaking

1 Let's go _____ . Have you got a snorkel?

2 I love _____ but I haven't got a paddle.

3 Have you got a fishing rod? I want to go _____ .

4 You need a life jacket when you go _____ .

5 Let's go _____ . Have you got riding boots?

2 **Read. Then circle.**

Hi. I'm Jo. I live near the sea and I love surfing. In summer I go surfing with my friends every weekend. I've got a new surf board. It's white and red. In autumn I'm fond of kayaking on the sea. I've got a kayak, a paddle and a life jacket. My kayak and my surfboard are in a hut in my garden. I also often go horse-riding but I'm bored with it now. I want to do something new. My friends go rock climbing but I'm terrified of climbing. I love water sports and there's a river near my house. Maybe I can try rafting!

1 Jo lives

   a in the mountains.

   b near to the sea.

   c in a valley.

2 She goes surfing

   a in the mornings.

   b every afternoon.

   c with her friends.

3 She

   a hasn't got a paddle.

   b has got a kayak.

   c hasn't got a hut in her garden.

4 Jo is

   a terrified of rock climbing.

   b bored with rock climbing.

   c crazy about rock climbing.

3 **Unscramble and write.**

1 snorkelling / let's / go / !

_____

2 life / a / you / got / have / jacket / ?

_____

3 this / going / you / what / are / to / do / summer / ?

_____

4 going / he's / go / to / next / surfing / summer / .

_____

4 **Plan a weekend holiday. Then write about what you're going to do.**

Friday	Saturday	Sunday

On Friday I'm going to _____ .

On _____ .

_____

1 **Read. Then write.**

1 Let's go _____ . Have you got a fishing rod?

2 I love _____ but I haven't got a snorkel.

3 Have you got riding boots? I want to go _____ .

4 You need a paddle when you go _____ .

5 I need to get my surfboard. I'm going to go _____ tomorrow.

2 **Read and circle.**

Hi. I'm Fran. I live next to a river in a forest. There are lots of hills and valleys in the forest. In the spring I often go rafting on the river with my friend, Val. We've got life jackets and paddles. My dad loves fishing and goes fishing on the river. In the summer I go horse-riding through the forest. I go with my brother and sister. We've got three small horses. We've also got riding hats and riding boots. We're crazy about riding. In autumn my brother and sister go rock climbing in the mountains. I'm fond of walking in the mountains but I'm not fond of rock climbing. I'm scared of it.

1 Fran lives
  a in the mountains.
  b in a valley.
  c next to a river.

2 She often goes rafting
  a in the autumn.
  b in the spring.
  c with her dad.

3 Her dad
  a goes fishing on the river.
  b hasn't got a fishing rod.
  c is bored with fishing.

4 Fran's brother and sister
  a are crazy about the forest.
  b haven't got riding boots.
  c have got horses.

5 Her brother and sister
  a go rock climbing in the mountains.
  b go fishing.
  c are scared of the mountains.

6 Fran
  a is scared of rivers.
  b is fond of rock climbing.
  c is scared of rock climbing.

3 **Write.**

1 _____ (let's / snorkelling)
_____ (sorry / don't like)

2 _____ (have got / riding boots / ?)
_____ **(✗)**

3 _____ (let's / horse-riding)
_____ (great idea / love)

4 _____ (have got / a life jacket / ?)
_____ **(✓)**

4 **Plan a week holiday. Then write about what you're going to do.**

Monday	
Tuesday	
Wednesday	
Thursday	
Friday	

On Monday I'm going to _____ .

On _____ .

_____

_____

_____

1 (4:32) **Listen. Then match.**

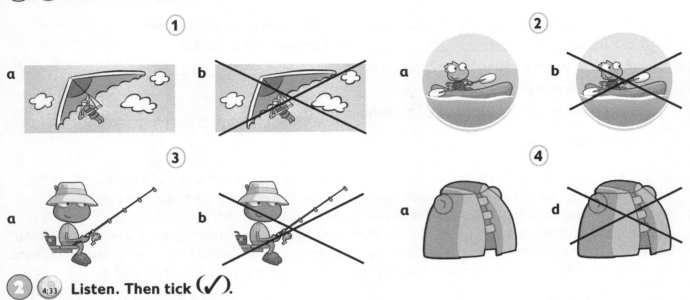

① a b ② a b

③ a b ④ a d

2 (4:33) **Listen. Then tick (✓).**

	diving	beach volleyball	sailing	rock climbing	bungee jumping	fishing
bored with						
scared of						
terrified of						
crazy about						

3 **Look at the activities. Then talk about what you're *crazy about*, *scared of* and *bored with*.**

What are you … ?   I'm crazy about …   I'm bored with …   I'm scared of …

1 **Listen. Then match.**

1 Let's go ...
  a swimming
  b horse-riding.
  c snorkelling.

2 Sorry, ...
  a I'm bored with horses.
  b I'm scared of horses.
  c I'm crazy about rock climbing.

3 I'm ...
  a crazy about surfing.
  b crazy about sailing.
  c crazy about horses.

4 Have ...
  a you got a life jacket?
  b you got a paddle?
  c you got a surfboard?

2 **Listen. Then tick (✓).**

	snorkelling	beach volleyball	sailing	rock climbing	bungee jumping	fishing
bored with						
terrified of						
scared of						
crazy about						

3 **Make notes about activities and your feelings about them. Then talk.**

fond of	_____
crazy about	_____
bored with	_____
scared of	_____
terrified of	_____

What are you ... ?

I'm ... about / of / with ...

1 Read. Then match.

1 What do you like doing?
2 What do your brother and sister like doing?
3 Does Dan like playing hockey?
4 Do monkeys eat fruit?
5 What do crabs eat?
6 How many teeth have gorillas got?
7 What's the weather like today?
8 What was the weather like last weekend?

a Yes, they do.
b It was wet and warm.
c They like painting.
d No, he doesn't.
e They've got 32.
f It's stormy.
g I like skiing.
h They eat worms.

2 Read. Then draw.

1 Sally is taller than Tim. Sally likes reading the newspaper. Tim likes playing the guitar.

2 It's stormy. There's lightning and thunder.

3 Pandas live in forests. They eat leaves.

4 I go camping in spring with my mum and dad. We like looking at the flowers.

3 Read. Then write.

1 What do you like doing at the weekend? _____
2 Do you like painting? _____
3 Where do camels live? _____
4 Do giraffes eat fish? _____
5 What's the weather like today? _____
6 What was the weather like last weekend? _____

4 Read and tick (✓) or cross (✗). Then correct the words.

1 sking ☐ _____

2 skeightboarding ☐ _____

3 grasslands ☐ _____

4 croccodile ☐ _____

5 degrees ☐ _____

6 humide ☐ _____

5 Read. Then sort.

thunder desert grassland autumn summer rainforest
warm humid spring degrees forest winter

Weather	Habitats	Seasons

6 Write about what you and your family like doing.

I like / don't like ...   My ... likes / doesn't like ...

Free Time

_____
_____
_____
_____
_____
_____
_____
_____
_____
_____
_____

1 **Read. Then match.**

1 What do you do on Thursdays?	**a** Yes, I do.
2 When does Rosie have ballet lessons?	**b** He wants to be a builder.
3 Does she want to be a lawyer?	**c** It's past the waterfall.
4 Do you want to be a builder?	**d** On Fridays at half past four.
5 Why do you want to be a carpenter?	**e** No, we couldn't.
6 Where's your hut?	**f** I do karate.
7 Could you go through the forest?	**g** Because I like making chairs.
8 What does Harry want to be?	**h** No, she doesn't.

2 **Read. Then draw.**

1 Tim practises the violin at a quarter to five.

2 Charlie wants to be a basketball player.

3 The monkey is between the crocodile and the hut.

4 I could swim across the lake towards the waterfall.

3 **Read. Then write.**

1 What do you do on Sundays? _____
2 When do you study Maths? _____
3 How do you go to school? _____
4 Do you want to be a film star? _____
5 What do you want to be? Why? _____
6 Where's your school? _____

4 Read and tick (✓) or cross (✗). Then correct the words.

1 gymnestics ☐ _____

2 midday ☐ _____

3 journolist ☐ _____

4 machanic ☐ _____

5 thruogh ☐ _____

6 coast ☐ _____

5 Read. Then sort.

> over   nest   lawyer   across   waterfall   model   towards
> vines   hut   around   photographer   singer

Rainforest	Prepositions	Jobs

6 Write about your week.

> have   learn to   study   practise   in   on   at
> a quarter past   half past   a quarter to

My week

_____

1 Read. Then match.

1 Why are you blushing?
2 Let's go sailing!
3 What's the matter?
4 How do you feel?
5 What makes you feel nervous?
6 Have you got a paddle?
7 What are you going to do tomorrow?
8 It's John's birthday.

a I'm going to go hang gliding.
b I feel relaxed.
c No, I haven't.
d Let's give him a present.
e Because I'm embarrassed.
f English tests!
g I'm worried.
h Great idea!

2 Read. Then draw.

1 She's crying because she's sad.

2 He feels happy because it's his birthday.

3 The man is fishing. He's got a fishing rod.

4 The woman is crazy about surfing.

3 Read. Then write.

1 How do you feel? _____
2 What makes you feel embarrassed? _____
3 What are you fond of? _____
4 Have you got a life jacket? _____
5 What are you going to do this weekend? _____
6 What's your family going to do tonight? _____

4 **Read and tick (✓) or cross (✗). Then correct the words.**

1 shakking ☐ _____

2 nervious ☐ _____

3 surprised ☐ _____

4 kayking ☐ _____

5 paddle ☐ _____

6 tereffied ☐ _____

5 **Read. Then sort.**

> snorkel   embarrassed   rafting   life jacket   nervous   sailing
> snorkelling   worried   surfboard   excited   surfing   riding boots

Extreme sports	Feelings	Things
_____	_____	_____
_____	_____	_____
_____	_____	_____
_____	_____	_____

6 **Write about your next family holiday.**

> I'm going to …   We're going to …   I'm fond of / crazy about / scared of …

My holiday

_____

_____

_____

_____

_____

_____

_____

_____

_____

_____

_____

_____

1 **Read. Then circle.**

> John: What's the matter, Kim?
>
> Kim: I'm worried. I have an English test and I'm terrified of tests.
>
> John: Don't worry. You're good at English.
>
> Kim: Yes, you're right but tests make me scared. How about you, John? How are you?
>
> John: I'm excited. We're going to the rainforest on holiday next week.
>
> Kim: Wow! That's very exciting. What are you going to do?
>
> John: We're going to go bungee jumping and we're going to go hiking. I want to see gorillas. They're my favourite animals. But I don't want to see any snakes! I'm scared of snakes. Anyway, good luck with your test.
>
> Kim: Thanks. Have fun on your vacation.

1 Kim is
   a embarrassed.
   b worried.
   c excited.

2 Kim is
   a terrified of gorillas.
   b terrified of tests.
   c bored of tests.

3 On holiday John is going to go
   a bungee jumping and hang gliding.
   b hiking and water skiing.
   c hiking and bungee jumping.

4 John's favourite animals are
   a snakes.
   b birds.
   c gorillas.

2 **Read. Then write _T_ (_True_) or _F_ (_False_).**

> I'm Bill. It's summer and I'm holiday. It's sunny and windy and the temperature is 20 degrees. We're going to go sailing this afternoon. We often go sailing in the summer on the lake near my house. My mum and dad have got a small boat and I've got my own life jacket.
>
> Yesterday we hiked through the forest. There were many birds. Then we walked across a bridge and to a lake. We could walk around the lake but we couldn't swim across it.
>
> Tomorrow I'm going to play basketball with my friends. It's going to be a lot of fun because I love basketball. I want to be a famous basketball player when I grow up.

1 It's spring. ☐

2 The temperature is 20 degrees. ☐

3 Bill has got a life jacket. ☐

4 Yesterday they hiked in the desert. ☐

5 There were many monkeys. ☐

6 Bill is going to play basketball tomorrow. ☐

3 **Read the text in Activity 2 again. Then answer the questions.**

1 What's the weather like today? _____

2 When do they often go sailing? _____

3 Could they swim across the lake? _____

4 What does Bill want to be? _____

1 **Read. Then circle.**

John: What's the matter, Kim?

Kim: I'm worried. I have an English test and I'm terrified of tests.

John: Don't worry. You're good at English.

Kim: Yes, you're right but tests make me scared. How about you, John? How are you?

John: I'm excited. We're going to the rainforest on holiday next week.

Kim: Wow! That's very exciting. What are you going to do?

John: We're going to go bungee jumping and we're going to go hiking. I want to see gorillas. They're my favourite animals. But I don't want to see any snakes! I'm scared of snakes. Anyway, good luck with your test.

Kim: Thanks. Have fun on your holiday.

1 Kim is
   a surprised.
   b excited.
   c worried.

2 Kim is
   a terrified of tests.
   b terrified of gorillas.
   c scared of snakes.

3 John is
   a terrified.
   b excited.
   c embarrassed.

4 John is going to go
   a bungee jumping and hiking.
   b hiking and snorkelling.
   c hiking and diving.

5 John doesn't want to see
   a gorillas.
   b snakes.
   c the rainforest.

6 John's favourite animals are
   a birds.
   b snakes.
   c gorillas.

2 **Read. Then write *T* (*True*) or *F* (*False*).**

I'm Katherine. I'm going to stay at my uncle and aunt's house this summer. They live next to the sea and they love sailing. They've got a small boat and they're going to teach me how to sail it. I often feel a little seasick on the boat but not always. Mum is going to get me a life jacket. We've got to wear a life jacket on the boat.

I often go fishing with my uncle. I don't like fishing but I like looking for crabs. They eat little sea animals and worms. I'm a little scared of big crabs but I like little crabs.

Last summer I visited the desert with my aunt and uncle. It was very hot and sunny! One day it was 38 degrees! We looked at camels and walked to some hills. We could walk around them but we couldn't walk over them. They were too big and it was too hot!

1 Katherine lives next to the sea. ☐

2 Her uncle and aunt like sailing. ☐

3 She hasn't got a life jacket. ☐

4 The sea often makes her feel sick. ☐

5 Her uncle likes looking for crabs. ☐

6 Katherine is scared of big crabs. ☐

7 Last summer she visited the desert. ☐

8 It was cool and windy in the desert. ☐

3 **Read the text in Activity 2 again. Then answer the questions.**

1 What does 'seasick' mean? _____

2 Why do you think they have got to wear a life jacket? _____

3 Which does Kim like more – fishing or looking for crabs? _____

4 Do you think it is warmer next to the sea or in the desert? _____

1 **Read. Then write.**

1 When do you study English? _____

2 What's the weather like today? _____

3 What do you like doing? _____

4 What are you scared of? _____

5 What are you going to do after school? _____

2 **Read. Then write the questions.**

1 _____ She's laughing because she's happy.

2 _____ It was warm and sunny.

3 _____ Tests make me feel nervous.

4 _____ He wants to be a farmer.

5 _____ Monkeys eat bananas.

3 **Read. Then write about a place you want to go on holiday.**

A place to visit

Where do you want to go? _____

_____

_____

Why? _____

_____

_____

What can you do there? _____

_____

_____

What can you see there? _____

_____

_____

What's the weather like there? _____

_____

_____

1 **Read. Then write.**

1 What do you do at the weekend? _____

2 What was the weather like yesterday? _____

3 What do your parents like doing? _____

4 What makes you embarrassed? _____

5 What are you going to do next winter? _____

6 Where's your house? _____

2 **Read. Then write the questions.**

1 _____ I'm relieved.

2 _____ It's 23 degrees.

3 _____ Rock climbing makes me scared.

4 _____ No, I don't want to be a journalist.

5 _____ He wants to be a dancer because he likes dancing.

6 _____ She's crying because she's sad.

3 **Read. Then write about a place you want to live.**

> Where do you want to live? Why?
> What can you see and do there?
> What's the weather like?

A place to live

_____

_____

_____

_____

_____

_____

_____

_____

_____

_____

_____

_____

_____

1 (4:36) **Listen. Then match.**

is going to go hiking		is going to walk the dog
likes spring	Julie	likes autumn
wants to be a ballet dancer	Ben	wants to be a builder
is shouting at the dog		is laughing at the dog

2 (4:37) **Listen. Then circle.**

1 She likes (*reading the newspaper / playing computer games*).
She doesn't like (*riding a scooter / cooking*).

2 Zebras and pandas are (*black and white / herbivores*).
(*Monkeys / Birds*) live in trees.

3 The woman asks about the weather in (*spring / autumn*).
The weather then is (*cloudy and wet / sunny and warm*).

4 He has gym lessons every morning at a (*quarter to / quarter past*) nine.
On Sundays he (*reads and does homework) / reads and learns to cook*).

3 (4:38) **Listen. Then write *True* or *False*.**

1 First you go on a road past a forest. _____

2 Then you go over a hill. _____

3 Next you go across a bridge. _____

4 The house is at the top of a mountain. _____

4 (4:39) **Listen. Then write a tick (✓) or cross (✗).**

✓ = likes   ✗ = doesn't like

	horse-riding	fishing	hiking	sailing
John				
Ron				
Judith				
Sue				

1 (4:40) **Listen. Then match.**

is going to play hockey

is going to play beach volleyball

plays tennis in spring and summer

does karate

practises before school

loves lakes and waterfalls

Janet

Billie

is going to chat online

is going to go hang gliding

usually plays volleyball in summer

plays piano

practises Tuesday, Thursday and Saturday

loves the sea and coast

2 (4:41) **Listen. Then circle.**

1 In spring she likes (*walking in the park / going on holiday*).
She (*likes / doesn't like*) autumn.
She (*likes / doesn't like*) winter.

2 They've got some (*crocodiles / gorillas*).
There's a (*lake / hill*) in the park.
They've also got some (*hippos / lions*).

3 The woman asks about the weather in (*spring / winter*).
It's usually (*cloudy and humid / sunny and cool*).
There's usually storms in the (*afternoon / morning*).

4 He (*likes / doesn't like*) the morning.
He can (*watch TV / chat with friends*) in the evenings.
He (*always / never*) goes to the park after school.

3 (4:42) **Listen. Write *True (T)* or *False (F)*. Then correct.**

1 First you go past the lake. ☐ _____

2 Next you go through the forest. ☐ _____

3 Then go along the river and past the waterfall. ☐ _____

4 Walk for 10 minutes. The parrots are in some trees. ☐ _____

4 (4:43) **Listen. Then write a tick (✓) or cross (✗).**

✓ = likes   ✗ = doesn't like

	skateboard	ski	play football	watch films
Silvia				
Joanne				
Pete				
Lenny				

5 **Look at Activity 4. Then write.**

1 Silvia doesn't like _____ .

2 Joanne likes _____ .

3 Pete doesn't like _____ .

4 Lenny doesn't like _____ .

① **Look and talk. Then find five differences.**

| under | across | next to | between | toward | near | rainy | sunny |
| trees | crocodile | snake | kayak | paddle | rainforest | river |

There is / are ...

I can / can't see ...

Is / Are there ... ?

Where is / are ... ?

1 **Look and talk. Then say five differences.**

There is / are ...

I can / can't see ...

Is / Are there ... ?

Where is / are ... ?

1 **Look and read. Then write.**

paddle

elephant

thunder

firefighter

bridge

watching tv

1 You use this to kayak. _____

2 I help people. _____

3 You use this to go across a river. _____

4 It lives in grasslands. _____

5 People like doing this in the evening. _____

6 You hear this after you see lightning. _____

2 **Look and read. Then write *yes* or *no*.**

1 One boy is surfing. _____

2 Two children are sailing. _____

3 A boy is horse-riding on the beach. _____

4 One girl is fishing. _____

5 One boy is wearing a life jacket. _____

6 The cat hasn't got a paddle. _____

3 Read. Then tick (✓) the best answer.

Ian is talking to his friend John.

1

Ian: Hi, John. You look happy. Why are you smiling?

John: **a** Because I'm sad.   ☐

       b Because I'm going on holiday.   ☐

       c Playing basketball makes me feel happy.   ☐

2

Ian: When are you going?

John: **a** This weekend.   ☐

       b Last summer.   ☐

       c I want to go next year.   ☐

3

Ian: What are you going to do?

John: **a** We hiked in the rainforest.   ☐

       b We hike in the rainforest.   ☐

       c We're going to go hiking in the rainforest.   ☐

4

Ian: The rainforest. Wow! Do monkeys live in the rainforest?

John: **a** Yes, they do.   ☐

       b They eat fruit.   ☐

       c No, I don't.   ☐

4 Read the story. Then write words to complete the sentences.

I'm Dennis. Next weekend I'm going to go to the mountains with my family. I'm going to stay in a small hut in a forest. The hut is next to a small river and a lake. I'm going to go fishing with my dad. I've got my fishing rod and some worms. We always go fishing in the morning and evening when there are lots of fish. My dog Sandy likes swimming. She often swims towards the fish. They are scared of her and they swim away!

1 Dennis is going to go to the _____ next weekend.

2 The hut is next to a river and a _____ .

3 Dennis is going to go _____ with his dad.

4 They _____ go fishing in the morning and evening.

5 Sandy is a _____ .

6 The fish are _____ of Sandy.

1 (4:44) **Listen and draw lines.**

| Bob | Nikki | Billy | Paul | Susan |

2 (4:45) **Listen and write.**

Book survey

1 Book title: _____
2 What book is about: _____
3 Favourite character: _____
4 Favourite part: _____
5 How many pages a day: _____

3 (4:46) **Listen and draw a line from the day to the correct picture.**

What's Barry going to do next week?

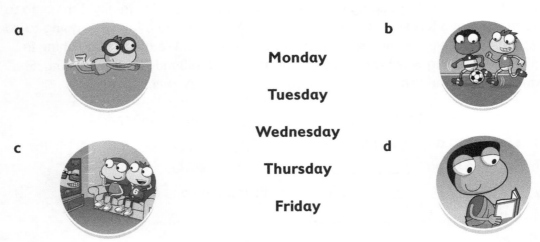

a

b

Monday

Tuesday

Wednesday

c

d

Thursday

Friday

4 (4:47) **Listen. Then tick (✓).**

1 What's the weather like?

a    **b**    **c**

☐   ☐   ☐

2 What animals does Jack see in the rainforest?

a    **b**   **c**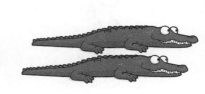

☐   ☐   ☐

5 (4:48) **Listen, colour and write.**

1 Look and read. Then write.

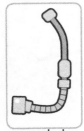
snorkel

crocodile

lightning

police officer

mountain

skateboarding

1 He or she wears a uniform and helps us to be safe. _____

2 You see this before you hear thunder. _____

3 This helps you breathe underwater. _____

4 This lives in rivers. It's a carnivore. _____

5 This is bigger than a hill. _____

6 This activity is fun and fast. _____

2 Look and read. Then write *yes* or *no*.

1 The baby is smiling. _____

2 The dog has got a shirt. _____

3 The birds are eating. _____

4 One man is angry at the dog. _____

5 The man with the sandwich is excited. _____

6 The woman with the bird is happy _____

3 **Read. Then tick (✓) the best answer.**

Myra is talking to her friend Hilary.

1 Myra: What's the matter, Hilary?

   Hilary: **a** She's nervous. ☐

   b I'm tired. ☐

   c I'm smiling. ☐

2 Myra: Why is that?

   Hilary: **a** Because I walked all day yesterday. ☐

   b Because I'm scared of tests. ☐

   c Because he can't sleep. ☐

3 Myra: Where were you?

   Hilary: **a** They were on the coast. ☐

   b She was in the rainforest. ☐

   c I was in the forest. ☐

4 Myra: What was the weather like?

   Hilary: **a** It's sunny and warm. ☐

   b It was warm. ☐

   c It's 23 degrees. ☐

4 **Read the story. Then write words to complete the sentences.**

I'm Susan. Tomorrow it's going to be warm and sunny. I'm going to go to the coast with my family. I love the sea. I'm going to go swimming and snorkelling. My mum has got a small boat and paddles and I've got my snorkel. I can jump into the sea and look at the fish. I'm a little scared but only a little. Last month I practised snorkelling in the swimming pool. I practised every Tuesday and Thursday. The water in the pool was warm. The water in the sea is colder but I'm ready. The journey to the coast is one and a half hours. There are mountains between my house and the sea. Dad is going to go on a road over the mountain. It's faster than going around the mountain. I'm very excited to see the fish! It's going to be amazing.

1 Susan is going to the _____ tomorrow.

2 She is going to go _____ and _____ .

3 Her mum has got a boat and _____ .

4 Last month Susan practised every _____ and _____ .

5 The _____ is one hour and a half.

6 The road over the mountain is _____ than the road around the mountain.

1 (4:49) **Listen and draw lines.**

| Vicky | Phil | Jane | Ian | Sam |

2 (4:50) **Listen and write.**

Wildlife park survey

1 Name: _____

2 Where is the park: _____

3 Animals in the park: _____

4 Time of lunch: _____

5 Name of a teacher: _____

3 (4:51) **Listen and draw a line from the day to the correct picture.**

Where was Charlie last week?

a

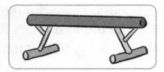

Monday

Tuesday

Wednesday

Thursday

Friday

b

c

d

Exam preparation

4 **Listen. Then tick (✓).**

1 What does Greg want to be?

a  ☐

b  ☐

c  ☐

2 What's Harry going to do tomorrow?

a  ☐

b  ☐

c  ☐

5 **Listen, colour and write.**

1 Look at the story. Then say what is happening.

© Pearson Education Ltd. 2012

Look at the pictures. Say which one is different, and why.

1
a
b
c
d

2
a
b
c
d

3
a
b
c
d

4
a
b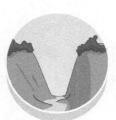
c
d

Say five differences.

4 **What do you want to be? Draw a mind map. Then talk.**

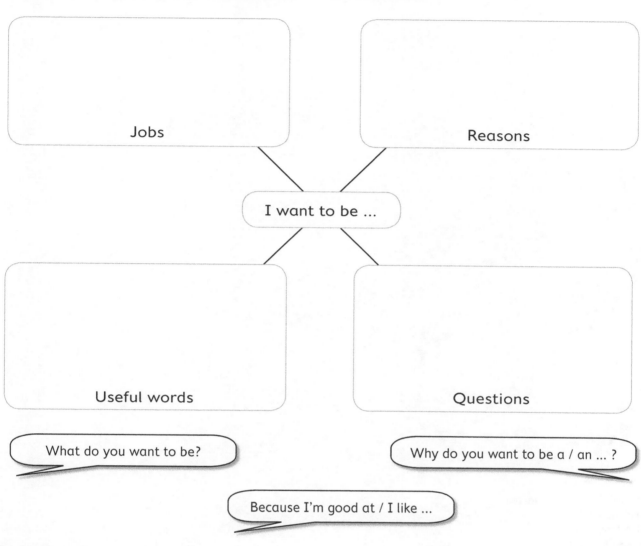

Jobs

Reasons

I want to be ...

Useful words

Questions

What do you want to be?

Why do you want to be a / an ... ?

Because I'm good at / I like ...

5 **Ask and answer questions.**

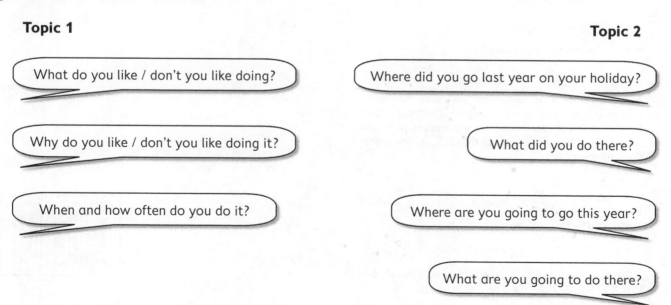

Topic 1

What do you like / don't you like doing?

Why do you like / don't you like doing it?

When and how often do you do it?

Topic 2

Where did you go last year on your holiday?

What did you do there?

Where are you going to go this year?

What are you going to do there?

Pearson Education Limited
Edinburgh Gate
Harlow
Essex CM20 2JE
England
and Associated Companies throughout the world.

www.islands.pearson.com

Written by Kerry Powell

First published 2012
Third impression 2017
Fourth impression 2017
ISBN: 978-1-4082-9057-6

Printed in Great Britain by Ashford Colour Press Ltd

All illustrative artworks © Pearson Education Limited 2012

ISBN 978-1-4082-9057-6

9 781408 290576